LIBRARY OF NEW TESTAMENT STUDIES

696

Formerly Journal for the Study of the New Testament Supplement Series

Editor
Chris Keith

Editorial Board
Dale C. Allison, Lynn H. Cohick, Kylie Crabbe, R. Alan Culpepper,
Craig A. Evans, Jennifer Eyl, Robert Fowler, Juan Hernández Jr.,
John S. Kloppenborg, Michael Labahn, Matthew V. Novenson, Love L. Sechrest,
Robert Wall, Catrin H. Williams, Brittany E. Wilson

THE SPATIOTEMPORAL ESCHATOLOGY OF HEBREWS: PRIESTLY PARTICIPATION IN THE HEAVENLY TABERNACLE

Luke Woo

t&tclark

LONDON • NEW YORK • OXFORD • NEW DELHI • SYDNEY

T&T CLARK
Bloomsbury Publishing Plc, 50 Bedford Square, London, WC1B 3DP, UK
Bloomsbury Publishing Inc, 1359 Broadway, New York, NY 10018, USA
Bloomsbury Publishing Ireland, 29 Earlsfort Terrace, Dublin 2, D02 AY28, Ireland

BLOOMSBURY, T&T CLARK and the T&T Clark logo
are trademarks of Bloomsbury Publishing Plc

First published in Great Britain 2024
Paperback edition published 2026

Copyright © Luke Woo, 2024

Luke Woo has asserted his right under the Copyright, Designs and Patents Act, 1988,
to be identified as Author of this work.

For legal purposes the Acknowledgments on p. xiii constitute an extension of this copyright page.

All rights reserved. No part of this publication may be: i) reproduced or transmitted in any form, electronic or mechanical, including photocopying, recording or by means of any information storage or retrieval system without prior permission in writing from the publishers; or ii) used or reproduced in any way for the training, development or operation of artificial intelligence (AI) technologies, including generative AI technologies. The rights holders expressly reserve this publication from the text and data mining exception as per Article 4(3) of the Digital Single Market Directive (EU) 2019/790.

Bloomsbury Publishing Plc does not have any control over, or responsibility for, any third-party websites referred to or in this book. All internet addresses given in this book were correct at the time of going to press. The author and publisher regret any inconvenience caused if addresses have changed or sites have ceased to exist, but can accept no responsibility for any such changes.

A catalogue record for this book is available from the British Library.

Library of Congress Cataloging-in-Publication Data

Names: Woo, Luke, author.
Title: The spatiotemporal eschatology of Hebrews : priestly participation
in the heavenly tabernacle / Luke Woo.
Description: 1. | London : T&T Clark, 2024. | Series: Library of New Testament studies; 696 |
Includes bibliographical references and index.
Identifiers: LCCN 2023051370 (print) | LCCN 2023051371 (ebook) |
ISBN 9780567714978 (hardback) | ISBN 9780567715005 (paperback) |
ISBN 9780567714985 (pdf) | ISBN 9780567714992 (ebook)
Subjects: LCSH: Bible. Hebrews–Criticism, interpretation, etc. |
Eschatology–Biblical teaching. | Space and time–Biblical teaching.
Classification: LCC BS2775.52 .W66 2024 (print) | LCC BS2775.52 (ebook) |
DDC 227/.8706–dc23/eng/20240607
LC record available at https://lccn.loc.gov/2023051370
LC ebook record available at https://lccn.loc.gov/2023051371

ISBN: HB: 978-0-5677-1497-8
PB: 978-0-5677-1500-5
ePDF: 978-0-5677-1498-5
ePUB: 978-0-5677-1499-2

Series: Library of New Testament Studies, volume 696
ISSN 2513-8790

Typeset by: Trans.form.ed SARL

For product safety related questions contact productsafety@bloomsbury.com

To find out more about our authors and books visit www.bloomsbury.com
and sign up for our newsletters.

CONTENTS

Figures ix
Tables xi
Acknowledgments xiii
Abbreviations xv

PART I
THE HEAVENLY TABERNACLE

Chapter 1
HEAVENLY TABERNACLE ESCHATOLOGY — 3
1.1. Spatiotemporal Eschatology and the Heavenly Tabernacle — 3
    1.1.1. Spatiotemporal Eschatological Language in Hebrews — 7
    1.1.2. Reconciling Eschatological Space and Time in Hebrews — 12
1.2. Survey of Scholarship on the Heavenly Tabernacle — 14
    1.2.1. Tabernacle as Dualistic Representations
        (The Platonic/Philonic and Cosmological Views) — 15
    1.2.2. Tabernacle as Social and Community Participation — 20
    1.2.3. Tabernacle as a Rhetorical, Literary Device — 23
    1.2.4. Tabernacle Bifurcated into Future-Spatial
        and Present-Spiritual Realities — 27
    1.2.5. Tabernacle as Spatially Realized — 30

Chapter 2
APPROACHING TABERNACLE SPACE — 35
2.1. Methodology: Tripartite Critical Spatial Theory — 35
    2.1.1. Reconciling Space — 36
    2.1.2. Applying Edward Soja's Thirdspace — 41
2.2. Thirdspace in Biblical Studies — 43
    2.2.1. Against an Anthropocentric Critical Spatiality — 45
2.3. Thirdspace and the Heavenly Tabernacle — 48
2.4. Excursus: Cynthia Westfall's "Space and Atonement in Hebrews" — 52

Chapter 3
THE BACKGROUND OF THE TABERNACLE 54
   3.1. The Heavenly Tabernacle in the Context of Hebrews 54
      3.1.1. Historical Context 54
      3.1.2. Literary Context 61
      3.1.3. Structure 62
   3.2. Spatial and Temporal Limitations of the Earthly Tabernacle 64
      3.2.1. Mt. Sinai's Limited Access 65
      3.2.2. Spatial Limitation 66
      3.2.3. Temporal Limitation 69

PART II.
FIRSTSPACE AND SECONDSPACE

Chapter 4
HEAVENLY ASCENT: HEBREWS 4:14 AND 6:19–20 75
   4.1. Firstspace: Passing through the Created Heavens 76
      4.1.1. Passed through the Heavens 77
      4.1.2. Depicting the Heavenly Journey in the Earthly Tabernacle ... 82
   4.2. Secondspace: Clearing the Heavenly Path 86

Chapter 5
THE ARCHETYPAL PATTERN:
HEBREWS 8:5 (EXODUS 25:40) 91
   5.1. Firstspace: A Standing Structure in the Heavens 94
      5.1.1. The Context of Hebrews 8:5 and Exodus 25:40 ... 94
      5.1.2. Exodus 25:9 and 40 in Early and Late Judaism ... 98
      5.1.3. The Interpretative Tradition of Exodus 25:40 ... 107
   5.2. Secondspace: Showcasing the Heavenly Tabernacle 114
      5.2.1. Intensification of Tabernacle Revelation in History ... 114
      5.2.2. Centering on the Heavenly Home 117

Chapter 6
THE GREATER AND MORE PERFECT TENT:
HEBREWS 9:1–14 119
   6.1. Firstspace: Entering Once and for All 119
      6.1.1. Through the Tabernacle or By Means of the Tabernacle? ... 122
      6.1.2. The Antithetical Schema of Hebrews 9:1–10 and 11–14 ... 127
      6.1.3. On the Character of the Transcendent Heavens ... 133
   6.2. Secondspace: From the Cross to the Sanctuary 135
   6.3. Summary 143

PART III.
THIRDSPACE

Chapter 7
BELIEVERS' SPATIAL AWARENESS — 149
   7.1. Complete Access and Full Entry — 150
   7.2. First-, Second-, and Thirdspace Interplay — 161
      7.2.1. The Grounding of Firstspace — 161
      7.2.2. Mutual Cooperation of Spatial Trialectics — 163
   7.3. Upward- and Forward-Looking — 167

Chapter 8
THIRDSPACE PRIESTLY ACTIVITY — 173
   8.1. Thirdspace Cultic Language — 176
      8.1.1. προσέρχομαι and εἰσέρχομαι — 178
      8.1.2. λειτουργός and λατρεύω — 186
   8.2. Confidence, Boldness, and Conscience — 190
   8.3. Thirdspace Movement — 196
      8.3.1. Vertical or Horizontal Priestly Service — 199
      8.3.2. Vertical and Horizontal Priestly Service — 205

Chapter 9
CONCLUSION — 211
   9.1. Part 1: The Heavenly Tabernacle — 211
   9.2. Part 2: Firstspace and Secondspace — 212
   9.3. Part 3: Thirdspace — 213
   9.4. Contributions, Implications, and New Avenues of Research — 214

Bibliography — 216
Index of References — 235
Index of Authors — 244

FIGURES

2.1	Spatial Trialectics Across Heaven and Earth	49
4.1	Macrolevel Itinerary of Jesus' Heavenly Spatial Movement	80
6.1	Rhetorical Analysis of Hebrews 9:11–14	130
7.1	Spatial Overlap of the Heavenly Tabernacle	166

TABLES

1.1	Movement Passages in Hebrews with Spatial and Temporal Language	8
5.1	The Textual Tradition of Exodus 25:9	109
5.2	The Textual Tradition of Exodus 25:40	110
5.3	The Textual Traditions of Exodus 25:9 and 40 in Hebrews	110
6.1	Architectural Descriptions of the Earthly and Heavenly Tabernacles	132

ACKNOWLEDGMENTS

This monograph is a slightly revised version of my PhD dissertation submitted to Westminster Theological Seminary in 2022. First, I want to express my gratitude to Chris Keith, Sarah Blake, Katherine Jenkins, and the LNTS team at Bloomsbury T&T Clark for their assistance in bringing this work to publication.

Immense gratitude goes to my supervisor, Dr. David E. Briones, who guided me through each step of the writing process. I am honored to have studied under someone who models both scholarly excellence and Christ-honoring character. I also want to thank Dr. Brandon D. Crowe and Dr. Thomas Keene for their guidance throughout my doctoral studies and for their helpful comments during the revision process. I am also thankful for my dear friend and fellow postgrad, Dr. Paul J. Park, who has been an engaging conversation partner in all aspects of theology.

This work would not have been possible without the love and care of a supportive community. Deep appreciation goes to my colleagues and friends on the Main Line: Bill Smith, Daniel Lui, Daniel Whang, Joe Hyun, Juwon Suh, Sam Hwang, Samantha Kim, and Tim and Julia Lee. I am especially thankful for Betty Suh in collating my dissertation chapters while I was overseas. David and Lynn Kim were also a tremendous help in obtaining resources from the campus library.

I am grateful to my parents-in-law, Soon-Yeol Kim and Bog-Soon Lee, for their hospitality in South Korea, which allowed me to concentrate on my studies. My sister, Heejin Woo, and my brother-in-law, Stephen McFate, have given me ongoing support in all that I do. My sincere appreciation also goes to my parents, Hyung Sik and Jae Yol Woo, who sacrificed so much to help me be who I am today.

Finally, I want to thank my beloved wife, Joanna, for her unwavering love and encouragement these past years. Your patience and kindness encourage me daily to be a better husband and father for our family. To my son, Elliot, and my daughter, Brooklyn—you have given me so much joy in more ways than you know. I am humbled and thankful to have you all in my life.

ABBREVIATIONS

4Q11	paleoGenesis-Exodus (4QpaleoGen-Exod)
4Q301	Mysteries (4QMyst)
4Q403–405	Songs of the Sabbath Sacrifice (4QShirShabb)
4Q417, 4Q418	Sapiential Work A or Secret of the Way Things Are (4QInstruction)
11Q19	The Temple Scroll^a (11QT^a)
AB	Anchor Bible
ABD	*Anchor Bible Dictionary*. Edited by David Noel Freedman. 6 vols. New York: Doubleday, 1992.
AGJU	Arbeiten zur Geschichte des antiken Judentums und des Urchristentums
ALGHJ	Arbeiten zur Literatur und Geschichte des hellenistischen Judentum
AnBib	Analecta biblica
ANRW	*Aufstieg und Niedergang der römischen Welt: Geschichte und Kultur Roms im Spiegel der neueren Forschung*. Edited by Hildegard Temporini and Wolfgang Hause. Berlin: de Gruyter, 1972–.
Ant.	*Jewish Antiquities* (Josephus)
ASE	*Annali di Storia dell'Esegesi Zeitschrift*
ASOR	American Society of Overseas Research
AUSDDS	*Andrews University Seminary Doctoral Dissertation Series*
AUSS	*Andrews University Seminary Studies*
AYBC	Anchor Yale Bible Commentary
BBR	*Bulletin for Biblical Research*
BDAG	Danker, Frederick W., Walter Bauer, William F. Arndt, and F. Wilbur Gingrich. *Greek-English Lexicon of the New Testament and Other Early Christian Literature*. 3rd ed. Chicago, IL: University of Chicago Press, 2000.
BDB	Brown, Francis, Samuel Rolles Driver, and Charles Augustus Briggs. *Enhanced Brown-Driver-Briggs Hebrew and English Lexicon*. Oxford: Clarendon Press, 1977.
BECNT	Baker Exegetical Commentary of the New Testament
BibInt	*Biblical Interpretation*
BIOSCS	Bulletin of the International Organization for Septuagint and Cognate Studies
BIS	Biblical Interpretation Series
BJS	Brown Judaic Studies
BR	*Biblical Research*
BRI	Biblical Research Institute

BSac	*Bibliotheca Sacra*
BST	Basel Studies of Theology
BTB	*Biblical Theology Bulletin*
BZ	*Biblische Zeitschrift*
BZNW	Beihefte zur Zeitschrift für die Neutestamentliche Wissenschaft
CAL	The Comprehensive Aramaic Lexicon Project at Hebrew Union College-Jewish Institute of Religion
CBC	Cornerstone Biblical Commentary
CBQ	*Catholic Biblical Quarterly*
CBQMS	Catholic Biblical Quarterly Monograph Series
CCGNT	Classic Commentaries on the Greek New Testament
CLLP	Clarendon Library of Logic and Philosophy
CRINT	Compendia rerum Iudaicarum ad Novum Testamentum
CurBR	*Currents in Biblical Research*
DARCOM	Daniel and Revelation Committee Series
DBL	*Dictionary of Biblical Imagery*. Edited by Leland Ryken, James C. Wilhoit, and Tremper Longman III. Downers Grove, IL: InterVarsity Press, 2000.
DLNT	*Dictionary of the Later New Testament and Its Developments*. Edited by Ralph P. Martin and Peter H. Davids. Downers Grove, IL: InterVarsity Press, 1997.
EDNT	*Exegetical Dictionary of the New Testament*. Edited by Horst Robert Balz and Gerhard Schneider. 3 vols. Grand Rapids, MI: Eerdmans, 1990–93.
EKKNT	Evangelisch-katholischer Kommentar zum Neuen Testament
ErFor	Erträge der Forschung
ESV	English Standard Version
ETR	*Études théologiques et religieuses*
EvQ	*Evangelical Quarterly*
ExpTim	*Expository Times*
FRLANT	Forschungen zur Religion und Literatur des Alten und Neuen Testaments
HCSB	Holman Christian Standard Bible
HNTC	Harper's New Testament Commentary
HTR	*Harvard Theological Review*
ICC	The International Critical Commentary
INT	*Interpretation*
ISBE	*International Standard Bible Encyclopedia*. Revised edition. Edited by Geoffrey W. Bromiley et al. 4 vols. Grand Rapids, MI: Eerdmans, 1979–88.
JATS	*Journal of the Adventist Theological Society*
JBL	*Journal of Biblical Literature*
JSJSup	Supplements to the Journal for the Study of Judaism
JSNT	*Journal for the Study of the New Testament*
JSNTSup	Journal for the Study of the New Testament Supplement Series
JSOT	*Journal for the Study of the Old Testament*
JSOTSup	Journal for the Study of the Old Testament Supplement Series

JTS	*Journal of Theological Studies*
KD	*Kerygma und Dogma*
KEK	Kritisch-exegetischer Kommentar über das Neue Testament (Meyer-Kommentar)
KJV	King James Version
L&N	*Greek-English Lexicon of the New Testament: Based on Semantic Domains*. 2nd ed. Edited by Johannes P. Louw and Eugene A. Nida. New York: United Bible Societies, 1989.
LBRS	Lexham Bible Reference Series
LCL	Loeb Classical Library
LEB	Lexham English Bible
LHBOTS	Library of Hebrew Bible/Old Testament Studies
LNTS	Library of New Testament Studies
LXX	Septuagint (the Greek tradition as a whole); *Septuaginta*. Edited by Alfred Rahlfs and Robert Hanhart. Stuttgart: Deutsche Bibelgesellschaft, 2006.
LXX^A	Codex Alexandrinus to the Septuagint
LXX^B	Codex Vaticanus to the Septuagint
MSU	Mitteilungen des Septuaginta-Unternehmens
MT/BHS	*Biblia Hebraica Stuttgartensia*. Edited by Karl Elliger and Wilhelm Rudolph. Stuttgart: German Bible Society, 1997.
NA^{28}	*Novum Testamentum Graece*. 28th ed. Edited by Barbara and Kurt Aland, Johannes Karavidopoulos, Carlo M. Martini, Bruce M. Metzger. Stuttgart: Deutsche Bibelgesellschaft, 2012.
NAC	The New American Commentary
NASB	New American Standard Bible
Neot	*Neotestamentica*
NETS	New English Translation of the Septuagint
NICNT	New International Commentary on the New Testament
NIDOTE	*New International Dictionary of Old Testament Theology and Exegesis*. Edited by W. A. VanGemeren. 5 vols. Grand Rapids, MI: Zondervan, 1997.
NIGTC	New International Greek Testament Commentary
NIV	New International Version
NIVAC	New International Version Application Commentary
NLT	New Living Translation
NovT	*Novum Testamentum*
NovTSup	Novum Testamentum Supplements
NRSV	New Revised Standard Version
NSBT	New Studies in Biblical Theology
NTC	New Testament Commentary
NTL	The New Testament Library
NTS	*New Testament Studies*
Op. Mund.	*On the Creation* (Philo)
OTL	The Old Testament Library
OTP	*Old Testament Pseudepigrapha*. Edited by James H. Charlesworth. 2 vols. New York: Yale University Press, 1983, 1985.

PNTC	Pillar New Testament Commentary
PRJ	*The Puritan Reformed Journal*
PRS	*Perspectives on Religious Studies*
Quaest. In Exod.	Questions and Answers on Exodus (Philo)
RB	*Revue biblique*
RBS	Resources for Biblical Study
ResQ	*Restoration Quarterly*
RevExp	*Review and Expositor*
RevQ	*Revue de Qumran*
RTR	*Reformed Theological Review*
SBL	Society of Biblical Literature
SBLAIL	SBL Ancient Israel and Its Literature
SBLDS	SBL Dissertation Series
SBLSCS	SBL Septuagint and Cognate Studies
SBLSP	SBL Seminar Papers
SJCL	Studies in Jewish and Christian Literature
SJT	*Scottish Journal of Theology*
SNT	*Studien zum Neuen Testament*
SNTSMS	Society for New Testament Studies Monograph Series
Somn.	*On Dreams* (Philo)
Spec. Leg.	*On the Special Laws* (Philo)
StBibLit	Studies in Biblical Literature
STDJ	Studies on the Texts of the Desert of Judah
SubBib	Subsidia Biblica
SWJT	*Southwestern Journal of Theology*
TDNT	*Theological Dictionary of the New Testament*. Edited by Gerhard Kittel and Gerhard Friedrich. Translated by Geoffrey W. Bromiley. 10 vols. Grand Rapids, MI: Eerdmans, 1964–67.
TDOT	*Theological Dictionary of the Old Testament*. Edited by G. Johannes Botterweck, Helmer Ringgren, and Heinz-Josef Fabry. Translated by J. T. Willis, D. E. Green, and D. W. Scott. 15 vols. Grand Rapids, MI: Eerdmans, 1977–2012.
TENT	Texts and Editions for New Testament Study
TNTC	Tyndale New Testament Commentary
TOTC	Tyndale Old Testament Commentary
TrinJ	*Trinity Journal*
TynBul	*Tyndale Bulletin*
TZ	*Theologische Zeitschrift*
USQR	*Union Seminary Quarterly Review*
UTRS	University of Toronto Romance Series
Vit. Mos.	*On the Life of Moses* (Philo)
War	*Jewish Wars* (Josephus)
WMANT	Wissenschaftliche Monographien zum Alten und Neuen-Testament
WUNT	Wissenschaftliche Untersuchungen zum Neuen Testament
ZNW	*Zeitschrift für die neutestamentliche Wissenschaft und die Kunde der älteren Kirche*

PART I
THE HEAVENLY TABERNACLE

Chapter 1

HEAVENLY TABERNACLE ESCHATOLOGY

1.1. Spatiotemporal Eschatology and the Heavenly Tabernacle

Jesus' death and resurrection has ushered in a state of latter-day eschatology for New Covenant believers. This eschatological prevalence can be seen in the New Testament in both the Pauline letters[1] and the non-Pauline letters such as the Epistle to the Hebrews.[2] Within the New Testament notion of eschatology, two realities co-exist both temporally and spatially,[3] with "heaven as the higher world over against earth."[4] Yet, it is in heaven where the "provisionally-realized final state" resides,[5] that is, the consummate kingdom and heavenly inheritance that believers will receive during Christ's second advent exists presently, yet provisionally in heaven.[6] This "latter-day new creation" has been inaugurated in the present,

---

1. Geerhardus Vos, *The Pauline Eschatology* (Princeton, NJ: Princeton University Press, 1930).

2. C. K Barrett, "The Eschatology of the Epistle to the Hebrews," in *The Background of the New Testament and Its Eschatology: Essays in Honour of C. H. Dodd*, ed. W. D. Davies and D. Daube (Cambridge: Cambridge University Press, 1956), 363–93.

3. By "temporal," I do not mean existing for a limited time (i.e., temporary). Rather, I refer to a reality that *presently* exists and will continue to exist along the axis of time according to God's eternality. By "spatial," I mean that it is (1) localized and occupying an identifiable, coordinate place and (2) materialized and consisting of physicality. I discuss what this entails in Section 6.1.3.

4. Andrew T. Lincoln, *Paradise Now and Not Yet: Studies in the Role of the Heavenly Dimension in Paul's Thought with Special Reference to His Eschatology*, SNTSMS 43 (New York: Cambridge University Press, 1981), 171; cf. Vos, *Pauline Eschatology*, 37–39. Vos recognized that heaven offered the advantage of expressing that the provisionally realized final state lies on a higher plane than the preceding world-development (Lincoln, 171).

5. Ibid.

6. It is the intent of this study to investigate in what *sense* this provisionally realized final state exists by way of the heavenly tabernacle.

and at least spiritually, the "already" is present in believers and the visible church. Therefore, eschatology is not limited to mere future events.[7]

The next question is how eschatology is present for believers, which indeed includes the spiritual benefits conferred in Christ's redemptive work. However, much scholarly attention has been given to the temporal, horizontal referent of eschatology[8] at the expense of the spatial, vertical referent.[9] With regards to the latter, it is often emphasized *that* such an eschatological reality presently exists, but without delving into *what* that is or *how* and *where* it is.[10] Therefore, scholars

---

7. Not all scholars believe in a physical consummation regarding the future eschaton. For example, Christopher Rowland interprets Revelation 21 as a non-literal vision and therefore rejects the idea of the new Jerusalem existing as a physical entity in heaven (*The Open Heaven: A Study of Apocalyptic in Judaism and Early Christianity* [London: SPCK, 1982], 56).

8. By horizontal I mean the time-bound progression of redemptive events that culmimnates in Christ's future return. Vertical eschatology corresponds to the present, spatial standing that believers share with Christ in the heavenly places. This is, at a minimum, a locative space in the transcendent heavens. Horizontal eschatology speaks of the believer's salvific reality in temporal terms (i.e., what they were, who they are now, and what they will be). Vertical eschatology does so in spatial terms (i.e., where they are and who they are with). Generally, horizontal eschatology discusses what takes place here on earth and vertical eschatology describes what takes place in heaven. This corresponds with G. K. Beale's definitions: "One striking feature of the eschatology of Hebrews, though also a trait of New Testament eschatology elsewhere, is that of its two-dimensional nature: it is characterized both by a vertical and horizontal plane, or both a spatial and temporal element. The preceding discussion has focused on the temporal aspect that the 'end-times' had begun in Christ's past work but also the final 'end' was still to come in the future. In the light of the spatial perspective, the end-time temple, for example, can be viewed both as a reality in present time and as being in a spatial dimension different from that of the material, earthly dimension (Heb. 9.1–10.26) because of the work of Christ" (*John's Use of the Old Testament in Revelation*, JSNTSup 166 [Sheffield: Sheffield Academic Press, 1998], 141).

9. Eric Stewart writes, "Nowhere is the privileging of time over space more apparent than in New Testament studies" (*Gathered around Jesus: An Alternative Spatial Practice in the Gospel of Mark* [Eugene, OR: Cascade, 2009], 41). In a similar vein, Patrick Schreiner writes that scholarship around the kingdom of God has also been neglectful to stress only the temporal question instead of the "where" or "space" of the kingdom (*The Body of Jesus: A Spatial Analysis of the Kingdom in Matthew*, LNTS 555 [New York: T&T Clark, 2016], 3, 7). Cf. also Annang Asumang, *Unlocking the Book of Hebrews: A Spatial Analysis of the Epistle to the Hebrews* (Eugene, OR: Wipf & Stock, 2008), 40.

10. Those who do discuss the inaugurated eschatological realities focus on the ethical and faithful obedience of believers. For example, in his discussion of believers' entry into the Holy of Holies and their approach to the throne of grace (cf. Heb. 4:16; 8:1), Georg Gäbel likens these events with the obedience of believers in the manner of Christ's obedience exhibited in his earthly life (*Die Kulttheologie des Hebräerbriefes: Eine exegetisch-religionsgeschichtliche Studie*, WUNT 2/212 [Tübingen: Mohr Siebeck, 2006],

like Andrew Lincoln call for the equalizing of the playing field in New Testament eschatological studies by stating, "Both sorts of language are to be given their full weight."[11] He continues, "Such flexibility will enable the reader to avoid the simplistic approach of those who would reduce the possibility of definition to two options by asserting that these eschatological realities are *either* in time *or* timeless, [or] they are *either* in space *or* spaceless."[12]

While the New Testament and especially the Pauline letters dedicate significant space elaborating the temporal aspects of eschatology (i.e., what believers spiritually possess now and what they will possess in consummate form in the future),[13] the letter to the Hebrews is an invaluable source in which an eschatology of both time and space is prevalent in the present. It is only in Hebrews that the higher plane of heaven is extensively presented with Christ as high priest ministering in heavenly space.[14] Regrettably, scholarship even in Hebrews has divorced the vertical and horizontal elements of its eschatology by pitting them against one another.[15] Leonhard Goppelt writes, "But was it really the case that Hebrews

---

209). For other examples of inaugurated, eschatological ethics, see G. K. Beale, "The Expanding Purpose of Temples in the Old Testament," in *The Temple and the Church's Mission: A Biblical Theology of the Dwelling Place of God*, NSBT 17 (Downers Grove, IL: InterVarsity Press, 2004), 81–122; "The Spirit as the Transforming Agent of the Inaugurated Eschatological New Creation" and "The Commencement of the Spirit's Building of Believers into the Transformed Temple of the End-Time New Creation," in *A New Testament Biblical Theology: The Unfolding of the Old Testament in the New* (Grand Rapids, MI: Baker Academic, 2011), 559–649; Geerhardus Vos, "The Religious and Ethical Motivation of Paul's Eschatology," in *Pauline Eschatology*, 62–71.

11. Lincoln, *Paradise Now and Not Yet*, 5.

12. Ibid.; emphases original.

13. For example, Rom. 8:19-25; 13:11-14; 1 Cor. 2:6-7; 3:12-15; 7:29-31; 15:20-28; 2 Cor. 4:16-18; 1 Thess. 4:13-18; 2 Thess. 2:4-8; Phil. 3:20-21; Col. 3:1-4; 1 Tim. 6:17-19; cf. Vos, *Pauline Eschatology*, 26–27. Vos notes that the concept of a higher *kosmos* is not found in Paul because of its associations with this evil world (ibid., 38).

14. Marie E. Isaacs, *Sacred Space: An Approach to the Theology of the Epistle to the Hebrews*, JSNTSup 73 (Sheffield: Sheffield Academic Press, 1992), 149.

15. For example, Ceslas Spicq does not see a "chronological continuity with the present world" (*continuité chronologique avec le monde présent*) as that of Jewish apocalyptic literature and, instead, contemporaneous only in terms of "spiritual, divine realities" (*réalités spirituelles, divines*) (*L'Épitre aux Hébreux*, 2 vols. [Paris: Gabalda, 1952], 1:268).

Richard M. Davidson states "that most recent studies of biblical typology have concentrated on horizontal typology and completely ignored the vertical typological patterns" (*Typology in Scripture: A Study of Hermeneutical* ΤΥΠΟΣ *Structures*, AUSDDS 2 [Berrien Springs, MI: Andrews University Press, 1981], 99). See also his chapter, "Typology in the Book of Hebrews," in *Issues in the Book of Hebrews*, ed. Frank B. Holbrook, DARCOM 4 (Silver Spring, MD: BRI, 1989), 148. Although there are select studies in Hebrews where a vertical typology "can hardly be avoided," Davidson notes that the majority of scholars such as Leonhard Goppelt "downplays the significance of vertical typology in Hebrews,

thought primarily, as it were, in this vertical cosmic-Hellenistic dualism, or did it think like Jesus and Paul in terms of the salvation-historical horizontal dimension?"[16] To such questions, we may respond by asking: Are the vertical and horizontal features of Hebrews mutually exclusive? Must eschatology likewise be bifurcated in such a manner?

This study argues the following thesis: The author of Hebrews presents the heavenly tabernacle along with all its high priestly activity, to eschatologically situate, orient, and ground believers both spatially and temporally. This enables believers to actualize in practice their heavenly, priestly identity by serving as priests on earth. This spatiotemporal eschatology, as we will call it, incorporates both spatial and temporal features of the heavenly tabernacle, which contributes to the author's holistic presentation of eschatology and carries ethical (and communal) implications in the letter to the Hebrews. I hope to offer two primary contributions to Hebrews scholarship. (1) The first contribution is methodological, utilizing insights from Edward Soja's Tripartite Critical Spatial Theory and applying them to all explicit references to the heavenly tabernacle in Hebrews.[17] (2) The second contribution is theological, amending the dichotomy of spatial

---

regarding it only as an aid to the better expounding of horizontal typology" (*Typology in Scripture*, 99; cf. Leonhard Goppelt, "Τύπος, Ἀντίτυπος, Τυπικός, Ὑποτύπωσις," *TDNT* 8:258–59).

16. Leonhard Goppelt, *Theology of the New Testament*, 2 vols. (Grand Rapids, MI: Eerdmans, 1982), 2:246. Similarly, ever since Albert Vanhoye introduced the question of a supposed horizontal/vertical dualism, it has been a premier challenge in Hebrews scholarship. David M. Moffitt writes, "In other words, the heart of the debate centers on what the nature of the eschatological world will be. Will it be a release of the spirit from the world of earthly matter into the realm of spirits, or will it involve some kind of transfer such that human beings will continue to have human bodies, but will nonetheless be fully able to dwell in God's presence?" (*Atonement and the Logic of Resurrection in the Epistle to the Hebrews*, NovTSup 141 [Leiden: Brill, 2013], 68–69). One's position impacts their view in the rest of their reading of Hebrews. For example, Vanhoye sees οἰκουμένη as a specialized term in Hebrews referring to a spiritual, eschatological realm in contrast to κόσμος ("L'οἰκουμένη dans l'Épître aux Hébreux," *Biblica* 45 [1964]: 253): "*Kosmos* désigne le monde visible, matériel; *oikouménè* évoque une réalité spirituelle, le monde des relations entre personnes" (emphases original). This is also noted by Moffitt, *Atonement*, 64.

17. The only application of Soja's theory on the heavenly tabernacle is Cynthia Wests fall's short chapter entitled "Space and Atonement in Hebrews," in *So Great a Salvation: A Dialogue on the Atonement in Hebrews*, ed. Jon C. Laansma, George H. Guthrie, and Cynthia Long Westfall, LNTS 516 (New York: T&T Clark, 2019), 228–48, which I discuss in Section 2.4. Apart from Westfall's chapter, the only comprehensive work on the spatiality of the entirety of Hebrews is Asumang's *Unlocking Hebrews*. However, Asumang's primary focus is on the wilderness people of God in Numbers and, in turn, on the people of God in Hebrews, and is not a dedicated work on the heavenly tabernacle. Furthermore, Asumang does not apply Soja's Tripartite Theory nor does he interpret the heavenly tabernacle as a physical, localized structure in the heavens, which is the position I defend in Part 2 of this study.

and temporal eschatology by arguing for and drawing attention to the heavenly tabernacle's spatial features that presently reside in heaven in a localized fashion. This tabernacle space is a real and actual place that believers spiritually occupy through Christ's high priestly access. This heavenly occupancy not only enables but also empowers the recipient believers to live out their priestly identity in their current already/not-yet eschatological situation on earth.

1.1.1. Spatiotemporal Eschatological Language in Hebrews

While Andrew Lincoln's cry for equalizing the playing field of both spatial and temporal characteristics of eschatology rings true for the entire New Testament, as Annang Asumang states, it is especially in Hebrews that "[t]here has been an academic debate as to whether the thought processes of the author of Hebrews are primarily spatial or temporal and whether it is cosmology or eschatology that structures the author's thought."[18] That there is an ongoing debate shows that Hebrews is not immune to the dichotomy of space and time when it comes to biblical themes such as eschatology. Such is the case when anything spatial in Hebrews is associated with cosmology, while eschatology has to do with time.[19] Because the debate has been set up along these two axes, a pendulum effect arises, asserting that the author of Hebrews is more spatial in his thought (i.e., Platonic or cosmological), or that he is more temporal (i.e., what is often meant to be eschatological). Asumang continues:

> This debate, however, betrays a false dichotomy that is made between space and time in academic discussions of the theology of Hebrews… [T]here is a very close interchangeable relationship between space and time… Space and time are in a continuum, and hence there is no question about any clumsy mixture of apocalyptic eschatology with platonic cosmology in Hebrews.[20]

It must be maintained that spatiality in Hebrews does not necessarily equate to Platonic or Philonic cosmology. Earlier biblical scholars who have asserted a Platonic/Philonic influence did so by observing the spatial features of the letter.[21]

---

18. Asumang, *Unlocking Hebrews*, 182.

19. Perhaps this is due to the commonly found scholarly assumption that the Bible itself is more concerned with time than space (Johan Marie Brinkman, *The Perception of Space in the Old Testament: An Exploration of the Methodological Problems of Its Investigation, Exemplified by a Study of Exodus 25 to 31* [Kampen: Kok Pharos, 1992], 22). Brinkman attributes this to the Bible paying "more attention to generations, to events… [and] is more concerned with history than with geography" (ibid.). While this study does not set out to challenge this assumption for the entirety of Scripture, I hope to show that the spatial features of the heavenly tabernacle in Hebrews is an important characteristic along with its temporal, eschatological dimension.

20. Asumang, *Unlocking Hebrews*, 182.

21. More on these scholars in Section 1.2.

They were right to draw attention to its spatial qualities. However, the problem lies in asserting the more difficult claim that the author of Hebrews' spatial concepts derived from or depended on a Platonic framework. This does not mean we must abandon Hebrews' rich spatial features altogether. Rather, we must investigate how these spatial features are interweaved with temporal features, especially when it comes to the believers' eschatological situation.

Therefore, the unhelpful dichotomy between space and time must be challenged. Does the author of Hebrews present his eschatology strictly in a temporal fashion? I answer in the negative, in that the author does not create such a dichotomy of space and time regarding key concepts in his letter.[22] In fact, the force of what he communicates is accented by the interweaving of both spatial and temporal language to communicate important ideas and themes.[23] See Table 1 for passages that reflect this:

Table 1. Movement Passages in Hebrews with Spatial and Temporal Language

Concept or Theme	Spatial Language	Temporal Language
Christ's Seating on the Throne after Having Made Purification of Sins	ἐκάθισεν ἐν δεξιᾷ τῆς μεγαλωσύνης ἐν ὑψηλοῖς (1:3d)[24]	καθαρισμὸν τῶν ἁμαρτιῶν ποιησάμενος (1:3c)[25]
Christ Made Lower than the Angels for a Little While	παρ' ἀγγέλους ἠλαττωμένον (2:9a)	τὸν δὲ βραχύ τι (2:9a)
Holy Spirit's Warning to Enter Rest "Today"	εἰ εἰσελεύσονται εἰς τὴν κατάπαυσίν μου (3:11b)	σήμερον ἐὰν τῆς φωνῆς αὐτοῦ ἀκούσητε (3:7b)

---

22. Scott D. Mackie, "Introduction to Part 2," in *The Letter to the Hebrews: Critical Readings*, ed. Scott D. Mackie, T&T Clark Critical Readings in Biblical Studies (London: T&T Clark, 2018), 141, who writes that "these spatial and temporal dimensions have occasionally been separated and/or individually prioritized by some scholars."

23. Movement passages in Hebrews "clearly permeate and dominate the whole language" of Hebrews (Asumang, *Unlocking Hebrews*, 40). Furthermore, he notes that verbs of movement are the traversing of space within a given time (i.e., movement = space + time). Hence, they are inseparable.

24. Throughout this study, unless otherwise noted, I follow the NT Greek text found in NA[28] and the OT Hebrew in *BHS*. For the LXX, see my discussion in Section 3.1.1. For the English Bible, I utilize the translation from the *New American Standard Bible* (La Habra, CA: The Lockman Foundation, 1995) unless otherwise noted.

25. The temporal participle ποιησάμενος communicates the completion of cleansing before he sits on the throne. Also 1:13b: κάθου ἐκ δεξιῶν μου, ἕως ἂν θῶ τοὺς ἐχθρούς σου ὑποπόδιον τῶν ποδῶν σου.

Entering Rest While the Promise Remains (After Having Believed)	εἰσελθεῖν εἰς τὴν κατάπαυσιν αὐτοῦ (4:1c) εἰσερχόμεθα[26] γὰρ εἰς τὴν κατάπαυσιν οἱ πιστεύσαντες (4:3a)[27]	μήποτε καταλειπομένης ἐπαγγελίας (4:1b)
Christ Entering the Veil as the Eternal High Priest	ὅπου πρόδρομος ὑπὲρ ἡμῶν εἰσῆλθεν Ἰησοῦς (6:20a)	ἀρχιερεὺς γενόμενος εἰς τὸν αἰῶνα (6:20b)
Contrasts between the Levitical Priesthood against Christ's Priesthood	ὑψηλότερος τῶν οὐρανῶν γενόμενος (7:26c) εἰς μὲν τὴν πρώτην σκηνὴν διὰ παντὸς εἰσίασιν (9:6b) ἅπαξ τοῦ ἐνιαυτοῦ μόνος ὁ ἀρχιερεὺς εἰσίασιν (9:7a) ὥσπερ ὁ ἀρχιερεὺς εἰσέρχεται εἰς τὰ ἅγια (9:25b)	ὃς οὐκ ἔχει καθ' ἡμέραν ἀνάγκην... ὑπὲρ τῶν ἰδίων ἁμαρτιῶν θυσίας ἀναφέρειν (7:27a–b) εἰς μὲν τὴν πρώτην σκηνὴν διὰ <u>παντὸς</u> εἰσίασιν (9:6b) <u>ἅπαξ τοῦ ἐνιαυτοῦ</u> μόνος ὁ ἀρχιερεὺς (9:7a) κατ' ἐνιαυτὸν ἐν αἵματι ἀλλοτρίῳ (9:25c)
The Standing Tabernacle for the Present Time	ἔτι τῆς πρώτης σκηνῆς ἐχούσης στάσιν (9:8c)	ἥτις παραβολὴ εἰς τὸν καιρὸν τὸν ἐνεστηκότα (9:9a)

26. Codices Alexandrinus and Ephraemi Rescriptus have the subjunctive εισερχωμεθα, which may have been introduced due to another nearby textual variant, ουν (ℵ, A, C), in place of γὰρ. Note that εισερχωμεθα and ουν are present in these same two witnesses (A and C). If γὰρ is the better reading due to the earlier witnesses (i.e., 𝔓[13,46] and B), then the indicative form, εἰσέρχομαι, is preferred ("for we have entered" instead of "therefore, let us enter"). Bruce M. Metzger also comments that the subjunctive is "quite inappropriate" with the following οἱ πιστεύσαντες (*A Textual Commentary on the Greek New Testament*, 2nd ed. [Stuttgart: Deutsche Biblegesellschaft, 1994], 596). The addition of τὴν may have been an insertion to signify and match the κατάπαυσιν that the author introduces in verse 1, which does not impact the meaning of this verse.

27. Similar verses can also be referenced throughout Hebrews 4 (e.g., 4:5, 10–11).

Contrast between Levitical Priests Standing Daily and Christ's Once-for-All Seating	Καὶ πᾶς μὲν ἱερεὺς[28] ἕστηκεν καθ' ἡμέραν λειτουργῶν (10:11a) ἐκάθισεν ἐν δεξιᾷ[29] τοῦ θεοῦ (10:12c)	Καὶ πᾶς μὲν ἱερεὺς ἕστηκεν <u>καθ' ἡμέραν</u> λειτουργῶν (10:11a) προσενέγκας θυσίαν εἰς τὸ διηνεκὲς (10:12b)
Believers' Exhortation to Enter and Draw Near as the Day Draws Near	παρρησίαν εἰς τὴν εἴσοδον τῶν ἁγίων (10:19b) προσερχώμεθα[30] μετὰ ἀληθινῆς καρδίας ἐν πληροφορίᾳ πίστεως (10:22a)	βλέπετε ἐγγίζουσαν τὴν ἡμέραν (10:25c)

The eschatology of Hebrews, like the concepts and themes listed above, is also described in language marked with both spatial and temporal features. In fact, this characteristic is what makes the eschatology of Hebrews so immanent, yet forward-looking.[31] It describes the present reality that exists for believers in the heavens, while also exhorting them to strive in faithful obedience in line with their coming future inheritance. But to see this eschatology strictly on a temporal plane is to adopt an under-realized eschatology that looks at the present only as "not-yet." Such a temporal-only eschatology requires mutually exclusive understandings of the two ages and makes it difficult to comprehend how the two can be contemporaneous with one another.[32] Hence, a spatial eschatology is important

---

28. The earlier witnesses of 𝔓[46], 𝔓[79] and ℵ support the reading of ἱερεὺς compared to the variant αρχιερευς found in Codices A and C. It is possible that copyists inserted αρχ- due to the discussion of the high priest in Heb. 8:3 and 9:7–11, 25 for the sake of clarification.

29. The variant, εκ δεξιων, may be from the influence of Ps. 109:1 LXX (ἐκ δεξιῶν μου) also found in Heb. 1:13. The text, ἐν δεξιᾷ, is supported by the earlier witnesses 𝔓[13], 𝔓[46], and 𝔓[79].

30. The variant reading προσερχομεθα in the indicative is strongly attested (𝔓[13] and 𝔓[46]) but may have arisen "from the very common confusion between homophonous ω and o" (Paul Ellingworth, *The Epistle to the Hebrews:* A Commentary on the Greek Text, NIGTC [Grand Rapids, MI: Eerdmans, 1993], 522). See also the participial forms found in 10:1 and 11:6, which also contain the omicron and not the omega.

31. This is known as the already/not-yet eschatological reality that believers participate in with the ushering in of the latter days in light of Christ's resurrection (see G. K. Beale's chapters, "The Eschatological Storyline of the Old Testament in Relation to the New Testament" and "Further Reflections on the Nature of the Eschatological New Testament Storyline," in *A New Testament Biblical Theology*, 129–86).

32. This is partly the reason why Hebrews is a challenge to understand in passages where believers are said to have entered God's rest (4:3), while only a couple of verses earlier, the promise of entering his rest remains (4:1). Our understanding of the past, present,

since it can be used to describe two concurrent realities being true in different places.³³

Geerhardus Vos similarly observes the advantages of a spatial eschatology: "[F]or here the existence of one does not exclude the contemporary existence of another, and there is nothing logically impossible either in the believer's belonging to both or at least preeminently to one rather than to the other."³⁴ Hence, adopting a full-orbed spatiotemporal eschatology of the tabernacle allows believers to have stronger confidence in their positional heavenly standing since that standing takes place in an actual place and in the present. This is especially true in Hebrews where the believer's positional standing corresponds to Christ's physical entry into the heavenly sanctuary. Therefore, one can say of Hebrews, "As soon as the direction of the actual spiritual life-contact becomes involved, the horizontal movement of thought on the time-plane must give way immediately to a vertical projection of the eschatological interest into the supernal region."³⁵

Tabernacle spatial language has often been associated with a cosmological interpretation, which identifies the tabernacle as either heaven itself or parts of heaven in a one-to-one fashion (i.e., the constituent parts and artifacts of the heavenly tabernacle refer to elements of the cosmos).³⁶ More recently, a reaction against the cosmological view has unfortunately brought upon another misinterpretation—either consciously or unconsciously—against a spatial view of the tabernacle altogether. While C. K. Barrett's influential article, "Eschatology of the Epistle to the Hebrews" (1956)³⁷ rightly stressed the importance of recognizing Hebrews' two-age, redemptive-historical presentation of believers' salvation, we must not go too far in favoring a temporal understanding of eschatology at the expense of the spatial.

For example, Kenneth Schenck writes that "the framework of Hebrews' thought is the narrative of *salvation history*, a plot that is fundamentally *horizontal* and teleological in orientation."³⁸ Thomas Keene argues against Otto Michel's

---

and future being mutually exclusive creates interpretive difficulties in such passages. For a more in-depth study on this topic, see David Peterson, *Hebrews and Perfection: An Examination of the Concept of Perfection in the "Epistle to the Hebrews,"* SNTSMS 47 (New York: Cambridge University Press, 2005).

33. This idea is found in other NT writings. For example, it is possible to speak of a believer being in two worlds (Jn 8:23) because Christian believers are *spiritually* seated with Christ in the heavenly places (Eph. 2:6) but *physically* on earth to live in faithful obedience (1 Pet. 1:17; cf. Phil. 1:24–26).

34. Vos, *Pauline Eschatology*, 37.
35. Ibid.
36. See my discussion on those who hold the cosmological view in Section 1.2.1.
37. Barrett, "The Eschatology of the Epistle to the Hebrews," 363–93.
38. Kenneth L. Schenck, "Philo and the Epistle to the Hebrews: Ronald Williamson's Study After Thirty Years," in *SPhiloA: Studies in Hellenistic Judaism*, BJS 14 (Providence, RI: Brown University Press, 2002), 116; emphases original. Schenck's aim in this particular work is to argue against a Philonic reading by dismissing spatial features altogether.

tabernacle divisions in Hebrews 9:6–10 as "illustrations or allegories for divisions in the heavens," which is strictly a cosmological interpretation. However, we need not conclude that the tabernacle divisions are strictly temporal either. Keene rightly suggests the utilization of eschatology as a better interpretive framework but focuses primarily on eschatology's temporal aspects. He concludes that the "contrast between the Mosaic and the Heavenly is not primarily cosmological and metaphysical but temporal and eschatological."[39] This study, in part, aims to further advance Keene's work which introduces the eschatological framework of the heavenly tabernacle. I intend to do this by presenting tabernacle eschatology as being spatial, but not necessarily cosmological; the heavenly tabernacle as eschatological, but not primarily horizontal (temporal) over the vertical (spatial); and finally, the heavenly tabernacle as doctrinal, but also exhortational.

1.1.2. Reconciling Eschatological Space and Time in Hebrews

Why is it important to reconcile eschatological space and time? It is because a strictly future eschatological hope is, in fact, a diminished hope. It can be likened to Old Testament believers who only proleptically received salvific benefits and could only look forward to that to which the signs and types pointed. The full potential of eschatological hope is realized when, in addition to the future consummation of things unseen, there is access to believers' eschatological reality in the present, albeit in heavenly spiritual form and in earthly ethical practice. It is only when we have a taste of the sample of what is to come that one can effectively wait in anticipation for its fullness. Furthermore, that sample must be real and the same *in kind* to its future counterpart. Without such a taste, a future-only eschatology has the potential danger to dismiss all that Christ has already accomplished and ushered in through the Holy Spirit (Heb. 2:4; 6:4; 9:14) or even to make believers' heavenly status a detached concept that resides somewhere in the Platonic realm.

The already/not-yet eschatological reality is prevalent throughout the New Testament. For example, Paul points to how believers have *every* spiritual blessing in the heavenly places (Eph. 1:3). Believers' possession of the Holy Spirit is the guaranteed down payment (ἀρραβὼν, Eph. 1:14) of their heavenly inheritance, and this Spirit then serves as a present hope and motivator while they look forward to the fullness of that inheritance. A similar already/not-yet eschatological "tension" is present in Hebrews.[40] The discontinuity is indeed affirmed; the new heavens

---

39. Thomas Keene, "Heaven Is a Tent: The Tabernacle as an Eschatological Metaphor in the Epistle to the Hebrews" (PhD diss., Westminster Theological Seminary, 2010), 122; cf. Otto Michel, *Der Brief an Die Hebräer*, 12th ed., KEK 13 (Göttingen: Vandenhoeck & Ruprecht, 1966). The conversation has been established such that any spatial language is associated with Platonic allegorical idealisms or cosmological divisions of heaven. I intend to take a step further by doing so without the neglect of space.

40. This is not limited to the heavenly tabernacle. For example, when discussing the topic of the final Sabbath, the author of Hebrews uses both the future and present

and the new earth will be, in a sense, nothing like what heaven and earth are like today. However, we must acknowledge the continuity of the already/not-yet, because in that same eschatological sense, believers possess aspects of the new heavens and new earth in the present. Furthermore, they themselves are actors who participate in this new creation. Both already-existing and yet-to-come realities must be understood to appreciate the eschatological tension of Hebrews.

Among the various eschatological themes in Hebrews, this study focuses on the heavenly tabernacle for the following reasons. First, along with Christ as the heavenly high priest, the heavenly tabernacle is a unique reality found nowhere else in the New Testament.[41] Second, the heavenly tabernacle is a prime example of how scholarship has overlooked Hebrews' spatial eschatology in favor of the temporal or has reduced it to Platonic or cosmological categories.[42] Others have interpreted the tabernacle according to a strictly rhetorical or social framework that limits us from appreciating its spatiality holistically.[43] While there are some who have recognized the importance of spatiality in Hebrews—albeit, not under the schema of eschatology—scholarship has had difficulty in reconciling the temporal and spatial elements of the heavenly tabernacle.[44] Finally, as this study hopes to show, the heavenly tabernacle serves as a heuristic tool to promote a holistic eschatology that gives weight to both its temporal and its spatial features. If believers grasp the indicative of their already-obtained access and standing with God in the localized heavenly tabernacle, then they no longer have to look on earth for a lasting city (Heb. 13:14). They can look upon their earthly

progressive tenses to signify believers' eschatological rest. As the people of God, they look forward to dwelling in the heavenly country (Heb. 13), while at the same time dwell with their high priest in the heavenly sanctuary.

41. There may be implicit references to the heavenly tabernacle in Rev. 13:6, 15:5, and 21:3, which remain outside the scope of this study.

42. There is a trend in Hebrews scholarship to interpret the heavenly places according to the framework of either a Platonic-Philonic cosmology or Jewish apocalypticism (David Moffitt, "Serving in the Tabernacle in Heaven: Sacred Space, Jesus's High-Priestly Sacrifice, and Hebrews' Analogical Theology," in *Hebrews in Contexts*, ed. Gabriella Gelardini and Harold W. Attridge, AGJU 91 [Leiden: Brill, 2016], 266; cf. also Eric F. Mason, "'Sit at My Right Hand': Enthronement and the Heavenly Sanctuary in Hebrews," in *A Teacher for All Generations: Essays in Honor of James C. VanderKam*, ed. Eric F. Mason et al., JSJSup 153 [Leiden: Brill, 2012], 2:901–16).

43. Cf. Sections 1.2.2–3.

44. For example, Nicholas J. Moore writes, "[Heavenly] access is portrayed as rest, the future goal of a pilgrim people (Heb. 3–4), but also as a sanctuary, the present possession of a priestly people (Heb. 5–10). Such a dual portrayal is at best confusing, and at worst contradictory" ("'In' or 'Near'? Heavenly Access and Christian Identity in Hebrews," in *Muted Voices of the New Testament: Readings in the Catholic Epistles and Hebrews*, ed. Katherine M. Hockey, Madison N. Pierce, and Francis Watson, LNTS 565 [New York: T&T Clark, 2017], 185).

communities—not as a place they call home, but as a place where they mediate the presence of God as heavenly priests on earth.

1.2. Survey of Scholarship on the Heavenly Tabernacle

There has been a fair amount of scholarship on the earthly tabernacle, as presented in the Old Testament, intertestamental and Jewish literature, and the New Testament.[45] Yet, when one gets to the Epistle to the Hebrews, the unique concept of the heavenly tabernacle becomes somewhat "enigmatic."[46] The reason for this lies in the challenge of understanding (1) the relationship between the tabernacle and Israel's cultic institutions and, closely related, (2) the background for the letter's tabernacle imagery.[47] Hence, these two challenges set the terms for how we should approach the heavenly tabernacle in Hebrews. They are certainly important in investigating the author of Hebrews' intent and usage of the heavenly tabernacle for his theological, and as I will argue later, his exhortational arguments.

Nevertheless, focusing on these two challenges does not take into consideration the full value of the heavenly tabernacle's features. In other words, they search for answers to the question of *how* the heavenly tabernacle is being used in Hebrews before it asks the question, "What is the heavenly tabernacle?" I suggest, once the *what* question is answered, then we can better understand the *how* question. Therefore, I intend to contribute to the discussion around the heavenly tabernacle by approaching it with constitutive questions first—namely, its spatial features.

We will begin by assessing how the heavenly tabernacle has thus far been understood in biblical scholarship. In my survey of scholars' discussion around the heavenly tabernacle, I identify five categories of approaches: (1) the tabernacle as dualistic representations of heaven itself either by ideals and forms, or as the entire cosmos (the Platonic/Philonic view); (2) the tabernacle as a place of social and community participation; (3) the tabernacle as a rhetorical, literary device; (4) the tabernacle identified strictly as either a future, spatial reality or a present, spiritual-only reality; and (5) the tabernacle as a spatially realized structure in the transcendent heavens, which is the view I defend in this study. This survey will focus on representative works beginning in the 1900s.[48]

---

45. Craig R. Koester, *The Dwelling of God: The Tabernacle in the Old Testament, Intertestamental Jewish Literature, and the New Testament*, CBQMS 22 (Washington, DC: Catholic Biblical Association of America, 1989) is the most recent and comprehensive study to date.

46. Ibid., 152.

47. Ibid.; cf. also Benjamin J. Ribbens, *Levitical Sacrifice and Heavenly Cult in Hebrews*, BZNW 222 (Berlin: de Gruyter, 2016), 85–99.

48. For a summary of earlier, traditional views of the tent, including those of the early Church, see Keene's discussion on Heb. 9:11–12. These views include: (1) the heavenly tabernacle as Jesus' body, either pre- or post-resurrection (allegorical and/or typological interpretations); and (2) the heavenly tabernacle as the church (ecclesiological interpretation) in "Heaven Is a Tent," 81–104.

1.2.1. Tabernacle as Dualistic Representations (The Platonic/Philonic and Cosmological Views)

This view has been prominent throughout the entire history of Hebrews interpretation.[49] In its most basic understanding, it sees the heavenly tabernacle as a representation of the heavens or cosmos in contradistinction to the earthly tabernacle.[50] Such a dualistic understanding stems from a Platonic metaphysics and philosophy, which most likely came through the writings of Philo.[51] Thus, beginning with Hugo Grotius in 1644, based on his reading of Hebrews 4:11, numerous scholars have observed the author's usage of Philonic terms and ideas.[52] After Grotius, two influential scholars that substantially discuss Hebrews and Philo are Ceslas Spicq[53] and Ronald Williamson.[54] After a thorough examination of Philo's and Hebrews' literary features as well as thought patterns,[55] Spicq

---

49. The most notable being Spicq, *L'Épitre aux Hébreux*, esp. 1:39–91; cf. Gareth Lee Cockerill, *The Epistle to the Hebrews*, NICNT (Grand Rapids, MI: Eerdmans, 2012), 29. Others who affirm a Platonic/Philonic influence to varying degrees include Wilfried Eisele, *Ein unerschütterliches Reich: Die mittelplatonische Umformung des Parusiegedankens im Hebräerbrief*, BZNW 116 (Berlin: de Gruyter, 2003); Ernst Käsemann, *The Wandering People of God: An Investigation of the Letter to the Hebrews*, trans. R. A. Harrisville and I. L. Sundberg (Minneapolis, MN: Augsburg, 1984); and Gerd Theissen, *Untersuchungen zum Hebräerbrief*, SNT 2 (Gütersloh: Gerd Mohn, 1969) as cited by Cockerill, *Hebrews*, 29.

50. Not only the tabernacle, but other key terms and themes found in Hebrews may be allegorized such as the Pentateuch, Melchizedek, and the Logos (Spicq, *L'Épitre aux Hébreux*, 1:63–64).

51. Ronald Williamson, *Philo and the Epistle to the Hebrews*, ALGHJ 4 (Leiden: Brill, 1970), 557. James Moffatt writes, "The philosophical element in his view of the world and God is fundamentally Platonic. Like Philo and the author of Wisdom, he interprets the past and the present alike in terms of the old theory (cp. on 8:5; 10:1) that the phenomenal is but an imperfect, shadowy transcript of what is eternal and real." *A Critical and Exegetical Commentary on the Epistle to the Hebrews*, ICC (Edinburgh: T&T Clark, 1924), xxxi.

52. Ellingworth, *Hebrews*, 45; Spicq, *L'Épitre aux Hébreux*, 1:39, who provides a history of earlier interpreters who held similar views.

53. In addition to Spicq's most well-known work, *L'Épitre aux Hébreux* (1952), his earlier article "Ἄγκυραν et Πρόδρομος dans Hébr VI. 19–20," *ST* 3 (1951): 185–87 introduces his views.

54. As noted by Robert W. Thurston, "Philo and the Epistle to the Hebrews," *EvQ* 58.2 (1986): 133; cf. Ronald Williamson's three works: "Background of the Epistle to the Hebrews," *ExpTim* 87.8 (1976): 232–37; *Philo and the Epistle to the Hebrews*; and "Philo and New Testament Christology," in *Studia Biblica 1978 III: Papers on Paul and Other New Testament Authors. Sixth International Congress on Biblical Studies*, ed. E. A. Livingstone, JSNTSup 3 (Sheffield: JSOT Press, 1980), 439–45.

55. Spicq compares with Philo the following features: *vocabulaire, paronomases (paronyms) et métaphors, arguments et exégèse, thèmes et schèmes,* and *psychologies* (Spicq, *L'Épitre aux Hébreux*, 1:41–91). Ellingworth provides a helpful summary of Spicq's investigation of these literary features (Ellingworth, *Hebrews*, 46 nn. 29–34).

concludes that the author of Hebrews was probably an Alexandrian compatriot who followed Philo's teachings.[56] He even goes on to argue that the author was "a Philonist converted to Christianity."[57]

In response, Ronald Williamson argues that no Philonic doctrine or teaching is evident in Hebrews.[58] In fact, the two teachings are sometimes in "direct conflict" with each other.[59] The arguments that challenge Philonic dependence are as follows: (1) While it is possible, there is no chronological certainty of Hebrews' dependence on Philo.[60] (2) The influence of Philo found in many contemporaneous writings, especially those in proximity with Alexandria, cannot be denied. Nevertheless, Philo's works are so voluminous that "some points of contact with Hebrews are to be expected."[61] (3) But the strongest argument comes from looking at the context and actual usage of seemingly similar terms. Usage of similar terms does not necessarily mean dependence or derivation.[62] At closer observation, Williamson has shown that the "differences between their systems are as fundamental as the affinities are peripheral."[63]

---

56. Spicq, *L'Épitre aux Hébreux*, 1:87: "mais elle s'expliquerait au mieux si ce dernier [l'auteur de l'épître] était l'un de ses compatriots et s'il avait suivi son enseignement personnel." All French translations my own unless otherwise noted.

57. "Au total, nous souscrivons… '([l'auteur de l'épître] est un philonien converti au christianisme" (ibid., 1:91).

58. Williamson, *Philo and Hebrews*, 36, 228, 294, 301, 332, 383. Lincoln D. Hurst strengthens Williamson's contention in his work *The Epistle to the Hebrews: Its Background of Thought*, SNTSMS 65 (New York: Cambridge University Press, 1990).

59. Thurston, "Philo and Epistle to Hebrews," 133.

60. Ellingworth, *Hebrews*, 47; cf. R. P. C. Hanson, *Allegory and Event: A Study of the Sources and Significance of Origen's Interpretation of Scripture* (London: SCM Press, 1959), 85–86. Philo died around 50 CE while the composition of Hebrews was likely after 60 CE (William L. Lane, *Hebrews 1–8*, WBC 47A [Dallas, TX: Word, 1991], lxii). I discuss the authorship and dating of Hebrews in Section 3.1.1.

61. Ellingworth, *Hebrews*, 47.

62. Samuel Sandmel, "Parallelomania," *JBL* 81.1 (1962): 1–13; Moisés Silva, *Biblical Words and Their Meaning: An Introduction to Lexical Semantics*, 2nd ed. (Grand Rapids, MI: Zondervan, 1994), esp. 138–59. See Gäbel's comparison between Philo and Hebrews (Gäbel, *Kulttheologie*, 112–27). In his concluding remarks, Gäbel states that Philo's understanding of τύπος is "substantially different" (*wesentlich verschieden*) and that Hebrews is far from the "epistemological idealism" (*erkenntnistheoretischen Idealismus*) we find in Platonic texts (ibid., 126).

63. Philip E. Hughes, "Review of Philo and the Epistle to the Hebrews by Ronald Williamson," *WTJ* 35.3 (1973): 349–50; cf. Williamson, *Philo and Hebrews*, 576–80; Isaacs, *Sacred Space*, 55–56.

A. Subview 1: Tabernacle as Immaterial Heaven

The tabernacle in Hebrews has been at the heart of the Platonic/Philonic debate.[64] A Platonic, dualistic framework results in a likewise dualistic representation of the tabernacle, expressed in either of two ways: (1) the heavenly tabernacle as the immaterial heavenlies, or (2) the heavenly tabernacle as the material heavenlies—this latter view being commonly referred to as the "cosmological view." Both views stem from Philo's emphasis on "cosmic truths" being depicted in the temple "since he accepts the Greek theory that men and the universe stand in the relation of microcosm to macrocosm (*Op. Mund.* 82; *Vit. Mos.* 2:135)."[65]

The first subview, especially when observing "Philonic" terms such as ὑπόδειγμα, σκιά, and χρηματίζω in Hebrews 8:5's usage of Exodus 25:40, makes a sharp dichotomy between the two tabernacles. The earthly tabernacle lies in the phenomenal realm and is an imperfect, shadowy transcript of what is eternal and real. Therefore, for the author of Hebrews, who is "trained in the Alexandrian philosophy of religion, the present world of sense and time stands over against the world of reality, the former being merely the shadow and copy of the latter."[66] Spicq writes, "Leur temple est au sanctuaire du ciel ce que l'image est au modèle, l'ombre à la réalité… A la vérité, cet exemplaire du temple céleste est bien imparfait, une ombre… une représentation voilée…"[67]

Philo indeed saw direct correlations between the earthly tabernacle's constituents with abstract ideas.[68] Hence, when we read that the high priest enters the Holy of Holies, "the mystic heavenward soar of the mind toward divine things

---

64. Alan Marshall Fairhurst, "Hellenistic Influence in the Epistle to the Hebrews," *TynBul* 7 (1961): 20.

65. Sidney G. Sowers, *The Hermeneutics of Philo and Hebrews: A Comparison of the Interpretation of the Old Testament in Philo Judaeus and the Epistle to the Hebrews*, BST 1 (Richmond, VA: John Knox, 1965), 62.

66. Moffatt, *Hebrews*, xxxiii; cf. Williamson, *Philo and Hebrews*, 562. Philo's *Vit. Mos.* 2:74–76 is representative of how Philo sees the heavenly archetype consisting of immaterial and invisible forms or ideas imprinted on the mind of Moses (cf. Keene, "Heaven Is a Tent," 109; Isaacs, *Sacred Space*, 209).

67. "Their temple is for the sanctuary of heaven what the image is to the model, the shadow to the reality… Truly, this copy of the heavenly temple is quite imperfect, a shadow…a veiled representation" (Spicq, *L'Épitre aux Hébreux*, 2:236). He also writes, "Celui-là, étant le modèle de celui-ci, est donc plus parfait et meilleur, comme l'idéal et la réalité par rapport à la participation et à l'ombre." Spicq continues in claiming that the sanctity of the earthly tabernacle *depended* on the heavenly: "Cette reproduction du sanctuaire supra-céleste, demeure divine, assurait la sainteté de la tent mosaïque" (ibid., 2:256).

68. In his discussion of Exod. 26:33b, Philo makes a distinction within the tabernacle: (1) The simple parts correlate to a sense-perceptible heaven; (2) the inner Holy of Holies correlates with the intelligible world. This "incorporeal world" is separated by the "Logos as by a veil" (Philo, *Quaest. in Exod.* 2:94; I utilize the Greek and the translated text of Philo from LCL unless otherwise noted). Furthermore, he speaks of the "temple of the soul" and

is thereby signified (*Som.* 2:231-233; *Gig.* 52; *Mig.* 104)."[69] Such statements imply that the location of Jesus' sacrifice was made in a timeless sphere.[70] But if the heavens can be penetrated only by intellect, what does it mean for the physical, resurrected body of Jesus who has entered the sanctuary once and for all? (Heb. 9:12). Or, why does the author of Hebrews describe at times, in literal detail, attributes of the heavenly tabernacle (cf. Heb. 9:1–5)? It is extremely difficult to make a clear-cut distinction between what is material/literal and what is immaterial/ideal because the author skillfully interweaves both into his presentation of the heavenly tabernacle. The conclusion stands then, for the heavenly tabernacle, that the presence of such "Philonic" terms does not necessarily mean dependence or even derivation.[71]

This does not mean that the earthly and heavenly tabernacles are to be conflated. Rather, the distinctions between the earthly and heavenly constructions of the tabernacle have their source not from Plato/Philo, but from the Old Testament.[72] The distinction between the earthly and heavenly tabernacle was certainly present in Old Testament Jewish thought before the writings of Plato and Philo. As this study hopes to show, the author uses spatial descriptions that are motivated by eschatology, not by philosophy.[73]

B. Subview 2: Tabernacle as the Cosmos

The cosmological view, originating from Josephus, sees the earthly tabernacle referring to the *material* heavens as its archetype rather than Philo's *immaterial*

---

how the "rational faculty" may correspond to the high priest and the temple's functions (Sowers, *The Hermeneutics of Philo and Hebrews*, 62).

69. Ibid., 63.

70. Moffatt, *Hebrews*, xliii; also Asumang, *Unlocking Hebrews*, 29; Fairhurst, *Hellenistic Influence in Hebrews*, 23. It is in the Holy of Holies where Philo contends that one retains a "midway place until he comes out again to the realm of body and flesh." In that sanctuary, he must dedicate the mind to the "incense of consecrated virtues" (*Som.* 2:232; cf. Lev. 16.11–17).

71. Williamson, *Philo and Hebrews*, 563; Kenneth Schenck, *Cosmology and Eschatology in Hebrews: The Settings of the Sacrifice*, SNTSMS 143 (New York: Cambridge University Press, 2007), 5. Some scholars "believe that Hebrews uses Platonic language without that language contributing to the author's thought in any significant way" (ibid., 5 n. 16).

72. Otto Michel proposes that the LXX is the "key" to understanding the background of Hebrews given that far too much has been examined under Philo. "Die LXX ist der Schlüssel zu mancher Frage, die bisher viel zu sehr von Philo her beleuchtet wurde" (Michel, *Der Brief an Die Hebräer*, 85).

73. Philo was driven by the philosophical necessity (or question) of how to reconcile the immaterial, transcendent God with a material universe like that which we find in Platonism. "On that assumption, Philo's presentation of mediatorial figures such as angels, Moses and the high priest is conditioned by a philosophical necessity, wherein God Himself is unable to act directly in the world" (Isaacs, *Sacred Space*, 130).

heavens and ideas.⁷⁴ The cosmological view was held by notable figures from the early church such as Theodoret of Cyrus and Origen,⁷⁵ although since the Reformation, many have distanced themselves from allegory and imported a more typological emphasis.⁷⁶ Even currently, the cosmological view is the most prominent position among modern scholars.⁷⁷

The problem with this view arises when we read Hebrews at face value. As Thomas Keene states, "This is because such cosmological reflections do not appear to be the main point of Hebrews. Hebrews' main objective is parenetic, not philosophical, and its overarching perspective is redemptive-historical and Christological, not cosmological."⁷⁸ Hence, we must be careful not to ascribe too much dependence on ANE cosmological traditions in Israel's understanding of

---

74. *Ant.* 3:123–50, 179–87; Josephus sees the outer court representing the earth and the sea while the inner court refers to heaven, where God dwells (cf. Schenck, *Cosmology and Eschatology*, 131–32, 151–52). However, Philo, at times, seems to admit "that the highest and πρός ἀλήθειαν temple of God is the universe… So the priests correspond to God's angels, the votive ornaments to the stars, and the Holy of Holies to the Heavens (*Spec.* 1 66f.)" (Sowers, *The Hermeneutics of Philo and Hebrews*, 57). Sowers also notes the following places where Philo sees the "specifications of the tabernacle to lay out the holy cosmic symbolism": *Spec. Leg.* 1:75–77; *Vit. Mos.* 2:77f, 88, 101–102; *Cong.* 116f; *Her.* 197, 221–25, 226; and especially *Quaest. in Exod.* 2:75–78 (ibid., 57–58). Craig Koester also sees remnants of this thought in Josephus' *War* 5.5.5 but the only explicit mentioning of cosmic figures is the reference to the seven lamps as representing the planets. Following, Koester has a helpful chart that references the places where Philo and Josephus attribute the tabernacle furnishings with cosmological significance (*Dwelling of God*, 60).

75. Keene, "Heaven Is a Tent," 101–13. Others include Clement of Alexandria and Jerome. Origen also saw the tabernacle illustrating various virtues of life (Koester, *Dwelling of God*, ix).

76. See Michael Kibbe's article which surveys the general course of Reformed and Catholic interpretations of Jesus' priesthood and, related, the tabernacle, in "Is It Finished? When Did It Start? Hebrews, Priesthood, and Atonement in Biblical, Systematic, and Historical Perspective," *JTS* 65.1 (2014): 25–61; cf. also Benjamin J. Ribbens, "Ascension and Atonement: The Significance of Post-Reformation, Reformed Responses to Socinians for Contemporary Atonement Debates in Hebrews," *WTJ* 80.1 (2018): 1–23.

77. As noted by Keene, "Heaven Is a Tent," 104. Keene and Schenck respectively provide a helpful summary of various scholars and their representative positions (ibid., 106–18; Schenck, *Cosmology and Eschatology*, 151 n. 21). For recent examples, see G. K. Beale, "Eden, the Temple, and the Church's Mission in the New Creation," *JETS* 48.1 (2005): 16–18; *The Temple and the Church's Mission*, 29–60.

78. Keene, "Heaven Is a Tent," 115. Another issue is that a portable tabernacle does not seem to fit with the Platonic characteristic of permanence in the heavenly realm (ibid., 118). Also, the cosmology in Hebrews is "latent" and the author of Hebrews seldom makes explicit cosmological statements; hence, to formulate a theory of Hebrews cosmology will present "obscurities and apparent contradictions" (Paul Ellingworth, "Jesus and the Universe in Hebrews," *EvQ* 58.4 [1986]: 339).

the tabernacle.[79] Keene and Schenck are correct in pointing out that in Hebrews, the metaphorical language in describing the tabernacle *as* heaven cannot be pushed too far.[80] Furthermore, the cosmological view does not explain the author's use of certain descriptions of the tabernacle such as the explicit statement, οὐ χειροποιήτου, τοῦτ' ἔστιν οὐ ταύτης τῆς κτίσεως (9:11b).[81] Therefore, while we can appreciate the spatial focus of a cosmological approach, identifying heaven or the entire cosmos as the referent cannot account for all the detail, activity, and theological import that Hebrews places in the heavenly sanctuary.

In Chapter 4 of this study I will discuss aspects of the cosmological view that are compatible with the structure-in-heaven view—meaning, that the tabernacle/temple as an existing structure, heaven may *also* represent the larger cosmos.[82] However, Hebrews presents the heavenly sanctuary and its cultic activity in a way that suggests the tabernacle is more than that.[83] In addition to its correlation to the cosmos, I propose that the tabernacle is also a localized place that resides above or past the *created* heavens and in the *transcendent* heavens.[84]

1.2.2. Tabernacle as Social and Community Participation

In this view, scholars see the author of Hebrews using the tabernacle concept as a means for the Christian community to participate in Christ's suffering whereby a

---

79. For example, Jon Levenson argues that the temple cosmogony of Judaism is essentially the same as Marduk's cosmology in the Enuma Elish (Jon D. Levenson, *Creation and the Persistence of Evil: The Jewish Drama of Divine Omnipotence* [Princeton, NJ: Princeton University Press, 1994], 95–99). Also see John H. Walton, *Ancient Near Eastern Thought and the Old Testament: Introducing the Conceptual World of the Hebrew Bible* (Grand Rapid, MI: Baker Academic, 2006), 146-49, 224-26, who makes strict parallels between the Jewish temple and Egyptian, Mesopotamian, and Akkadian texts. For a well-written refutation against such dependence on non-canonical sources, see Elías Brasil de Sousa, "Sanctuary: Cosmos, Covenant, and Creation," *JATS* 24.1 (2013): 25–41.

80. As a result, they both affirm the symbolic depiction of heaven as a whole in Heb. 8:1-2 but are also sympathetic to 8:5 and perhaps 9:6–10 suggesting a "structure *within* heaven" (Keene, "Heaven Is a Tent," 116; emphasis original; cf. Schenck, *Cosmology and Eschatology*, 172).

81. Albert Vanhoye, "Par la tente plus grande et plus parfaite (He 9,11)," *Biblica* 46.1 (1965): 27.

82. Elías Brasil de Sousa writes, "Correlations and analogies between the sanctuary and the world, creation, cosmos, etc. should not obliterate Scripture's foundational perception that the heavenly sanctuary is the ultimate locus of God's activity in favor of the human race and the place where Christ performs his priestly ministry" ("The Heavenly Sanctuary/Temple Motif in the Hebrew Bible: Function and Relationship to the Earthly Counterparts," [PhD diss., Andrews University, 2005], 39).

83. This will be the majority of my discussion in Part 2: Firstspace and Secondspace.

84. I make a distinction between the created and transcendent heavens in Chapter 4 and Section 6.1.3.

relationship with God is experienced. All the while, an actual heavenly tabernacle is nonexistent or inaccessible.[85] They claim that this notion does not diminish the importance of the heavenly tabernacle, because the author's *usage* of the heavenly tabernacle motif is what is important and maintained. Hence, it is not important to argue for the tabernacle's actual existence or make-up, but for how it enables the community to see themselves occupying tabernacle space to cope with their situation and how it stirs them up to social participation in Christ's suffering.

Jon Berquist argues that when it comes to the whereabouts of the heavenly temple or tabernacle, like that of Jesus' body, it is outside of humanly experienced time. Therefore, a shared temporal plane with Jesus' body and the earthly is not available for the community.[86] Nevertheless, the means through which the community can participate with Jesus lies in the "absent spaces" of Hebrews. To occupy these spaces is to occupy them with Christ via community participation in believers' earthly suffering. Gabriella Gelardini suggests that Moses' departure from the camp (Exod. 33:7–11) is the primary context for Hebrews 13:7–19, which is a departure from defilement. Hence, when the author reminds the community of their heavenly altar and urges them to join Christ "outside the camp" (13:10–11), he is "alluding initially to this temporary Tabernacle: an undefiled meeting-place bare of any cultic furnishing, a space with the sole function of enabling reconciliation with God."[87] This meeting place is not an actual space in the heavenly sanctuary, but a metaphorical one that consists of persecution and suffering at the hands of the Gentile (i.e., Greco-Roman) community.

Ellen Aitken argues that the author of Hebrews employs metaphors of movement to describe Jesus' journey to earth and then heaven. The result is a semiotically complex landscape, which contains sacrifice, offerings, and cultic ritual. This combined with the cityscape of Flavian Rome deploys a reimagining or "'reassembling' of the tabernacle in a radically new space with different material and personnel, that is, with different spatial practices."[88] Therefore, Aitken advances the community participation argument further by asserting that Hebrews *reassembles* the true tabernacle in response to Flavian rulers after the First Jewish War.[89]

---

85. See Ellen Aitken, "The Body of Jesus Outside the Eternal City: Mapping Ritual Space in the Epistle to the Hebrews," in Gelardini and Attridge, eds, *Hebrews in Contexts*, 194–209; "Reading Hebrews in Flavian Rome," USQR 59.3-4 (2005): 82–85; Jon Berquist, "Critical Spatiality and the Book of Hebrews," in Gelardini and Attridge, eds, *Hebrews in Contexts*, 181–93; Gabriella Gelardini, "Charting 'Outside the Camp' with Edward W. Soja: Critical Spatiality and Hebrews 13," in Gelardini and Attridge, eds, *Hebrews in Contexts*, 210–37; Mark K. George, *Israel's Tabernacle as Social Space*, SBLAIL 2 (Leiden: Brill, 2009).

86. Berquist, "Critical Spatiality and the Book of Hebrews," 185–87.

87. Gelardini, "Charting 'Outside the Camp,'" 230.

88. Aitken, "Body of Jesus Outside the Eternal City," 205.

89. Ibid., 207.

Mark George focuses his study of the earthly tabernacle in Exodus 25–31 and 35–40 to argue that Israel's tabernacle is ultimately a social space. He takes an "agnostic position on the question of the historical existence of the tabernacle"[90] because what is important in the priestly narratives of the tabernacle is the social ordering of Israelite society.[91] For George, the tabernacle's material existence is irrelevant to the more important question of how the tabernacle helps us understand the priestly writers' views and perspectives on Israelite society. In other words, the tabernacle concept is that of an anthropologically created space.[92]

What all these scholars have in common is how they handle the absence or the inaccessibility of a physical tabernacle/temple space. This especially arises in the Hebrews context if there is reason to believe that the Second Temple had been destroyed.[93] Berquist's, Gelardini's, and Aitken's responses are to fill those absent spaces with socially created ones—namely, community participation of suffering under Roman rule. George responds by dismissing the physical altogether and utilizing only the *concept* of the tabernacle by defining it as socially created space. However, I suggest that what is physically absent on earth need not be absent in heaven. We cannot dismiss the detailed descriptions of either the earthly tabernacle in Exodus or the heavenly tabernacle in Hebrews (e.g., 8:5; 9:1–14). Furthermore, the rhetorical, theological, and exhortational impact for community participation in any kind of suffering becomes diminished if believers' occupancy in the heavenly sanctuary is merely a conceptual one.[94]

Dismissing the notion of an actual heavenly tabernacle space removes the security needed for believers to persevere in faithfulness. Persecuted believers are able to joyfully accept the seizure of their earthly property and homes *knowing* (γινώσκοντες) that they have for themselves a better possession and a lasting one (Heb. 10:34). If the believers understood the "better and lasting possession" to be true *only* through the ethical and socially created space within the community,

---

90. George, *Israel's Tabernacle*, 12.

91. He does, however, suggest that the narratives give material plausibility to the tabernacle, based on how the "Priestly writers appropriated such objects in their narratives," referring to material parts of the tabernacle and its furnishings (ibid., 13).

92. George's understanding of space removes the necessity of a physical structure, since people can fill in the void of empty spaces through their thoughts, values, practices, and emotions, or what he calls "spatial poetics" (George, *Israel's Tabernacle*, 14). To reiterate, George is not necessarily arguing that the earthly tabernacle did not exist; in fact, he maintains that the *plausibility* of physical space must be affirmed. However, what is more important to consider are the mental and symbolic features of space, which he deems as true tabernacle space (ibid., 17–18).

93. The timing of the writing of Hebrews is debated, especially whether it was written prior or after the destruction of the Jerusalem Temple in 70 CE. See my position in Section 3.1.1.

94. I discuss later how the motivation behind believers' perseverance and obedient, priestly living is dependent on a co-shared occupancy with Christ in the presence of God (Chapters 7–8).

then how can such a heavenly place be better?⁹⁵ A truly better and lasting possession is one that possesses all three necessary aspects of space: the physical, the symbolic, and the ethical.

1.2.3. Tabernacle as a Rhetorical, Literary Device

This third approach argues that the author of Hebrews uses the heavenly tabernacle as a literary or heuristic device to communicate doctrinal concepts such as Jesus' high priestly Christology.⁹⁶ Representative scholars in this category include Philip Church, Mayjee Philip, Kenneth Schenck, and Annang Asumang.⁹⁷ While

---

95. This is similar to Jesus' explanation to his disciples that there are *presently* (εἰσιν) many rooms in his Father's house. If it were not so, why would Jesus tell them that he is going there to prepare (πορεύομαι ἑτοιμάσαι) a place for them? (Jn 14:2). On his commentary on this particular verse, D. A. Carson writes that "the words presuppose that the 'place' exists before Jesus gets there. It is not that he arrives on the scene and then begins to prepare the place; rather, in the context of Johannine theology, it is the going itself, via the cross and resurrection, that prepares the place for Jesus' disciples" (*The Gospel According to John*, PNTC [Grand Rapids, MI: Eerdmans, 1991], 489–90). In the socially created schema, it would be as if Jesus told his disciples that there is a place for them only in theory or in concept, or that they are ultimately responsible for creating such heavenly spaces.

96. Under the rhetorical approach we may also include those who see the tabernacle as metaphorically referring to other entities. First, there is the traditional, Christological view of the tabernacle as Jesus' body and its more recent variations (cf. Keene, "Heaven Is a Tent," 83–88). Examples include the tabernacle as Christ's humanity (Aelred Cody, *Heavenly Sanctuary and Liturgy in the Epistle to the Hebrews: The Achievement of Salvation in the Epistle's Perspectives* [St. Meinrad, IN: Grail, 1960]); Christ's glorified body (Vanhoye, "Par la tente," 10–12, 21–28; Christ's glorified *Eucharistic* body (James Swetnam, "Greater and More Perfect Tent: A Contribution to the Discussion of Hebrews 9:11," *Biblica* 47.1 [1966]: 91–106). Another metaphorical view identifies the tabernacle as the "New Covenant people of God" such that of B. F. Westcott and F. F. Bruce (Keene, "Heaven Is a Tent," 94–100).

97. Philip Arthur Frederick Church, "Jesus the High Priest of the Heavenly Temple: Temple Symbolism in Hebrews 4:14–10:25," in *Hebrews and the Temple: Attitudes to the Temple in Second Temple Judaism and in Hebrews*, NovTSup 171 (Leiden: Brill, 2017), 369–432; "Wilderness Tabernacle and Eschatological Temple: A Study in Temple Symbolism in Hebrews in the Light of Attitudes to the Temple in the Literature of Middle Judaism" (PhD diss., University of Otago, 2012); Mayjee Philip, *Leviticus in Hebrews: A Transtextual Analysis of the Tabernacle Theme in the Letter to the Hebrews* (Oxford: Peter Lang, 2011); Kenneth Schenck, "An Archaeology of Hebrews' Tabernacle Imagery," in Gelardini and Attridge, eds, *Hebrews in Contexts*, 238–58; Schenck, *Cosmology and Eschatology in Hebrews*; Annang Asumang, "The Tabernacle as a Heuristic Device in the Interpretation of the Christology of the Epistle to the Hebrews" (ThM diss., The South African Theological Seminary, 2005); *Unlocking Hebrews*, 80–118; Annang Asumang and

this approach is not categorically incorrect,[98] such literary readings may overlook the spatial features of the heavenly tabernacle or deem them as non-accessible or unimportant.[99] Cynthia Westfall therefore correctly observes that "the classification and analysis of spatial references as typology, thought, or metaphor are often applied without consideration of the meaning of space/place apart from their assumed function as abstract symbols."[100]

By utilizing a narrative critical (rhetorical) approach, Kenneth Schenck establishes two contrasting thoughts—the eschatological and cosmological, which respectively correspond to time and space.[101] According to this contrasting schema, he asserts a strict distinction between a physical, earthly tabernacle that is visible against a spiritual, heavenly one that is invisible.[102] He believes that a literal heavenly tabernacle cannot account for all the references that are made in the epistle. Furthermore, the author of Hebrews "uses the heavenly tabernacle in several different metaphorical ways that do not necessarily cohere with one another" and therefore, the tabernacle imagery defies "any simple, literal referent in heaven."[103] He concludes the following, "In the end, the best explanation for Hebrews' varied tabernacle imagery and rhetoric is that the primary significance of the tabernacle is located in the rhetorical purposes of the author's broader high priestly metaphor."[104]

Mayjee Philip maps out the multi-layered relationships between Hebrews and Leviticus by utilizing Gérard Genette's five categories of transtextuality.[105] She argues that the author merely utilizes the heavenly tabernacle concept based on its appropriation in Leviticus in order to establish the more important idea of Jesus'

Bill Domeris, "The Migrant Camp of the People of God: A Uniting Theme for the Epistle to the Hebrews," *Conspectus* 3 (2007): 1–33; "Ministering in the Tabernacle: Spatiality and the Christology of Hebrew," *Conspectus* 1 (2006): 1–25.

98. The heavenly tabernacle can serve as both the original type and a metaphor. See my discussion on the analogical view of metaphors in Section 5.1.3.

99. Matthew Sleeman draws similar conclusions when considering the narrative reading of Christ's ascension in the book of Acts; hence, he hopes to apply "geographical theory to inform a richer spatial understanding of the ascension" (*Geography and the Ascension Narrative in Acts*, SNTSMS 146 [New York: Cambridge University Press, 2009], 22).

100. Westfall, "Space and Atonement," 231.

101. Schenck, *Cosmology and Eschatology*, esp. 115–81; cf. also "An Archaeology of Hebrews' Tabernacle Imagery," 238–58. Note how from the onset, Schenck assumes a space (cosmology) vs. time (eschatology) framework.

102. Schenck, *Cosmology and Eschatology*, 115.

103. Ibid.

104. Ibid., 180.

105. Philip, *Leviticus in Hebrews*, 24–25; cf. Gérard Genette, *Palimpsests: Literature in the Second Degree*, trans. Channa Newman and Claude Doubinsky, Stages 8 (Lincoln, NE: University of Nebraska Press, 1997).

better and greater sacrifice.[106] She writes, "In Hebrews, transformation is applied to metaphors of sacrifice that are central to Leviticus; the author transforms aspects of the levitical system for his purpose of presenting Jesus as the ultimate sacrifice for sin."[107] Instead of subordinating the heavenly tabernacle under the sacrificial concept, I suggest that in a mutually reciprocated fashion, the heavenly characteristics of the heavenly tabernacle befit the location of Christ's high priestly ministry and, in turn, Christ's occupancy of the heavenly tabernacle makes the heavenly tabernacle better and greater than the levitical one (Heb. 9:11).

Annang Asumang argues that the heavenly tabernacle is a literary heuristic device—drawing on its background from the narrative structure of Numbers—to communicate Hebrews' Christology without delving into its spatial features (i.e., its cosmology).[108] The spatial representations of the tabernacle lay out the semiosphere or "the intellectual scaffolding" of its doctrinal expositions such as the Christological presentation of Jesus as high priest.[109] However, "the cosmological aspect of this interpretation of the sacrifice of Christ, is not to be pressed too far, certainly not as much as the sacrificial template which governs the staged explanation of Christ's death."[110] This leads him to metaphorically correspond certain parts of the tabernacle according to time periods or "ages"[111] rather than the constituent parts of an actual tabernacle. Elsewhere, he equates the Holy of Holies as a metaphor for heaven itself.[112] Similar to those under the social, community participation view, Asumang is concerned with how the author of Hebrews heuristically uses the tabernacle motif rather than investigating first what the tabernacle is according to the author. He concludes that we should "not push the interpretation of Hebrews to the extreme and imagine a physical tabernacle or material blood being sprinkled in it and so on."[113]

---

106. Philip, *Leviticus in Hebrews*, 62.

107. Ibid., 79.

108. Asumang's larger thesis is that Hebrews is rhetorically organized based upon the spatial structure of the tabernacle as portrayed in the book of Numbers. "This literary structure served as a mnemonic that enabled Hebrews and his first readers to piece the message of the sermon together in their minds" (Asumang, *Unlocking Hebrews*, 25–26). See also Asumang, "Tabernacle as Heuristic Device for Christology," 127, where he argues that the author of Hebrews draws on the multi-dimensional role of the tabernacle as the organizing principle for God's people (cf. also Asumang and Domeris, "Ministering in the Tabernacle," 1–25 and "The Migrant Camp of the People of God," 1–33).

109. Asumang, *Unlocking Hebrews*, 40.

110. Asumang, "Tabernacle as Heuristic Device for Christology," 86–87. This statement reveals Asumang's belief that to see the tabernacle as an actual place is to equate it to a cosmological description of the heavenlies.

111. Ibid., 88 n. 39.

112. Ibid., 104; Asumang, *Unlocking Hebrews*, 107–108.

113. Asumang, *Unlocking Hebrews*, 107.

I suggest, however, the heavenly tabernacle can be both heuristic *and* physical. There are many incidences when God uses physical symbols to communicate or reveal aspects of his nature (e.g., the unburning bush, the Ark of the Covenant, Eden/Mt. Sinai, temple artifacts). Jesus himself uses symbols and signs that were real and actualized, while at the same time describing the kingdom of heaven (e.g., the multiplication of bread and fish). All these examples were both physical while metaphorically conveying a deeper meaning. I suggest that the heavenly tabernacle can also be interpreted in such a manner.

A. The Heavenly Tabernacle as Metaphor

A more nuanced approach is one that appreciates the rhetorical strategy and metaphorical language of the heavenly tabernacle, yet without dismissing its material and locative presence in the heavenly sphere. Thomas Keene argues that the tabernacle metaphor is central in the author's overall argumentative strategy. His understanding of the tabernacle is influenced by his definition of typology, which he shares with Kenneth Schenck as being "more horizontal and narratival while allegory is more vertical and philosophical."[114] However, we can expand this definition of typology to not *only* have a horizontal and narratival usage, but a typological usage that is both forward-pointing and upward-pointing.[115] Such an understanding best corresponds to an eschatological tabernacle. If such is the case, I agree with Keene's proposal that eschatology is the tabernacle's prominent characteristic, which is then described using metaphorical language.[116]

Keene notes the author's intentional lack of cosmological precision regarding the tabernacle's location or what constitutes the heavenly tabernacle. There are only cosmological overtones, which he refers to the tabernacle's spatial features.[117] Therefore, he states that "[a]ssociating the tabernacle with a heavenly pattern does not necessitate a strictly spatial description" because "Second Temple conceptions of heaven, and especially NT conceptions [including Hebrews], are not purely spatial in character."[118] He is correct in that heaven itself is not described in full spatial terms, nor is the heavenly tabernacle described in comprehensive spatial detail. However, there are such explicit spatial descriptions of the heavenly tabernacle found in passages such as 9:11–14, which puts forth the notion of a physical,

---

114. Keene, "Heaven Is a Tent," 77 n. 50.
115. Not necessarily allegorical or philosophical in the Platonic sense.
116. Hence Keene's dissertation title, "The Tabernacle as an Eschatological Metaphor."
117. Ibid., 128. I prefer not to use the term, "cosmological," because it implies an intent to specify a distinct cosmology of the heavens and the universe. I argue, and agree with Keene, that this is not the intent of the author; however, I am suggesting a spatiality to the heavenly tabernacle that is not primarily referring to the physical cosmos.
118. Ibid., 119. Elsewhere he asserts that the "spatial and temporal are woven together in a tapestry" (ibid., 125) and that "the greater tabernacle symbolizes a new age…[that is] expressed in both temporal and spatial categories" (ibid., 126). Here, Keene describes the tabernacle as having both "temporal and spatial characteristics."

materialized structure in the heavenlies.¹¹⁹ Furthermore, as this study hopes to show, spatial trialectics allows us to include Keene's metaphorical emphasis on the heavenly tabernacle within a holistic understanding of time *and* space.

I suggest that we not draw a hard line between a spatial interpretation of the tabernacle and a metaphorical. Rather, we can appreciate the metaphorical usage of a heavenly localized, spatial tabernacle. The author of Hebrews indeed utilizes a rhetorical strategy in describing the heavenly tabernacle. Yet, we can provide further existential and constitutional grounding to the metaphorical usage in a way that affirms and appreciates its spatial features. In other words, if the metaphorical usage corresponds to the Secondspace dimension of the tabernacle, I want to provide both the Firstspace and Thirdspace dimensions while also observing the interplay amongst all three.¹²⁰

1.2.4. Tabernacle Bifurcated into Future-Spatial and Present-Spiritual Realities

This fourth approach includes those who bifurcate the heavenly tabernacle into two separate realities: a spatial one that lies in the future, against a spiritual, abstract one that is presently accessible to believers. While modern scholarship has dismissed the idea that the author of Hebrews wrote strictly in Platonic categories,¹²¹ vestiges of a physical–spiritual dualism are present according to this approach.¹²² Such readings are misleading in that they make a presently accessible Hebrews eschatology to be strictly spiritual while only the future, realized one is physical.¹²³ This is an example of the problem stated earlier, that eschatology itself has been separated into two parts according to its spatial and temporal axes. The heavenly tabernacle falls victim to this bifurcation.

In 1978, George MacRae published an article entitled, "Heavenly Temple and Eschatology in the Letter to the Hebrews," which argues for an eschatological schema of Hebrews.¹²⁴ In regards to the heavenly tabernacle, this schema assumes

---

119. I investigate these spatial features in Chapter 6 of this study.

120. This will be the bulk of my arguments in Parts 2 and 3.

121. For example, Asumang and Domeris, "Ministering in the Tabernacle," 18.

122. Cynthia Westfall astutely observes, "In the history of interpretation, the heavenly tabernacle has been interpreted in Platonic terms and categories, and those interpretations continue to cast a shadow over how Hebrews is read" (Westfall, "Space and Atonement," 230). She continues, "We generally agree that the author of Hebrews is not Platonic, but fail to recognize that we are Platonic in our understanding of space, or, at least, more a product of Platonism in our worldview in this area than a product of the text and the biblical worldview" (ibid., 231).

123. This is similar to what is seen in Jewish apocalyptic writings by those who await the physical reestablishment of the temple. Those under this category include Marie E. Isaacs ("Hebrew 13:9–16 Revisited," *NTS* 43.2 [1997]: 268–84 and Albert Vanhoye ("L'οἰκουμένη," 248–53).

124. George W. MacRae, "Heavenly Temple and Eschatology in the Letter to the Hebrews," *Semeia* 12 (1978): 179–99. MacRae affirms and builds on C. K. Barrett's

that the author of Hebrews was influenced by two schools of thought: Hellenistic Judaism (Philo and Josephus) and Jewish apocalypticism.[125] This is MacRae's response to the prevalent argument of his day, concerning whether Hebrews had predominantly a Platonic or a Jewish apocalyptic influence.[126] The former sees the temple as abstractly constituting heaven itself, and the latter sees the temple as a literal "container" or structure within heaven. Instead of choosing one, MacRae conflates the two in an approach which he coins "Hellenistic Temple Symbolism." Both views are present in Hebrews: the apocalyptic in 8:1–5, 9:23, 9:11–12; and the Hellenistic in 9:24, 10:19–20, and perhaps 6:19-20.[127] The author's reason for doing so was to conflate "his own Alexandrian imagery with [the recipients'] apocalyptic presuppositions" in an effort to strengthen their hope.[128]

Against this, one does not need to overstate the author's Alexandrian influence in order to introduce an eschatological hope that is presently accessible to believers. Instead, a present eschatological hope resides—albeit at times in latent and shadowy form—in the heavenly sanctuary ever since Moses' revelation of it in Exodus 25:9. Therefore, while MacRae is correct in putting forth an eschatological dimension of the heavenly tabernacle, he regards it as (1) being in the future or (2) present *only* in an abstract Alexandrian/Platonic sense. Participation in a localized heavenly sanctuary remains only in the future for the Hebrews audience.[129] Such a view disconnects the organic unity between the exposition (i.e., the present participation of believers in the heavenly sanctuary) and the exhortation to remain faithful until the consummation of their eschatological hope.[130] Therefore, while I agree with MacRae in the eschatological schema for

---

influential article, "The Eschatology of the Epistle to the Hebrews" (1956), which argues that an eschatological, apocalyptic Judaism lies in the background of Hebrews over a Platonic idealism.

125. Even further, MacRae makes the distinction that the author of Hebrews was Alexandrian and more sympathetic to the Platonic worldview whereas the recipients of the epistle held to a future, apocalyptic eschatology (ibid., 179, 190–91, and 196).

126. Ibid., 180.

127. Ibid., 179. Marie Isaacs holds a similar stance in which the two views are conflated (*Sacred Space*, 61). See also Knut Backhaus, who argues that Hebrews represents both Jewish-Christian monotheism and the metaphysical tradition of Middle Platonism (*Der sprechende Gott: gesammelte Studien zum Hebräerbrief*, WUNT 240 [Tübingen: Mohr Siebeck, 2009], 302; cf. also 49–76).

128. MacRae, "Heavenly Temple and Eschatology," 179. Another concept that MacRae stresses, which will be applicable for us in Chapter 8, is the relation of the apocalyptic, eschatological features of the "homily" to the exhortation of the people to perseverance (13:22) (ibid., 191). However, he goes too far in thinking that the "paraenesis…determines the purpose of Hebrews" even over the doctrinal (ibid.).

129. Ibid., 188.

130. As David Moffitt writes from his understanding of Second Temple literature, "[T]hey did not appear to envision a spiritual/material dichotomy" (Moffitt, *Atonement*, 82) and that "a dichotomy between the spiritual realm and the material realm was neither

Hebrews, I disagree with his bifurcation of Hebrews eschatology into two separate Alexandrian and Jewish apocalyptic constituents. Rather, the heavenly tabernacle is evidence that Hebrews eschatology is physical and spiritual, *both* in the present and in the future.

Marie Isaacs, by focusing on the social situation of the Hebrews audience, believes that Hebrews was written in response to the destruction, and therefore the absence, of the Jerusalem Temple. The author of Hebrews, in writing to "a group feeling bereft of one of the major means of drawing near to God, offers the consoling thought that Jesus has opened for them a new and better way."[131] She argues that, as a result, the author directs the mournful recipients' attention away from a physical space to a heavenly, sacred space.[132] Therefore, Hebrews gives a way for the believers to cope with the loss of Jerusalem and for the author to "attempt to reinterpret the Scriptures to meet the specific needs of his audience."[133] To do so, the author turns to the tabernacle to relocate the believers' concept of sacred space towards heaven.[134] The problem is that, for Isaacs, the physical, heavenly tabernacle lies only in the future. There is no present, physical tabernacle that localizes believers' spiritual positioning before God.[135]

Isaacs is correct in observing how the author points his readers upward (and if I may add, *forward*) to reorient their understanding of sacred space, as opposed to looking backwards into the past, or into the present situation of an absent temple. However, she does not discuss *what* they are looking at but only *where* to look. I agree with A. C. Perriman, who remarks that Isaacs disregards what the activity is in this sacred space (i.e., the person and the work of Christ) and thus, "is not really connected to the spatial motif."[136] While her study is not on the heavenly tabernacle *per se*, she claims that the tabernacle and the language of heaven ultimately function as a "religious metaphor," which, "as such, defies all attempts at systematization."[137] However, similar to those in the rhetorical device camp, it

constitutive of nor necessary for the eschatological hope of at least some Jews of this time period" (ibid., 117). Acknowledging such a background, Moffitt concludes for Hebrews the following statement: "If this is an accurate assessment of Hebrews' eschatology, the probability that the homily does not rely upon a spiritual/material dualism greatly increases. When the author speaks of the unseen city, land, and heavenly tabernacle, and links the Son's entry into the οἰκουμένη with his ascension into the realm of heaven and God's presence, it need not be the case that he posits the kind of spiritual/material dualism he is often thought to have assumed" (ibid., 118).

131. Isaacs, *Sacred Space*, 77–78.
132. Ibid., 62.
133. Ibid., 67.
134. Ibid.
135. She writes that "heaven is not so much a geographical location as a symbol of the divine" (ibid., 205; cf. also 222).
136. Andrew C. Perriman, Review of *Sacred Space: An Approach to the Theology of the Epistle to the Hebrews* by Marie Isaacs," *Themelios* 20.1 (1994): 29.
137. Isaacs, *Sacred Space*, 206.

seems lacking to suggest that the author of Hebrews would redirect the believers' upwards into an empty, metaphorical or abstract space.[138]

These scholars have contributed to the shift in Hebrews scholarship that favors the temporal dimension of Hebrews eschatology over the spatial.[139] Yet problems arise when associating a heavenly tabernacle vision with a future-only emphasis. Cynthia Westfall aptly states that "interpreters of Hebrews often ascribe metaphorical, symbolic, or otherwise abstract significance to the references to places, treating them as if they were references to time (e.g., most often in eschatological/apocalyptic future) or assigning them to a theological category or idea (e.g., exaltation)."[140] In conclusion, many scholars have assumed an eschatology that is primarily temporally future, or they have dismissed the tabernacle's spatial character by only acknowledging its spatial overtones within a cosmological grid. On the contrary, the spatial and temporal characteristics of the heavenly tabernacle—both in the present and in the future—give the eschatological nature of Hebrews its full value.

1.2.5. Tabernacle as Spatially Realized

Against these previous approaches, I affirm a fifth view, in which a spatially realized heavenly tabernacle structure exists for the believers in their current eschatological situation. This approach is not recent and had been proposed by the likes of Otrfried Hofius in 1972.[141] This position recognizes the affinity between the tabernacle's spatial features and features of Jewish apocalyptic literature.[142] Thus heaven is presented as a container that holds a concrete temple/tabernacle. Others are sympathetic to this approach due to the logical implications of Jesus' bodily presence and activity in the heavenly sanctuary.[143] Nevertheless, these

---

138. While she affirms the tension of the already/not-yet eschatological reality of the believers (cf. ibid., 58–59), she at times diminishes what the believers currently possess. For example, because the consummation of the heavenly sanctuary lies only in the future, she writes, "Thus for humanity, salvation lies not in the present but in the imminent future" (ibid., 219).

139. Scott D. Mackie, *Eschatology and Exhortation in the Epistle to the Hebrews*, WUNT 2/223 (Tübingen: Mohr Siebeck, 2007), 31.

140. Westfall, "Space and Atonement," 228–29.

141. Moffitt, *Atonement*, 222 n. 7. For the Seventh Day Adventist position, see William G. Johnsson, "The Heavenly Sanctuary—Figurative or Real?," in Holbrook, ed., *Issues in the Book of Hebrews*, 35–51. Affirming a physical heavenly tabernacle does not necessarily connote the Seventh Day Adventist doctrine of Jesus' two-phase high priestly ministry. This doctrine goes starkly against how the author of Hebrews describes Jesus' once-for-all efficacy that has been manifested at the consummation of the ages (Heb. 9:26; esp. 7:27). There is no mention of a second phase but the next sequential progression of redemptive history points only to Christ's second return (9:28).

142. Scholars such as Scott Mackie, C. K. Barrett, and Cynthia Westfall.

143. Two representative scholars are David Moffitt and R. B. Jamieson.

scholars' works either are not primarily concerned with the heavenly tabernacle,[144] nor do they utilize Edward Soja's Tripartite schema of the heavenly tabernacle, which this study attempts to do.

Scott Mackie argues that the heavenly sanctuary must be "real" for both the author of Hebrews and his audience.[145] This is especially true given the "community facing a crisis of commitment, resulting from both societal pressures and a waning sense of God's involvement in their lives."[146] In response, the author provides "vivid, evocative descriptions of the heavenly sanctuary and Jesus' sacral actions therein," so that the community would "'see' the exalted Jesus (2:9; 3:1; 9:24–8; 12:2) and their involvement in the enthronement/adoption ceremony (2:13; 10:24–5)."[147] He writes elsewhere, "Despite our inability to ascertain the exact 'cosmographic' shape of the author's universe, we can however safely surmise that at the center of his construction of the heavenly realm resides an actual temple."[148] Cynthia Westfall also affirms that the author and his readers would have understood the tabernacle and the act of atonement as happening in a concrete space.[149]

Georg Gäbel can loosely be categorized under this view. Although he does not discuss the metaphysical nature of the heavenly tabernacle, he rightly stresses the importance of recognizing both the vertical (for him, the ontological) and horizontal (redemptive-historical) aspects of the tabernacle typology.[150] Such statements suggest that Gäbel affirms an "ontological" existence of the heavenly tabernacle, which itself is the basis for its "soteriological quality" (*soteriologische Qualität*).[151] However, he does not delve into any metaphysical discussions of the tabernacle other than the fact that Moses (cf. Heb. 8:5 [Exod. 25:40]) is shown the "heavenly sanctuary itself and not just an intelligible model."[152]

---

144. Often the main focus of study is the atonement, or the background or situational setting of the author of Hebrews.

145. Mackie, *Eschatology and Exhortation*, 158–59; cf. also 91–92, and especially Scott D. Mackie, "Heavenly Sanctuary Mysticism in the Epistle to the Hebrews," *JTS* 62.1 (2011): 82–83, where he references several Second Temple Jewish texts to state that the Hebrews "author clearly believes that an actual temple stands at the centre of the heavenly realm."

146. Ibid., 78.

147. Ibid., 79.

148. Mackie, *Eschatology and Exhortation*, 158.

149. Westfall, "Space and Atonement in Hebrews," 228–30, where she states that the author of Hebrews "represents the heavenly tabernacle as a concrete real place," just as Jesus is a "real and concrete high priest." More on Westfall's position will be discussed in Section 2.4.

150. Gäbel, *Kulttheologie*, 242: "Typologischer (verheißungsgeschichtlich-horizontaler) und ontologischer (vertikaler) Aspekt der Urbild-Abbild-Beziehung sind daher untrennbar verschränkt." All German translations my own unless otherwise noted.

151. Ibid., 244.

152. Ibid., 243: "des irdischen Heiligtums um das himmlische Heiligtum selbst und nicht nur um ein intelligibles Modell."

For David Moffitt, the heavenly sanctuary is the most sacred space within the heavens, which is part of an extended metaphor (analogical)[153] of the high priest's entry into the earthly sacred space of the tabernacle. The strongest evidence for this understanding lies in Jesus' physical, resurrected, glorified body, in which he is depicted as having entered God's heavenly presence (Heb. 6:19–20; 9:11–12, 24). In maintaining the physicality of both Christ's body and the heavenly tabernacle, Moffitt argues against an "earthly versus spiritual" dualism in understanding either concept. Following John J. Collins,[154] he affirms a Jewish apocalyptic eschatology that includes both a temporal and spatial horizon for the heavenly tabernacle. He writes, "The 'coming world' of Heb. 2:5 and the 'coming age' of 6:5 refer to the same eschatological reality—a new time and space."[155] My study will partly respond to Moffitt's follow-up question of "how the glorified body and the mortal body (and, by the same token, the perishing world and the world to come) relate to each other."[156] He states summarily, "Jesus entered the true tabernacle located in heaven. This tabernacle is neither the created heavens nor part of the created heavens, but a structure that exists above and beyond the realm of this creation. Jesus went through this heavenly structure and entered into its most holy place."[157]

R. B. Jamieson, in his works, "When and Where Did Jesus Offer Himself" (2017) and later, *Jesus' Death and Heavenly Offering in Hebrews* (2019), presents a schema of views that address the time and location of Jesus' self-offering. He holds to a view that sees Christ's self-offering as a unified sequence encompassing death on earth and entrance into heaven.[158] Under such a view, Hebrews depicts "the

---

153. Moffitt prefers the term "analogical" over "metaphor," because the prior assumes an actual model to exist. This is his specialized usage, which is based on Janet Soskice's homeomorphic model (analogy of structure). "That is, the elements of a homeomorphic model are structured to one degree or another such that they are located in relation to one another according to the structural relations among the elements of the source being depicted. Obviously such models are not metaphors, not least because they are not linguistic acts" (Moffitt, "Serving in the Tabernacle in Heaven," 262). I utilize insights from the homeomorphic model and apply it to the tabernacle's Secondspace features in Chapter 5.

154. John J. Collins, "Towards the Morphology of a Genre: Introduction," *Semeia* 14 (1979): 1–20.

155. Moffitt, *Atonement*, 81 n. 83.

156. Ibid.

157. Ibid., 223. He follows Otfried Hofius in drawing strong connections to Jewish apocalyptic texts that "imagine multiple heavens with a tabernacle or temple structure located in the highest heaven" (Moffitt, "Serving in the Tabernacle in Heaven," 274; cf. also *Atonement*, 221 n. 7).

158. "When and Where Did Jesus Offer Himself? A Taxonomy of Recent Scholarship on Hebrews," *CurBR* 15.3 (2017): 349; *Jesus' Death and Heavenly Offering in Hebrews*, SNTSMS 172 (New York: Cambridge University Press, 2019), 24.

heavenly sanctuary as the description of a real albeit transcendent place, which Christ entered bodily, and where he remains until his return."[159] In his examination of Hebrews 8:1-5, and 9:24 and 28, Jamieson writes:

> Hebrews envisions the heavenly tabernacle as an actual structure in heaven. Though heaven is a transcendent realm, in Hebrews it is a realm housing a tabernacle in which a glorified human ministers… Making all due allowance for transcendent aspects of Hebrews' depiction of heaven, its heavenly tabernacle must be "real" enough for the resurrected Jesus to be there now.[160]

However, Jamieson, along with Moffitt, is primarily concerned with the location and timing of the atonement. I intend to argue for a localized heavenly tabernacle which is sympathetic to their emphases on Christ's physical resurrected body that is integral to the atonement.

Finally, Benjamin Ribbens argues for a created, actualized heavenly tabernacle in order to argue for the legitimacy of the earthly, levitical cultic system. That system, he argues, was modeled after the heavenly one, and was efficacious based on the proleptic priestly ministry of Christ.[161] Therefore, there was not only a temporal and spatial correspondence between the earthly and heavenly sanctuaries (cultic location); but there was a correspondence between the cultic activity that took place in them (cultic activity).

In conclusion to this chapter, these varying approaches to the heavenly tabernacle have merit. The dualistic representation view (Section 1.2.1) affirms a verticality to the heavenly tabernacle, which is quite different from (and better) than the earthly tabernacle. It is indeed wholly other (Heb. 9:11b, τοῦτ' ἔστιν οὐ ταύτης τῆς κτίσεως). The social and community participation view (Section 1.2.2) is concerned with the historical situation of the epistle and seeks to appropriate how the heavenly tabernacle impacts the day-to-day lives of New Covenant believers. The rhetorical, literary device view (Section 1.2.3) is correct in that the heavenly tabernacle is being utilized to communicate important salvific realities for the believer. It is certainly compatible with, and strengthens the arguments for, presenting a high priestly Christology along with the continuities (or discontinuities) of the levitical sacrifices. Also, the progress in associating the heavenly tabernacle with a Jewish apocalyptic background has provided a rich landscape in how we can understand the tabernacle's heavenly characteristics (Section 1.2.4). It is also significant that scholars have begun to affirm an actual, materialized

---

159. Jamieson, "When and Where," 350.
160. Jamieson, *Jesus' Death and Heavenly Offering*, 53–54.
161. Although Ribbens' work is a study of the heavenly and levitical cult, he devotes one chapter to the tabernacle entitled, "Heavenly Tabernacle and Cult in Hebrews," in which he argues for an actualized heavenly tabernacle based on early, mystical apocalyptic texts as its conceptual background (Ribbens, *Levitical Sacrifice and Heavenly Cult*, 82–148, esp. 105–29 and 129 n. 211).

heavenly tabernacle while distancing themselves from the traditional, cosmological view (Section 1.2.5). It seems, then, that the next step in advancing Hebrews tabernacle studies is to synthesize these merits into a holistic understanding of the heavenly tabernacle—one that does justice to all the concerns of these views. It is this study's contention that spatial trialectics can lead us in the right direction.

Chapter 2

APPROACHING TABERNACLE SPACE

2.1. Methodology: Tripartite Critical Spatial Theory

To understand what it means for the tabernacle to be spatially realized, we must first understand what space is and how it is perceived. Most of the scholars discussed in the previous chapter hardly disagree *that* the tabernacle is spatial; but they come to different conclusions as to *how* it is spatial. Therefore, it will be helpful to trace the progress of spatial studies ("Critical Spatiality," or "Critical Spatial Studies")[1] and their impact on biblical studies. The purpose of this section is not to present a comprehensive presentation of geography and spatial studies from Aristotle to the present,[2] but to give a basic overview of the same, and to

---

1. Critical Spatiality is often defined as viewing space as a social or cultural product that comes about from individuals and communities (Schreiner, *Body of Jesus*, 48). However, Edward W. Soja himself shifts the emphasis for it to be more of a balanced, ontological triad of sociality, historicality, and spatiality (*Thirdspace: Journeys to Los Angeles and Other Real-and-Imagined Places* [Cambridge, MA: Blackwell, 1996], 171; cf. Schreiner, *Body of Jesus*, 49 n. 49). In other words, space as a social product cannot be defined *as* Critical Spatiality but only as one necessary aspect of it. Schreiner makes a similar disclaimer that "space and place are not *merely* social constructions...but within the structures of place that the very possibility of the social arises. This, I think, is what critical spatiality is getting at, but some may conclude that the theory emphasizes the social construction aspect at the expense of other realities" (ibid., 163; emphasis original).

2. See the following for helpful surveys: Jon Berquist, "Critical Spatiality and the Construction of the Ancient World," in *Imagining Biblical Worlds: Studies in Spatial, Social, and Historical Constructs in Honor of James W. Flanagan*, ed. David M. Gunn and Paula M. McNutt, JSOTSup 359 (New York: Sheffield Academic Press, 2002), 14–29; Edward S. Casey, *Getting Back into Place: Toward a Renewed Understanding of the Place-World*, 2nd ed., Studies in Continental Thought (Bloomington, IN: Indiana University Press, 2009); Mark K. George, "Space and History: Siting Critical Space for Biblical Studies," in *Constructions of Space I: Theory, Geography, and Narrative*, ed. Jon L. Berquist and Claudia V. Camp, LHBOTS 481 (New York: T&T Clark, 2007), 19–20. Schreiner also provides a helpful analysis on how the scientific and mathematical revolutions of Einstein, Galileo, and Newton

note two specific challenges that arise when spatial considerations are applied to the heavenly tabernacle.

The first is the challenge of reconciling the tabernacle's static structure with the dynamic, social implications that surround it. Along with this lies the question of how the tabernacle's static space creates this dynamic. The second challenge deals with the reconciliation of time and space. Can the heavenly tabernacle be understood as spatial along with its temporal characteristics? Addressing these two challenges will enable us to better apply Critical Spatial Theory to the heavenly tabernacle, and, as a result, to Hebrews' spatiotemporal eschatology.

2.1.1. Reconciling Space

A. Reconciling Static and Dynamic Space

Historically, there have been two different approaches to space. The first originated with Plato's designation of space as a "receptacle that receives matter and gives matter form, without having form itself." It was then followed by Aristotle's designation of space as the "boundary between a containing body and the thing contained" which was more compatible to "experience and common sense."[3] Mark George is correct in saying that these two approaches "were a significant influence on the discussion about space and place for the next two thousand years in the Western world."[4] Plato's approach tended towards thinking of space through reason, and defined it by its structural make-up or occupancy of a coordinate area. On the other hand, Aristotle's approach emphasized the experiencing of space.[5]

These two approaches have led to debates in how space is to be understood.[6] This can be seen in the range of views from Newton's absolute, fixed space to Gottfried Leibniz's relational view[7] to Descartes' relative, varied space.[8] It is in response to this problem that Immanuel Kant attempted to reconcile absolute

---

have impacted the way history has viewed space and geography studies that followed ("Space, Place and Biblical Studies: A Survey of Recent Research in Light of Developing Trends," *CurBR* 14.3 [2016]: 342–51).

3. As noted by George, "Space and History," 18. "If then a body has another body outside it and containing it, it is in place, and if not, not" (Aristotle, *Physics, Volume I: Books 1–4*, trans. P. H. Wicksteed and F. M. Cornford, LCL 228 [Cambridge, MA: Harvard University Press, 1957], 4.5.212a32–212b3). "Plato viewed space as a receptacle (ὑποδοχή); Aristotle had a volumetric conception of space (τὸ πόσον or μέγος)" (Schreiner, *Body of Jesus*, 40 n. 9).

4. George, "Space and History," 18. Johan Marie Brinkman makes similar observations but distinguishes them as *perception* and *experience* (*The Perception of Space*, 16).

5. George, "Space and History," 18.

6. Schreiner, "Space, Place, and Biblical Studies," 341.

7. Schreiner, *Body of Jesus*, 42.

8. George, "Space and History," 19–20. The successes of Newton, Galileo, and Einstein in their respective fields further solidified the prevalent view that space is an "infinite

and relative space. His solution was to separate the two into the noumenal and phenomenal realms, which, unsurprisingly, correlates to the two approaches of space that Plato and Aristotle proposed, respectively. Both are affirmed, albeit without interrelation. Following Kant, philosophers and geographers have oscillated between these two approaches to space—either an objective understanding of space as a fixed, structural construct that fills an area or a subjective understanding of occupied space that comes about through experience.[9]

Until the 1960s, it was the positivist, space-as-container approach that was most prominent, partly due to the modernist and Enlightenment movements of the decades preceding.[10] James Flanagan writes, "In recent centuries, Kantian philosophy, Newtonian physics, and Euclidean geometry combined to support confidence in a so-called modernist Cartesian space and time grid. In that perception, three-dimensional space was calibrated on x, y, and z axes as a static 'container' in which events occur throughout time, the fourth dimension."[11] This can be seen in the prevalence of how people tend to view geography as merely concerning Cartesian points as on a map—hence, what postmodern geographers have called a reductionistic or positivist approach to geography.[12] Michel Foucault, often known as the pioneer of postmodern spatial studies, was one of the first to challenge this approach. He introduced the concept of "heterotopia," which are "spaces of liberty outside of social control,"[13] and challenged the "closed-ended object–subject dialectic that controls the modernist perception" of space.[14]

---

container, volume, or body," in contrast to the "local and subjective views of space and place" (Schreiner, "Space, Place, and Biblical Studies," 342).

9. Henri Lefebvre notes that philosophers have also contributed to the problem of this "schism" by viewing space as abstract (metaphysical) in a homogeneous, infinite manner (*The Production of Space*, trans. Donald Nicholson-Smith [Cambridge, MA: Basil Blackwell, 1991], 14). I will use the English translation of Lefebvre's book written in French except when interacting with key quotes, terms, and phrases: *La production de l'espace*, 2nd ed. (1974; repr., Paris: Éditions Anthropos, 1981).

10. Schreiner, "Space, Place, and Biblical Studies," 344; *Body of Jesus*, 44; Sleeman, *Geography and Ascension*, 24. This perception of location was "developed on a Platonic trajectory fueled in part by the Scientific Revolution, the age of exploration, and even the exploration of space" (Westfall, "Space and Atonement," 231; cf. Casey, *Getting Back into Place*, 3–8). As evidence for this observation, Soja engages with Lefebvre's work, *La production de l'espace* (1974), which culminated out of the sixties (Soja, *Thirdspace*, 73).

11. James W. Flanagan, "Space," in *Handbook of Postmodern Biblical Interpretation*, ed. A. K. M. Adam (St. Louis, MO: Chalice Press, 2000), 239; cf. also Berquist, "Critical Spatiality and the Construction," 15; Schreiner, "Space, Place and Biblical Studies," 342–44.

12. Soja, *Thirdspace*, 76.

13. David Harvey, *Justice, Nature, and the Geography of Difference* (Cambridge, MA: Blackwell, 1996), 230; cf. Michel Foucault and Jay Miskowiec, "Of Other Spaces," *Diacritics* 16.1 (1986): 22–27.

14. Flanagan, "Space," 241.

Ever since the onset of these reactions against the notion of geography as simply concerning fixed points as on a map, since the 1980s, space and geography have expanded into numerous other discussions, particularly those of social theory and interdisciplinary studies.[15] The direction and momentum of spatial studies have led many to subsume spatial studies under social or humanistic studies.[16] "Place and space, in this view, develop through time and are not static concepts. Humanistic geography began to connect space to the phenomenological and existential experiences of particular people."[17] The development of all these insights culminated in what is commonly called in postmodern geography the "spatial turn."[18]

15. Berquist, "Introduction: Critical Spatiality and the Uses of Theory," in Berquist and Camp, eds, *Constructions of Space I*, 1–2.

16. One can also assert that space as a social construct was stipulated by Émile Durkheim whose view on space is summarized by the following statement: "Space is the external expression of human consciousness, with the symbolisms, organizations, arrangements, and other aspects derived from social structures and meanings" (George, "Space and History," 25); cf. Emile Durkheim, *The Elementary Forms of Religious Life*, trans. Karen E. Fields (New York: Free Press, 1995), esp. 10–18. Durkheim believes that space, along with the sacred and profane categories of religion, are social constructions—"products of collective thought" (ibid., 9). Another key figure is Yi-Fu Tuan who emphasized that the *experience* of space is highly dependent on the one observing it (Berquist, "Critical Spatiality and Construction of the Ancient World," 18). Yi-Fuan Tuan is considered to have introduced the concept of "humanistic geography" (*Space and Place: The Perspective of Experience*, 7th ed. (Minneapolis, MN: University of Minnesota Press, 2011). James Flanagan also writes that "sociology goes hand in hand with architecture" ("Space," 240). Other notable postmodern geographers/theorists include David Harvey, *The Condition of Postmodernity: An Enquiry into the Origins of Cultural Change* (Cambridge, MA: Blackwell, 1989), esp. 201–326; Doreen B. Massey, *For Space* (Thousand Oaks, CA: Sage, 2005); *Space, Place, and Gender* (Minneapolis, MN: University of Minnesota Press, 1994); Robert David Sack, *Conceptions of Space in Social Thought: A Geographic Perspective*, Critical Human Geography (London: Macmillan, 1980). See Flanagan, "Space," 239–40, for an overview of notable scholars' contributions. For a more comprehensive treatment of "key thinkers" on space and place, see Phil Hubbard and Rob Kitchin's *Key Thinkers on Space and Place*, 2nd ed. (Los Angeles, CA: Sage, 2011).

17. Schreiner, "Space, Place, and Biblical Studies," 344.

18. See *The Spatial Turn: Interdisciplinary Perspectives*, ed. Barney Warf and Santa Arias, Routledge Studies in Human Geography 26 (New York: Routledge, 2009), esp. Edward Soja's "Taking Space Personally," 23–25; cf. also Matthew Sleeman, "Critical Spatial Theory 2.0," in *Constructions of Space V: Place, Space and Identity in the Ancient Mediterranean World*, ed. Gert T. M. Prinsloo and Christl M. Maier, LHBOTS 576 (New York: T&T Clark, 2013), 51. Key figures who contributed to the Spatial Turn include Henri Lefebvre, Michel Foucault, David Harvey, and Edward W. Soja (Halvor Moxnes, "Landscape and Spatiality: Placing Jesus," in *Understanding the Social World of the New Testament*, ed. Dietmar Neufeld and Richard E. DeMaris [New York: Routledge, 2010], 90–106). Schreiner

From this spatial turn, Henri Lefebvre attempted to resolve the tension between positivist and humanist camps, which set the stage for "Critical Spatiality."[19] According to Mark George, Lefebvre asserts that "[s]ocial space (understandings of space shaped by social ideas) produces real, tangible effects in (and on) the material, physical world. Thus, for Lefebvre, to study one type of space, be that physical space or mental space, without the other is to ignore something central about the nature of social space."[20] There was no such thing as absolute or static space, for it is the activity of humans to colonize space that makes space what it is.[21] This was the first component of the notion that people *produced* space—through phenomena such as language, movement, and other social interactions which all contribute to the production or reproduction of space—hence, space being a social product. This process is dialogical (or dialectic) involving the relations amongst the inhabitants in their local communities with the physical space around them.[22]

From these observations, Lefebvre developed a spatial triad: (1) spatial practice (*la pratique spatiale*), (2) representations of space (*les représentations de l'espace*), and spaces of representation (*les espaces de représentation*).[23] This triad can also be understood as *l'espace perçu, l'espace conçu,* and *l'espace vécu* (perceived space, conceived space, and lived space).[24] In simpler terms, they correspond to the physical, the mental, and the social:

> The fields we are concerned with are, first, the *physical*—nature, the Cosmos; secondly, the *mental,* including logical and formal abstractions; and, thirdly, the *social*. In other words, we are concerned with logico-epistemological

also provides a summary of factors that led to this Spatial Turn in Chapter 3, "Spatial Theory," in *The Body of Jesus*, 38–55.

19. *La production de l'espace* (1974) paved the way for Critical Spatiality by interacting with Foucault's *heterotopia* and developing a spatial trialectic. Lefebvre takes Durkheim's definition along with Hegel's idea of self-consciousness and Marx's concept of human production to believe that it is people who produce (real) space (George, "Space and History," 25–26).

20. Ibid., 25. Lefebvre begins by stating that up until recently, "the word 'space' had a strictly geometrical meaning: the idea it evoked was simply that of an empty area" (*Production of Space*, 1).

21. Schreiner, "Space, Place, and Biblical Studies," 346; cf. Henri Lefebvre, *The Survival of Capitalism: Reproduction of the Relations of Production,* trans. Frank Bryan (New York: St. Martin's Press, 1976), 17–18. Lefebvre particularly utilizes the example of capitalism and how people create city/town centers from which peripheral, social (spatial) activity derives.

22. Ibid., 18.

23. Lefebvre, *Production of Space*, 33–38.

24. Lefebvre, *La production de l'espace*, 49. It is "imperative" that a subject can traverse through this trialectic experience without being "lost." "Que le vécu, le conçu, le perçu se rejoignent, de sorte que le 'sujet,' le membre de tel groupe social, puisse passer de l'un à l'autre sans s'y perdre, cela s'impose" (ibid., 51).

space, the space of social practice, the space occupied by sensory phenomena, including products of the imagination such as projects and projections, symbols and utopias.[25]

This triad ultimately sets up the framework for Edward Soja's tripartite schema of Thirdspace, which will be utilized in this study.[26]

The spatial turn offered a corrective in affirming space's intrinsic, static features while acknowledging its dynamic, social ones. However, a problem arises when we view space as dialectic[27] without (1) considering the more complex relationships that space has among the physical, mental, and social or (2) acknowledging the importance of people and the reciprocal impact that they have *on* space. It is in response to this problem that a spatial trialectics comes onto the scene.

B. Reconciling Space and Time

The second challenge lies in reconciling *time* along with our understanding of space. Previously it was stated that time had taken precedence over space in eschatology studies. The same tendency is evident in the modern era, even in secular scholarship.[28] Jon Berquist goes so far to say that philosophers in the past two centuries have observed that time has been "annihilating space."[29] Even now, the current status of and interest in spatial studies are partly the result of what philosophers, including the likes of Karl Marx, have observed regarding the prominence of time over space.[30] This, too, has made its way into biblical studies.[31]

---

25. Lefebvre, *Production of Space*, 11–12; emphases original.

26. As presented in his book, *Thirdspace*. Soja's earlier thoughts and especially his critique of traditional geographies were published in his *Postmodern Geographies: The Reassertion of Space in Critical Social Theory* (New York: Verso, 1989).

27. Meaning only two parties are involved.

28. "For at least the past century, time and history have occupied a privileged position in the practical and theoretical consciousness of Western Marxism and critical interpretation of social life and practice" (Soja, *Postmodern Geographies*, 1). Soja agrees with Foucault by quoting, "Space was treated as the dead, the fixed, the undialectical, the immobile. Time, on the contrary was richness, fecundity, life, dialectic" (Michel Foucault, "Questions on Geography," in *Power/Knowledge: Selected Interviews and Other Writings*, trans. Colin Gordon [New York: Pantheon Books, 1980], 70 cited in Soja, *Postmodern Geographies*, 10). Soja introduces his trialectics by first tracing the history of philosophy and geography and how it has neglected space in Chapter 3: "The Socio-spatial Dialectic" (ibid., 76–93).

29. Berquist, "Introduction: Critical Spatiality and the Uses of Theory," 1.

30. Brinkman, *The Perception of Space*, 12. Hegel, Heidegger, Sartre, and other critical social theorists have made "muted efforts to reactivate space more centrally" (Soja, *Thirdspace*, 71).

31. "In line with modernity's way of thinking, however, Christian theology has tended to privilege the temporal sequencing of arguments and narratives over their spatial arrangement" (Asumang, *Unlocking Hebrews*, 40).

Pitting space and time against each other inevitably deems one to be more important than the other. Instead of seeing them as substantially different realities or relinquishing one to a subordinate status, space and time must go hand-in-hand. As Lefebvre writes, "Time is known and actualized in space" and "space is known only in and through time."[32]

One of the most notable thinkers to regret the disproportionate interest and focus of time over space was Michel Foucault. This difference of interest is unsurprising if space is seen as static; interest in it pales in comparison to that of time. Space, however, must be seen as dialectic, dynamic, and essential to people, societies, and the unfolding events of history. By this redefinition, time is held to be inherent in one's definition of space. Lefebvre adopted this dynamic definition by proposing spatiality as consisting of both space and time while maintaining their distinctive properties. He writes, "Time is distinguishable but not separable from space…" Furthermore, "[p]henomena which an analytical intelligence associates solely with 'temporality,' such as growth, maturation, and aging, cannot in fact be disassociated from 'spatiality' (itself an abstraction). Space and time thus appear and manifest themselves as different yet unseverable."[33] Affirming these insights, I propose that within biblical studies, a spatiotemporal eschatology is a prime candidate to reconcile time and space in Hebrews.

2.1.2. Applying Edward Soja's Thirdspace

Although Lefebvre advanced spatial studies by utilizing the notion of Foucault's heterotopia ("lived spaces"), he approached it as a Marxist philosopher and sociologist whose intent was to investigate how "particular ideas of space are creations of political practice, social system, division of labor and mode of production."[34] Edward Soja takes Lefebvre's notion of lived spaces and reapplies it as an urban planner, who "shifts the grounding from Lefebvre's explicit Marxist concentration on modes of production (including material, social and ideological effects) into a more postmodern intellectual context."[35] He believes that in Lefebvre's *Production of Space,* there is an additional theme that is "embedded deeply" but

---

32. Lefebvre, *Production of Space*, 219. This is one helpful way of thinking about the interrelatedness of space and time (as well as of matter and energy). For example, Albert Einstein's theory of relativity asserts that these aspects of reality are all relative to one another (Berquist, *Critical Spatiality and Construction*, 15).

33. Although people cannot see time as they see space, they do "live time" and are "in time" (Lefebvre, *Production of Space*, 95; also 175, 219). "Yet all anyone sees is movements. In nature, time is apprehended within space—in the very heart of space…" (ibid).

34. Berquist, "Critical Spatiality and Construction," 19; cf. Lefebvre, *Production of Space*, 36–37.

35. Berquist, "Critical Spatiality and Construction," 20; cf. Soja, *Thirdspace*, Chapter 1: "The Extraordinary Voyages of Henri Lefebvre," 26–52. Soja recognizes Lefebvre's "meta-Marxism" and "spatial politics" that he sees as an "incessant theme that is summarily captured and intoned in that repeated phrase: the social production of social space"

"never systematically extrapolated," which Soja coins, "Thirding-as-Othering." Soja writes:

> I then use this method [Thirding-as-Othering] to re-describe and help clarify what I think Lefebvre was writing about in the thematic "Plan" of *The Production of Space* fugue: a trialectics of spatiality, of spatial thinking, of the spatial imagination that echoes from Lefebvre's interweaving incantation of three different kinds of spaces: the *perceived* space of materialized Spatial Practice; the *conceived* space he defined as Representations of Space; and the *lived* Spaces of Representation.[36]

By doing so, Soja frees Lefebvre's heterotopia from its Marxist framework and allows for a more unbiased application. Soja's outcome is Tripartite Critical Spatial Theory.[37] Soja proposes that space cannot be understood in a reductionistic, dialectical fashion in either static (positivist) or dynamic (social) categories. While Soja recognizes and affirms both properties, he distinguishes them from its experiential, lived-out properties. Soja, building on the work of previous geographers and philosophers, and especially Foucault and Lefebvre,[38] has influenced the way that space is understood: "In short, geographers, anthropologists, and sociologists now describe space in a tri-part division; the physical world in which people exist, the ideological underpinnings of understanding places, and the lived practices of people within those places that sometimes challenge and sometimes reaffirm the expected uses of such places."[39] He argues that space has three interrelated properties: *First-*, *Second-*, and *Thirdspace*.[40]

Soja defines Firstspace as the physical, concrete, mappable and measurable geographies of our lifeworlds. Secondspace is our mental projections or representations onto an empirical world from imagined or projected geographies.[41] He regrets that the modern world tends to view space in either First or Secondspace categories at the neglect of Thirdspace—in other words, a binary notion of space

(*Thirdspace*, 60; cf. also 106–107). Soja has a different agenda as an urban planner who applies Lefebvre's insights for the city mapping of Los Angeles.

36. Soja, *Thirdspace*, 10; cf. Chapter 2: "The Trialectics of Spatiality," esp. 66–82.

37. See Soja's *Postmodern Geographies* (1989), esp. Chapter 2: "Spatializations: Marxist Geography and Critical Social Theory," 43–75.

38. Soja has the same concerns as Lefebvre. "Lefebvre's Marxist-inspired scholarly program…was in large part an effort to erase this binary split between pure and impure, imagined and real, or theoretical and empirical" (Berquist, "Introduction," 4). It is the space where the "real and imagined are intertwined" (Flanagan, "Space," 243). Regarding Michel Foucault's heterotopologies, Soja admits they are "frustratingly incomplete, inconsistent, [and] incoherent," while at the same time, provide a "marvelous incunabula of another fruitful journey into Thirdspace" (Soja, *Thirdspace*, 162).

39. Schreiner, "Space, Place, and Biblical Studies," 341.

40. Soja, *Thirdspace*, 10.

41. Such projections can then be articulated in blueprint designs, texts, and maps.

that is physical versus theoretical. His "Third-as-Othering" trialectic is a "means of escaping the binarisms, dialectics, and opposition that lead to a 'closed logic of either/or' that capture physicalist (materialist) and mentalist (idealist) geographers in a hopelessly closed, mutually reinforcing exchange."[42] Therefore, he proposes the necessity of Thirdspace, which allows us to view space as trialectic while incorporating both the physical and imagined.

He writes, "*Thirdspace* too can be described as a creative recombination and extension, one that builds on a Firstspace perspective that is focused on the 'real' material world and a Secondspace perspective that interprets this reality through 'imagined' representations of spatiality."[43] It is much more than "wrapping texts in appealing spatial metaphors."[44] In the previous survey in Section 1.2, all the views acknowledged an aspect of the heavenly tabernacle that can be affirmed. For example, the concrete descriptions of the tabernacle found in the cosmological view and its rhetorically rich spatial metaphors both must be acknowledged. But only when the tabernacle's physical, symbolic, spiritual, and ethical characteristics come together in "creative recombination and extension" can we progress in our understanding of the eschatological, heavenly tabernacle.

2.2. Thirdspace in Biblical Studies

When it comes to biblical studies, there are many benefits to the advances made in spatial studies. As Mark George writes, "Space is not simply the neutral medium in which biblical and related narratives and events took place."[45] It was over the space of the promised land that created the backdrop for Israel's wilderness journeys. It was the devastation over the lost space of Jerusalem and the temple that set the scene for Israel's woes and prophetic laments. In the New Testament and especially in the Epistle to the Hebrews, it is the question of occupied heavenly space that has a direct impact on how believers occupy and live out of their earthly space.

There lies much potential in utilizing insights from modern geography and spatial studies in biblical studies, because it allows for the "interweaving of physical and historical geography with social and ideological representations, which are shaped further by the immediacy of lived experience."[46] Soja's tripartite schema has branched into other fields, and biblical studies is no exception.[47]

---

42. Flanagan, "Space," 241–42; cf. Soja, *Thirdspace*, 60.
43. Soja, *Thirdspace*, 6.
44. Ibid., 96.
45. George, "Space and History," 29.
46. Thomas B. Dozeman, "Biblical Geography and Critical Spatial Studies," in Berquist and Camp, eds, *Constructions of Space I*, 105.
47. Soja, "Taking Space Personally," 23–24. Other than geography, areas such as the social sciences and humanities are where the Spatial Turn has had its deepest effect (ibid., 24–25). Soja himself states from the outset that Thirdspace is "trandisciplinary in scope

In fact, Soja records how surprised he was when he, at a conference at the Chicago Divinity School, saw his spatial perspective utilized in the "reconceptualization of Nature…in the esoteric field of eschatology."[48] He recalls the following:

> It was explained to me that eschatologists were using Thirdspace (1996) and my concepts of critical thirding-as-othering and trialectics as a means of opening up new ways to explore the multiplicity of dimensions through which heaven and hell could be described as putative lived spaces. The Spatial Turn had seemingly reached its outer limits.[49]

The application of Critical Spatial Theory in biblical studies has its roots in the ASOR/SBL consultation in 1988 entitled, "Constructs of Ancient History and Religion," which culminated in James Flanagan's presidential address entitled, "The Trialectics of Biblical Studies" in 1996. This eventually formed the "Construction of Ancient Space Seminars" in 2000.[50] After various works and applications of Critical Spatiality to biblical texts,[51] the progress and momentum of biblical spatial studies is "irreversible and ongoing."[52] Altogether, these resulted in a specialized field of Critical Spatial Biblical Studies which has recently produced a variety of helpful works.[53]

[because it] cuts across all perspectives and modes of thought, and is not confined solely to geographers, architects, urbanists and others for whom spatial thinking is a primary professional preoccupation (Soja, *Thirdspace*, 3). Schreiner provides a helpful review of the "scholars who have appropriated what they call 'critical spatiality' to historical, sociological, and narratival readings," especially those who describe space in the tri-part division as this study attempts to do with the heavenly tabernacle ("Space, Place and Biblical Studies," 351–60). See also his section entitled, "A Spatial Turn and Biblical Studies" (*Body of Jesus*, 11–14).

48. Soja, *Taking Space Personally*, 28.
49. Ibid.
50. James W. Flanagan, "Ancient Perceptions of Space/Perceptions of Ancient Space," *Semeia* 87 (1999): 15–43. Prior to this address, Flanagan had already been working on how to incorporate social theory models into biblical studies since 1987. Five volumes were published based on these seminars, entitled *Constructions of Space* (2008–2013). For further overview of how Critical Spatial Theory was introduced into biblical studies, see Gunn and McNutt's introduction in *Imagining Biblical Worlds*, 6–8.
51. Some representative works in NT studies include Halvor Moxnes, *Putting Jesus in His Place: A Radical Vision of Household and Kingdom* (Louisville, KY: Westminster John Knox, 2003); Patrick Schreiner's *The Body of Jesus* (2016); Matthew Sleeman's *Geography and the Ascension Narrative in Acts* (2009); Eric Stewart's *Gathered Around Jesus* (2009); Karen J. Wenell, *Jesus and Land: Sacred and Social Space in Second Temple Judaism*, LNTS 334 (New York: T&T Clark, 2007).
52. Sleeman, "Critical Spatial Theory 2.0," 64.
53. Two recent compilations have been published: David M. Gunn and Paula M. McNutt, eds., *Imagining Biblical Worlds: Studies in Spatial, Social, and Historical Constructs*

While the terminology and concepts behind Critical Spatial Theory are innovative and modern, the dynamics of space that it describes is not a novel or foreign concept. To apply this method is not to suggest that the author of Hebrews had Soja's trialectics in mind at the time of his writing. We must appreciate the historical trajectory of how space has been understood. Nevertheless, the dynamics of space and geography have been contemplated on prior to the writing of Hebrews through the likes of Plato and Aristotle.[54] Furthermore, Soja's trialectics is not creating innovative spatial features that were not previously present. Rather, it is a "way of understanding" what he describes has always been a "distinct mode of critical spatial awareness."[55] This stems out of his concern for the "theoretical rebalancing of spatiality, historicality, and sociality as all-embracing dimensions of human life."[56] In other words, spatial theory is not *prescribing* a new way of looking at space but *describing* ways in which people, both ancient and modern, have viewed space all along.[57] Before we move on to the theory's application to the heavenly tabernacle, I address one concern regarding the anthropocentric focus that Critical Spatiality tends to espouse.

2.2.1. Against an Anthropocentric Critical Spatiality

Postmodern geographers were right to react against a positivist approach to geography. Spatiality cannot merely be limited projections or constructs that simply occupy space. One cannot deny the impact that space has had on ideas and people, and, in turn, the impact that ideas and people have had on space. Space is not only static but also dynamic. On the other hand, postmodern geography has swung to the other side of the pendulum by defining space as being entirely a social construct. Hence, scholarship in geography has shifted from a positivist approach, to environmental determinism (the idea that geography *determines* the social characteristics of the people), to human agency (space is neutral and separate from human social relations), to finally, a socially produced understanding of

---

in Honor of James W. Flanagan, JSOTSup 359 (New York: Sheffield Academic Press) and the collection of articles in *Constructions of Space: Vols. 1–5* (2007–2016).

54. For a study on how the concept of space has been perceived in the Greek classical and Hellenistic era, see Keimpe Algra, *Concepts of Space in Greek Thought*, Philosophia Antiqua 65 (New York: Brill, 1995).

55. Soja, *Thirdspace*, 10.

56. Ibid.

57. Cf. Mark K. George, "Introduction," in *Constructions of Space IV: Further Developments in Examining Ancient Israel's Social Space*, ed. Mark K. George, LHBOTS 569 (New York: T&T Clark, 2013), xi; Victor H. Matthews, "Physical Space, Imagined Space, and 'Lived Space' in Ancient Israel," *BRB* 33.1 (2003): 12–20; and Sleeman's discussion on how ancient writers did not see space as mere settings for history, and that "spatialised reading does not compete with, or seek to replace, historical readings" (*Geography and Ascension*, 50). Similar observations are also made by Katherine Clarke, *Between Geography and History: Hellenistic Constructions of the Roman World* (Oxford: Clarendon Press, 1999).

space.⁵⁸ This final stage believes that "society constructs and shapes the framework of knowledge in the human mind,"⁵⁹ which ultimately includes our understanding of space altogether.

Admittedly, Edward Soja's and Henri Lefebvre's spatial models stemmed from a socially created view of space apart from divine agency. Nevertheless, divine intrusion and "eschatological impulses assume and demand a different 'thirding' within their construals of space."⁶⁰ The spatial turn applied to biblical studies is not only a social turn at the human level. It is a divine one. As such, "[b]iblical eschatologies variously restructure spatial relations and, within their texts' persuasive frames, reflect an inbreaking which is both within and from beyond earthly, secular spaces."⁶¹ In other words, when it comes to biblical studies, Thirdspace cannot be anthropocentric, but must instead be theocentric.

Unfortunately, many biblical spatial studies have adopted this anthropocentric approach.⁶² Jon Berquist, a scholar who has greatly advanced Critical Spatial Biblical Studies, writes, "Space has a genealogy and a history; it exists as a constructed category within the framework of human experience. Space is something we make, create, produce, shape, reshape, form, inform, disform and transform. All these human activities are operations upon space, leaving traces that mark its history and its shape."⁶³ Hence, space naturally will be socially contested by the people(s) who vie to control space.⁶⁴ Therefore, as an example, in his utilization of spatial trialectics in Hebrews, Berquist reverses the proper order—that is, our participation in Firstspace (1S) and our understanding of the

---

58. Eric Clark Stewart, "New Testament Space/Spatiality," *BTB* 42.3 (2012): 140–41.

59. George, "Space and History," 25. It is also worth noting that the shift of emphasis towards the participant of space correlates with the reader-oriented approach of linguistic interpretation such as Stanley E. Fish, *Is There a Text in This Class? The Authority of Interpretive Communities* (Cambridge, MA: Harvard University Press, 1980) and Peter L. Berger and Thomas Luckmann, *The Social Construction of Reality: A Treatise in the Sociology of Knowledge* (New York: Anchor Books, 1990).

60. Sleeman, "Critical Spatial Theory 2.0," 56.

61. Ibid., 57.

62. Notable exceptions include Matthew Sleeman's *Geography and the Ascension Narrative in Acts* (2009) and Patrick Schreiner's *The Body of Jesus: A Spatial Analysis of the Kingdom in Matthew* (2016). In Sleeman's work, Jesus' ascension shaped the believers' spatiality and "understanding of space both within and beyond the church" (*Geography and Ascension*, 5). Schreiner argues that the kingdom of God in the Gospel of Matthew is not limited to God's "reign" or "rule" but also "logically necessitates a spatial territory and people over which he reigns" (Schreiner, *Body of Jesus*, 36). This results in Jesus breaking in and making a new, earthly kingdom with the presence of his body.

63. Berquist, "Critical Spatiality and Construction," 14–15.

64. "Critical spatiality encompasses those theories that self-consciously attempt to move beyond modernist, mechanistic, essentialist understandings of space; thus, critical spatiality understands all aspects of space to be human constructions that are socially contested" (ibid.).

Secondspace (2S) are what enables us to live out the Thirdspace (3S). He, on the other hand, argues that in Hebrews, believers' suffering (3S) is what constructs their 1S and 2S.[65] This comes from his notion of "absent spaces," which is that the heavenly temple and the body of Jesus are outside of "human-experienced time." A shared temporal plane between Jesus' body and the earthly realm is not available for the community. "Instead, both the temple and the body of Jesus are absent in Firstspace but present in Secondspace, as memory and representation. The problem of these two spaces is that they are gone; thus, the entire Book of Hebrews lacks any grounding in a real physical Firstspace."[66]

However, it is more correct to say that believers' participation in Firstspace and Secondspace is what creates their Thirdspace situation of suffering and enables them to faithfully live it out. I propose we observe how First- and Secondspaces are presented theologically within the author of Hebrews' argument to then see the social and community implications that necessarily result from it. Schreiner views similarly in writing, "[I]t seems that more theological and narrative work needs to be done in this area rather than just social or cultural, although the two interact."[67]

Unfortunately, there are currently no works dedicated to a comprehensive study of the heavenly tabernacle in Hebrews using Soja's categories.[68] Utilizing insights from this method, I propose that Firstspace spatial features of the heavenly tabernacle and its Secondspace semiotics come together for believers to live Thirdspace according to the exhortation to live as priests in their eschatological situation. However, a careful distinction must be made. The lived experience of believers does not itself *create* heavenly tabernacle Thirdspace, but rather enables believers to *participate* in it as they *imagine* its practices on earth.[69] This distinction is what sets this study apart methodologically from the anthropocentric approach to Critical Spatiality seen in the likes of Jon Berquist and Mark George. The heavenly tabernacle space is metaphysically a divine creation while its participation and its lived experience in that space produces a re-imagining of the tabernacle through believers' priestly practices in their earthly communities.

---

65. In believing that space is socially produced, he takes the social situation of believers (3S) to draw implications on Firstspace and Secondspace. Thus, believers themselves create space through their active participation in Thirdspace.

66. Berquist, "Critical Spatiality and the Book of Hebrews," 185–87. Because of this absence, Hebrews presents "suffering as the means for transfer between [the material and divine] realms" (ibid., 187).

67. Schreiner, "Space, Place, and Biblical Studies," 361.

68. Apart from Cynthia Westfall's short chapter discussed in Section 2.4.

69. We must adjust our understanding of "imagining," not as "inventing," but as a "way of knowing things that can be known no other way" and has the "power to make us *see*" and taking our minds "beyond positions justified by reasons, to conclusions which come to govern our behavior" (Schreiner, *Body of Jesus*, 14; emphasis original).

2.3. Thirdspace and the Heavenly Tabernacle

We now specifically turn to Edward Soja's trialectics in our study of the heavenly tabernacle in Hebrews. With Soja's trialectics, we can study the heavenly tabernacle itself as a spatial entity, which allows us to consider its multiple dimensions in its eschatological nature. Firstspace is concerned with the "material and materialized 'physical' spatiality that is directly comprehended in empirically measurable *configurations*."[70] This leads us to look closely at the records of empirical observations and descriptions of the heavenly tabernacle—to which both Hebrews and much of Jewish apocalyptic literature attest. Secondspace is the "explanatory concentration on [the] conceived rather than perceived space."[71] *Conceived* does not necessarily mean that the mind originates such projections; oftentimes, it is done in response to and in correlation with the perceived, material space. Therefore, "the knowledge of this material reality is comprehended essentially through, as *res cogito*, literally 'thought things.'"[72] It is how believers acknowledge, understand, and embrace their heavenly status as being spiritually present with the resurrected Christ in a materialized, heavenly tabernacle. This "empowers the mind" so that the Secondspace "explanation becomes more reflexive, subjective, introspective, philosophical, and individualized."[73] This has profound implications in believers' self-understanding and their social ethics on earth.

This perceived configuration allows us to physically ground the heavenly tabernacle in place (Firstspace), which then strengthens believers' assurance of their positional standing with Christ before God's heavenly throne (Secondspace). We can then consider how these physical and spiritual realities transform their self-understanding into that of being heavenly priests, who actualize this identity into that of earthly priests (Thirdspace) in limitless possibilities and potential.[74] Furthermore, in reciprocal fashion, their priestly practice and their consciousness of their priestly identity feed back into and further inform what constitutes the heavenly tabernacle, since they themselves are occupants of that tabernacle space. This is an example of how the interplay of a space's multiple dimensions mutually inform one another.[75] Rather than taking a static approach to studying the tabernacle, we can appreciate the dynamic nature of the eschatological tabernacle along with its occupants. This takes into consideration Soja's precaution against a binary dialectic in our view of the tabernacle (literal vs. metaphorical, present vs. future, ethical vs. doctrinal).

---

70. Soja, *Thirdspace*, 74; emphasis original.
71. Ibid., 78.
72. Ibid., 79.
73. Ibid.
74. Soja notes how Lefebvre would see spaces such as cities as a "possibilities machine" (ibid., 3).
75. I discuss this interplay in Section 7.2.

A visualization of these concepts across the heaven–earth landscape can be seen in Figure 2.1. While the distance between heaven and earth is immeasurable, the grounding of believers' Firstspace standing in the heavenly tabernacle allows for Secondspace to bridge the gap, allowing for the simultaneous physical and spiritual realities to take place. It is having an accurate Secondspace understanding which then allows and enables believers to serve as priests on earth, which is the outworking of their heavenly, priestly identity.

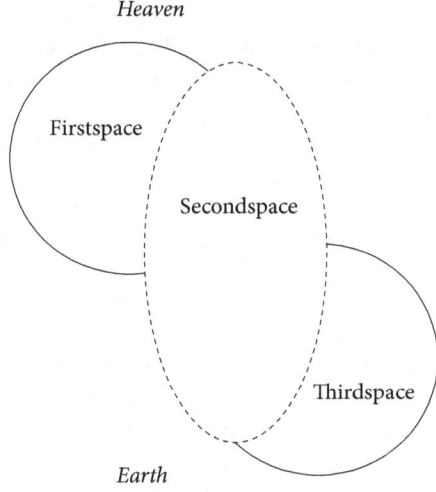

Figure 2.1. Spatial Trialectics Across Heaven and Earth

The benefit of Tripartite Critical Spatial Theory is that it allows us to look at the heavenly tabernacle with a holistic understanding of space. As previously mentioned, space and geography have traditionally been reduced to an immovable, absolute, Cartesian notion of space. This resulted in reducing space to only physical terms (i.e., Firstspace). The spatial turn brought to attention humanistic interpretation and subjectivity—hence, "humanistic geography," the "complex relationship between people and place."[76] Space is also concerned with the values that are attached to physical places and the social interactions that people have with the communities around them.[77] In sum, the theory allows us to admit that

---

76. Schreiner, "Space, Place and Biblical Studies," 344.
77. The reason for my adaptation of Soja's and Lefebvre's spatial theory is due to their primary concern with political practices and, for Lefebvre, the Marxist divisions of labor and power. What is useful for this study is (1) their expanding the notion of space to surpass geographic, physical constructions and (2) the interplay among the physical, mental, and ethical spheres as it comes to a particular space. "[S]pace is ineluctably all three at once" (Berquist, "Critical Spatiality and Construction," 20; cf. also Schreiner, "Space, Place and Biblical Studies," 341, 360).

space is "not neutral or objective"[78] and that meaning and practice are not simply projected or attached to space, but also constitute space. We cannot think of the heavenly tabernacle apart from what it signifies for Old Testament believers, which is intensified for New Testament believers. Furthermore, we cannot envision a heavenly tabernacle that does not, in turn, impact and influence the social, lived practices of those who occupy it spiritually while they remain on earth.

The application of spatial trialectics to the heavenly tabernacle constitutes the bulk of this study. I will present Firstspace by arguing for a spatially realized tabernacle using contextual exegesis and tracing the heavenly tabernacle motif in the Old Testament (e.g., the use of Exod. 25:40 in Heb. 8:5) and intertestamental literature. I then evaluate the tabernacle's Secondspace: the heavenly tabernacle's symbolic depictions in light of Christ's high priestly work on behalf of believers. To do so, I incorporate insights from David Moffitt's "analogical model," which developed out of Janet Soskice's homeomorphic versus paramorphic models of metaphors.[79] The texts considered are Hebrews 4:14; 6:19-20; 8:1-5; 9:1-14 (Chapters 4–6 of this study). Once Firstspace and Secondspace realities ground the believers' spiritual presence in the heavenly tabernacle and their identification with Jesus Christ, the heavenly high priest, believers then possess a clear conscience and the confidence (4:16; 9:14; 10:19–22) to identify and serve as priests. This I refer to as heavenly tabernacle Thirdspace (Chapters 7–8).

I will also discuss the interplay of First-, Second-, and Thirdspace for the tabernacle, because these interactions give believers the confidence to actualize their priestly activity due to having a clean conscience (Heb. 4:16; 9:14; 10:1–3, 19–25). This mutual interaction of First-, Second-, and Thirdspace gives believers a spatial orientation that is both heavenly and earthly. Furthermore, they follow Soja's proposal that space exists as places of transformation through social praxis of resistance.[80] This interplay of First-, Second-, and Thirdspace is necessary for believers to participate in priestly activity both spiritually in heaven and ethically on earth. Therefore, the earthly spaces that believers occupy become places of transformation, motivated by believers' positional standing in the heavenly sacred space.

In this arrangement, the metaphorical and rhetorical power of the heavenly tabernacle is reinforced by the fact that it is locally actualized in the heavens. Believers' knowledge of an actualized place in the tabernacle contributes to their present assurance in Jesus' high priestly activity, especially as it concerns their clear conscience obtained through him (Heb. 10:22). If this physical spatiality is relegated only to a future-based reality, it weakens the ongoing motivation that arises from their heavenly occupancy. Hence, a fully accessible spiritual Secondspace reality must be grounded in physical Firstspace. Furthermore, the believers'

---

78. Berquist, "Critical Spatiality and Construction," 22.

79. Moffitt, "Serving in the Tabernacle in Heaven," 259–82.

80. Soja, *Postmodern Geographies*, 122. In Hebrews, this "resistance" refers to believers' encounter with the secular worldview and lifestyle that is antagonistic to their faith (Heb. 10:25, 32–34; 12:14; 13:13).

priestly participation in Thirdspace in (1) vertical worship and (2) horizontal, social, and ethical practice is grounded in both First and Secondspace.[81] I will argue that this participation is a priestly one—hence, a general priesthood of believers in Hebrews.

The following preliminary conclusions are proposed: (1) The heavenly tabernacle serves as a prime example of a holistic eschatology that incorporates both temporal and spatial features. Hence, the author of Hebrews uses the heavenly tabernacle to communicate eschatological realities for believers to ground their identities as priests and to act as priests in their communities. (2) Second, this study stresses the importance of Christ's high priestly role and activity in order for these eschatological realities to be accessible for the believer. Believers are allowed access to the inner parts of the heavenly sanctuary *via* an identification with the high priest, Jesus. (3) Third, the spatiotemporal eschatological tabernacle adds support to how Hebrews eschatology can be one of the binding concepts that hold together the doctrinal and hortatory features of the letter without neglecting them or reading them in isolation.[82] Other themes, such as Christ's supremacy and superiority, the parenetic warnings to the wilderness generation, the attention dedicated to Christ's heavenly movement and presence in the Most Holy Place, and the exhortation for believers to draw near and to hold fast can all be harmonized under Hebrews' eschatology.

Defining space according to Soja's categories allows us to have a more robust understanding of the heavenly tabernacle's eschatological features. The believers' spiritual occupancy in a spatially realized heavenly tabernacle (doctrinal) provides the motivation necessary to faithfully carry out the instructions as priests (hortatory).[83] These conclusions support my thesis that the author of Hebrews intentionally presents the heavenly tabernacle to eschatologically situate, orient,

---

81. I pay careful attention to not contend that believers' Thirdspace activity is what constitutes their First- and Secondspace status in heaven. This I believe reverses the order of how the author of Hebrews presents the believers' positional First- and Secondspace standing with Christ in heaven (8:1–10:18) *and then* delineates how they live out those realities in Thirdspace (10:19–13:25).

82. A reoccurring question in Hebrews scholarship is how one reconciles the ethical instructions in Hebrews 13 with the doctrinal arguments that precede it (James W. Thompson, "Insider Ethics for Outsiders: Ethics for Aliens in Hebrews," *ResQ* 53.4 [2011]: 207–19).

83. In addition, other interpretive implications may be considered. For example, there is a recurring question as to why the author of Hebrews uses the tabernacle motif instead of the temple. Based on this, some have conjectured that this is due to the presence or absence of the Second Temple. In other words, "Why the tabernacle and not the temple?" This study may show that the author of Hebrews' use of the tabernacle motif is not strictly tied to the historical situation of his audience (i.e., the presence or destruction of the Second Temple either pre- or post 70 CE); rather, the author utilizes the heavenly tabernacle motif because it better represents the current eschatological situation of the believers than does a future-oriented temple.

and ground believers both spatially and temporally. They are spiritually present in the heavenly tabernacle with Christ and yet physically serve as priests on earth by actualizing their heavenly status through social and ethical obedience within their community. As a result, Hebrews scholarship can benefit both methodologically and theologically: (1) The application of Edward Soja's Tripartite Critical Spatial Theory on the heavenly tabernacle in Hebrews and (2) a holistic understanding of Hebrews eschatology, achieved by reconciling the spatial and temporal features of the heavenly tabernacle. Furthermore, these insights can be a benefit to present-day believers as they bear the author's word of exhortation (13:22), which is grounded in their identification with Christ, the heavenly high priest who ministers in the holy places (8:1).

2.4. Excursus: Cynthia Westfall's "Space and Atonement in Hebrews"

In Chapter 1 of this study, five approaches to understanding the heavenly tabernacle were presented. However, one recent and helpful work that does not neatly fit into any of those approaches is Cynthia Westfall's chapter entitled "Space and Atonement in Hebrews," in *So Great a Salvation: A Dialogue on the Atonement in Hebrews* (2019).[84] To date, it is the only application of Soja's Tripartite Critical Spatial Theory to the heavenly tabernacle in Hebrews. Nevertheless, she, like many recent scholars, is engaged in the conversation surrounding the atonement rather than eschatology. She expresses her intent by writing, "The central argument of this chapter is that the author of Hebrews was interpreting the atonement of Christ by correlating, disambiguating, and applying a form of spatial interpretation to the description of the place of atonement in the LXX."[85] When it comes to locating the atonement, she suggests drawing attention away from the time of the atonement to its location. While the location and timing of the atonement is an important topic, I hope to contribute to the understanding of the eschatological framework of the letter by focusing particularly on the heavenly tabernacle. Furthermore, Westfall's short chapter of twenty pages does not delve into specific, heavenly tabernacle texts in Hebrews, but instead presents only a broad understanding of the heavenly tabernacle.[86] More importantly, her conclusions on the heavenly tabernacle's Second and Thirdspace are different from mine.[87]

For example, for Westfall, heavenly tabernacle Secondspace is not the symbolic or mental representation that arises from an empirical Firstspace; rather, it is the actual earthly tabernacle (temple) up to the point of its destruction. She argues

---

84. Westfall, "Space and Atonement in Hebrews," 228–48.
85. Ibid., 234.
86. Westfall's focus is on investigating the spatial features of the place of atonement to determine the timing of the atonement, and not on presenting the tabernacle itself as a key feature to communicate the believers' eschatological situation.
87. However, as previously mentioned, Westfall and I hold to similar views regarding the physical, concrete reality of a heavenly sanctuary structure (ibid., 235–36).

that the earthly tabernacle was itself "a symbol that points to the reality and a map from which the heavenly space can be described."[88] She deduces this from Hebrews 8:5, which references Exodus 25:40 "to show that the [earthly] 'sanctuary' in which the Levitic priests serve is Secondspace. It is a copy (ὑποδείγματι) and shadow (σκιᾷ) of what is in heaven."[89] When taking these terms literally, it can be understood why Westfall would depict the earthly tabernacle as the "blueprint" and therefore as the heavenly tabernacle's Secondspace. However, it is doubtful that Edward Soja means Secondspace to be the actual, physical "blueprint" of an architectural design. Rather, Secondspace is the symbolic meaning of *what* a particular Firstspace represents, which *can* be captured by, though is not limited to, a blueprint or a model. In Hebrews, would the author's intent in presenting the heavenly tabernacle really be to draw focus backwards to the symbolic significance of the earthly tabernacle?

This, in fact, seems to be the opposite of what is written in chapters 7–10 of Hebrews, in which the levitical sacrifices are described as inferior and a shadow of what was to come with the heavenly. Instead of literally applying the terms "copy" and "shadow" to strictly align with Soja's Secondspace definition of "representation," the heavenly tabernacle's Secondspace is its "conceived space or its perception" as Westfall herself defines it.[90] I argue that Firstspace is the heavenly tabernacle, and Secondspace encompasses the tabernacle's soteriological significance, which results in priestly implications for believers. Westfall understands tabernacle Thirdspace to be the occupation of believers "outside the camp" (Heb. 13:13) as a marginalized community, living as those called to collective resistance against Rome.[91] I present heavenly tabernacle Thirdspace, which includes Westfall's notion of co-suffering with Christ, but is expanded to include Christlike obedience and ethical behavior[92] while holding onto the spatiotemporal eschatological realities of Christ's high priestly work.[93]

---

88. Ibid., 236.
89. Ibid., 237.
90. Ibid., 232.
91. Furthermore, her chapter does not discuss *how* her Firstspace and Secondspace depictions contribute to or enable the community to live in Thirdspace. The question is, "How are heavenly tabernacle Firstspace and Westfall's earthly tabernacle Secondspace related to her Thirdspace marginalized living?" The relationships and the interactions that Firstspace, Secondspace, and Thirdspace have with one another, emphasized by Soja, seems to be missing.
92. I recognize that while Westfall exclusively discusses participation in Christ's suffering, obedience and ethics are closely related and could also be assumed by her.
93. Similarly with Berquist, she also reverses the order from Firstspace to Secondspace to Thirdspace. For her, it is the believers' participation with Jesus "outside the camp" that entails their occupying the true tabernacle as priests (ibid., 242). As I will argue, it is in fact believers' present occupation with Christ in the heavenly tabernacle (Firstspace and Secondspace) that enables them to live and function as priests, as Thirdspace.

Chapter 3

THE BACKGROUND OF THE TABERNACLE

3.1. The Heavenly Tabernacle in the Context of Hebrews

Admittedly, the Epistle to the Hebrews does not describe the heavenly tabernacle in comprehensive, spatial detail. Yet, this does not diminish the importance of the spatial language that the author of Hebrews does use for the heavenly tabernacle. We will examine three important passages that utilizes such spatial language: First, Hebrews 4:14 and 6:19–20 depict Jesus as having physically traversed through the created heavens to arrive at the heavenly tabernacle (Chapter 4). Second, Hebrews 8:5 draws upon the revelation that God had shown to Moses (Exod. 25:40) that affirms an actualized tabernacle as the model (τύπον/תַּבְנִית) for the earthly one (Chapter 5). And thirdly, Hebrews 9:1–14 further describes key spatial features of the heavenly tabernacle, which houses the celestial liturgy that takes place within (Chapter 6).

Utilizing Soja's spatial trialetics, we will examine the heavenly tabernacle's Firstspace and Secondspace features for each passage and then utilize our collective findings to investigate its Thirdspace properties that become realized in the believers' ethical and priestly living (Chapters 7–8). But before delving into these specific passages, in this chapter, we will orient our study of the heavenly tabernacle with an overview of the historical, literary, and structural features of Hebrews. Furthermore, we will note important characteristics of the Old Testament tabernacle that are carried over into the New Testament—namely, its temporal and spatial limitations with respect to one's access to God's presence.

3.1.1. Historical Context

It is not within the scope of this study to provide an exhaustive introduction to Hebrews, yet it is helpful to consider the pertinent context of the heavenly tabernacle. The "epistle" to the Hebrews is best classified as a "word of exhortation"[1]

---

[1] The same phrase, τοῦ λόγου τῆς παρακλήσεως, appears in Acts 13:15 when the synagogue officials press Paul to give a "word of exhortation" (λόγος παρακλήσεως) to the people. For more on this classification, see Mackie, *Eschatology and Exhortation*, 19–25;

(Heb. 13:22) or "sermon"[2] written by an unknown author[3] with a thorough understanding of the Greek Old Testament.[4] This is supported when observing

Michel, *Der Brief an die Hebräer*, 27; James Swetnam, "On the Literary Genre of the 'Epistle' to the Hebrews," *NovT* 11.4 (1969): 261–69. Furthermore, Lawrence Wills argues that an identifiable three-part pattern exists in Acts 13:14–41 (indicative or "exempla," conclusion, and exhortation) and the term "word of exhortation" likely took on a "fixed meaning" for sermons ("The Form of the Sermon in Hellenistic Judaism and Early Christianity," *HTR* 77.3–4 [1984]: 278–80). See also C. Clifton Black, "The Rhetorical Form of the Hellenistic Jewish and Early Christian Sermon: A Response to Lawrence Wills," *HTR* 81.1 (1988): 1–18, who argues Acts 13:13–41 is even closer to the conventions of Greco-Roman rhetoric than Wills presents. For our purposes, we note that the exact phrasing is used in both Hebrews and Acts 13 with the latter clearly showing Paul delivering a persuasive and hortatory address.

2. One of the distinguishing features of Hebrews is how the author interweaves the doctrinal and hortatory material and has in mind the situation of a specific group of believers (cf. David J. MacLeod, "The Literary Structure of the Book of Hebrews," *BSac* 146.582 [1989]: 185–97; Jeremy Punt, "Hebrews, Thought-Patterns and Context: Aspects of the Background of Hebrews," *Neot* 31.1 [1997]: 121; Spicq, *L'Épître aux Hébreux*, 1:27; Steve Stanley, "The Structure of Hebrews from Three Perspectives," *TynBul* 45.2 [1994]: 247–49). Furthermore, Hebrews lacks the standard introduction that we commonly find in letters from that time period (Lane, *Hebrews 1–8*, lxx). There is no formal identification of the author or the recipients, nor is there a prelude of blessing or thanksgiving like that which we normally find in Paul's letters (William L. Lane, "Hebrews: A Sermon in Search of a Setting," *SWJT* 28.1 [1985]: 13–18).

3. For a summary of proposed authors, see Charles Cutler Torrey, "The Authorship and Character of the So-Called 'Epistle to the Hebrews,'" *JBL* 30.2 (1911): 137–56; Cockerill, *Hebrews*, 7–10; Ellingworth, *Hebrews*, 3–20; Lane, *Hebrews 1–8*, xlix; Spicq, *L'Épître aux Hébreux*, 1:197–219. The most common candidates include Paul, Clement of Rome, Luke, Apollos, Barnabas, Peter, and Jude. When specific individuals are not proposed, it has been suggested that the author may have been educated in the Alexandrian tradition with a religious-historical knowledge of Judaism (rabbinic apocalyptic) and Hellenism (gnostic philosophy). For example, "Wir haben wohl einen alexandrinisch gebildeten juden-christlichen Lehrer vor uns. Wie die johanneische Literatur verlangt auch der Hebr die religionsgeschichtliche Kenntnis des Judentums (Rabbinat, Apokalyptik) und des Hellenismus (Gnosis, Philosophie)" (Michel, *Der Brief an Die Hebräer*, 35 n. 1).

4. F. F. Bruce, *The Epistle to the Hebrews*, NICNT (Grand Rapids, MI: Eerdmans, 1990), 5, 20; Hurst, *Hebrews*, 4, 12. The author quotes the OT thirty-five times including repeated quotations and depends primarily on the LXX (Ellingworth, *Hebrews*, 11, 37; cf. Radu Gheorghita, *The Role of the Septuagint in Hebrews: An Investigation of Its Influence with Special Consideration to the Use of Hab 2:3-4 in Heb 10:37-38*, WUNT 2/160 [Tübingen: Mohr Siebeck, 2003], especially pp. 1–6 and 31–38; Iutisone Salevao, *Legitimation in the Letter to the Hebrews: The Construction and Maintenance of a Symbolic Universe*, JSNTSup 219 [New York: Sheffield Academic Press, 2002], 101). For potential non-Christian backgrounds that may have influenced the author, see Hurst, *Hebrews*, 1–86.

the author's dependence (either verbatim or near verbatim) on the LXX[5] in places where he explicitly quotes the Old Testament.[6] It can further be said that the author of Hebrews had a "remarkable command of the Jewish sacred writing" and that he used the Jewish Scriptures "with much more uniformity and precision than most of the other NT writers."[7]

Therefore, it is the assumption of this study that the author of Hebrews depended on the LXX as his *Vorlage* for the Old Testament.[8] This is not to propose with certainty any one homogenous translation of the MT in the Old Greek (i.e.,

---

5. By LXX, I refer to the Greek OT—itself a collection to the traditions of translations of the Hebrew OT—in circulation by the time of the writing of Hebrews for the early Christian communities "as far as it can be reconstructed from evidence" (J. K. Aitken, ed., *T&T Clark Companion to the Septuagint* [New York: T&T Clark, 2015], 2). See also Gheorghita, *Role*, 1, 6–7 and R. Timothy McLay, *The Use of the Septuagint in New Testament Research* (Grand Rapids, MI: Eerdmans, 2003), 7, who prefer to use the term "Jewish Scriptures." For a history of the origins of the term and its usage, see E. E. Ellis, "The Old Testament Canon in the Early Church," 678–79 and Emmanuel Tov, "The Septuagint," 161–64 both in *Mikra: Text, Translation, Reading, and Interpretation of the Hebrew Bible in Ancient Judaism and Early Christianity*, ed. M. J. Mulder and Harry Sysling, CRINT 1 (Minneapolis, MN: Fortress Press, 1990); Peter J. Gentry, "The Septuagint and the Text of the Old Testament," *BBR* 16.2 (2006): 193–94. For the LXX's importance and use for NT research, see McLay, *The Use of the Septuagint*.

6. Heb. 1:6 (Deut. 32:43 LXX), esp. noting that the command to worship God (προσκυνησάτωσαν αὐτῷ) is absent in the MT; Heb. 1:7 (Ps. 103:4 LXX); Heb. 1:10–12 (Ps. 101:26–28 LXX); Heb. 2:6–8 (Ps. 8:5–7 LXX); Heb. 2:12 (Ps. 21:23 LXX); Heb. 3:2–5 (Num. 12:7 LXX); Heb. 3:7b–11 (Ps. 94:7–11 LXX); Heb. 8:5 (Exod. 25:9, 40 LXX); Heb. 10:5b–7 (Ps. 39:7–9 LXX; cf. footnote 11 below); Heb. 10:30 (Deut. 32:35, 36 LXX); Heb. 10:37–38 (Hab. 2:3–7 LXX); Heb. 11:21 (Gen. 47:31 LXX), esp. noting the author's choice of *staff* (LXX) over *bed* (MT); Heb. 12:5 (Prov. 12:5 LXX). While it is true that the author of Hebrews depended on the LXX, "it is incorrect to characterize the quotations in Hebrews as *always* Septuagintal" since "some agree with a known Hebrew text, either whole or in part, against the Septuagint" (George E. Howard, "Hebrews and the Old Testament Quotations," *NovT* 10.2–3 [1968]: 215; emphasis mine).

7. Gheorghita, *Role*, 2.

8. Ibid.; also David M. Moffitt, "The Interpretation of Scripture in the Epistle to the Hebrews," in *Reading the Epistle to the Hebrews: A Resource for Students*, ed. Eric F. Mason and Kevin B. McCruden, RBS 66 (Atlanta, GA: SBL, 2011), 78; Angela Rascher, *Schriftauslegung und Christologie im Hebräerbrief*, BZNW 153 (Berlin: de Gruyter, 2007). Alison Salvesen writes, "The LXX is itself a faithful translation of the Hebrew" and furthermore, that the author of Hebrews has "repeated and consistent use of the Greek textual tradition of the Scriptures, the Septuagint" ("Exodus," in Aitken, ed., *T&T Clark Companion to the Septuagint*, 30, 6). For a study arguing for the author's faithfulness in citing and referring to the OT Scriptures, see Susan E. Docherty, *The Use of the Old Testament in Hebrews: A Case Study in Early Jewish Bible Interpretation*, WUNT 2/260 (Tübingen: Mohr Siebeck, 2009), esp. 132–42.

Theodotian, Aquila, Symmachus or its recensions). Scholars agree that "there is no one Septuagint, not only in terms of the books included, but in terms of the text itself."[9] As is the case with septuagintal studies, we must consider possible readings for each instance considering the "number of versions that have left their mark on our text and manuscripts."[10] Therefore, references to the Old Testament in Hebrews call us to identify any intentional redactions or divergences from the MT or LXX tradition.[11]

There are complex debates over the version of the LXX that the author used. First of all, it is unknown whether the author primarily drew from biblical manuscripts[12] or from memory, although a combination of both may be possible.[13]

9. Aitken, *Companion*, 2. See esp. discussion by Leonard J. Greenspoon, "The Use and Abuse of the Term 'LXX' and Related Terminology in Recent Scholarship," *BIOSCS* 20 (1987): 21–29; also Docherty, "Use of OT in Hebrews," 122–23; Georg Walser, *Old Testament Quotations in Hebrews: Studies in Their Textual and Contextual Background*, WUNT 2/356 (Tübingen: Mohr Siebeck, 2013), 3–4.

10. Aitken, *Companion*, 5; also Julio C. Trebolle Barrera, *The Jewish Bible and the Christian Bible: An Introduction to the History of the Bible* (Grand Rapids, MI: Eerdmans, 1998), 437; Gheorghita, *Role*, 6.

11. In some passages, there may be debates over the author's intentional redaction of the LXX against the *Vorlage* he utilized. For example, in Heb. 10:5b–7, the author renders the tradition of Ps. 39:7-9 (σωμα δὲ κατηρτίσω μοι, "you prepared a body for me") over the MT's Ps. 40:7-9 (אָזְנַיִם כָּרִיתָ לִּי, "ears you have dug/opened for me") which either reflects an early LXX messianic interpretation of the psalm or the author's intentional redaction. The literal translation of ωτια over σωμα is reflected in both Rahlfs-Hanhart and the Göttingen translation as well as Aquila, Symmachus, and Theodotion (Karen H. Jobes and Moisés Silva, *Invitation to the Septuagint* [Grand Rapids, MI: Baker Academic, 2000], 195–98). For further discussion, see Attridge, *Hebrews*, 274; Ellingworth, *Hebrews*, 500–501; J. C. McCullough, "The Old Testament Quotations in Hebrews," *NTS* 26.3 (1980): 363–79; Karen H. Jobes, "Rhetorical Achievement in the Hebrews 10 'Misquote' of Psalm 40," *Biblica* 72 (1991): 387–96; Moffatt, *Hebrews*, 138–39; Spicq, *L'Epître aux Hébreux*, 1:336–38; Walser, *Old Testament Quotations*, 90–102. Ronald H. van der Bergh, "A Textual Comparison of Hebrews 10:5b–7 and LXX Psalm 39:7–9," *Neot* 42.2 (2008): 355–57, argues for σωμα as the original reading due to the lack of external evidence for ὠτία found only in the Gallican Psalter and LaG, a sixth-century Western text, along with minuscules 142 and 156 (ibid., 355). On the other hand, Karen Jobes suggests the author's intentional redaction to σωμα based on first-century rhetoric which latter scribes "corrected" back to ὠτία ("Rhetorical Achievement," 388–96). In light of such difficulties, while it is accepted that the author relied on the LXX as his *Vorlage*, we must not immediately take this at face value in all instances.

12. "Die alttestamentlichen Zitate des Hebr folgen aufs Ganze gesehen der LXX, und zwar vielfach derart wörtlich, daß man zu der Vermutung kommen konnte, der Verfasser habe nicht nach dem Gedächtnis, sondern aus einer schriftlichen Vorlage zitiert" (Michel, *Der Brief an Die Hebräer*, 155).

13. Moffitt, "Interpretation of Scripture," 78. The author of Hebrews quotes Jer. 38:31–34 LXX in 8:8–12, the longest citation of the OT in the NT, as well as an extended

Nevertheless, proposed candidates include what we find in Alexandrinus (LXX^A),[14] a combination of both Alexandrinus and Vaticanus (LXX^A and LXX^B),[15] a tradition underlying LXX^A and LXX^B,[16] or some other non-extant tradition.[17] Martin Karrer captures the situation in his statement: "In many cases Hebrews goes with A against B, in others with B against A, in a third set of cases with lesser manuscripts, and about fifteen times it differs from virtually all known LXX manuscripts."[18] While it is agreed that the author utilized the LXX, there are no definitive conclusions as to what *form* of the LXX he utilized.[19] For example, the author's reference to Daniel 6:23 in Hebrews 11:33 suggests Theodotion's (or Proto-Theodotion's) translation (ἐνέφραξεν τὰ στόματα τῶν λεόντων, "[God] shut the mouths of lions")[20] over the

citation of Ps. 94:7-11 LXX in 3:7-11. This does suggest that he had manuscripts of at least two bodies of texts available (Martin Karrer, "The Epistle to the Hebrews and the Septuagint," in *Septuagint Research: Issues and Challenges in the Study of the Greek Jewish Scriptures*, ed. Wolfgang Kraus and R. Glenn Wooden, SBLSCS 53 [Atlanta, GA: SBL, 2006], 342). Spicq also observes the precision with which the author of Hebrews cites these extended passages and concludes the following: "Elle reproduit de longs textes de l'Écriture…et d'une façon si généralement exacte que l'on est en droit de penser qu'elle copie un manuscrit et ne se contente pas d'une réminiscence" (*L'Épître aux Hébreux*, 1:334).

14. First suggested by Friedrich Bleek, *Der Brief an Die Hebräer: Erläutert Durch Einleitung Uebersetzung und Forlaufenden Commentar*, 2 vols. (Berlin: F. Dümmler, 1828), 1:374; Richard Longenecker, *Biblical Exegesis in the Apostolic Period*, 2nd ed. (Grand Rapids, MI: Eerdmans, 1999), 150; Moffatt, *Hebrews*, lxii. Spicq also writes that the author generally adopts Codex A but not as we have it (*L'Épître aux Hébreux*, 1:336): "Il adopte en général les leçons du codex A, mais non pas tel que nous le possédons."

15. H. J. B. Combrink states that it is "generally accepted that Hebrews usually cites according to the LXX (and not the MT), with approximately two-thirds of the readings from LXX^A and one third from LXX^B" ("Some Thoughts on the Old Testament Citations in the Epistle to the Hebrews," *Neot* 5 [1971]: 23).

16. Hans Hübner writes that "[m]any quotations are based on the A-text, while some are based on the B-text," but also raises the possibility of a "recension based on traditions which were later taken up in codices A and B" ("The OT Quotations in the New Testament," *ABD* 4:1103).

17. Markus Barth notes that, at times, the OT text used by the author of Hebrews are not found in either Vaticanus or Alexandrinus ("The Old Testament in Hebrews," in *Current Issues in New Testament Interpretation: Essays in Honour of Otto A. Piper*, ed. William Klassen and Graydon F. Snyder [London: SCM Press, 1962], 55). See also the discussion in Kenneth J. Thomas, "Old Testament Citations in Hebrews," *NTS* 11.4 (1965): 321-24.

18. Karrer, "Hebrews and the Septuagint," 344.

19. Moffitt, "Interpretation of Scripture," 78.

20. Emanuel Tov, *The Parallel Aligned Hebrew-Aramaic and Greek Texts of Jewish Scripture: Alexandrinus and Theodotion Variants* (Bellingham, WA: Lexham Press, 2003).

3. The Background of the Tabernacle

Old Greek tradition found in Rahlfs' edition (σέσωκέ με ὁ θεὸς ἀπὸ τῶν λεόντων, "God has saved me from the lions").²¹

Kenneth Thomas, in his assessment of Old Testament citations in Hebrews, concludes that the differences between LXX^A and LXX^B "probably originated in the transmission of the LXX rather than in Hebrews" and that "there is no evidence that the author knew two different readings in these instances and chose between them."²² While "there is overwhelming evidence that the author of Hebrews used a LXX text of a generally primitive nature," the particular LXX^(A/B) readings in Hebrews represent the text of the LXX used by the author of Hebrews in these instances."²³ Therefore, while recognizing the complexity involved in the "quest for the assumed LXX *Vorlage*"²⁴ in Hebrews, I utilize Rahlfs-Hahnart's *Septuaginta* (2006) while considering textual issues and variants found in the Göttingen's critical editions where available.²⁵

---

21. Jobes and Silva, *Invitation*, 42. Although this may be a case when the author considered the MT's rendering over the LXX (אַרְיָוָתָא פֻּם וּסְגַר). While the author of Hebrews used the LXX for the source of the Jewish Scriptures, we must not quickly assume that he had no exposure or access to the MT. At the least, he may have had a Hebrew consonantal text that was similar to or later became the MT (McLay, *Use of the Septuagint*, 8; also Rascher, "Schriftauslegung und Christologie," 15): "Allerdings kann aus der Nichtbenutzung des Masoretischen Textes nicht gefolgert werden, dass der Hebr diesen Text nicht kannte."

22. Thomas, "Old Testament Citations," 320.

23. Ibid., 321; cf. also 324.

24. As noted in Gert Steyn's title, *A Quest for the Assumed LXX Vorlage of the Explicit Quotations in Hebrews*, FRLANT 235 (Göttingen: Vandenhoeck & Ruprecht, 2011). See also his article, "An Overview of the Extent and Diversity of Methods Utilised by the Author of Hebrews When Using the Old Testament," *Neot* 32.2 (2008): 327–52 and his chapter, "Which 'LXX' are We Talking about in NT Scholarship?," in *Die Septuaginta: Texte, Kontexte, Lebenswelten*, ed. Martin Karrer and Wolfgang Kraus, WUNT 219 (Tübingen: Mohr Siebeck, 2008), 697–707; cf. also Moffitt, "Interpretation of Scripture," 78. Gheorghita writes that "the data on the history of the Greek translation of the Hebrew Scriptures and its history of transmission is far from being conclusive" (*Role*, 7). This complexity can also be seen in Peter J. Gentry's guidelines concerning the relationship between the LXX and the MT especially in relation to other OT witnesses found in the Dead Sea Scrolls, Syriac, Targums, and the Vulgate ("The Septuagint and the Text of the Old Testament," 193–218).

25. As opposed to a *diplomatic* approach. However, note that the Rahfls-Hanhart's edition itself is primarily based on Codices Vaticanus, Alexandrinus, and Sinaiticus. Important for this study (esp. Chapter 5) is that the "text of Exodus in Codex Vaticanus shows hardly any revision towards MT" (Salvesen, "Exodus," 30; cf. also John William Wevers, *Text History of the Greek Exodus*, MSU 21 [Göttingen: Vandenhoek & Ruprecht, 1992], 40). "Attempts to find the Author's *vorlage* from one of the major codices have been abandoned for the present time. Therefore, an eclectic approach, based on a careful assessment of the textual variants in each case, is the preferred way forward" (Gheorghita, *Role*, 29).

This does not mean to say that the purpose is to solely discover an underlying witness of the LXX or MT text,[26] but to note the importance of studying the author's understanding and interpretation of the Jewish scriptures through his use of them. Therefore, utilizing the eclectic text will give us "the closest approximation to what was originally written."[27] What is important for our purposes is to recognize that while the author was a second-generation believer (Heb. 2:1–3),[28] he had a thorough and impressive knowledge of the Old Testament considering that the "argument of Hebrews is marked by reference to the OT cultus."[29]

Without certainty of what the author of Hebrews meant by "those from Italy" send you greetings (13:24), the identity of the letter's recipients range from Judea in the east to Spain in the west,[30] although Rome is a likely candidate considering how Paul's Roman epistle is similarly seeped with Old Testament citations and allusions.[31] Nevertheless, the letter's recipients—without limiting them to only either Jews or Gentiles[32]—were "thoroughly acquainted with OT persons, institutions (especially cultic institutions)."[33] Regarding the letter's dating, the external evidence of Hebrews 1:3-7 embedded in 1 Clement 36:1-5 supports an

---

26. Gheorghita, *Role*, 4, who along with Julio Trebolle Barrera notes the importance of the "eclipsed exegetical value of the LXX," and to not overlook that "[s]ince it is a translation, the LXX is also a work of interpretation" (Barrera, *The Jewish Bible and the Christian Bible*, 436, 438).

27. McLay, *Use of Septuagint*, 13; also Docherty, "Use of OT in Hebrews," 123; McCullough, "OT Citations in Hebrews," 363. Gheorghita writes that "the Göttingen Septuagint provides the needed textual information to help establish with a reasonable degree of certainty what might have been the Author's *Vorlage*" (*Role*, 29).

28. The author distinguishes himself apart from the original apostles—"*those* who first heard from the Lord" and "confirmed to *us* by those who heard" (v. 3).

29. Ellingworth, *Hebrews*, 10; cf. also 37.

30. Bruce, *Hebrews*, 10; John Dunnill, *Covenant and Sacrifice in the Letter to the Hebrews*, SNTSMS 75 (New York: Cambridge University Press, 1992), 22–29; Ellingworth, *Hebrews*, 28; Patrick Gray, "Hebrews Among Greeks and Romans," in Mason and McCruden, eds, *Reading the Epistle to the Hebrews*, 14–15; Mackie, *Eschatology and Exhortation*, 9–17.

31. When we consider sections such as Romans 9–11, there is undoubtedly a "significant Jewish element in the church in Rome" (Ellingworth, *Hebrews*, 23). For a history of research on the topic of the OT in Hebrews from the late nineteenth century onward, see Docherty, "Use of OT in Hebrews," 9–82. For the argument that the letter originated in Rome, see Régis Burnet, ""La finale de l'épître aux Hébreux: une addition alexandrine de la fin du II siècle?," *RB* 120.3 (2013): 423–40.

32. Geerhardus Vos, *The Teaching of the Epistle to the Hebrews*, ed. Johannes G. Vos (Philipsburg, NJ: Presbyterian & Reformed, 1956), 11–23. Hebrews contain arguments and illustrations that appeal to both Jewish and Gentile or "God-fearing" readers.

33. Ibid. In the author's use of Psalm 95, he refers to prior Israelite generations as their "fathers," which suggest that the recipients were predominantly Jewish Christians. Furthermore, the author repeatedly refers to the OT as their "natural *alternative* identity-base"

upper limit of 96 CE.[34] The internal evidence shows that Hebrews was written to second generation believers who had heard the gospel from those who had direct interaction with Jesus.[35] An even earlier date is possible if the references to persecution are tied to Nero in 65 CE and the discussion of temple activity as if it was ongoing—hence a pre-70 CE writing.[36] For the arguments presented in this study, a standing, localized heavenly tabernacle does not depend on the presence or absence of the Second Temple since the author's comparisons draw upon the cultic institutions established in the past. Nevertheless, if the earthly temple had been destroyed (post-70 CE), it is difficult to imagine why the author did not refer to its destruction to further his argument regarding the superiority of the heavenly tabernacle.

3.1.2. Literary Context

The epistle begins by establishing the supremacy of Jesus Christ in his revelatory disclosure, his ontological oneness with God, and his providential power over the universe (1:1–13). This provides the Christological backdrop for the author's later arguments concerning Jesus' high priestly ministry. The revelation spoken in God's Son (ἐλάλησεν ἡμῖν ἐν υἱῷ, Heb. 1:2a) is the terminal endpoint by virtue of *who* Jesus is as God in the exact imprint of his nature, his revelation, ministry, and rule. Therefore, Jesus' revelation is far better than that of the prophets and the angels (1:3–4). In light of the divine authoritative nature of this revelation, the church must heed the message of salvation that was proclaimed to them (2:1). They are likened to the Israelites who wandered in the wilderness and are urged to avoid acting out in rebellion like their ancestors. They must strive to enter the promised, eschatological rest (3:1–4:13).

Until the consummation of that rest, Christ sympathizes with his people as the great high priest and mediates their relationship with God. He is qualified to do so because he is without sin and perfect, being the source of eternal salvation (5:9). As the divinely appointed high priest in the order of Melchizedek, Jesus is the guarantor of a better covenant (7:22). Next, the author delineates the reasons for Jesus' better and high priestly ministry. His mediatory role is eternal because he holds his priesthood permanently and lives forever. Jesus' blood sacrifice is a far better sacrifice that does not require repetition. It is more than sufficient to save those who draw near to God through him (7:25).

---

who are susceptible to turning back to that alternative (Dunnill, *Covenant and Sacrifice*, 24; emphasis original).

34. Bruce, *Hebrews*, 13; Ellingworth, *Hebrews*, 29; Donald Guthrie, *Hebrews: An Introduction and Commentary*, TNTC 15 (Downers Grove, IL: InterVarsity Press, 1983), 30.

35. Heb. 2:3; cf. Bruce, *Hebrews*, 20–21.

36. Ibid., 21. This is often suggested in light of the present force of the verbs in the priestly acts (e.g., Heb. 8:6–13); cf. also Cockerill, *Hebrews*, 39; Ellingworth, *Hebrews*, 32–33; Lane, *Hebrews 1–8*, lxvi. Scholars are evenly divided on a pre-70 and post-70 date (cf. Church, *Hebrews and the Temple*, 14 n. 65; Ellingworth, *Hebrews*, 33).

In Hebrews 8:1, the author reiterates his previous exposition while beginning a new "rhetorically marked section" (κεφάλαιον) in his argument[37] that extends into 10:18 by entering a doctrinal discourse on the levitical sanctuary and priesthood. Jesus is the mediator of a new and better covenant and, as such, performs his priestly ministry in the heavenly tabernacle. All the previous types and promises, such as the tabernacle that Moses built, pointed to their fulfillment in Jesus' high priestly ministry. The earthly tabernacle was a model of the true and real heavenly tabernacle, where Christ enacts the new and better covenant as promised by the prophet Jeremiah (8:8–12; cf. Jer. 38:31–34 LXX). Through Jesus' role as high priest, the true and genuine people of God have direct access to this heavenly space. In turn, the author calls his readers to persevere and continue to live as faithful exiles in the present age as they look towards their heavenly country (10:19–13:25).

3.1.3. Structure

With respect to the structure of Hebrews, there have been many approaches, though without a unified consensus.[38] One overlooked feature is how the epistle's structure aligns with believers' entry into the heavenly sanctuary and their earthly living in light of that reality. Viewing Hebrews as a tripartite structure,[39]

---

37. Lane, *Hebrews 1–8*, 202.

38. Barry Clyde Joslin summarizes eight difference approaches to the structure of Hebrews and concludes no such consensus ("Can Hebrews Be Structured? An Assessment of Eight Approaches," *CurBR* 6.1 (2007): 99–129. See also Stanley, "Structure of Hebrews," 245–71; Albert Vanhoye, "Discussions sur la structure de l'Épître aux Hébreux," *Biblica* 55.3 (1974): 349–80; *Structure and Message of the Epistle to the Hebrews*, SubBib 12 (Rome: Editrice Pontificio Istituto Biblico, 1989). For a recent, comprehensive study on Hebrews' structure using discourse analysis, see George H. Guthrie, *The Structure of Hebrews: A Text-Linguistic Analysis*, NovTSup 73 (New York: Brill, 1994), especially his historical survey on Hebrews' structure (pp. 3–20); also MacLeod, "Literary Structure," 185–97. Cynthia Long Westfall similarly utilizes discourse analysis and yet comes to different conclusions than Guthrie (*A Discourse Analysis of the Letter to the Hebrews: The Relationship between Form and Meaning*, LNTS 297 [New York: T&T Clark, 2005]). Guthrie stresses the importance of separating the expository and hortatory sections while affirming a logical relationship between the two throughout the epistle. However, Westfall argues that Guthrie's method diminishes the continuity and integrity of the entire discourse (ibid., 19–20).

39. Wolfgang Nauck, "Zum Aufbau des Hebräerbriefes," in *Judentum, Urchristentum, Kirche; Festschrift Für Joachim Jeremias*, ed. Walter Eltester, BZNW 26 (Berlin: Töpelmann, 1960), 199–206, who groups the three sections correlating with hortatory commands. Note that the exhortations Nauck designates to his second and third sections have spatial characteristics: "Tretet herzu zu Gott und haltet fest am Bekenntnis, denn Jesus Christus hat diesen Weg eröffnet" and "Stehet fest und folgt Jesus Christus nach, der der Anfänger und Vollender des Glaubens ist!" (ibid., 204–205).

inclusios in 4:14-16 and 10:19-31[40] mark the beginning and end of the central section (5:1-10:18) that deals with Christ's high priestly, heavenly ministry, which "has enabled access to the presence of God for his followers."[41] Furthermore, this tripartite structure with spatiality in mind allows us to see how doctrine and exhortation are intertwined not only within specific passages, but on a macrolevel as well.[42] Hebrews 4:14 begins with the movement of Christ who ascends through the heavens to his heavenly dwelling.[43] Coupled with Christ's movement is the believers' encouragement to likewise participate in movement by drawing near to the throne of grace with Christ as their forerunner (6:20). In the central section, the author expounds the high priestly ministry that takes place in this heavenly space (5:1-10:18), which is where believers spiritually reside. In the third section, the focus shifts onto the believers' confidence (10:18), which results in their ethical communal living—all in light of their joint standing with Christ in the heavenly sanctuary as a result of their entry.

This structure fits well with the passages to be examined throughout this study. In Chapter 4, we examine Hebrews 4:14-16, which marks the beginning of the central section with Christ's movement into heavenly space; Hebrews 8:1-5, which marks the rhetorical highpoint of the author's description of Christ's high priestly ministry that takes place in the heavenly tabernacle (Chapter 5); and finally, Hebrews 9:1-14, which expounds what activity takes place in the heavenly tabernacle (Chapter 6). In Chapters 7-8, we see the boldness and confidence that result in believers' identification as heavenly priests (10:19-25) who practice their priestly ministry on earth through their ethics and communal living by way of exhortation.

---

40. Ibid., 200-204; also Erich Grässer, *An Die Hebräer*, 3 vols., EKKNT 1-3/17 (Zürich: Benziger, 1990-97), 1:240. Guthrie notes the presence of cohesion shifts and verbal parallels in both of these passages. Believers have a priest (ἔχοντες οὖν ἀρχιερέα μέγαν, 4:14; εχοντες οὖν...ἱερέα μέγαν 10:21) named Jesus (Ἰησοῦ, 4:14; 10:19) who has led the way into the heavens (διεληλυθότα τοὺς οὐρανούς, 4:14; διὰ τοῦ καταπετάσματος, 10:19) and as a result, believers should draw near to God (προσερχώμεθα, 4:16; 10:22) (*Structure of Hebrews*, 79); cf. also Harold W. Attridge, *The Epistle to the Hebrews: A Commentary on the Epistle to the Hebrews*, Hermeneia (Philadelphia, PA: Fortress Press, 1989), 14-15. Other proponents of a tripartite schema are Jon C. Laansma, "Hidden Stories in Hebrews: Cosmology and Theology," in Laansma, Guthrie, and Westfall, eds, *So Great a Salvation*, 9; and Stanley, "The Structure of Hebrews," 245-71, who marks his tripartite schema as 1:5-7:28; 8:1-10:39; 11:1-13:19.

41. Church, *Hebrews and the Temple*, 12; cf. Cockerill, *Hebrews*, 61-62.

42. As opposed to Guthrie's strict division of doctrine and exhortation at 10:18 (Guthrie, *Structure*, 58; cf. Ellingworth, *Hebrews*, 50).

43. Verses 14-16 recapitulate the theme of Christ's priesthood first introduced in 2:17-3:1 (Spicq, *L'Épître aux Hébreux*, 2:91; also Michael Bachmann, "Hohepriesterliches Leiden: Beobachtungen zu Heb 5:1-10," *ZNW* 78.3-4 [1987]: 254).

3.2. Spatial and Temporal Limitations of the Earthly Tabernacle

Hebrews has the greatest number of formal Old Testament quotations in the New Testament[44] and is also seeped in Old Testament references, allusions, and echoes.[45] Therefore, it is necessary to consider what features of the Old Testament tabernacle lie in the background of the author and his recipients. The tabernacle itself was one of the ways that allowed for continuity across the many generations throughout Israel's history.[46] Hence, it is appropriate to assume that features of the earthly tabernacle lie in the background of thought for the recipients of Hebrews. Instead of performing an entire survey of the tabernacle motif throughout the Old Testament,[47] for our purposes, we draw our attention to two features that are helpful in our investigation of the heavenly tabernacle.

First, the earthly tabernacle was a visible and physical manifestation of inaccessibility. The segregation of the various courts and sanctuaries of the tabernacle communicated that access to God was limited both spatially and temporally. Only certain Israelites were allowed access to the tabernacle's inner parts only at appointed times in accordance with God's revealed instructions.

Second, in response to its inaccessibility, by God's own initiative, the tabernacle also stood for accessibility. After establishing and making known its inaccessibility, that very same tabernacle becomes the means through which the Israelites have access, though limited, to God's presence. It is through the role of the levitical

---

44. Guthrie, "Old Testament in Hebrews," *DLNT*, 841–42. While different criteria result in varied counts, a conservative number would be Cockerill's twenty-five OT passages (thirty-two if counting multiple uses) being quoted with an introductory formula of speech such as λέγων (Cockerill, *Hebrews*, 42–43; esp. p. 42 n. 85 in comparison with other scholars). In comparison, Spicq counts thirty-six citations (Spicq, *L'Épître aux Hébreux*, 1:331). See also R. T. France, "The Writer of Hebrews as a Biblical Expositor," *TynBul* 47.2 (1996): 246; George H. Guthrie, "Hebrews' Use of the Old Testament: Recent Trends in Research," *CurBR* 1.2 (2003): 272.

45. With perhaps the exception of Revelation, it is the most "permeated" with older-covenant texts (George H. Guthrie, "Hebrews," in *Commentary on the New Testament Use of the Old Testament*, ed. G. K. Beale and D. A. Carson [Grand Rapids, MI: Baker Academic, 2007], 919. Gheorghita writes that current scholarship "has reached an undeniable consensus regarding the importance of the Jewish Scriptures and their contribution to the theology of the Epistle to the Hebrews" (*Role*, 1). Spicq goes as far to say that Hebrews' extensive reference of the OT makes it "d'une étude générale des citations bibliques" (*L'Épître aux Hébreux*, 1:330).

46. Koester, *The Dwelling of God*, 74–75.

47. Craig Koester traces tabernacle references in the OT, intertestamental Jewish literature, and the NT in his work, *The Dwelling of God*. See also Church, "Wilderness Tabernacle and Eschatological Temple," 35–248; Myung Soo Suh, *The Tabernacle in the Narrative History of Israel from the Exodus to the Conquest*, StBibLit 50 (New York: Peter Lang, 2003).

priesthood taking part in cultic sacrifices and rituals within the tabernacle that Israelites can have their sins atoned for and their relationship with Yahweh restored.

Therefore, in our investigation of the spatial and temporal properties of the heavenly tabernacle, we first assert that the Old Testament tabernacle was a place of access, albeit a limited access, by way of its spatial characteristics and the timing of the cultic institutions that took place within. This symbolic backdrop allows us to better appreciate the author's theological argumentation for how Jesus' high priestly entry and ministry have granted believers full, spatial access into the heavenly tabernacle for all eternity.

3.2.1. Mt. Sinai's Limited Access

The challenge of accessing God's presence did not begin at the onset of the construction of the earthly tabernacle. Even before the tabernacle instructions were given on top of Mt. Sinai in Exodus 25, the preceding context portrays this spatial limitation during Moses' ascent. Therefore, Mt. Sinai served as a precursor to the tabernacle[48] and "the paradigm for access to the presence of God under the first covenant."[49] The Sinai mountaintop was accessible only to Moses. Not only was it off-limits to the rest of the people, but there was also the threat of death for anyone who approached the base of the mountain (Exod. 19:12-16, 21). But due to Moses' mediatory and representative role on behalf of the Israelites, there was access, albeit a limited access, to God who met with him on the mountaintop. This limitation was spatial, as can be seen in the physical, vertical gradations of the mountain.[50] This limitation was also temporal. Before Moses' ascent, the Lord instructs the people to consecrate themselves for two days and to be ready on the third day (vv. 10–11). Only at the Lord's appointed time is Moses able to bring the people near the base of the mountain, and then only he may ascend it.

It is significant that during this mountaintop experience, Moses receives the instructions for the tabernacle. Hence, the limited accessibility of Mt. Sinai and its significance get transferred to the tabernacle. "Indeed, inasmuch as the Sinai narrative aims at the book of Leviticus, we may also state—and much more aptly—that it aims at the tabernacle cultus."[51] The Lord descended (ירד) upon Mt.

---

48. G. K. Beale, "The Descent of the Eschatological Temple in the Form of the Spirit at Pentecost: Part 1 The Clearest Evidence," *TynBul* 56.1 (2005): 100–102; de Sousa, "The Heavenly Sanctuary/Temple Motif," 158–59.

49. Gäbel, *Kulttheologie*, 382: "Die Siniaoffenbarung wird damit zum Paradigma der Verwehrung des Zugangs zur Gottespräsenz unter der ersten διαθήκη."

50. L. Michael Morales distinguishes a tripartite division of the mount based on three bands of holiness described in Exod. 19:20; 24:12, 16–18 (top); 19:24; 24:1–2, 9–15 (midsection); 19:12, 17 (base) (*Who Shall Ascend the Mountain of the Lord? A Biblical Theology of the Book of Leviticus*, NSBT 37 [Downers Grove, IL: InterVarsity Press, 2015]), 87.

51. Ibid., 95.

Sinai in chapter 19 and dwelled (שׁכן) upon the mountaintop (Exod. 19:18, 20, 25) and, similarly, he dwelled (שׁכן) among them via the tabernacle (Exod. 29:45–46).[52]

Moses, as Israel's prophet and mediator, was granted access to God via the Sinai mountaintop experience; however, he was prohibited from entering the tent of meeting once the tabernacle was constructed. His access was limited because God's cloud and glory had settled on it (Exod. 40:35), which prohibited the presence of any man. As Michael Morales points out, it is significant that the book of Exodus ends with the crisis that if Israel's mediator, Moses, is not able to enter, who is able? How are God's people able to enter God's presence?[53] Hence, this question lies in the backdrop of Leviticus, which provisionally grants that sought-after access through the cultic system of the tabernacle. The tabernacle also points forward to the need for the once-for-all provision of Christ who performs the ultimate cultic ritual of his death and atonement in the heavenly tabernacle.

3.2.2. Spatial Limitation

The Old Testament tabernacle is physically divided into two sections: the Most Holy Place (קֹדֶשׁ הַקֳּדָשִׁים), which is separated from the Holy Place (הַקֹּדֶשׁ) by a veil to prevent access (Exod. 26:1, 31–35; 36:8, 35). This is reinforced by images of the cherubim on the veil, representing God's agents guarding its entry.[54] The massive curtain, which had to cover the Holy Place, measuring twenty by ten by ten cubits, was an intimidating barrier that hung on four acacia wood supports.[55] A third section can be included if one considers the outer courtyards and even a fourth if including the wilderness outside of the camp.[56]

The spatial designations of this limitation are further portrayed by the materials used. From the tabernacle's exterior to its interior, the materials reflect concentric circles of increasing holiness.[57] This is represented by the materials that make up the artifacts, as well as how elaborate those artifacts were relative to their

---

52. Morales also draws similarities between the tripartite division of the tabernacle with the three sections of the mountain with both having an altar through which a representative can approach God (ibid., 96–100).

53. Ibid., 107, 111.

54. Phillip J. Long, "Holy of Holies," ed. John D. Barry et al., *The Lexham Bible Dictionary* (Bellingham, WA: Lexham Press, 2016), Logos Bible Software.

55. Ibid. The limitation of access continued to be shown spatially even in later constructions of the temple, which were enforced by "walls of partition which limited access to the courts of God" (Stephen Westerholm, "Temple," *ISBE* 4:769).

56. The later temple is surrounded by three square courtyards (cf. 1 Kgs 7:12).

57. Beale, *The Temple and the Church's Mission*, 32–36; Menahem Haran, *Temples and Temple-Service in Ancient Israel: An Inquiry into Biblical Cult Phenomena and the Historical Setting of the Priestly School* (Winona Lake, IN: Eisenbrauns, 1985), 158–69; Craig R. Koester, *Hebrews: A New Translation with Introduction and Commentary*, AYBC 36 (New Haven, CT: Yale University Press, 2008), 402–403; Paul A. Nierengarten, "Temple Scroll," in *The Lexham Bible Dictionary*, Logos Bible Software. The gradually descending scale of

distance from the ark.[58] Gold was used in the inner sanctuary, silver in the Holy Place, and bronze for all other areas such as the pillars in the courtyard.[59] These sections also housed various artifacts, which themselves signified varying levels of holiness. Gold was used for the overlay of the ark, the cherubim, and the mercy seat, which all resided in the inner sanctuary. Other materials, such as the various leathers and hairs, reflected a decreasing value further away from the sanctuary.[60] Furthermore, the color of the curtains was a dark blue or purple,[61] colors which were rare and precious as they could only be extracted from particular species of shellfish.[62] The twisted linen itself was of a "superior Egyptian variety"[63] (Exod. 36:7; 38:16-18, 23; 39:2-8). Visibly, the colors would stand out amongst the rest of the tabernacle and the camp.

Altogether, these spatial barriers created concentric circles of holiness designated by the courts and the service that took place within them. They reflected the heightened levels of holiness as one progresses from the eastern end toward the inner portions.[64] For example, Israelites without priestly designation, both male and female, were able to enter the tabernacle courtyard when they brought their sacrifices and offerings, or gathered to hear God's instructions through Moses.[65]

holiness from the center correlates with the "careful and deliberate use of gold, silver, or bronze, or violet purple, reddish purple, crimson red, or white materials, and the offices of the high priest (=Aaron), priests, and Levites in connection with the tent sanctuary" (Klaus Koch, "אֹהֶל," *TDOT* 1:129). Cf. also John I. Durham, *Exodus*, WBC 3 (Dallas, TX: Word, 1987), 373.

Philip P. Jenson develops an entire work dedicated to the structural organization of the priestly writings, 'P' in Exod. 25–31, 35–40, and Leviticus, and eschews a kergymatic approach (*Graded Holiness: A Key to the Priestly Conception of the World*, JSOTSup 106 [Sheffield: JSOT Press, 1992]). His categories are the spatial dimension, personal dimension, ritual dimension, and the dimension of time (ibid., 35). While I do not agree with his conclusion that "graded holiness" is *the* organizing principle behind these passages, he provides a helpful description of how the composition of the tabernacle adheres to a holiness spectrum in Chapter 4, "The Spatial Dimension," 89–114.

58. Haran, *Temples and Temple-Service*, 165.
59. Stephen Westerholm, "Tabernacle," *ISBE* 4:698; cf. Exod. 38:19-20.
60. Durham, *Exodus*, 354.
61. A further distinction is made when observing that a "pure blue" cloth covered the ark during the tabernacle's journeys while the outer sanctuary furniture was covered in purple, which was "considered slightly coarser and cheaper than blue" (Haran, *Temples and Temple-Service*, 158-59).
62. Ibid.
63. Westerholm, "Tabernacle," 4:699, who notes that "the Israelites in the wilderness would scarcely have had at their disposal all the materials listed in the quantities required."
64. Edward Stuart Talbot, "Tabernacle (Jewish)," in *The Oxford Dictionary of the Christian Church*, ed. F. L. Cross and Elizabeth A. Livingstone (New York: Oxford University Press, 2005), 1584.
65. Westerholm, "Tabernacle," 4:702.

The Holy Place was accessible only to the priests (Exod. 28:43), while entrance into the Most Holy Place was possible for the high priest once a year (Lev. 16:34).[66] Outside the tabernacle courts, residual wastes from ritual sacrifices (Exod. 29:14; Lev. 4:12; 8:17; 9:11; 16:27; Deut. 23:10), unclean and rebellious Israelites (Lev. 13:46; 24:14; Num. 5:1), and those cursed (Lev. 24:14) were cast outside of the camp (cf. Heb. 13:13).

Altogether, the considerations of a person's identity (i.e., Israelite, priest, Levite) and the materials and designs that make up the artifacts connote the idea that God's holiness increased from the outer courts to the inner sanctuary. As a result, one's accessibility was limited depending on one's location relative to the inner sanctuary. In such a way, God communicated the intensity of his holiness through spatial means. It was geographical—based on one's proximity to the inner sanctuary. It was also material—based on the quality of the resources used to make the artifacts. If God used these spatial designations in the earthly tabernacle to communicate his holiness and the restrictions governing one's approach to his presence, then it is feasible that the physical, spatial designations of the heavenly firmament functions in a similar way.[67]

All this shows that prominent, physical designations were made by way of the specified locations of each tabernacle section and the materials that comprised them. Thus, the tabernacle communicated a limitation of access through its spatial markers. As seen in the account of Nadab and Abihu, the repercussions for violating these visible markers were immediate death (Lev. 10:1-2).[68] This is why Aaron was again warned that he could not enter "at just any time or in any manner within the veil, lest he die (in like manner to his sons)."[69] Interestingly, God's threatening responses to even inadvertent advancements towards the inner sanctuary are consistent with his glory. Through these fatal events, he shows himself to be holy, and thus is glorified before the entire congregation.[70]

This created a conundrum for the Israelites. The Israelites "longed, naturally enough, for some sort of closeness to God, a closeness that would be physical as well as moral."[71] This closeness was prevented by their sinful natures before a holy

---

66. Timo Eskola, *Messiah and the Throne: Jewish Merkabah Mysticism and Early Christian Exaltation Discourse*, WUNT 2/142 (Tübingen: Mohr Siebeck, 2001), 56-57. Non-Levites could not even approach the furniture of the tabernacle nor its outer altar except when the sacred furniture was covered (Num. 18:3) (Haran, *Temples and Temple-Service*, 181).

67. Vern Poythress notes that both the visible heaven and the tabernacle's "Holy Place" correspond to one another, which express "degrees of inaccessibility" (*The Shadow of Christ in the Law of Moses* [Phillipsburg, NJ: Presbyterian & Reformed, 1995], 18).

68. Morales suggests that the primary reason for their deaths was likely their entrance into the inner sanctuary (*Who Shall Ascend?*, 147).

69. Ibid.

70. Haran, *Temples and Temple-Service*, 188.

71. Cody, *Heavenly Sanctuary and Liturgy*, 12, who also notes this longing in Moses' request to physically be in God's presence and see his face (Exod. 33:18).

and righteous God. Nevertheless, out of God's benevolence and mercy, he also granted his people mediated access. Through the high priest's federal representation, to physically move across from the outside towards the inner sanctuary allowed them, at least proleptically and typologically, to have their longings satisfied. Michael Morales' analysis summarizes the situation well:

> Understanding YHWH to be the fountain of life, the spectrum between life and death may be mapped out *spatially*, with life and ordered cosmos at one end, and death and chaos at the other end… Keeping in mind how the tabernacle is an architectural mountain of God and model of the threefold cosmos, the holy of holies corresponds to the clouded summit of the mountain, the heavenly abode of God. As the place of God's Presence, the holy of holies represents the uttermost source of life. At the opposite end of the spectrum is the wilderness, which corresponds to the unruly waters surrounding the mountain, underneath which lies Sheol, the realm of chaos and death.[72]

3.2.3. Temporal Limitation

In addition to the limitation of access signified via its spatial features, the tabernacle and its associated rituals and festivals were also limited temporally. Even for Israelites who were qualified by office to enter the inner parts of the sanctuary, they could not enter whenever they wished. Morales writes:

> One might ask, for example, what good it is to have a sanctuary-like cosmos (sacred space) with a priestly humanity (sacred status), apart from appointed times of fellowship with God (sacred time)? Similarly, without appointed Sabbaths and festivals for fellowship with God, the tabernacle, along with its priesthood and rituals for drawing near, would have no telos or purpose.[73]

It was only during the appointed festivals and Sabbaths that the Israelites could utilize the space of the tabernacle to have access to God.

Rites such as the Day of the Atonement began only when access into the Holy of Holies was granted. In correlating fashion, spatial access for the high priest was granted only when temporal access was given. Nevertheless, this entry into the sanctuary amounted to a journey into the presence of God. While the individual

---

72. Morales, *Who Shall Ascend?*, 157; emphasis mine.
73. Ibid., 185. Leviticus also had a "major emphasis on sacred time," due to its connections with the creation account, and particularly, the Sabbath day which itself was "the appointed time for intimate dwelling with God" (ibid., 203). This explains why the entire final third of Leviticus "resounds with the festive gatherings of Israel's calendar" (ibid., 185). Morales also applies this to other books of the Pentateuch such as Exodus and Numbers showing how the chronological markers are no less significant than the locations visited throughout Israel's journey (ibid., 23–38).

cultic rituals performed during specific times and places are important (hence, the debate regarding the exact timing and location of Christ's atonement),[74] the ultimate focus and purpose of these cultic rituals were to re-establish a relationship with God. The atonement incorporated all these things, and yet is best summed up as a journey to God that takes place in the tabernacle. "Once more, the tabernacle was not merely the earthly house of God, but the way to God—the way of YHWH."[75] This journey not only takes time as one moves toward God, but it takes place during the appointed times and none other.

If the book of Leviticus and especially the tabernacle passages are centered around meeting and communing with God, then we must incorporate these important ideas when thinking about the heavenly tabernacle. It too is a place *and* time of meeting and communing with God but in a greater, eschatological sense. By analogy, it is a far greater space because the materials are not made with human hands. It houses a far greater priest in the glorified, resurrected person of Jesus Christ. And it is an ongoing experience for believers, not limited to appointed rites and festivals.

In conclusion, the tabernacle in the Old Testament was primarily about establishing access to God, which was at the same time, a limited access both spatially and temporally. The dilemma of reestablishing access with God was not a new concept with the Old Testament tabernacle. The "liturgical drama and logic for the tabernacle cultus" went back to the Eden narrative where Adam was created to serve as a figural high priest.[76] This notion of limited access from the earthly tabernacle prefigures both vertically (spatially) and horizontally (temporally) to the eschatological, heavenly tabernacle. Spatially, the heavenly tabernacle is not made with hands of this creation (Heb. 9:11, 24) and is constitutively far better and greater than the earthly one. Temporally, access to God in the heavenly tabernacle is not open merely at appointed times, but Christ entered the Holy of Holies and offered for all time one sacrifice for sins (Heb. 10:12). While sufficient during its place in redemptive history, the Old Testament tabernacle is insufficient when compared to the heavenly tabernacle given its limited times of access to God (sacred time), restricted access to the Holy of Holies (sacred space), and restriction of the persons allowed entrance (sacred status).

Carrying with us the importance of the earthly tabernacle's spatial features and how it was a place of both accessibility and inaccessibility, we can now appreciate the spatial features of the heavenly tabernacle found in the passages that we will investigate in the following chapters. First, in Heb. 4:14, Jesus in his glorified humanity, passes through the heavens to enter behind the curtain as the forerunner (πρόδρομος) on our behalf. Then in 8:1–5, God reveals to his people

---

74. See discussion on Moffitt's *Atonement and the Logic of Resurrection in the Epistle to the Hebrews* (2013) in Section 1.2.5.

75. Morales, *Who Shall Ascend?*, 176.

76. The atonement is the reversal of the expulsion of Adam out of Eden (eastward) via the tabernacle, which grants the high priest access (westward) into the Holy of Holies from the outer courts on behalf of the people (ibid., 174).

through Moses the spatial features of the heavenly tabernacle. This revelation is possible because of God's initiative shown through the Holy Spirit (9:8). And finally, in 9:1–14 we are told details of the heavenly tabernacle and how it serves towards believers' standing with God in that heavenly space. These passages combined reveal that there is no longer a temporal or spatial limitation seen in the earthly tabernacle; rather, it has been replaced by a full and continual access that has been granted through believers' spiritual union with Christ, the heavenly high priest.

PART II
FIRSTSPACE AND SECONDSPACE

Chapter 4

HEAVENLY ASCENT: HEBREWS 4:14 AND 6:19-20

The first passage in our investigation does not explicitly discuss the heavenly tabernacle; however, it provides essential preliminary information for the tabernacle's later spatial descriptions. As mentioned, Hebrews 4:14 marks the beginning of the central section of Hebrews, which shifts the focus to Christ's high priestly ministry. To draw attention to the locale of his ministry, the author depicts Jesus' movement from earth, through the "created heavens,"[1] and into the heavenly sanctuary. Therefore, not only does he transition into the central section thematically and by way of *inclusio*,[2] the author introduces a shift in spatial orientation similar to a change of scenery in between acts of a drama. This vertical shift moves away from horizontal, earthly discussions (i.e., entering Canaan in 4:1-6) to the heavenly.[3] Jesus is the high priest *who has passed through the heavens* (διεληλυθότα τοὺς οὐρανούς, v. 14). Questions naturally arise in light of this challenging verse: What do οὐρανούς entail? And related, what then does it mean for Jesus to pass through (διεληλυθότα) them?

This chapter attempts to answer these questions by examining these spatial terms under the categories of Firstspace and Secondspace. In Firstspace, Jesus as high priest is the resurrected Christ who in his physical, glorified state, passed through the created heavens to arrive at his destination, the heavenly tabernacle. When we note the vertical dimension of this spatial feat, Jesus ascended into God's presence in a manner that exceeds what Moses could do on Mt. Sinai. When considering Hebrews 4:14, two assertions are made: First, the great high priest in verse 14 refers to the resurrected Jesus who assumes the role of mediator for humanity by way of his descension and ascension. Second, οὐρανούς is the physical firmament that separates earth and the locale of God's transcendent

---

1. In distinction from the "transcendent heavens," which itself is the dwelling place of God and houses the heavenly sanctuary. On my view on the transcendent heavens, see Section 6.1.3.
2. Guthrie, *Structure of Hebrews*, 79-82.
3. William Lane describes this shift as providing another "dimension" in continuation of the "place of rest in 4:1-11" (*Hebrews 1-8*, 103).

presence—namely, the created heavens. Putting the two together, the high priest is the resurrected Jesus who, in his glorified state, passes through the physical heavens in his ascension. Establishing this allows us to maintain the spatial continuity of Jesus' itinerary in the journey from the physical earth, through the created heavens (Chapter 4 of this study), and into the actualized, heavenly sanctuary (Chapters 5-6 of this study). If the physical body of Jesus passes through the physical, created heavens, then we should expect to understand Jesus to have similarly arrived at a localized place in the heavenlies.

If this Firstspace understanding of Hebrews 4:14 is adopted, we may say that Secondspace draws upon the symbolic and spiritual implications of Jesus' spatial movement. This Firstspace itinerary that Jesus traveled[4] is the reason why believers are called to hold fast to their confession and *draw near* (προσερχώμεθα) with confidence to the throne of grace (vv. 4 and 16).[5] Believers understand that Jesus traversed along this itinerary—not only for his own personal relocation amongst the heavenly session,[6] but to foreshadow what will be the itinerary of believers. Jesus has entered into the sanctuary within the veil *as their forerunner* (πρόδρομος, 6:20). Hence, the Secondspace import for believers is highly motivating, which fits the tone of the immediate, exhortational context of these verses and the entirety of Hebrews (13:22). The immeasurable chasm that stood as believers' inaccessibility to God's presence has now been opened for believers through their association with this high priest.

4.1. Firstspace: Passing through the Created Heavens

Affirming Jesus' vertical journey to the heavenly sanctuary as one passing through the physical, created heavens allows us to uphold continuity between Jesus' earthly existence and his heavenly one. Importantly, this maintains that the origin and destination are actual places. Without doing so, there is difficulty in locating Jesus' physical body. His resurrected, glorified state either becomes ignored or dematerialized into the Platonic realm. The author of Hebrews, however, ensures that the spatial features of Jesus' heavenly ascent remain in view in 4:14. Earlier, I noted how space and movement permeate the language of Hebrews,

---

4. I purposely use the past tense to align with the author's use of the perfect and aorist (punctiliar) tenses in διέρχομαι (4:14) and εἰσέρχομαι (6:20), respectively. Although the aorist form does not primarily indicate time but rather, aspect (cf. Daniel B. Wallace, *Greek Grammar Beyond the Basics: An Exegetical Syntax of the New Testament* [Grand Rapids, MI: Zondervan, 1996], 202), the context suggests that the completed action of Jesus' entry into the heavenly sanctuary is the basis for the subjunctive hortatory commands for believers (i.e., κρατῶμεν [4:14] and παράκλησιν ἔχωμεν [6:18]).

5. In-depth discussion on the significance of the believer's entrance will be presented in Chapters 7 and 8.

6. Meaning, at the right hand of God's throne in the inner sanctuary of the heavenly tabernacle (Heb. 8:1; 12:2; Rev. 3:21).

and how understanding "these spatial movement references" is crucial in our understanding of the epistle.[7] If we adhere to Asumang's definition of "movement," which is comprised of the traversing of space over time, it is only natural to infer that Jesus' movement through the heavens was a movement through physical space. The previous references to an earthly promised land served to provide warning and exhortation to realign and reorient believers' view toward the upward direction via Jesus' heavenly movement.[8]

4.1.1. Passed through the Heavens

It is not new for Hebrews scholarship to interpret οὐρανούς in 4:14 as the physical, created heavens.[9] We take our cue from the author's ten uses of οὐρανός in Hebrews. At least three of these (1:10; 11:12; 12:26) are clear in that the designation is the physical firmament above the earth.[10] While there is a tendency for these designations to be made in the plural, the word's singular and plural forms may be interchanged (cf. 9:23–24).[11] When studying the context of these occurrences, οὐρανός is given two designations in Hebrews: (1) the physical, created firmament (the sky) or (2) a term to refer the transcendent dwelling place of God.[12] Against the second designation, the author of Hebrews is hardly saying that Jesus passed through the dwelling place of God to arrive at that very same place! Rather, Jesus passes *through* the heavens to arrive at that dwelling place.

This understanding of the term supports what the author clarifies later when he further describes the high priest's exalted status through spatial language in 7:26: "Jesus the high priest is *exalted above* (ὑψηλότερος) the heavens."[13] Against this interpretation, Philip Church argues that 4:14 refers to the transcendent (meaning, invisible or uncreated), dwelling place of God because the word's plural form normally refers to God's transcendent dwelling place.[14] However, there are

---

7. So Asumang, *Unlocking Hebrews*, 40.

8. Ibid., 39; Asumang notes the following language: to not drift away (2:1–4), to enter and go in (3:7–4:11), to leave and go on to perfection (5:11–6:12), and to enter and draw near (10:19–39).

9. Koester, *Hebrews*, 282.

10. This is especially true noting how Heb. 1:10–12 quotes Ps. 102:25–27. Hebrews 11:12 also alludes to the stars of *heaven* in the promise made to Abraham, and Heb. 12:26 quotes Hag. 2:6, which clearly references the physical heavens and the earth. A case can also be made for the reference to the heavens in Heb. 7:26 since the author portrays the separation of Christ and the sinners.

11. BDAG, 738; Cockerill, *Hebrews*, 224 n. 10; Philip E. Hughes, *A Commentary on the Epistle to the Hebrews* (Grand Rapids, MI: Eerdmans, 1977), 170 n. 2.

12. Unsurprisingly, these two definitions also apply for שָׁמַיִם, which the LXX translates as οὐρανούς (Jonathan T. Pennington, *Heaven and Earth in the Gospel of Matthew*, NovTSup 126 [Leiden: Brill, 2007], 41–45).

13. See also Eph. 4:10b: ὁ ἀναβὰς ὑπεράνω πάντων τῶν οὐρανῶν.

14. Church, *Hebrews and the Temple*, 372–78.

numerous instances where οὐρανός in the plural clearly refers to the physical, created heavens.[15] We see this in Matthew 3:16 and Mark 1:10: When Jesus came out of the water he immediately saw the οὐρανοί/οὐρανούς being torn open (cf. also Acts 2:34; 7:56; 2 Pet. 3:5, 7, 10, 13).[16]

Outside of the New Testament, a survey of the combinations of οὐρανούς with vertical, spatial language is not enough to draw strict parallels to any one intertestamental work. Yet, we can at least acknowledge that the idea of passing through the created heavens is present, namely in heavenly ascensions. For example, it is made explicit that in his ascent through the seven heavens, Isaiah goes up into each firmament, observes its activity, and then is subsequently taken above it (Mart. Ascen. Isa. 7.1–37;[17] cf. also T. Abraham (Rec. A) 10; 1 En. 14–19; 2 En. 1–23; T. Levi 2–5).[18] What differs in our passage is that the author of Hebrews does not have much to say regarding the quality or number of firmaments.[19] For example, in Jewish apocalyptic and rabbinic writings,[20] the number of heavens is widely varied: "two (2 En. 7.1), three (2 En. 8.1; cf. 2 Cor. 12.2-4), five (3 Bar. 11.1), seven (3 En. 1–2; 17.1-3; b. Hag. 12b), or ten (4 En. 20)."[21] Also, unlike

---

15. Furthermore, שָׁמַיִם (οὐρανούς) is often used in a way where both senses (created heavens and God's dwelling place) are present. At the very least, it is unlikely the author of Hebrews solely has God's dwelling place in view (Pennington, *Heaven and Earth*, 46 and 48).

16. Apart from Matthew, who has a particular usage of the plural, the rest of the NT has a mixed usage of the plural, in both aforementioned senses.

17. It may be argued that Isaiah likely was not in his physical body but this does not invalidate the idea that *what* he saw took place in the physical firmaments. Furthermore, although there are Christian additions to this work, "[I]t is so clearly based on earlier Jewish material and sources that parts of the work can be used as evidence for Jewish thinking" (Eskola, *Messiah and the Throne*, 111).

18. For comprehensive studies on the topic of heavenly ascent, consult the following works: Martha Himmelfarb, *Ascent to Heaven in Jewish and Christian Apocalypses* (New York: Oxford University Press, 1993); Rowland, *Open Heaven* (1982); Alan F. Segal, "Heavenly Ascent in Hellenistic Judaism, Early Christianity and their Environment," in 2.23.2, Part 2, 23.2, ed. Hildegard Temporini and Wolgang Haase (Berlin: de Gruyter, 1980), 1333–94. This shows that by at least the beginning of the second century BCE (or before), that ascent journeys through the created heavens were not uncommon (Rowland, *Open Heaven*, 55).

19. In both the LXX and in Hebrews, οὐρανοί is an assimilation of the Hebrew word שָׁמַיִם, which itself is plural (Hughes, *Hebrews*, 170 n. 2).

20. The existence of multiple heavens appears to be "standard Jewish belief" (Rowland, *Open Heaven*, 81).

21. Isaacs, *Sacred Space*, 206 n. 1; cf. also Lincoln, *Paradise Now*, 78; James D. Tabor, *Things Unutterable: Paul's Ascent to Paradise in Its Greco-Roman, Judaic, and Early Christian Contexts*, Studies in Judaism (Lanham, MD: University Press of America, 1986), 116; James Buchanan Wallace, *Snatched into Paradise (2 Cor 12:1-10): Paul's Heavenly Journey in the Context of Early Christian Experience*, BZNW 179 (New York: de Gruyter, 2011), 33.

1 Enoch 14, the author of Hebrews does not describe the environmental activity that takes place *within* the heavens.²²

Considering that these heavenly ascent journeys are variegated, there is not one conclusive formula on how to interpret the cosmologies of these ascents. However, we can at least affirm that the vertical upward ascent was indeed a spatial one through heaven's physical firmaments. That the intertestamental accounts of heavenly ascent had an influence in the New Testament is clearly seen in Paul's personal account of being caught up in the *third* heaven (ἁρπαγέντα τὸν τοιοῦτον ἕως τρίτου οὐρανοῦ, 2 Cor. 12:2).²³ Christopher Rowland aptly states, "The cosmological beliefs were such that it often became necessary for anyone who would enter the immediate presence of God to embark on a journey through the heavenly world, in order to reach God himself."²⁴ Our passage similarly contains spatial features and shares the concept of *movement* through the physical firmament that is described in Jewish apocalyptic literature. In fact, George Guthrie states, "Such movement between heaven and earth is perhaps the most distinguishing feature of apocalyptic literature of the era (e.g., 1 En. 39.3-4; 52.1; Wis. 4:10-11; Apoc. Mos. 37.3)."²⁵

This may explain why the author of Hebrews uses the word διέρχομαι to connote this movement, which occurs only once in the entire epistle. In the New Testament, this word occurs forty-one times and all but one instance refers to

---

Tabor states, "Scholars have tried, without much success, to precisely identify his language in Jewish texts from this period which mention a plurality of heavens" (*Things Unutterable*, 116).

For example, in b. Hag. 12b, the seven heavens are listed by name, with the fourth heaven housing heavenly structures: "where the heavenly Jerusalem, the Temple, and the altar are built, and Michael, principal prince, stands and offers an offering on it: 'I have surely built you a house of lofty above, a place for you to dwell in forever.'" Translation from Jacob Neusner, *The Babylonian Talmud: A Translation and Commentary* (Peabody, MA: Hendrickson, 2011), 7:49.

22. Enoch's journey is described with physical descriptions of his surrounding envivronment. Clouds (νεφέλαι) and mist (ὀμίχλαι) summon him (1 En. 14:8a). He sees stars (ἀστέρων) and lightning (διαστραπαί) running across the horizon (v. 8b). He arrives at a wall built with hailstones (λίθοις χαλάζης, v. 10). Furthermore, Enoch visits other geographical locations such as the mountains of the earth (1 En. 25.3; 77.1-9), which are not places of mythological geography but actual places (J. T. Milik and Matthew Black, *The Books of Enoch: Aramaic Fragments of Qumrân Cave 4* [Oxford: Clarendon Press, 1976], 16); also referenced in Rowland, *Open Heaven*, 125.

23. David Garland writes that a "three-heaven schema is the most well-established view in Jewish writings" (*2 Corinthians*, NAC 29 [Nashville, TN: Broadman & Holman, 1999], 514).

24. Rowland, *Open Heaven*, 80.

25. George H. Guthrie, *2 Corinthians*, BECNT (Grand Rapids, MI: Baker Academic, 2015), 582.

spatial movement across a geographical location.[26] Furthermore, while occasionally the word refers to movement *within* an area (Acts 13:6; 18:23), it more often denotes movement *through* an area and *beyond* it (Acts 14:24; 15:3, 41; 16:6; 19:1, 21; 20:2; 1 Cor. 16:5).[27] This is especially true when the verb is coupled with the accusative form of a place (τοὺς οὐρανούς).[28] Therefore, "it gives the reader the sense of a spatial journey that penetrates through heavenly realms" and aligns well with Hebrews' latter "similar spatial image"[29] including the spatial descriptions of the heavenly sanctuary.

There is additional support for this understanding of a heavenly journey when looking at our passage from a wider, contextual level within the epistle. Hebrews 4:14's placement within the epistle correlates with Jesus' spatial movement that spans from heaven to earth (incarnation, 2:5–9), up through the heavens (ascension, 4:14), and arriving at God's throne (session, 7:26). Prior to Hebrews 2, Jesus' preincarnate existence with God is in view (1:1–14) and immediately after in 7:26, Jesus' spatial position is reinforced by introducing Jesus as the high priest "who has taken his seat at the right hand of the throne of the Majesty in the heavens" (8:1).

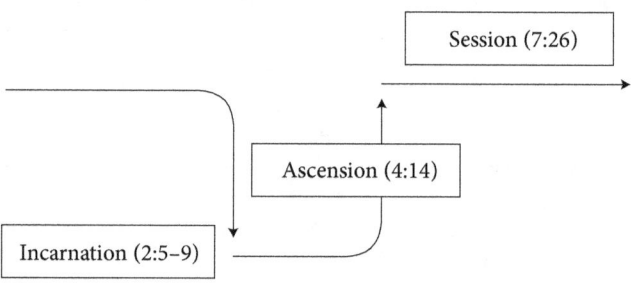

Figure 4.1. Macrolevel Itinerary of Jesus' Heavenly Spatial Movement

---

26. See BDAG, 244. It is used once to connote a non-physical concept (i.e., death) *spreading* to all men who sinned (Rom. 5:12).

27. Ellingworth, *Hebrews*, 267; cf. also Lane, *Hebrews 1–8*, 94, 103. A list of other scholars who support this view can be found in Church, *Hebrews and the Temple*, 371 n. 9.

28. Philip Church prefers "moving about an area," so that v. 14 translates into the high priest ministering about in the heavenlies (*Hebrews and the Temple*, 373–74). However, he does not consider the use of διέρχομαι *with* the accusative, which discounts his claim for support in Acts 20:25. In Acts 20:25, the word διῆλθον is in the aorist active without a direct object, while in Heb. 4:14, the word is διεληλυθότα (perfect, participle) with the accusative τοὺς οὐρανούς.

29. Luke Timothy Johnson, *Hebrews: A Commentary*, NTL (Louisville, KY: Westminster John Knox Press, 2012), 139.

If Hebrews 4:14 draws attention to Jesus' vertical movement upwards, the opposite spatial movement downward from heaven to earth is first introduced in 2:5–9. Hence, these two passages indicate a spatial complement with one another.[30] That Jesus' incarnation is in view is confirmed by the immediate mention of his earthly suffering and death and the explicit phrase, "little while lower than angels" (βραχύ τι παρ' ἀγγέλους, Heb. 2:9).[31] Hence, Jesus' spatial movement from heaven to earth in his incarnation provides the backdrop of his ascension introduced in 4:14.[32] Furthermore, Jesus's ascension, and believers' ascension with him, are foreshadowed immediately following: "For it was fitting for him...*in bringing many sons to glory* (πολλοὺς υἱοὺς εἰς δόξαν ἀγαγόντα), to perfect the author of their salvation" (2:10). Hebrews 4:14, then, continues this line of thought by introducing Jesus' corresponding ascension and exaltation. In a comparable way to how Jesus traversed the heavens down to earth in his incarnation, he has traversed the heavens up to God's dwelling place.[33]

Now, Jesus having traveled through the created heavens, other passages in Hebrews affirm Jesus' locale as being *above* the heavens.[34] The author begins by locating Jesus as the one who passed through the heavens (4:14) but is now *exalted above the heavens* (ὑψηλότερος τῶν οὐρανῶν γενόμενος, 7:26; cf. also 8:1). In both verses, the author associates space with Jesus' high priestly status. In sum, the itinerary is presented as follows: In Heb. 4:14, Jesus' heavenly journey brings

---

30. Ellingworth, "Jesus and the Universe in Hebrews," 341.

31. This hardly means Jesus was constitutively or ontologically lower than angels (cf. Heb. 1:4), but that he was locationally so in his incarnation. While it can be debated whether βραχύ τι is spatial or temporal, either of these designations refer to Jesus' incarnation. Earlier, it was made clear in Heb. 1:8 that "it is no less than God himself who declares through Scripture the Son's superiority to the angels. And yet—in view of the use of Ps. 44:7 [LXX] in Heb. 1:8—it would be more precise to say that God declares his own superiority to the angels in the person of the Son" (Kavin Rowe, "The Trinity in the Letters of St. Paul and Hebrews," in *The Oxford Handbook of the Trinity*, ed. Gilles Emery and Matthew Levering [New York: Oxford University Press, 2011], 7).

32. One may argue that Jesus did not physically traverse downward at his birth, which I agree with. However, at the least, and without speculating on the metaphysical conception of the eternal Son in Mary's physical womb, Jesus' incarnation does imply that the physical nature of the world is in view, which, in turn, is locationally below the heavens (cf. Rom. 10:6–7; Eph. 4:9–10). Note also that Ps. 8:3–5 lies in the background of Heb. 2:6–8. In this psalm, David "looks up" (spatially) at the heavens and states that God "made the son of man lower" (spatially) than the heavenly beings. In other words, I am simply affirming a locational starting and endpoint (heaven and earth) in Jesus' incarnation.

33. What I will present as Secondspace in the next section is the astonishing fact that in Jesus' ascension, he will bring many with him as their "forerunner."

34. Ott Kuss acknowledges that the heavens in 4:14 appear as a kind of "intermediate stage" to God's presence (*Der Brief an Die Hebräer*, 2nd ed., RNT 8 [Regensburg: Friedrich Pustet, 1966], 70): "[H]ier erscheinen 'die Himmel' als eine Art Zwischenstufe, jenseits derer sich erst Gottes Thron befindet."

into view his ability to cross the insurmountable chasm between earth and heaven to God's presence. In Heb. 7:26, it locates him as having completed that journey (ascension) and above those heavens—now seated at the right hand of God in the heavenly sanctuary (heavenly session). If Hebrews 4:14 stresses the vertical axis of Jesus' spatial movement, Hebrews 6:19–20 (εἰσερχομένην εἰς τὸ ἐσώτερον τοῦ καταπετάσματος) introduces the horizontal movement *into* the heavenly sanctuary,[35] and then finally shows him having arrived to take his seat in the heavenly session in 7:26. The descriptions of the heavenly sanctuary and its heavenly cultic activity is expounded in 9:1–14.

4.1.2. Depicting the Heavenly Journey in the Earthly Tabernacle

Conceptually, Jesus' heavenly journey corresponds with what took place in the Old Testament during the high priest's movement across the divided sections of the earthly tabernacle.[36] Jesus passed through the heavens, just as the high priest moved from the front court, through the Holy Place, and into the Most Holy Place.[37] This movement through the earthly tabernacle would have visually depicted a movement through the heavens when considering the various ornaments and decorations in each tabernacle section. As G. K. Beale writes:

> The curtains of the holy place were blue, purple, and scarlet, representing the variegated colors of the sky, and figures of winged creatures were woven into all the curtains throughout the tabernacle, enforcing the imagery of the visible heavens… [I]f people were to peer into the holy place, they would see seventy lights [lampstands], which against the darker setting of the curtains of the tabernacle and temple would resemble the heavenly light sources (stars, planets, sun, and moon).[38]

---

35. See Mt. 27:51; Mk 15:38; Lk. 23:45; Heb. 9:3; 10:20. Here I refer to a horizontal, spatial, movement, which is distinct from the horizontal, *temporal* element of Hebrews eschatology. It is worth mentioning, however, that the horizontal, temporal element does exists in 6:20 in Jesus "having become a high priest *forever* (αἰῶνα) according to the order of Melchizedek."

36. It is easy for modern readers to overlook the dramatic effect of cultic service and participation. Reading descriptions of what took place in the tabernacle does not fully encapsulate the experience and effect of actually seeing and participating in those sacrifices and rituals.

37. Koester, *Hebrews*, 282.

38. Beale, *New Testament Biblical Theology*, 628. Here Beale limits this analogy for the Holy Place to *only* the future heavens and not the current visible heavens. However, his analogy can apply to the present, created heavens, for Beale himself notes the temple-heaven analogy with Isa. 66:1: "Heaven is My throne, and the earth is My footstool," which clearly refers to the presently created heavens and earth. Beale takes the cosmological view of the earthly tabernacle/temple, meaning that the heavenly tabernacle itself is a metaphor for the entirety of the cosmos (*Temple and Church's Mission*, 29–60). While I agree that the

Even the censer created a cloud of incense smoke, which visually shielded the priest's eyes when entering the Most Holy Place. If such a place is the "counterpart to the heavenly throne room of God," then such an entrance dramatically enacts how "the high priest indeed entered 'heaven' with the clouds."[39] In 1 Enoch, not only is Enoch's final destination described as an actual heavenly palace of crystal, but chapters 17, 33–36, and 72–82 also describe the "peregrinations of the heavenly luminaries through the portals of heaven."[40] That Enoch is describing a physical experience can be seen as he recounts the winds that were causing him to fly and rush him up high into heaven (14:8–9).[41] If we consider that the objects in the earthly tabernacle symbolized heavenly objects, then the heavenly referents themselves are actual entities in the sky. Hence, we see similar descriptions of tabernacle ornaments in apocalyptic ascents. For example, in an earlier part of Enoch's ascent, he observes the rotation of the luminaries (i.e., lampstands) that "rise and set in order each in its season" and "all the works of God" on the whole earth (1 En. 2.1–3; cf. 72.1–37). This coheres with Vern Poythress' observation that the intentional positioning of artifacts such as the tabernacle lampstands communicates aspects of the heavenly skies.[42]

A. The Created Heavens as the Gateway to God's Transcendent Dwelling

In the New Testament, various passages support the idea that the created heavens serve as the gateway to the transcendent dwelling place of God and his heavenly court. Unsurprisingly, each time the heavens *open up*, it is in association with

---

earthly tabernacle and temple do indeed have an analogical counterpart to the cosmos, this does not dismiss the possibility that a separate, heavenly tabernacle structurally exists. As I will argue later, in Heb. 8:1–5 and 9:1–14, the author describes the heavenly sanctuary and its heavenly cultic activity such that the cosmological view is insufficient. Nevertheless, Heb. 4:14 by itself is compatible with the cosmological view.

39. Morales, *Who Shall Ascend?*, 172; cf. Beale, *New Testament Biblical Theology*, 628; *Temple and Church's Mission*, 36–37. Josephus also notes how the inner sanctuary was clouded to prevent its visibility: "But the inmost part of the temple of all was of twenty cubits. This was also separated from the outer part by a veil. In this there was nothing at all. It was inaccessible and inviolable, and not to be seen by any; and was called the Holy of Holies" (Josephus, *War* 5:219). Translation taken from William Whiston's *The Works of Josephus: Complete and Unabridged* (Peabody, MA: Hendrickson, 1987), 707.

40. John G. Gammie, "Spatial and Ethical Dualism in Jewish Wisdom and Apocalyptic Literature," *JBL* 93.3 (1974): 368.

41. Timo Eskola writes that the "physical nature of his ascension is unique" compared to later apocalyptic writings (*Messiah and the Throne*, 72). This corresponds with the tradition that Enoch was physically taken up into heaven (Gen. 5:24; cf. Segal, "Heavenly Ascent," 1359).

42. The lampstand on the south side of the Holy Place shows that the Israel's point of view, north of the equator, would see the circuit of heavenly lights to the south (Poythress, *Shadow of Christ*, 18).

either Jesus' incarnation or his ascension. The angels travel up into the created heavens and down from it when they pronounce Jesus' birth (Lk. 2:15), while the heavenly host's singing can be audibly heard from the heavens (v. 13). The heavens open up during Jesus' baptism (Mt. 3:13–17; Mk 1:9–11; Lk. 3:21–23; Jn 1:32–34), which is associated with the inauguration of Jesus' earthly ministry (i.e., his incarnational ministry). Later, in Acts 1:9–11, Jesus ascends into the created heavens and the clouds received him out of the disciples' sight (v. 9). While the disciples keep staring up into the sky an angel comes to provide commentary for what took place: "This Jesus, who has been taken up from you into heaven, will come in just the same way as you have watched Him go into heaven" (v. 11b). This connotes the idea of a physical ascension and, later, a physical advent of Jesus' second return. Lastly, during his martyrdom, Stephen gazes into what is likely the created heavens (the sky) when he beholds the heavens opening up (τοὺς οὐρανοὺς διηνοιγμένους) and he sees Jesus at the right hand of God (Acts 7:56). All these passages weave together what Aelred Cody refers to as the *transitus* of Christ, which includes his incarnation, passion and death, resurrection, ascension, and session as "one great mystery of salvation, the one celestial liturgy, in which each mystery has its part to play on the way toward the celestial Holy of Holies."[43]

The investigation thus far raises the question of the author of Hebrews' implied cosmology. Like the other New Testament writings, the author does "not offer enough information to reconstruct a uniform 'early Christian view' of the physical universe."[44] It is unlikely that the author's intent was to depict a distinct cosmology. Although Hebrews may have the most "extended meditation on cosmic structures in the NT," it is "clearly focused on theological concerns."[45] Nevertheless, he did have a conceptualized understanding of the cosmos as it relates to Christ's ascension and high priestly session and believers' joint itinerary with Christ. In general, this may be assumed based on early Judaism at least having "shaped the theology of the New Testament writers"[46] and that the author of Hebrews' cosmology "would have been considered traditional by Christians steeped in the Old Testament. It would be consistent with the idea that this writer derives his cosmology more from his Scriptures as filtered through (by now) traditional christology than from either empirical observation or philosophical speculations..."[47]

More specifically to Hebrews 4:14, the author makes a distinction between the "created" and "transcendent" heavens. David Peterson believes that the author of

---

43. Cody, *Heavenly Sanctuary and Liturgy*, 6.

44. Jonathan T. Pennington and Sean M. McDonough, "Conclusion," in *Cosmology and New Testament Theology*, ed. Jonathan T. Pennington and Sean M. McDonough, LNTS 355 (London: T&T Clark, 2008), 189.

45. Ibid.

46. Ibid.

47. Jon C. Laansma, "The Cosmology of Hebrews," in Pennington and McDonough, eds, *Cosmology and New Testament Theology*, 141.

Hebrews follows the three-part heaven model that we find in Enoch and Paul (cf. 2 En. 8.1 and 2 Cor. 12.2-4, respectively): (1) The created and transitory heavens (1:10-12; 12:26), (2) the heavens that Jesus passes through (4:14; 9:11-12), and (3) heaven as the dwelling place of God (9:24).[48] From the observations made above, there need not be such a sharp distinction between the "created and transitory heavens" and the "heavens that Jesus passes through."[49] Peterson is, however, correct in wanting to stress a distinct heaven(s) as the space that Jesus passes through in his ascension (cf. Eph. 4:8-10 and 1 Pet. 3:22).

Earlier, I introduced Edward Soja's Firstspace which is defined as the physical, concrete, mappable, and measurable geographies of our lifeworlds. Using his categories, I propose the following conclusions for the Firstspace features in Hebrews 4:14. It includes the mappable vertical ascent into and through the created firmaments of the sky. These physical features are the spatial backdrop of Jesus' heavenly ascent. This backdrop, as we will see in the next section, conveys the immeasurable distance that separates God and man. It is this chasm that must be traversed in order for man to enter God's presence—a chasm that only Jesus Christ, the heavenly high priest, has crossed.

Affirming the Firstspace, physical features of Christ's heavenly ascent will support the later assertion (Chapters 5 and 6 of this study) that the heavenly tabernacle is not the heavens themselves but a physical structure within the transcendent heavens, or in other words, a destination either in or past the created heavens. This idea is not unique nor is it novel.[50] Even prior to Qumran, it was not uncommon to think of "a celestial tabernacle" which is "situated above the firmament of the cherubim"[51] or the "tabernacle of highest loftiness," which itself is a sanctuary in the "highest realm of heaven."[52] Before delving into spatial descriptions of the tabernacle and the liturgical activity that takes place inside, we now consider the Secondspace features of Hebrews 4:14.

---

48. Peterson, *Hebrews and Perfection*, 143. See Otto Michel's commentary on Heb. 9:11 who holds a similar tripartite view of the heavens: "(1) die zu dieser Schöpfung gehören und deshalb vergänglich sind (1:10-12); durch die Christus hindurchschreitet (4:14; 9:10-12); den Himmel als den eigentlichen Wohnort der Gottheith (9:24) (Michel, *Der Brief an Hebräer*, 311-12). However, neither Michel nor Peterson provide information as to why (1) and (2) cannot be the same. Michel views the heavens in 4:14 in an apocalyptic-Gnostic sense (*apokalyptisch-gnostischem*), which may contribute to his understanding (ibid., 205).

49. Laansma similarly writes that what we can distill from Hebrews regarding the cosmos is that of a visible earth and heaven (sky) with the invisible heaven (God's abode) above. In his study of Heb. 2:6-9, "it is not clear that the writer has an intermediate *sphere* between earth and heaven in mind" ("Cosmology of Hebrews," 133).

50. See Section 1.2.5.

51. Koester, *Dwelling of God*, 37.

52. For example, see 4Q403 f1ii:10-16. See also in Koester, *Dwelling of God*, 38, who states that the tabernacle is a "special locus of divine glory *within* the heavenly realms" (ibid., emphasis mine).

4.2. Secondspace: Clearing the Heavenly Path

The previous section argued that the heavenly ascent in Hebrews 4:14 involves the traversal of the physical, created heavens. Earlier we considered how the earthly tabernacle served as a model of the universe, with the outer courts representing earth and the inner courts representing heaven. This may lead us to think that the inward movement in the tabernacle is primarily about relocation. However, this inward movement does much more than depict a displacement from one location to another (i.e., from earth to heaven). It is, first and foremost, a movement of relationship to and towards God who resides in the transcendent heavens. In other words, heaven is not the goal; rather, the goal includes the heavenly traversal that is necessary to enter into God's presence and draw near to him (4:16). This goal must stay in our purview when we read in Hebrews 4:14 how Jesus traversed the vertical chasm from earth to heaven to enter into God's presence. If he is the forerunner (πρόδρομος) who goes before believers (Heb. 6:20), then the hope is that believers, too, can traverse through heaven to be with God. This is the astonishing Secondspace feature of Jesus' heavenly ascent.

As discussed earlier in Section 3.2, spatial limitations are intrinsic to the earthly tabernacle. Hence, when the author of Hebrews boldly states that this high priest has gone into the inner place within the veil in Hebrews 6:19–20, they hear it in contrast to the explicit prohibition that God gave to Moses and Aaron (Exod. 40:1–33). The only time that access through the veil was granted was on the Day of Atonement (Exod. 26:31–35 LXX, καταπέτασμα; Lev. 16:2–12; Num. 18:7 LXX, καταπετάσματος). Out of the three possible designations of "veil" in the earthly tabernacle, 6:19–20 refers to the innermost veil that prevents entry into the Most Holy Place.

In addition to the arguments set forth by Roy Gane, there is also the explicit mentioning of Jesus as ἀρχιερεύς.[53] The high priest was the only one allowed into the Most Holy Place during the Day of Atonement. Furthermore, εἰς τὸ ἐσώτερον τοῦ καταπετάσματος in our verse is present in Exodus 26:33 and Leviticus 16:2, 12, and 15, which all refer to the inner veil. Physically and spatially, access to the inner sanctuary was not possible. This explains why prior to Jesus' exaltation, the heavenly ascents in the Old Testament and intertestamental literature were "extraordinary and demonstrate that open access to God in his heavenly temple was commonly perceived as exceptional, if not even impossible."[54]

---

53. Roy E. Gane, "Re-Opening Katapetasma ('Veil') in Hebrews 6:19," *AUSS* 38.1 (2000): 5–8; cf. Norman H. Young, "'Where Jesus Has Gone as a Forerunner on Our Behalf' (Hebrews 6:20)," *AUSS* 39.2 (2001): 165–73. Gane also notes that unlike καταπέτασμα, פָּרֹכֶת "unambiguously denotes the inner veil" ("Re-Opening Katapetasma," 6).

54. Scott D. Mackie, "Heavenly Sanctuary Mysticism," 93. For example, in Ezek. 41:1–3, Ezekiel does not enter into God's dwelling place but, in v. 3, the angel enters in (וּבָא) (Nicholas J. Moore, "Heaven's Revolving Door? Cosmology, Entrance, and Approach in Hebrews," *BBR* 29.2 [2019]: 204). Harold Attridge goes so far as to assert that concerning the descriptions of Christ's salvific activity, "the dominant image is one of movement out of the

This impossibility did not prevent humanity from aspiring and even attempting to reach God's dwelling place (cf. Gen. 11:4). This was their response due to their longing "for some sort of closeness to God, a closeness that would be physical as well as moral."[55] When these efforts failed, God descended to dwell with his people. During the construction of the tabernacle and temple, the point was not to simply memorialize Yahweh's greatness but for humanity to ascend into God's dwelling place.[56] In the New Covenant, Jesus crossed through the Firstspace created heavens. This shows that the impossible chasm between God and man, depicted by the immeasurable distance between heaven and earth, has been traversed. The dwelling place of God can now be accessed, which means that God himself is accessible. Proleptically, the earthly tabernacle in its journey from the wilderness to the inner parts of the sanctuary depicted the journey from earth to God's dwelling place. What the Israelites saw in dramatic fashion symbolically in the movement within the earthly tabernacle, believers now see in Jesus' heavenly, vertical movement into God's presence. To see Jesus traverse the actual heavens is to see what Old Testament believers could only see by way of imagination when they observed the physical movement from outside the earthly tabernacle to its inner parts.[57]

This idea of the tabernacle/temple as the meeting place with God continues into the New Testament. In John's Gospel, before Jesus' death Peter asks Jesus where he is going. Jesus answers, "Where I go, you cannot follow me now; but you will follow later" (Jn 13:16). Shortly after, Jesus consoles the disciples, not with empty words, but with an eschatological promise that is rich with Jewish tradition. As James McCaffrey notes, the terminology used to designate the Father's house may rightly be interpreted with the heavenly temple in view as the goal of eschatological salvation. Thus, this "image aptly describes for the disciples of a life-with God in the promised temple of the eschatological age."[58] Jesus' heavenly ascent to

world in its present state into the transcendent sphere of God's presence" (*Essays on John and Hebrews*, WUNT 264 [Tübingen: Mohr Siebeck, 2010], 306). There is an instance in the Testament of Levi when Levi "saw the Holy Most High sitting on the throne" (T. Levi 5:1) but this is a special circumstance where he is given the "blessing of the priesthood" for the sake of Israel. This coincides with my later argument that entrance into the (heavenly) sanctuary denotes a priesthood (cf. Section 8.1).

55. Cody, *Heavenly Sanctuary*, 12.

56. During the Old Covenant era, the Israelites never physically ascend; rather, God descends (Exod. 40:34; Num. 9:15–23).

57. "Ce qu'aucun Israélite ne pouvait espérer, pénétrer à la suite du grand prêtre dans le Saint des Saints, les chrétiens le réalisent. Pécheurs, is seront néanmoins introduits dansle sanctuaire divin, grâce au très sacrifice du Christ, à l'exercice permanent de ses fonctions sacerdotales" (Spicq, *L'Épître aux Hébreux*, 2:166). Here Spicq draws attention to the contrast between those under the Old and New Covenants by the use of the sanctuary's cultic, liturgical background.

58. James McCaffrey, *The House with Many Rooms: The Temple Theme of Jn. 14, 2-3*, AnBib 114 (Rome: Editrice Pontificio Istituto Biblico, 1988), 129.

the Father is gate liturgy into the eschatological, heavenly temple.[59] The remarkable promise lies in Jesus' latter statement: "You will follow later."[60]

All along, the intent had been for God's people to dwell with him in what Michael Morales calls the new exodus—"to lift humanity up into God's heavenly situation."[61] Hence, the disciples miss the point when trying to establish manmade tabernacles on the mount of Jesus' transfiguration (Lk. 9:33). In the case of Acts 1:9–11, the disciples looking up into the sky communicates the immeasurable, physical distance that stands between them and Jesus. They understood Jesus not as having disappeared, but as having traveled vertically through the physical heavens to arrive at some transcendent location. Their sadness at seeing this impassable chasm is met with the comforting words of the angel, who assures them that just as Jesus physically went up into heaven, he will physically return.[62]

During his transfiguration in Luke 9:28–36, Jesus refuses the disciples' proposal to dwell on the earthly mountain because he already has in mind a heavenly dwelling fit for him and his disciples. In Hebrews 6:19, Jesus enters that dwelling place as their πρόδρομος. Though this word only occurs here in the New Testament, and previous occurrences do not provide a unified consensus to its meaning, the context implies that Jesus' going is precedent for a following that comes after.[63] In one instance in Numbers 13:20 LXX, πρόδρομοι is used to describe the "first ripe" or "firstfruit" grapes, which indicate a representative portion of the crops to follow. In respect to persons, the sense is that of one who pioneers "on behalf of someone else" or for one's "benefit"[64] and therefore implies that there will be a following of believers into the sanctuary after Jesus.[65] Hence, believers' spatial movement into the sanctuary is unequivocally tied to Jesus' already-made entrance.[66] In 4:14, they currently possess (ἔχοντες)[67] Jesus as their high priest, which grounds the two exhortations that follow in verses 14–16.[68]

---

59. Morales, *Who Shall Ascend?*, 265.

60. Jesus' entrance is both "exemplary" and "mimetic" in its roles of bringing believers into heavenly glory (Scott Mackie, "Introduction to Part 1," in Mackie, ed., *The Letter to the Hebrews*, 19).

61. Morales, *Who Shall Ascend?*, 268.

62. Acts 1:1–2 also links Jesus' heavenly departure with words of exhortation or "teaching" (ἤρξατο ὁ Ἰησοῦς ποιεῖν τε καὶ διδάσκειν... ἄχρι ἧς ἡμέρας... ἀνελήμφθη, v. 2).

63. In v. 20, consider the πρό- prefix (Ellingworth, *Hebrews*, 348) and immediately after, ὑπὲρ ἡμῶν translated as "for us," which designate the body of believers who follow.

64. L&N 36.9.

65. Koester, *Dwelling of God*, 164.

66. I agree with Ellen Aitken that the language of movement stresses the solidarity that believers have with Jesus' itinerary; however, she bases it on Jesus' movement outside the gate (Heb. 13:14) and designates the final destination as a reimagining of Flavian Rome ("Body of Jesus Outside the Eternal City," 208).

67. Translated as "having" or "since we have" in consideration with the conjunction οὖν.

68. David L. Allen, *Hebrews*, NAC 35 (Nashville, TN: Broadman & Holman, 2010), 303.

4. Heavenly Ascent

As the forerunner and firstfruit (1 Cor. 15:20) of all who believe in him, Jesus now leads his people through the same itinerary into God's dwelling place (Heb. 4:16; 6:19–20; 10:19–20).[69] It details in spatial terms what the author introduces in 2:10: Jesus *bringing* many sons to glory (πολλοὺς υἱοὺς εἰς δόξαν ἀγαγόντα) as the founder (τὸν ἀρχηγὸν) of their salvation.[70] In this verse, the author qualifies the meaning of τὸν ἀρχηγὸν as someone who brings others into the glory of God.[71] The term in the Old Testament, τὸν ἀρχηγὸν (ראש) implies a community/household who follows after the head/leader/representative. For example, in Numbers 14:4, the Israelites want to appoint a "leader" (ἀρχηγὸν) to lead them out of the wilderness back to Egypt. In Numbers 13:2, a "representative" (ἀρχηγὸν) is chosen from each tribe who will first enter the land of Canaan. The assumption is that the rest of the tribe's members will follow after the leader once a secure pathway has been made.

Following Hebrews 2:10, comparisons with two Old Testament figures are made utilizing the wilderness narrative of Numbers. Jesus is the greater Moses (3:1–6) and greater Joshua (4:1–8), who brings his people into the presence of God's glory in ways the former pioneers could not. Given these connections, there is indeed a "firstfruit" sense in the usage of leader (ἀρχηγός) in Hebrews. Therefore, Jesus is not ἀρχηγὸν only by virtue of who he is, but also what he has done in clearing a forward path for others to follow.

Believers' shared itinerary with Christ does not take place in one redemptive sweep. What was true for Jesus in one act of his ascension is true in two stages for the believers. First, believers ascend spiritually by way of the spiritual union that they have with Christ.[72] In that sense, while the heavenly journey itself includes a physical traversal, believers remain physically here on earth. Only later in the second stage during his second advent will they follow Christ again physically (cf. 1 Thess. 4:16–17). Fitting with the already/not-yet schema of Hebrews, the believers' ascent is also already true but also not yet realized. Nevertheless, the path has been cleared and the believers' ascent through the heavens is possible. Morales' concluding statements on the Levitical tabernacle/temple ring true for the recipients of Hebrews:

---

69. "The death of Christ on earth has removed the demarcation between heaven and earth. The earth is now open to heaven, or the way on earth is now paved for those sanctified by his blood as a living way to heaven" (Ekkehard W. Stegemann and Wolfgang Stegemann, "Does the Cultic Language in Hebrews Represent Sacrificial Metaphors? Reflections on Some Basic Problems," in *Hebrews: Contemporary Methods, New Insights*, ed. Gabriella Gelardini, BIS 75 [Leiden: Brill, 2005], 19).

70. See also Heb. 12:2: Jesus, the author (τὸν ἀρχηγὸν) and perfector of our faith.

71. Hence, I agree with Cockerill that "pioneer" defined as "one who, by entering a new land, enables others to follow" is the most appropriate translation given the context of Hebrews (Cockerill, *Hebrews*, 137).

72. More on union with Christ will be discussed in Section 7.1.

Chiefly, through the outpoured Spirit, believers are united to the ascended Jesus Christ, born from above, and are enabled with all the church to make the heavenly ascent. The Spirit's descent, through which Jesus returns to his disciples, is the church's ascent, this journey itself led by the Son into the Father's house. And so this heavenly reality is tasted and renewed liturgically, in the corporate Spirit-enabled approach of God's people, as they ascend with Jesus to the heavenly Mount Zion, Lord's Day by Lord's Day, through the new and living way – the veil of Jesus' flesh.[73]

It is this Secondspace feature of Jesus' heavenly itinerary that allows the author to exhort his addressees "to follow the path 'through the heavens' that Christ blazed and take advantage of the access to God that he provides."[74] Two assertions deserve restating: (1) Jesus traverses the spatial chasm that lies between the physical heavens and earth. (2) And his heavenly journey, set in motion at the onset of his sacrificial death and resurrection, is tied to the fulfillment of his promise that he would bring many sons into glory (Heb. 2:10; cf. 12:2). His entrance into the heavenly sanctuary is unequivocally tied to believers' entrance. In reciprocal fashion, believers' entrance into the heavenly sanctuary is tied to their inseverable bond in Christ.

In conclusion, we have considered the Firstspace and Secondspace depictions of Jesus' heavenly ascent (4:14) and, closely associated with it, his entrance into the heavenly sanctuary (6:19–20). Firstspace is Jesus' heavenly ascension through the physical, created heavens. Its Secondspace comes into view when we consider how the distance between heaven and earth (God and man) was understood as an impossibility, yet Jesus the high priest traversed this chasm to reach God and entered into the holy sanctuary on behalf of believers. His heavenly itinerary is not self-serving; it is not reserved for Jesus alone. Rather, it is unequivocally tied to the believers' own itinerary by way of their inseparable union with Christ—first spiritually and later, physically. Establishing these spatial characteristics (First and Secondspace) will then be motivation for believers to live out Thirdspace as heavenly priests on earth as they realize their access and communion with God. Before we delve into Thirdspace implications (Chapters 7–8), we turn to the heavenly sanctuary structure in Hebrews 8:1–5 (Exod. 25:40).

---

73. Morales, *Who Shall Ascend?*, 283–84.
74. Attridge, *Hebrews*, 141.

Chapter 5

THE ARCHETYPAL PATTERN: HEBREWS 8:5 (EXODUS 25:40)

It is becoming more established that the Jewish apocalyptic genre is the more appropriate background for understanding Hebrews' "thought world."[1] That development comes as a result of recognizing the spatial characteristics of Jewish apocalyptic while being wary of transferring the entirety of Jewish cosmology upon Hebrews.[2] Hence, apart from the Old Testament, the most appropriate conceptual background for the cultic texts in Hebrews is the mystical, Jewish apocalyptic classification with "some modifications in light of the Christ event," and that "these texts do establish the closest parallels to Hebrews's understanding of a heavenly sanctuary."[3] Such an approach fits the eschatological message of Hebrews and rightly acknowledges the eschatological influence that the Jewish apocalyptic has on Hebrews.[4]

---

1. Laansma, "Cosmology of Hebrews," 130; also Alexander Stewart, "Cosmology, Eschatology, and Soteriology in Hebrews: A Synthetic Analysis," *BBR* 20.4 (2010): 546.

2. For example, William G. Johnsson argues that the apocalyptic writings did not have a metaphorical construal of the heavenly cultic but rather described a "realistic heavenly sanctuary and liturgy" ("The Heavenly Sanctuary—Figurative or Real?," 50). While other backgrounds have been considered for Hebrews, they are outweighed by difficulties more than any advantages (Hurst, *Hebrews*, 131; Ribbens, *Levitical Sacrifice*, 85).

I utilize John J. Collins' helpful definition of apocalyptic literature: "a genre of revelatory literature with a narrative framework, in which a revelation is mediated by an otherworldly being to a human recipient, disclosing a transcendent reality which is both temporal, insofar as it envisages eschatological salvation, and spatial insofar as it involves another, supernatural world" (*The Apocalyptic Imagination: An Introduction to Jewish Apocalyptic Literature*, 2nd ed. [Grand Rapids, MI: Eerdmans, 1998], 5). For a comprehensive study on apocalyptic studies in Judaism and early Christianity, see Christopher Rowland's *The Open Heaven* (1982).

3. Ribbens, *Levitical Sacrifice*, 99.

4. "Die Heiligtumstheologie des Hebr nimmt die Urbild-Abbild-Relation aus den frühjüdischen Kontexten auf und prägt sie um, um die aufgrund der Erhöhung Christi

There have, however, been varying opinions to the extent of that influence. Scholars have gone on to ascribe vertical aspects of the tabernacle exclusively to Platonic associations while holding that only the horizontal, forward-looking aspects align more closely with Jewish eschatology.[5] This notion has been recently challenged, and it has been argued that vertical/horizontal and spatial/temporal categories are not mutually exclusive to either worldview, and especially in Hebrews.[6] Still others argue that the author of Hebrews blends the two worldviews so that he can gain a sympathetic hearing from his audience.[7]

The challenge remains *how* to appropriate the Jewish apocalyptic tradition found in Hebrews. One path forward, as this chapter intends to show, is to recognize that the descriptions of the heavenly tabernacle align with the physical descriptions (Firstspace) of the tabernacle/temple in Jewish apocalyptic

---

im Himmel gegenwärtige unüberbietbare eschatologische Heilsfülle auszusagen" (Gäbel, *Kulttheologie*, 17).

5. Barrett, "The Eschatology of the Epistle to the Hebrews," 363–93; Hurst, *Hebrews*, 33–38; Lincoln D. Hurst, "How 'Platonic' Are Heb. VIII. 5 and IX. 23 f.?," *JTS* 34.1 (1983): 156–68. Ribbens writes that these two scholars "were the most prominent voices to challenge the Philonic background of Hebrews's heavenly sanctuary. While they promoted an apocalyptic background, they still considered spatial, vertical language to be Platonic and Hellenistic whereas temporal, horizontal distinctions were eschatological and apocalyptic" (Ribbens, *Levitical Sacrifice*, 90). For similar comments, see Ellingworth, *Hebrews*, 408; Lane, *Hebrews 1–8*, cviii and 207–208. However, Lincoln Hurst elsewhere qualifies that the author of Hebrews' use of vertical, spatial language is indeed Jewish-apocalyptic with Greek influence: "It is more likely that some amount of Greek influence has come into play, but it came into ground which was already prepared for it in which there was no great contrast between the two [Greek vs. Jewish-apocalyptic] traditions" ("Eschatology and 'Platonism' in the Epistle to the Hebrews," *SBLSP* 23 [1984]: 43).

6. Mackie, *Eschatology and Exhortation*, 6. David A. deSilva argues that Judeo-Christian views of cosmology and redemptive activity "intrude upon the static, unchanging notion of the ideal realm as found in Plato" ("How Greek Was the Author of 'Hebrews'? A Study of the Author's Location in Regard to Greek παιδεία," in *Christian Origins and Greco-Roman Culture: Social and Literary Contexts for the New Testament*, ed. Stanley E. Porter and Andrew W. Pitts, TENT 9 [Leiden: Brill, 2013], 637 n. 15). Cf. also Hurst, "Eschatology and 'Platonism,'" 43; Schenck, "Philo and the Epistle to the Hebrews," 114, 119; Ronald Williamson, "Platonism and Hebrews," *SJT* 16.4 (1963): 419. The argument proposed is that Jewish apocalyptic literature has numerous examples where vertical, spatial language is used prior to Greek influence upon the Judeo-Christian world. This is the view that I hold while acknowledging that an indirect Platonic influence may have existed during the author's time of writing. Yet it is my contention that the Jewish apocalyptic contains both vertical and horizontal characteristics (cf. Section 7.3 of this study).

7. MacRae, "Heavenly Temple and Eschatology," 179–99, who believes that while the author of Hebrews is primarily Platonic in thought, he uses the Jewish apocalyptic background to gain credibility with his Jewish hearers.

literature.⁸ Yet, while holding this notion, the spiritual import (Secondspace) and social/ethical implications (Thirdspace) are quite different.⁹ This approach prevents us from an "illegitimate totality transfer"¹⁰ of all that is Jewish-apocalyptic to Hebrews, but still recognizes its influence and commonly held beliefs of the recipients of Hebrews. Neither in apocalyptic literature nor in Hebrews will we find an explicit, comprehensive defense arguing for a physical, standing heavenly tabernacle. Yet, enough commonality exists between Jewish apocalyptic writings with the author of Hebrews' worldview that "they use the heavenly sanctuary and the understanding that they share with their audience to make their arguments."¹¹ On this assumption, we can affirm Craig Koester's conclusion in his survey of the tabernacle imagery: "In a setting where the differences between Christianity and Judaism were becoming increasingly clear, tabernacle imagery helped to establish continuity between Christianity and Israel's cultic heritage."¹²

This chapter will investigate the use of Exodus 25:40 in Hebrews 8:5, a key verse in understanding the relationship between the earthly and heavenly establishments of God's locality—the latter having been historically understood as referring either to heavenly cosmology or merely to the concept of transience.¹³ A key question will be: What does God mean when he refers to the "pattern" (τύπον/תַּבְנִית) from which the earthly tent was established? Hence its usage in Exodus 25 will be traced throughout the Old Testament and intertestamental

---

8. Recently, Kathryn Lopez applied Critical Spatial Theory to assess the spatial language in two apocalyptic judgment scenes in Daniel 7 and 1 Enoch 90. She writes, "Apocalyptic writings are strategic attempts to implement a worldview as a lived space… Critical spatial theory offers some helpful insights into the space that apocalyptic as a genre tries to define and normalize, and it provides some useful categories for analyzing the spatial strategies that apocalyptic writings use" ("Standing Before the Throne of God: Critical Spatiality in Apocalyptic Scenes of Judgment," in *Constructions of Space II: The Biblical City and Other Imagined Spaces*, ed. Jon L. Berquist and Claudia V. Camp, LHBOTS 490 [New York: T&T Clark, 2008], 139).

9. As Nicholas Moore writes, "It is important to be clear about how exactly such apocalyptic texts are being adduced—whether they are relied on primarily to contrast with or to confirm what we find in Hebrews—and to acknowledge that they exhibit both similarities (in terms of heavenly ascent and vision of a heavenly sanctuary) and also a number of differences from the letter" ("Heaven's Revolving Door," 203).

10. James Barr, *The Semantics of Biblical Language* (Oxford: Oxford University Press, 1961), 222.

11. Ribbens, *Levitical Sacrifice*, 98 n. 85.

12. Koester, *Dwelling of God*, 185–86.

13. For a presentation of views, see Jared Calaway, *The Sabbath and the Sanctuary: Access to God in the Letter to the Hebrews and Its Priestly Context*, WUNT 2/349 (Tübingen: Mohr Siebeck, 2013); Sakae Kubo, "Hebrews 9:11-12: Christ's Body, Heavenly Region, or…?," in *Scribes and Scripture: New Testament Essays in Honor of J. Harold Greenlee*, ed. David Alan Black (Winona Lake, IN: Eisenbrauns, 1992), 97–107.

literature to propose that the author of Hebrews refers to an eschatological tent that is spatially realized in the heavenlies. These findings will contribute towards a Firstspace understanding of the tabernacle structure located in the transcendent heavens, which then grounds its Secondspace implications for believers.[14] Such Secondspace implications include: (1) God's initiating act of revelation of his dwelling place and (2) that revelation conveying that an actual, physical place awaits believers to dwell with God.

5.1. Firstspace: A Standing Structure in the Heavens

5.1.1. The Context of Hebrews 8:5 and Exodus 25:40

Hebrews 8:5 lies within the centrally marked section introduced by κεφάλαιον in 8:1. There is debate whether κεφάλαιον is best translated as "in sum," "the chief point," or "crowning affirmation."[15] The third option is preferred considering that the author introduces a new rhetorically marked argument (*contra* "in sum"). Furthermore, he is not simply emphasizing one point out of many (*contra* "chief point"). Rather, the preceding presentation of how the prior levitical arrangement is deficient (7:11–28) leads to a climactic resolution in Jesus' heavenly ministry. Having now identified Jesus as the one who is exalted above the heavens, 7:26–28 introduces the concept of a heavenly high priest and the need for such a ministry.[16] His identity is then revealed in the triumphant announcement, "We do have

---

14. The following scholars specifically interpret Heb. 8:5 as something other than a standing heavenly structure: Asumang, *Unlocking*, 107–10; Church, *Hebrews and the Church*, 405–34; Cody, *Heavenly Sanctuary and Liturgy*, 16; Hughes, *Hebrews*, 295; Goppelt, "Τύπος, Ἀντίτυπος, Τυπικός, Ὑποτύπωσις," 8:257–58; Koester, *The Dwelling of God*, 174–83; Moffatt, *Hebrews*, xxxiv, 105; Peterson, *Hebrews and Perfection*, 131; Schenck, *Cosmology and Eschatology*, 171–72. See also my survey in Section 1.2.1–4.

Those who argue for a standing structure in heaven are Davidson, *Typology in Scripture*, 342–43; Eskola, *Messiah and Throne*, 252; Jamieson, *Heavenly Offering*, 51–57; Mackie, *Eschatology and Exhortation*, 158; "Heavenly Sanctuary Mysticism," 94–95; Moffitt, "Serving in the Tabernacle," 269–74; Ribbens, *Levitical Cult*, 89–99; King L. She, *The Use of Exodus in Hebrews*, StBibLit 142 (New York: Peter Lang, 2011), 132–33; Max Wilcox, "'According to the Pattern (Tbnyt)…': Exodus 25:40 in the New Testament and Early Jewish Thought," *RevQ* 13.1–4 (1988): 648–56. See also my survey in Section 1.2.5.

15. Bruce, *Hebrews*, 180 n. 1; Ellingworth, *Hebrews*, 399–400; Koester, *Hebrews*, 374–75.

16. Similarly, Keene argues that 8:1 is a climactic point that brings together the two ideas of Jesus' reign with the Father (i.e., his positional standing) and his identity as the great High Priest (Keene, "Heaven Is a Tent," 37). Hermut Löhr sees Heb. 8:1–6 as recapitulating prior themes (e.g., *Hoherpriester* and *Opfer*) while also introducing new ones (e.g., *Opferstätte* and *Kultordnung*) ("'Umriss' Und 'Schatten': Bemerkungen Zur Zitierung von Ex 25,40 in Hebr 8," *ZNW* 84.3–4 [1993]: 219).

such a high priest," in 8:1"[17] (τοιοῦτον ἔχομεν ἀρχιερέα), with a description of his ministry in verses 1–6 using what Franz Laub calls, "cult spatiality" (*kultischer Räumlichkeit*).[18] The next two sections (8:7–13 and 9:1–10) focus back on the prior levitical order while recapitulating Jesus' heavenly priesthood in 9:11.[19] Therefore, 8:1–2 "spatially foregrounds" the heavenly tabernacle as the locale for the exposition that is to follow through 10:18.[20]

Prior to the Exodus 25:40 citation in 8:5, the phrase καθὼς κεχρημάτισται Μωϋσῆς... φησιν[21] focuses on the Old Testament event of the tabernacle construction.[22] Although the author does not repeatedly use an introductory formula like Paul's καθὼς γέγραπται, he does use the conjunction καθώς with a speaking verb, such as λέγειν or in this case, φησιν. The effect is such that, without dismissing the author's stylistic features, the act of speaking is not limited to the past but God directly speaks now.[23] Next comes the formal citation further marked by the γάρ conjunction written in a "clear and unique verbal parallelism"[24] with Exodus 25:40.[25]

The citation of Exodus 25:40 reflects the LXX—itself a faithful translation of the MT,[26] with the exception of two changes: (1) The author inserts πάντα

---

17. "[T]he relative pronoun ὅς has correlative force, so that τοιοῦτον refers primarily to what follows (Lane, *Hebrews 1–8*, 204).

18. Franz Laub, "'Ein für allemal hineingegangen in das Allerheiligste' [Hebr 9:12]–Zum Verständnis des Kreuzestodes im Hebräerbrief," *BZ* 35.1 [1991]: 66–68. By this term Laub means the liturgy of the sanctuary of the "real tent," which houses the immediate presence of God (ibid.).

19. This recapitulation of Jesus' role in the "liturge du sanctuaire" is why Léopold Sabourin believes Heb. 8:2 and 9:11–12 are key verses that clarify the meaning of the entire epistle ("Liturge du sanctuaire et de la tente véritable," *NTS* 18.1 [1971]: 87).

20. Guthrie, *Structure*, 122–23; Jamieson, *Jesus' Death and Heavenly Offering*, 52.

21. Both Rahlf's and the Göttingen editions present the same reading for both Exod. 25:9 and 40. I utilize the versification of the MT and Rahlf's LXX of 25:9 over the Göttingen's versification (25:8) for the sake of consistency.

22. The reader would have been cued to this event earlier in v. 2 with the reference to the "real tent, which the Lord pitched" (Wilcox, "According to the Pattern," 656). Furthermore, v. 6b introduces the theme of διαθήκη, which makes the "place of worship" in vv. 2 and 5 to be what is "in fact innovative in the pericope" (Löhr, "Umriß und Schatten," 220).

23. Note the present, indicative tense of φησιν.

24. G. K. Beale, *Handbook on the New Testament Use of the Old Testament: Exegesis and Interpretation* (Grand Rapids, MI: Baker Academic, 2012), 29.

25. Richard Longenecker confirms this instance as one of the thirty-eight instances where an OT passage is quoted (Longenecker, *Biblical Exegesis*, 148).

26. The "general character" of the Exodus LXX is one that "adhered closely to a form of the Hebrew text similar to the MT" though it may be different at times in length and ordering (Larry J. Perkins, "Exodus," in *A New English Translation of the Septuagint*, ed. Albert Pietersma and Benjamin G. Wright [Oxford: Oxford University Press, 2007], 43).

before κατά and (2) the perfect passive δεδειγμένον changes to the aorist passive δειχθέντα. The addition of πάντα is due either to its reflecting a different witness (i.e., LXX Manuscript F[27] or the Lucian recension)[28] or a deliberate addition by the author.[29] The latter is more likely considering the presence of πάντα in Exodus 25:9 LXX, which the author likely had in mind based on his emphasis on the thoroughness of the instructions.[30] The change from δεδειγμένον to δειχθέντα is either stylistic or due to the author seeing the construction of the Mosaic tabernacle as a past event.[31] That both 25:9 and 25:40 were taken together for future citations can be seen in Philo's *Leg. All.* 3.102, where words from both verses are fused together. Philo uses κατὰ τὸ παράδειγμα and also includes πάντα as seen in 25:9, while using δεδειγμένον found in 25:40. This supports the possibility that Hebrews also had both verses in mind, which would allow him to insert πάντα.[32] Mary D'Angelo is therefore correct to suggest that the author refers to the entire context of Exodus 25–31, especially with the addition of πάντα.[33]

Exodus 1–18 contain the narrative of God's redemptive deliverance out of bondage from Egypt to prepare a holy nation living in communion with himself. The evidence of such a communion is to be seen in Israel's adherence to the Mosaic Law in their ethical conduct (Exod. 19–24) and their levitical services conducted in the tabernacle, which in turn prepare for God's glory to fill the tabernacle's presence (Exod. 25–40). Exodus 25–31 contain the instructions for the tabernacle's construction, given to Moses and later implemented by the

27. Guthrie, "Hebrews," 969.
28. Simon J. Kistemaker, *Psalm Citations in the Epistle to the Hebrews* (1961; repr., Eugene, OR: Wipf & Stock, 2010), 40.
29. It is common for the LXX to insert πάντα though not present in the MT (Ellingworth, *Hebrews*, 407).
30. There may also be a "more pleasing rhythm as well as the assonance" that comes from the final syllables *hora, panta,* and *kanta* (Guthrie, "Hebrews," 969). Löhr suggests that πάντα refers to the entire implementation of the cult being modeled after the heavenly one, similar with 9:1–5 ("Umriß und Schatten," 221). However, if the focus of verses 1–5 is the *location* of the cult as Löhr himself states (cf. ibid., 220), then it seems likely that the author of Hebrews more specifically has the structure and its artifacts in view.
31. Gert Steyn, "'On Earth as It Is in Heaven…' The Heavenly Sanctuary Motif in Hebrews 8:5 and Its Textual Connection with the 'Shadowy Copy' of LXX Exodus 25:40," *HTS Teologiese Studies/Theological Studies* 67.1 (2011): 4. Philo also retains the δεδειγμένον reflected in the LXX, which suggests either the existence of such a text (prior to 50 CE) or the author of Hebrews' intentional change.
32. *Contra* Steyn, who argues that both the author of Hebrews and Philo were together dependent on a different *Vorlage* (Steyn, "On Earth as It Is in Heaven," 4).
33. Mary Rose D'Angelo, *Moses in the Letter to the Hebrews*, SBLDS 42 (Missoula, MT: Scholars Press, 1979), 205–14.

craftsmen Oholiab and Bezalel for its construction (Exod. 35–40).[34] In Exodus 25, God instructs Moses to collect contributions from the Israelites as each heart is stirred to give (יִדְּבֶנּוּ לִבּוֹ, v. 2).

With the contributions ready, God commands Moses to make a sanctuary according to all that is shown him (כְּכֹל אֲשֶׁר אֲנִי מַרְאֶה אוֹתְךָ, v. 9). The details of the tabernacle's construction are given in three subsections: the ark of the testimony (vv. 10–22), the table for the bread of Presence (vv. 23–30), and the lampstand of pure gold (vv. 31–39). After these instructions, God repeats the command given in verse 9 by requiring that Moses make them after the pattern (תַּבְנִית) that was shown him on the mountain (v. 40). Thus, while the preceding chapters detail how God brings the Israelites into relationship with him, chapters 25–31 instruct how to maintain the presence of God through priestly service. John Durham writes, "As Exodus through chap. 24 is shaped by the promise of Presence, the proof of Presence, and the coming of Presence, so these chapters are shaped by the need to keep current and extend that same Presence through a carefully presented and interlocked sequence of symbols."[35]

In 24:18, Moses enters the cloud and ascends the mountain where he will reside for forty days and forty nights. Exodus 25:1 records the dialogue that takes place in God's tabernacle instructions beginning with the freewill contributions that serve as an introduction to the list of materials that will be later required for the tabernacle construction.[36] While 25:40 can be seen as concluding the subsection of the lampstand, it is better to see it concluding the three subsections (vv. 10–39) by repeating the summary instruction, "Make everything according to the pattern that I show you." The repeated use of this phrase throughout chapters 25–31 has confused scholars, who wonder if this vocabulary belonged to an older tradition. Brevard Childs goes as far as to trace an ancient, traditional use of this phrasing back to other ancient Near Eastern parallels that share similar ideas of their temple following a heavenly pattern.[37] Childs struggles with the question whether such a phrase is used to legitimize the sanctity and heavenly origin of the tabernacle *after the fact*, or whether it is the authentic record of divine revelation given to Moses by Yahweh. A simpler solution is more likely: Chapters 25–31 record the *instructions* for building the tabernacle while chapters 35–40 record its *actual building* with minor additions and/or deletions.[38]

---

34. Scholars who approach these chapters according to source tradition attribute chs. 25–31 to the priestly source (Brevard S. Childs, *The Book of Exodus: A Critical, Theological Commentary*, OTL [Philadelphia, PA: Westminster Press, 1974], 529; Durham, *Exodus*, 350).

35. Durham, *Exodus*, 353.

36. Peter Enns, *Exodus*, NIVAC (Grand Rapids, MI: Zondervan, 2014), 509.

37. Childs suggests that an ancient tradition preceded the priestly source and the two traditions were woven together, which explains what he sees as a tension between chs. 25–31 and 35–40 (Childs, *Exodus*, 535–37).

38. Enns, *Exodus*, 506.

5.1.2. Exodus 25:9 and 40 in Early and Late Judaism

Having oriented ourselves with the occasion of God's instructions to Moses, we now investigate how Moses and the Jewish tradition after him would have interpreted this revelatory event. But first, we must note that it is unlikely that Exodus 25:10–39 spells out every detail of the instructions Moses had heard and seen. Nor is it feasible to assess every description of tabernacle/temple furnishings in intertestamental literature. As Stephen Westerholm comments, "Many details—some quite essential—are left unspecified," and therefore, the citation is to be seen as a refrain that stresses the need for Moses to carry out every detail that was spoken to him.[39] However, because verses 9 and 40 are seen as summative refrains,[40] it is strategic to search for revelatory events of a tabernacle structure in the heavens and particularly for any occurrences of תַּבְנִית when tracing its interpretative usage throughout early and late Judaism.[41]

A. 1 Enoch 14:8–20 (Second Century BCE–First Century CE)[42]

The book of 1 Enoch is characteristic of apocalyptic revelation. It begins when Enoch's[43] "eyes were opened and he saw" a revelation where he sees God marching upon Mount Sinai (1 En. 1:2–4). This is similar to Moses' ascent to the mountaintop whereupon God instructs him to hear and see the heavenly revelation before him. Enoch, too, is commanded to "examine all the activities which take place in the sky" (2:1) and placed in a position where he can "look at the earth" (v. 2; cf. Deut. 26:15). In Enoch's apocalyptic vision, he is not given a series of unrelated visions; rather he is also given a tour of the heavenly places: "And I came into the tongues of the fire and drew near to a great house which was built of white marble, and the inner walks were like mosaics of white marble, the floor of

---

39. Stephen Westerholm, "Tabernacle," 4:699. Douglas Stuart similarly notes that the verbal description here is only a summation while the actual pattern and its details were communicated to Moses and later, Bezalel. He writes, "We cannot therefore know exactly what the lampstand was to be like; what we can know is generally its structure and motifs. The particulars were in the oral 'blueprints' Moses conveyed to the craftsmen from images revealed to him by God" (*Exodus*, NAC 2 [Nashville, TN: Broadman & Holman, 2006], 581).

40. Note another occurrence regarding the tabernacle in 26:30, albeit with a different word, מִשְׁפָּט for "plan." It occurs again after the instructions on the bronze altar in Exod. 27:8: "As it has been shown you on the mountain, so shall it be made."

41. For a word study on תַּבְנִית see Davidson, *Typology in Scripture*, 358–88; also his chapter, "Typology in the Book of Hebrews," 159–69. Davidson concludes that תַּבְנִית "allows for, and even leans toward, a heavenly original and/or miniature model of a heavenly original" (ibid., 163; cf. Ps. 144:12).

42. Ephraim Isaac, "1 (Ethiopic Apocalypse of) Enoch: A New Translation and Introduction," in *OTP* 1:5. Citations, translations, and references to the date of composition for apocryphal and pseudepigraphal works are taken from *OTP* unless otherwise noted.

43. Attributed to Enoch from Gen. 5:24.

crystal..." (14:10; cf. Ezek. 1:22).[44] As he enters the house, great fear and trembling fall upon him when he enters a second house which is "greater in its glory and greatness" (v. 16). It is here where he sees a "lofty throne" and hears the "voice of the cherubim" all to behold the "Great Glory" sitting upon it (vv. 19-20). The two "houses" mentioned correlate to the two sections of the heavenly tabernacle[45] (cf. Heb. 9:2, 8), which is "confirmed by the fact that the second room appears to be the Holy of Holies" where Enoch sees God's throne.[46]

Three notable features can be discerned in the way that Enoch's ascent relates to Moses' tabernacle revelation: (1) There is a combination of both auditory and visual (spatial) revelation. This is seen in the descriptive language used to describe the hallways, the floors, and the ceilings. He "observes and sees" these features, while at the same time *hearing* the cherubim's voice. (2) There is movement across the spatial divide between the first house and the second house. Furthermore, there is an intensification of God's glory as Enoch moves from one house to the next. This is reminiscent of the progressive levels of holiness from the tabernacle's outer courts to the Most Holy Place that contains the ark. It is not surprising that in the tabernacle's innermost sanctuary, Enoch comes upon God himself. (3) Thirdly, just as God reveals the pattern of the tabernacle after Moses' ascent on Mt. Sinai, Enoch's eschatological visions are given after his ascent into the heavenly sanctuary. Following the visions of the judgment that awaits the watchers, new visions reorient Enoch's position as he sees "mansions of the elect and the mansions of the holy" prepared for the righteous (1 En. 39:4; 41:1-2).[47]

B. *Wisdom of Solomon 9:8, 15b-17 (220 BCE–Mid-First Century CE)*[48]

A more explicit reference to Exodus 25:9 and 40 is present in the Wisdom of Solomon 9:8.[49] This section recalls the event where Solomon prays for wisdom to

---

44. An epilogue of a similar experience is also recorded in 1 En. 71:1-9, where there is a clear, crystal structure (v. 6) that houses angels who go in and out of that structure.

45. Philip Church and Jared Calaway minimize the amount of correspondence between the heavenly and earthly sanctuaries because of the lack of precision in detail (cf. Church, *Hebrews and the Temple*, 156; Calaway, *Sabbath and Sanctuary*, 120 n. 64). However, they both cite and depend upon Martha Himmelfarb who does affirm such a correspondence even while acknowledging a "limited correspondence of detail" (cf. Himmelfarb, *Ascent to Heaven*, 15).

46. Eskola, *Messiah and the Throne*, 73.

47. In Enoch's ascent there is a separation of visions: one that is future and earthly, and one that is present and heavenly. Chapters 39-41 are a parenthetical reference to the heavenly state of affairs and, in ch. 50, his vision resumes to the future earth again—specifically, the earthly resurrection of the elect.

48. David Winston, *The Wisdom of Solomon: A New Translation with Introduction and Commentary*, AB 43 (Garden City, NY: Doubleday, 1979), 20.

49. This may also be a harmonization with Exod. 25:9, 40 and 1 Chron. 28:11 (Koester, *Dwelling of God*, 177). Key words such as ἅγιος, σκηνή, and ὄρος are found in both in Wis. 9:8 and Heb. 8:2, 5 (Church, "Wilderness," 51-52).

govern the Israelites and, as a result, receives a revelation that he is to build a copy of the holy tent: "you said that I should build a shrine on your holy mountain, an altar in the city of your encamping, *a copy of the holy tent* that you prepared beforehand from the beginning" (μίμημα σκηνῆς ἁγίας, ἣν προητοίμασας ἀπ' ἀρχῆς).[50]

While this is not an exact citation of Exodus 25:40, the correspondence with that passage of building a copy of the heavenly temple on the mountain is clear.[51] In further support of such correspondence, later in 9:15b–17 Solomon confesses: "and the earthly tent weighs down a mind full of cares. With difficulty we make inferences about what is on earth, and what is at hand we find with labor, but who has *traced out what is in the heavens*? Who has learned your counsel unless you gave wisdom and sent your holy spirit from on high?"[52] Here, Solomon confesses the inadequacy of the earthly tent,[53] yet faces the dilemma that no earthly mind can trace out the things in the heavens. Therefore, as seen in his supplication, he looks to God to send wisdom (the Holy Spirit) from the heavenly locale (v. 10). Only then will his construction of the earthly temple—modeled after the heavenly one—be "acceptable" (v. 12). Similarly to the Moses account, God's earthly sanctuary must be constructed based on *God's* wisdom and knowledge of the heavenly tabernacle, which already houses God and his eternal wisdom.

C. Testament of Levi 3:1–10 (Mid-Second Century to First Century BCE)[54]

In the third chapter of the Testament of Levi, God commands Levi to "listen concerning the heavens which have been *shown to you*" (3:1).[55] This is another instance of the combined spatial and auditory revelation that is associated with the heavenly places. Levi is then taken directly into the Holy of Holies (v. 4) where he observes levitical activities in the heavenly sanctuary that are akin to the earthly levitical practices.[56] "In the uppermost heaven of all dwells the Great Glory

---

50. Emphasis added. I utilize the Greek text from Rahlfs-Hanhart's LXX and the English text from NETS.
51. Steyn, "'On Earth as It Is in Heaven...,'" 2.
52. Emphasis added.
53. 1 Kgs 8:27; Isa. 66:1–2.
54. H. C. Kee, "Testaments of the Twelve Patriarchs: A New Translation and Introduction," *OTP* 1:775.
55. Levi's ascent is another example of a belief in multiple heavens with the third one being the heaven of God's dwelling place.
56. *Contra* Philip Church who suggests the possibility that this is in reference to Levi being in the earthly tabernacle since "in this text, there is no rigid distinction between the earthly and the heavenly temple" (*Hebrews and the Temple*, 186). However, this goes against the description of Levi's itinerary, which describes the heavenly luminaries preceding his entrance. Furthermore, it is doubtful that the liturgical activity of the angels that are described is actually taking place in the earthly sanctuary.

in the Holy of Holies superior to all holiness. There with him are the archangels, who serve and offer propitiatory sacrifices to the Lord on behalf of all the sins of ignorance of the righteous ones" (vv. 3c–5). That Levi sees not simply a static image but inner *activity* confirms the visual and spatial orientation of his revelation of the heavenly sanctuary.[57]

D. 2 Baruch 4:1–7 and 59:1–12 (Early Second Century CE)[58]

In 2 Baruch, Baruch is comforted amid Jerusalem's destruction "by affirming the reality of the heavenly Jerusalem with its temple, which God showed Adam and Moses (2 Bar. 4:1–7) and which Nebuchadnezzar is powerless to attack."[59] Here, God reveals that the heavenly building (temple) was already "prepared" when he had initially created Paradise for Adam in Genesis 1–3. God further shares how he showed this building to Adam, and later to Abraham and Moses: "And again I showed it also to Moses on Mount Sinai when I showed him the likeness of the tabernacle and all its vessels. Behold, now it is preserved with me—as also Paradise" (4:5–6). What must be noted is that the intent of this revelation is to provide comfort in light of the destruction of the earthly temple. And in order to provide that comfort, God showcases an already-existing heavenly temple that was similarly revealed to faithful figures at various times throughout Israel's history—namely, for our purposes, Moses and his revelatory event in Exodus 25. Furthermore, the heavenly temple has continued to exist in the heavens along with Paradise, which itself is presented as a mappable place in the heavenly locale.[60]

2 Baruch 59:3–4 recounts an event when Moses was taken up to the heavens, and in that account, "the heavens which are under the throne of the Mighty One were severely shaken" (v. 3). Here, Baruch's revelation is associated with Moses' revelation through its three successive revelations: (1) Warnings and the ways of the law, (2) the end of time, and (3) the likeness of Zion which was to be made after the *likeness* of the present sanctuary.[61] Here, the revealed visions are heavenly and eschatological. That Baruch's revelation is likened to Moses' reveals how both incidents entail the visual showcasing of the tabernacle structure.

---

57. I discuss more on the heavenly cult in Chapter 8 of this study.

58. A. F. J. Klijn, "2 (Syriac Apocalypse of) Baruch: A New Translation and Introduction," *OTP* 1:615.

59. David A. deSilva, "Hebrews," in *The Bible Knowledge Background Commentary: John's Gospel, Hebrews-Revelation*, ed. Craig A. Evans and Craig A. Bubeck (Colorado Springs, CO: Victor, 2005), 225.

60. Lk. 23:43; 2 Cor. 12:3; Rev. 2:7.

61. In such eschatological revelations, both temporal (end time) and spatial features (tabernacle sanctuary) are present.

E. Lives of the Prophets 3:14–19 (First Century CE)[62]

In the Lives of the Prophets, Ezekiel is recorded to have been "snatched up," similar to how in Ezekiel 8:3, the Spirit lifted him up between earth and heaven. In describing how Ezekiel was snatched up (ἡρπάγη),[63] verse 15 compares this "snatching up" with that of Moses: "Like Moses, this man [Ezekiel] saw the pattern of the Temple, with its wall and broad outer wall, just as Daniel also said that it would be built." This supports a tradition that interpreted Moses' revelatory event as not existing in God's mind but required him to be physically displaced in order to see the pattern of the temple.

F. The Dead Sea Scrolls[64]

11Q19 (Temple Scroll)

While 11Q19 does not explicitly use the language of Exodus 25:9 or 40, the "compiler of 11QTempleᵃ [11Q19] probably used Exodus 25:31–40 as a basis for his discussion of the lampstand."[65] Thus, the Temple Scroll is an attempt to fill in the minor details that were not recorded in Exodus. The idea is that such a "temple scroll" was "handed down by God to Moses, by Moses to Joshua, by Joshua to the Elders, by the Elders to the prophets, by the prophets to David and by David to Solomon."[66] The detailed descriptions assume that what Moses received was not his own interpretation of a vague pattern, but an actual, descriptive revelation of an existing heavenly sanctuary.

4Q417 Frag. 1 i:16–17 (4QInstruction)

In 4Q417 frag. 1 i, instruction is given to reflect upon the wonders, mysteries, and revelations of God. These are given in the "vision of meditation and a book of remembrance" as an "inheritance" to Enosh along with a spiritual people according to the pattern (כתבנית)[67] of the holy ones (i:16–17).[68] The same word,

---

62. D. R. A. Hare, "The Lives of the Prophets: A New Translation and Introduction," in *OTP* 2:379.

63. The Greek text of *Liv. Pro.* is taken from Ken Penner and Michael S. Heiser, *Old Testament Greek Pseudepigrapha with Morphology* (Bellingham, WA: Lexham Press, 2008). Interestingly, the same word ἡρπάγη is used to describe Paul's ascent to the third heavens (τρίτου οὐρανοῦ) in 2 Cor. 12:4.

64. The Hebrew and English texts in this section are from Florentino García Martínez and Eibert J. C. Tigchelaar, eds., *The Dead Sea Scrolls Study Edition*, 2 vols. (Leiden: Brill, 1997–98) unless otherwise noted.

65. Steyn, "On Earth as It Is in Heaven," 2.

66. Wilcox, "According to the Pattern," 653.

67. Martínez and Tigchelaar, *Dead Sea Scrolls*, 2:860.

68. This is mentioned again in 4Q418 f43–45i:13 (כיא כתבנית קדושים יצרו).

כתבנית, from Exodus 25:9 and 40 is used not to describe a pattern of an architectural construction, but an actual holy group of people. The text does not specify the identity of the holy ones (קדושים יצרו), therefore further deductions cannot be made about the spatial characteristics of these figures. However, it can be assumed that these holy ones are already-existing beings (not existing in thought only). These existing beings served as the pattern and original for later ones to come. Hence, this shares the same sense with the tabernacle event where an existing heavenly pattern serves as the basis or original for the earthly one.

4Q403 Frag. 1 i:41 (4QSongs of Sabbath Sacrifice)

4QSongs of the Sabbath Sacrifice (4QShirShabb [4Q403]) Frag. 1 i:41 records the praise of the "foundations of the holy of holies, the supporting columns of the most exalted dwelling, and all the corners of his building."[69] This building is then later referred to as a "structure" (תבנית).[70] Here the heavenly construction evokes praise unto God, because God is the architect of the building. Other passages in this document also have references to a structure but are too incomplete to decipher the context (e.g., 4Q404 f5:8, f6:5;[71] 4Q301 f2b:5).[72]

Other Qumran Documents and Fragments

A handful of other Qumran documents (e.g., 1Q32, 2Q24, 5Q15) reflect a tradition where the "'writer' or 'seer' is taken on a guided tour of the heavenly or

---

69. Martínez and Tigchelaar, *Dead Sea Scrolls*, 2:820. Wise, Abegg, and Cook translate מבניתו as "structure" instead of building (Michael O. Wise, Martin G. Abegg Jr., and Edward M. Cook, *The Dead Sea Scrolls: A New Translation* [New York: HarperOne, 2005], 470).

70. See also 4Q403 f1ii:16: "the chiefs of the construction/structure (תבנית) of the gods. And they praise him in his holy inner shrine." Wise, Abegg Jr., and Cook's translation has "the chiefs of the divine building" (Wise, Abegg Jr., and Cook, *Dead Sea Scrolls*, 471).

71. This fragment can be viewed in Martin G. Abegg Jr.'s *Qumran Sectarian Manuscripts* (Bellingham, WA: Logos Bible Software, 2003).

72. Philip Church argues that the description of the heavenly structure in *ShirShabb* presents considerable detail on the structure and its contents, a level of detail which is absent in Hebrews. Therefore, it is "doubtful" in positing a "heavenly temple above that corresponds in some way to the earthly temple or tabernacle below" ("Wilderness Tabernacle," 126). While I agree with Church's caution against thinking that Hebrews depended on or derived its heavenly tabernacle understanding from Qumran, a common tradition can nevertheless be assumed. The lack of detail for the heavenly tabernacle in Hebrews is because the author emphasizes the high priest and his heavenly ministry that takes place *in* the heavenly sanctuary and not the intricacies of the sanctuary itself. This is why much of the detail of the tabernacle is excluded in 9:1–28 although enough is present to make a heavenly–earthly correlation between the tabernacles.

visionary city and given its detailed measurements and plan" and while "[t]hese texts however do not actually mention Exodus 25,9.40 so far as we can tell from the fragments presently available…, they do attest the currency of speculation about the nature and measurements of the 'heavenly' or 'new' Jerusalem and/or Temple in Jewish sectarian thought up to the late First Century A.D."[73] Two major insights arise from these references: (1) The concepts of eschatological space (vertical) and time (horizontal) were fluid. Visions of a spatial heavenly event are proleptic in that their contents signify that a better, "end-time" temple will be established.[74] In other words, the heavenly tabernacle is not only spatial and of divine origin; it is eschatologically oriented toward the end times. (2) Earlier, it was argued that Moses' reception of the tabernacle instructions was a revelatory event that combined both auditory and visual communication. The correspondence between the two shows that throughout the Second Temple period, the "showing of a 'pattern'" was understood as apocalyptic revelation[75] of what resides in the heavens.

G. Talmudim and Midrashim[76]

B. Menaḥoth 29A

A selection of passages from the Babylonian Talmud reflect the tradition that Moses had seen details of the tabernacle further than what is recorded in Exodus 25. In b. Menaḥoth 29A, Samuel b. Nahmani asks for clarification on the meaning of the "pure candlestick" and is answered, "It signifies that its pattern came down from the place of purity."[77] This is further explained by referencing Moses' account on Mt. Sinai in seeing the pattern of the heavenly tabernacle: "R. Yosé b. R. Judah, 'An ark of fire, a table of fire, and a candlestick made of fire came down from heaven; Moses saw them and copied the pattern: "And see that you make them after their pattern, which is being shown you in the mountain… And you shall rear up the tabernacle according to the fashion thereof that has been shown you in the mountain?"'"[78]

---

73. Wilcox, "According to the Pattern," 655.
74. Ibid., 656.
75. deSilva, "Hebrews," 225.
76. The dating of latter rabbinic sources does not guarantee a prior basis for later NT writings, but rather captures ideas that NT authors would have been familiar with during the time of their writing (Beale, *Handbook on NT Use of OT*, 41–44).
77. Translation from Eli Cashdan, *The Babylonian Talmud: Tractate Menaḥot* (London: Soncino Press, 1948), 187–88; emphasis added. Being "pure" is explained as not being susceptible to uncleanness, and hence a quality that can only be derived from heaven above.
78. Translation from Neusner, *The Babylonian Talmud*, 19:169. Note, Eli Cashdan uses the English word, "reproduce," instead of "copy," in his translation (*Babylonian Talmud*,

B. Shebu'oth 14b-15a (2:1, II.1.C) and B. Sanhedrin 16b (1:1, XXV.1.B)

The attention to the tabernacle artifacts is also seen in b. Shebu'oth 14b-15a and b. Sanhedrin 16b where a command is given to make a future tabernacle (or temple) according to how Moses had made the tabernacle in Exodus 25. B. Shebu'oth 14b reads, "Said R. Shimi bar Hiyya, 'Scripture has stated, "According to all that I show you, the pattern of the tabernacle [and the pattern of all the furniture thereof] even so shall you make it" (Ex. 25:9)—in the coming generations.'"[79] Thus, the instructions that Moses had received were a precedent for future revelations and for the future temple to serve Israel's future generations.[80] This fuels a debate as to whether anointing and consecration are also necessary for the physical vessels, which they deem not because of Moses' prior consecration of the vessels in the first tabernacle. From these passages, the tradition shows that even specific vessels were presented to Moses for him to visually see their patterns and, in this case, consecrate them.

Midr. Exodus 35:3-6 and Midr. Numbers 15:10

We find further support of a standing tabernacle that served as Moses' model in the Midrashim. In Midr. Exod. 35:3-6, Moses receives the attribution for building the tabernacle even though Bezalel and Oholiab were the ones who carried it out. When initially hearing God's command, he replies the following in 35:6: "'Lord of the Universe! Am I a God that I should be able to make one exactly like it?' The divine reply was: 'Make after their pattern in blue, purple, and scarlet; as thou hast seen above, copy the pattern below... If thou wilt make below a replica of that which is above, I will desert My heavenly assembly and cause My Shecinah to dwell among you below.'"[81] Midr. Numbers 15:10 is more explicit as to Moses' forgetfulness and inability to carry out its construction by stating: "Nevertheless,

---

187-88). Victor Aptowitzer contends that the rhetorical nature of the question implies that Moses saw no actual figure but only "forms" ("The Celestial Temple as Viewed in the Aggadah," in *Studies in Jewish Thought*, ed. Joseph Dan, Binah 2 [New York: Praeger, 1989], 11). Yet, the rhetorical question does not necessarily preclude an actual structure being shown. What is rhetorical is not the existence of the structure, but the *manner* of the construction: "Will you not make it according to what I have shown you" or "You are not intending to make it apart from what is being shown to you, are you?"

79. Neusner, *Babylonian Talmud*, 18:54.

80. Guthrie, "Hebrews," 969. There is a repetition of this dialogue also in b. Sanh. 16b (Neusner, *Babylonian Talmud*, 16:67).

81. Harry Freedman and Maurice Simon, eds., *Midrash Rabbah Exodus*, trans. S. M. Lehrman, vol. 3 (London: Soncino Press, 1939), 435. The addition of God's "Shecinah" to come down reflects the Targumic tradition where Neofiti 1, Onkelos, and Pseudo-Jonathan all add the phrase, "and I will let my presence/Shekinal rest/dwell among them (איקר שכינתי)" as well as Midr. Song 3:2 and Midr. Exod. 25:3-6.

Moses still found difficulty in understanding, and when he came down he forgot its construction. He went up again and said: 'Master! How shall we make it?'" After God reveals to him again, "still Moses experienced difficulty, and when he descended forgot."[82] This occurs again one more time when Moses is finally shown the model. This time, Moses is aware of what it looks like but "still found it hard to construct," which resulted in God instructing Moses to seek Bezalel for its construction.[83]

H. Philo of Alexandria

In *Questions and Answers on the Exodus*, Philo quotes Exodus 25:40, albeit in a different word order, and adds the adverb, πάντα.[84] He writes in *Quaest. in Exod.* 2:82:

> What is the meaning of the words, "Thou shalt make (them) according to the pattern which has been shown to thee on the mountain?" Through the "pattern" He again indicates the *incorporeal heaven*, the archetype of the sense-perceptible, for it is a visible pattern and impression and measure. He testifies to these things by saying "See," (thereby) admonishing (us) to keep the vision of the soul sleepless and ever wakeful in order to see incorporeal forms, since, if it were (merely a question of) seeing the sense-perceptible with the eyes of the body, it is clear that no (divine) command would be needed for this.[85]

Philo interprets the pattern to be the *incorporeal heaven*, and states that Moses needed to be commanded to *see* because if the vision was merely a physical sight, he would not need such a command. He comments similarly on Exodus 25:9 LXX (*Quaest. In Exod.* 2:52) that the unbegotten and uncreated God is the teacher of "incorporeal and archetypal things," who showed Moses the "forms of intelligible things."[86] Hence, the reason for Moses' elevation upon the mountain

---

82. Harry Freedman and Maurice Simon, eds., *Midrash Rabbah Numbers II*, trans. Judah J. Slotki, vol. 6 (London: Soncino Press, 1939), 650.

83. A similar account describing Bezalel's involvement is also found in Philo's *Leg. All.* 3.102–104. However, in Philo's account, Moses fashions the archetypes while Bezalel constructs the earthly copies: Μωυσῆς μὲν γὰρ τὰ ἀρχέτυπα τεχνιτεύει, Βεσελεὴλ δὲ τὰ τούτων μιμήματα. The Greek text is from Peder Borgen, Kåre Fuglseth, and Roald Skarsten, eds., *The Works of Philo: Greek Text with Morphology* (Bellingham, WA: Logos Bible Software, 2005).

84. Philo, *Questions and Answers on Exodus*, trans. Ralph Marcus, LCL 401 (Cambridge, MA; Harvard University Press, 1953), 131 n. h.

85. Ibid., 131–32; emphasis added.

86. Ibid., 99; emphasis added. Similar comparisons can be found in *Leg. All.* 3:102; *Vit. Mos.* 2:74–76, and 141; *Somn.* 1:206.

was to be free from the "dense and thick cloud that hinders reception" because the "nature of invisible things cannot be seen by corporeal eyes" but "by seeing rather figuratively" (*Quaest. In Exod.* 2:52).[87]

These examples confirm our earlier assessment of Philo's dualistic representation of the tabernacle (Section 1.2.1) where he draws a strict separation between heaven and earth. It is a hermeneutic principle that sense-perceptible objects of the material earth have their correspondence to an incorporeal and archetypal pattern.[88]

5.1.3. The Interpretative Tradition of Exodus 25:40

The survey of references and uses of Exodus 25:9 and 40 throughout intertestamental literature supports the following conclusions. (1) As reflected in the Wisdom of Solomon, the construction can only begin on the basis of God's existing knowledge of a standing heavenly tabernacle, which God initiates through a revelatory act to his chosen representative. It is this wisdom and knowledge of God that invokes praise in celebrating the glory of the heavenly structure (cf. 4QShirShabb).

(2) In the participant's movement across the spatial divides of the heavenly temple (1 Enoch), he discovers heavenly artifacts that correspond to the earthly tabernacle and levitical activity that takes place in the inner sanctuary (T. Levi). Qumran manuscripts "filled in the gaps" of Exodus 25 by inserting additional details of the sanctuary. It is the overwhelming amount of detail that causes Moses to forget and call upon Bezalel to help with the tabernacle's construction (b. Menaḥoth; Midr. Exod.; Midr. Numbers). And by virtue of the earthly tabernacle's basis upon the heavenly tabernacle, the *Shekinah* glory of God is able to dwell in the earthly tabernacle (Targummim; Midr. Exod.).

(3) In works such as the Lives of the Prophets, other figures (e.g., Ezekiel) take up the revelatory pattern of Moses. There is an expectation that similar revelations take place which draw attention to a future, eschatological tabernacle (b. Sheb. 14b-15; b. Sanh. 16b; 2 Bar. 4:1-7 and 59:1-12). Therefore, like Hebrews, the earthly tabernacle was never intended to be the focus of God's dwelling—rather, it typified the final, heavenly tabernacle where God immediately dwells.

One of the common arguments against a standing heavenly structure in Hebrews is the lack of detail in the tabernacle's descriptions.[89] In response, we must remember the author's rhetorical strategy in utilizing the tabernacle motif: He is locating the place of Christ's high priestly ministry and arguing that, in part, that ministry is far greater and better because it takes place in the heavens. It is

---

87. Ibid. Philo likens this to an elevation of Moses' soul.
88. See also Moffitt, "Serving in the Tabernacle," 269-71.
89. Asumang, *Unlocking Hebrews*, 107-108.

correct that the author does not intend to set forth a Hebrews cosmology or an architectural catalog of the heavenly tabernacle's contents; hence, the amount of detail is sparse compared to the Old Testament and intertestamental literature. Nevertheless, the author does provide points of references such as Hebrews 9:23 and the formal citation of Hebrews 8:5 to signify what he meant by the heavenly tabernacle.[90]

When we observe the Old Testament and intertestamental tradition, we see that the tabernacle revelation was not simply figurative language or a snapshot of God's mind.[91] It is only in Philo that we begin to see τύπος taking on the meaning "blueprint" without it referring to something or someone actually realized.[92] Furthermore, if all that Moses was shown was a figurative blueprint, then the question arises why he did not bring down at least copies of the plans similar to how he brought down the two tablets of the Ten Commandments. The immediate context suggests that "Moses was provided in vision with a view of something constructed, relating in vivid reality how the sanctuary was going to look."[93]

Therefore, this interpretation is not the result of early Judaism changing the original meaning of Exodus 25:9, 40 to devise an overly literal heavenly depiction. Those interpreters were careful to preserve the interpretive tradition of the heavenly tabernacle.[94] As can be seen in Tables 5.1–3, throughout the centuries, the translation of Exodus 25:9, 40 remains mostly unchanged. We can assume that, similarly, the interpretive tradition of Exodus 25 remains unchanged and is present in the backdrop of the believers who are addressed in the Epistle to the Hebrews.

---

90. This is similar to how the New Testament authors took portions of the OT to "illustrate or elucidate the meaning of the main section under consideration" (C. H. Dodd, *According to the Scriptures: The Sub-Structure of New Testament Theology* [London: Fontana Books, 1965], 126). If so, Heb. 8:5 "assume[s] on the part of their readers a knowledge of, and willingness to accept, an interpretation but part of the common stock of tradition shared by writer and readers; its presence in sources outside the Letter to the Hebrews confirms the plausibility of the finding" (Wilcox, "According to the Pattern," 650).

91. As seen earlier, it is only in Philo that we begin to see τύπος to mean a pattern conceived in God's mind (cf. *Leg. All.* 3:102; *Vit. Mos.* 2:74–76, and 141; *Som.* 1:206). Also note in Exod. 25:9, the *hifil* participle of ראה, suggesting that something *caused* Moses to "see" (cf. Davidson, *Typology in Scripture*, 375).

92. On the contrary, the tradition of τύπος meaning a heavenly original above is carried through and found in Acts 7:44 (Goppelt, "Τύπος, Ἀντίτυπος, Τυπικός, Ὑποτύπωσις," *TDNT* 8:257).

93. Davidson, *Typology in Scripture*, 376.

94. Koester, *Dwelling of God*, 185–86; Rowland, *Open Heaven*, 83.

5. The Archetypal Pattern

Table 5.1. The Textual Tradition of Exodus 25:9[95]

		Exodus 25:9			
MT	Tg. Ps.-J.[96]	Tg. Onq.[97]	Tg. Neof.[98]	4Q11[99]	
כְּכֹל אֲשֶׁר אֲנִי מַרְאֶה אוֹתְךָ אֵת תַּבְנִית הַמִּשְׁכָּן וְאֵת תַּבְנִית כָּל כֵּלָיו וְכֵן תַּעֲשׂוּ	ככל מה דאנא מחמי יתך ית צורת משכנא וית צורת כל מנוי והיכדין תעבדון	כְּכֹל דָאֲנָא מַחֲזֵי יָתָךְ יָת דְמוּת מַשְׁכְּנָא וְיָת דְמוּת כָּל מָנוֹהִי וְכֵן תַּעַבְדוּן	כל[100] מה די אנא מחזי יתך ית דמותא דמשכנא וית דמות כל מנוי וכדן[101] תעבדון	[ככל אשר אני מראה אותך את תב]נית המשכן ואת [תבנית כל כליו וכן תעשו]	
According to everything that I show you, the pattern of the tabernacle and the pattern of all its furniture, thus you shall make it.	According to all that I show you, the pattern of the tabernacle and the pattern of its utensils, so shall you make it.	According to all that I show you, the design of the sanctuary and the design of all its vessels, so you should do.	(According to)[102] whatever I will show you concerning the design of the tabernacle and concerning the design of all its utensils, thus you shall do.	According to everything that I show you, the pattern of the sanctuary and the pattern of all of its furniture, thus you shall make it.	

95. Though not listed, we can also include Acts 7:44 where Stephen cites the same citation: ἡ σκηνὴ τοῦ μαρτυρίου ἦν τοῖς πατράσιν ἡμῶν ἐν τῇ ἐρήμῳ καθὼς διετάξατο ὁ λαλῶν τῷ Μωϋσῇ ποιῆσαι αὐτὴν κατὰ τὸν τύπον ὃν ἑωράκει. A few verses later, Stephen quotes Isa. 66:1–2 to communicate that the created heavens and earth cannot contain God's presence because of their qualitative nature—namely, they are *earthly*. Note the question, "What kind (ποῖον) of house will you make for me?" This is in line with Stephen's polemical cry against the created, idolatrous tent of Moloch in v. 43. Hence, nothing in this universe can contain God (*contra* the cosmological interpretation). Rather, the quality of that which can house God most be wholly other; it must be heavenly.

96. Stephen A. Kaufman, ed., *Targum Pseudo-Jonathan to the Pentateuch*, CAL (Cincinnati, OH: Hebrew Union College, 2005), Logos Bible Software.

97. Stephen A. Kaufman, ed., *Targum Onqelos to the Pentateuch*, CAL (Cincinnati, OH: Hebrew Union College, 2005), Logos Bible Software. English translation from Martin McNamara, ed., *The Targum Onqelos to Exodus: Translated, with Apparatus and Notes*, trans. Bernard Grossfeld, vol. 7 (Collegeville, MN: Liturgical Press, 1990).

98. Stephen A. Kaufman, ed., *Targum Neofiti to the Pentateuch* (Cincinnati, OH: Hebrew Union College, 2005), Logos Bible Software.

99. This presents the best possible rendering of the Qumran text based on 4Q11 paleoGenesis-Exodus 1. Light gray portions are supplied with the English and Hebrew text from Ken M. Penner, *The Lexham Dead Sea Scrolls Hebrew-English Interlinear Bible* (Bellingham, WA: Lexham Press, 2016).

100. ככל is presented as a marginal secondary variant.

101. מאניי וכן is presented as a marginal secondary variant.

102. כ preposition is missing in the Neofiti marginal gloss.

Table 5.2 The Textual Tradition of Exodus 25:40

Exodus 25:40			
MT	Tg. Ps.-J	Tg. Onq.	Tg. Neof.
וּרְאֵה וַעֲשֵׂה בְּתַבְנִיתָם אֲשֶׁר אַתָּה מָרְאֶה בָּהָר	וחמי ועיבד בציוריהון דאנת מתחמי בטוורא	וחזי וְעִיבֵיד בדמותהון דְאַת מִתחזי בְטוּרָא	וחמי ועבד בדמותיהון די את חמי בטורא
And see that you make them after the pattern for them, which is shown you on the mountain.	See that you make (them) according to the patterns for them that you are being shown on the mountain.	Observe and make (them) according to their design, which you were shown on the mountain.	And see that you make (them) according to their designs which you see (saw) on the mountain.

Table 5.3 The Textual Traditions of Exodus 25:9 and 40 in Hebrews

25:40 MT	25:9 LXX	25:40 LXX	Heb. 8:5c NA[28]	Leg. All. 3.102[103]
וּרְאֵה וַעֲשֵׂה בְּתַבְנִיתָם אֲשֶׁר אַתָּה מָרְאֶה בָּהָר	καὶ ποιήσεις μοι κατὰ πάντα, ὅσα ἐγώ σοι δεικνύω ἐν τῷ ὄρει, τὸ παράδειγμα τῆς σκηνῆς καὶ τὸ παράδειγμα πάντων τῶν σκευῶν αὐτῆς, οὕτω ποιήσεις.	ὅρα ποιήσεις κατὰ τὸν τύπον τὸν δεδειγμένον σοι ἐν τῷ ὄρει	ὅρα γάρ φησιν, ποιήσεις πάντα κατὰ τὸν τύπον τὸν δειχθέντα σοι ἐν τῷ ὄρει	κατὰ τὸ παράδειγμα τὸ δεδειγμένον σοι ἐν τῷ ὄρει πάντα ποιήσεις
And see that you make them after the pattern for them, which is shown you on the mountain.	And you shall make for me according to everything that I am about to show you on the mountain—the example of the tabernacle and the example of all of its vessels, thus you shall make them.	See to it that you make [them] according to the pattern that had been shown to you on the mountain.	Saying, "See to it that you make everything according to the pattern shown to you on the mountain."	According to the example that was shown you on the mountain, you shall make everything.

---

103. Borgen, Fuglseth, and Skarsten, "The Works of Philo."

5. The Archetypal Pattern   111

This tradition of a standing heavenly tabernacle likely continued by the time of the composition of Hebrews. By itself, Hebrews 8:5 does not explicitly describe what constitutes the "heavenly things" (τῶν ἐπουρανίων) but the phrase is repeated in 9:23,[104] where it is specified that the heavenly things required better sacrifices for purification. Christ, similarly to figures such as Enoch, did indeed enter a specific place (v. 24).[105]

Shinya Nomoto also utilizes Hebrews 9:24 to inform his understanding of the sanctuary and tabernacle in 8:1–5. He argues that the reappearance of the sanctuary (ἅγια) in verse 24a is defined as "heaven itself" (αὐτὸν τὸν οὐρανόν) in verse 24b. Therefore, he suggests that this reference to Christ entering heaven in 9:24 should inform us to equate the "heavenly sanctuary" in 8:1–5 with the generic term, "heaven."[106] In my response, Nomoto overlooks the adversative conjunction, ἀλλά, between verses 24a and 24b, which informs us that the author of Hebrews is not equating the heavenly sanctuary with heaven itself.[107] Rather, the author contrasts the dwelling place of God—that is, "heaven" against a "holy place made with hands" (εἰς χειροποίητα, v. 24a), which is the earthly sanctuary. Furthermore, the "holy place" (τὰ ἅγια) in 9:12 suggests that the author is not utilizing the term in such a generic fashion as "heaven."

---

104. "In 9:23 the spatial preposition is significant: that on which the earthly tabernacle was patterned is located in heaven. This parallel sheds light on 8:5, confirming that the Levitical priests serve in a copy of the tabernacle in heaven" (Jamieson, *Jesus' Death and Heavenly Offering*, 55).

105. I will discuss Heb. 9:1–14 in more depth in the next chapter. In 8:2, I take καὶ as an exepegetical conjunction where τῆς σκηνῆς τῆς ἀληθινῆς is a further description of τῶν ἁγίων and refers to the same heavenly tabernacle (also Ellingworth, *Hebrews*, 402; Koester, *Hebrews*, 376).

106. "Zu beachten ist auch, daß er in Hebr. viii If das Bild vom himmlischen Heiligtum einführt, zur Interpretation der Stellvertretung des zur Rechten Gottes erhöhten Christus, um es dann in Hebr. ix 24 plötzlich fallen zu lassen und es durch den Begriff 'Himmel' als Ort der Stellvertretung Christi zu ersetzen" (Shinya Nomoto, "Herkunft und Struktur der Hohenpriestervorstellung im Hebräerbrief," *NovT* 10.1 [1968]: 17).

107. This is why Nomoto suggests that any vertical correspondence in 8:1–5 is in regard to the "image of the heavenly sanctuary" (*das Bild des himmlischen Heiligtums*) and that the comparison of the two sanctuaries is only in regards to a typological comparison of salvation history between the priestly acts of services in the Old and New Covenants (ibid.," 18): "Die Gegenüberstellung von irdischem und himmlischem Heiligtum hat also im Hebr. nur insofern Bedeutung, als sie dem heilsgeschichtlich-typologischen Grundvergleich von vergangenem Priesterdienst des alten Bundes und gegenwärtigem des neuen untergeordnet und dienstbar gemacht wird." While the typological (horizontal) comparison is indeed important (as indicated by the νυνὶ δὲ in Heb. 8:6), it cannot account for the spatial descriptions found in 9:1–5. Furthermore, we must consider the author of Hebrews' citation of Exod. 25:40 and its respective context. Moses was not merely given a glimpse into the future (i.e., a forward-looking typology), but a vertical one (i.e., the sanctuary in heaven) which will be the *place* of typological fulfillment in Christ.

While the author of Hebrews does not record *what* was seen in 8:5, he intentionally includes the imperative ὅρα, unlike the previous textual traditions, to reaffirm that Moses was not simply instructed about God's pattern for the tabernacle. He was commanded by God to directly *see* a structure which the Lord set up (ἣν ἔπηξεν ὁ κύριος).[108] Furthermore, the author adds πάντα which the LXX does not have.[109] This suggests that the author does not simply have in mind the revealing of the outer structure of the heavenly tabernacle, but also all of the tabernacle's constituent parts and the artifacts contained within it as attested in the intertestamental literature.

The author's rhetorical strategy is to draw comparisons between the levitical and heavenly institutions, which includes the earthly and heavenly tabernacle (also comparisons between earthly and heavenly priests and gifts/sacrifices in vv. 3–4).[110] Therefore, if we adopt a metaphorical interpretation of the heavenly tabernacle that is detached from its physical existence, then we are in danger of interpreting the heavenly priest figuratively as well.[111] We should not miss the focus of the author's comparisons: the efficacy between the earthly and heavenly sacrifices that is connected to the tabernacle's location. "*Now if* (εἰ μὲν) *He were on earth*, He would not be a priest at all" (v. 4a). This may be why the author begins

---

108. The language used here does not suggest a blueprint model contained in God's mind. Note the allusion to Num. 24:6 LXX: καὶ ὡσεὶ σκηναί, ἃς ἔπηξεν κύριος, where there is clearly a physical pitching of Israel's tents (cf. Josh. 18:1: καὶ ἔπηξαν ἐκεῖ τὴν σκηνὴν τοῦ μαρτυρίου). Radu Gheorghita writes that the "larger context in which this allusion must be read is the prominent tradition in early Judaism which refers to the heavenly City and Temple as the patterns in whose image the correspondent realities on Earth were modelled" (*Role*, 83).

109. Philo continues this tradition of adding πάντα in *Leg. All.* 3:102 and *Quaest. in Exod.* 2:52.

110. Another contrasting element is in view if we consider Heb. 3:1–6 as a basis of comparison (οἶκος): On the one hand, the author presents God and the heavenly tent, and Moses and the earthly sanctuary on the other (Löhr, "Umriß und Schatten," 229).

111. As discussed in Section 1.2.3., Spicq defines the *true* tent (τῆς σκηνῆς τῆς ἀληθινῆς) against the backdrop of John's usage as "authentique, génuine, parfaite, de nature ou d'origine divine" (cf. Jn 1:9; 6:32; 15:1; 1 Jn 2:8). However, he deems these traits to be incompatible with "matérielle" which itself is "imparfaite" and "transitoire" (Spicq, *L'Épître aux Hébreux*, 2:234). This is an example of Spicq's view that the author of Hebrews was dependent upon a Platonic worldview. While John's usage is helpful in communicating the idea of the tabernacle being genuine and authentic, it does not necessarily connote the idea of "immaterial" (e.g. "ἀληθής," BDAG, 43). In his discussion of ἀλήθεια, Hans Hübner warns against the import of a mythological Gnosticism that operates on a "dualism focused on substance," since such views "fail, in different ways, to recognize the importance of John 1:14a" ("ἀλήθεια," *EDNT* 1:60).

his discussion on Jesus' high priestly ministry (8:1–10:18) by first establishing Jesus' location in the heavens in Hebrews 1:1b–2 (cf. Ps. 110:1).[112]

This is not to dismiss the metaphorical characteristics of the author's language in describing spiritual realities. Rather, the comparison is grounding metaphorical language in that which concretely exists in heaven. David Moffitt argues that this approach, which he calls the "analogical metaphor" approach, best fits how the author of Hebrews utilizes tabernacle language.[113] Moffitt adopts Janet Soskice's "homeomorphic model" "in which the subject of the model is also its source (e.g., a model aeroplane or a dummy used to teach life-saving skills)."[114] In the analogical model, there is no abstraction or Platonizing of heavenly realities.[115] It assumes a standing heavenly tabernacle while concurrently affirming the spiritual significance of its earthly counterpart.[116] Hence, the heavenly tabernacle serves as an actual τύπος for the earthly tabernacle antitype in analogical correspondence, not as a figurative pattern.[117] Furthermore, this approach coheres with

---

112. Jamieson refers to this rhetorical relocation as a "spatial frame from earth to heaven where it remains throughout 8:3–10:18" (*Jesus' Death and Heavenly Offering*, 52). King She interestingly writes that the author "activates" Exod. 25:40 to draw their attention to the true tabernacle and true high priest in heaven (*Use of Exodus in Hebrews*, 34).

113. Moffitt, "Serving in the Tabernacle in Heaven," 259–82. This is similar to William Johnsson's "literalizing" manner which is different from a metaphorical or literalistic manner ("The Heavenly Sanctuary—Figurative or Real?," 35). A "literalizing" manner affirms the presence of an actual heavenly tabernacle but without all the precise details (literalistic).

114. Janet Martin Soskice, *Metaphor and Religious Language* (Oxford: Oxford University Press, 1985), 102. The opposite would be a paramorphic model, which Moffitt argues as the wrong approach to understanding Jesus' high priestly ministry. An example of this would be to understand Jesus' entrance into the heavenly tabernacle as "an extended metaphor that depicts the spiritual significance of Jesus's death in terms of the atoning ministry of the Jewish high priest" (Moffitt, "Serving in the Tabernacle in Heaven," 259).

115. For example, Kenneth Schenck writes that "we should not be surprised to find that the literal correspondent to the heavenly tabernacle in some cases is *the abstract sacred space where Christ's spiritual atonement takes place*" (*Cosmology and Eschatology*, 168; emphasis original).

116. This is not to say that the two counterparts are identical (i.e., that one is a replica of the other). A model airplane can be said to "fly" (e.g., a child holding it in the air) like an actual plane, but there is a qualitative difference between the two (Moffitt, "Serving in the Tabernacle in Heaven," 262–63).

117. This allows the author to interchange heavenly cultic language with the earthly tabernacle (cf. 8:5a; 9:6–7, 11). This is different from the traditional understanding of earthly types and heavenly antitypes. This is due to "denkt Hebr nicht vom Irdischen aus über das Himmlische, sondern umgekehrt vom Himmlischen aus über das Irdische nach" (Gäbel, *Kulttheologie*, 472).

understanding Jesus the high priest as actually existing and presiding in the heavenly sanctuary. Such an understanding better reflects the Jewish apocalyptic tradition, which we see reflected in the Epistle to the Hebrews. In sum, given the examples of the heavenly tabernacle tradition found in Jewish apocalyptic literature and evidence of the author of Hebrews continuing and utilizing this tradition, it is maintained that the heavenly tabernacle Firstspace is a standing, physical structure located in the transcendent heavens.

5.2. Secondspace: Showcasing the Heavenly Tabernacle

5.2.1. Intensification of Tabernacle Revelation in History

Earlier, I referenced Edward Soja's description of Secondspace as mental projections that arise from imagined or projected geographies. A potential problem arises when God's people are not able to ground their mental projections in a structure that is obscured from their sight.[118] Not only were the Israelites limited in their access to God's presence as seen in the Old Testament tabernacle, but they were also left without knowledge of God's heavenly dwelling itself. Hence, Hebrews 8:5 (Exod. 25:9, 40) is a response to this problem, which is its Secondspace feature: God initiates the revelation of the heavenly tabernacle to his people in order to center their spiritual, spatial occupancy with Christ in his dwelling place.

Unlike other ancient Near Eastern parallels where a cultic construction serves to invoke the presence of their god(s) or to localize a deity to manmade structures, Yahweh initiates the earthly tabernacle's assembly and procedures.[119] Exodus 25 begins with a characteristic repetition of God initiating dialogue with Moses, which reflects God's desire to dwell amongst his people. Out of the seven times that the phrase, "The Lord said to Moses," occurs in Exodus 25–31, six of them are concerned with the tabernacle's construction and its furnishings. Thus, in the construction of the earthly sanctuary, God is the one who designates its procedures precisely because it is *God* who desires to dwell with his people. The crux of the tabernacle account in Exodus 25–40 is not the *act* of building such a sanctuary, but God's divine initiative and desire to dwell amongst his people.[120]

---

118. Here I do not mean that the heavenly tabernacle is invisible, but rather that it is concealed and out of sight from an earthly perspective.

119. This stands in contrast to "The Temple Hymn of Gudea of Lagash," where Gudea receives instructions for building a divine residence but had to first purify the city and ensure that the building was without defect. Only when construction happened in such a way would the divinity be invoked to bestow favor upon them (Daniel Block, *The Book of Ezekiel, Chapters 25–48*, NICOT [Grand Rapids, MI: Eerdmans, 1997], 510).

120. One of the tabernacle's functions was to continue to be a place of divine revelation since God spoke from the mercy seat and the ark of testimony (Exod. 25:22) (Koester, *Dwelling of God*, 7). Furthermore, God's presence in the tabernacle itself is a revelation of God himself (Morales, *Who Shall Ascend?*, 102).

God's purpose is clear in verse 8: "Let them make me a sanctuary *so that* I may dwell (וְשָׁכַנְתִּי) in their midst."[121] The central feature of these chapters is not the tabernacle, but rather, God's presence.[122]

Exodus 25:40 begins with a hendiadys, "see and make" or "see that you make" (וּרְאֵה וַעֲשֵׂה; ὅρα ποιήσεις LXX), which reiterates the purpose for Moses' revelation. It also shows that this mountaintop experience was not simply an auditory revelation, but also a visual one.[123] It is revelatory in a full sense. This is further supported by the fact that תַּבְנִית is most often used to refer to a physical model throughout the Old Testament.[124] For example, this word is used three times in 1 Chronicles 28:11–18 when David gives the *plan* (תַּבְנִית) of the temple for Solomon and in 2 Kings 16:10 where King Ahaz provides Uriah with "a model of the altar and its *pattern* (תַּבְנִית), exact in all its details." Finally, the בְּ preposition in verse 40 is best taken as a standard of measurement or computation (cf. Gen. 1:26; Isa. 10:24, 26; Amos 4:10).[125] Therefore, the capacity of what Moses was shown was not "merely an *interpretation* of a general concept," but rather a "precise build-out of a *revealed* design… It was his design they followed precisely. They did not think up a house and offer it to him, but rather he revealed what his house was to be like and graciously allowed them to build it for him."[126]

Moses, serving as a prophet-priest, is one of the representative figures who receives God's tabernacle revelation. This is partly the meaning of the following: "Long ago, at many times and in many ways, God spoke to our fathers by the prophets" (Heb. 1:1a). Moses was faithful in this way as God's servant, who was to testify to the things that were to be spoken later (3:5). The author makes explicit that Moses served in typological function to Christ as "in these last days he has spoken to us in his Son" (1:2a). Furthermore, it is Jesus who would be faithful

---

121. The consecutive perfect tense verbs of וְעָשׂוּ and וְשָׁכַנְתִּי depend on the context for translating the phrase sequentially (Stuart, *Exodus*, 564 n. 331). According to this principle, the preceding context allows for a jussive meaning, followed by a volitive, purpose clause. The LXX instead uses the phrase, ὀφθήσομαι ἐν ὑμῖν, which emphasizes God's self-revelation over his dwelling presence.

122. Douglas Stuart calls this verse the "strongest statement in Exodus," which is "God's concern to center himself among his people and to have them organize themselves around him" (ibid., 564–65).

123. Note the choice and tense of the verb used immediately following: "that which is *shown you* (or being shown to you) on the mountain (מָרְאֶה בָּהָר)." A literal translation reflecting the *hoph'al* participle of ראה would be "which you are caused to see" (Bruce, *Hebrews*, 184 n. 28).

124. Out of twenty instances, four times the sense of the verb is taken to mean *form*, rather than *plan* or *pattern*. However, even *form* can have the sense of a physical model. For example, in Ezek. 10:8, the cherubim appeared to have the *visual form* (תַּבְנִית) of a human hand under their wings.

125. BDB 90.8.

126. Stuart, *Exodus*, 590.

over God's house not as a servant like Moses, but as God's Son (3:6).[127] However, we must not overlook the progression of this typological revelation leading up to Jesus' arrival through figures such as David and Ezekiel.

In 1 Chronicles 28:11–19, David provides for Solomon the *plan* (תַּבְנִית) of the porch of the temple (v. 11) and "the *plan* (תַּבְנִית) of all that he had in mind, for the courts of the house of the LORD" (v. 12a). After describing the temple's constituent parts, David shares with Solomon, "All this the LORD made me understand in writing by His hand upon me, all the details of *pattern* (תַּבְנִית)" (v. 19). The sense of תַּבְנִית captured by "pattern" as seen in Exodus 25:9 and 40 occurs only here in the Old Testament except for 2 Kings 16:10.[128] That David is given a divine revelation is seen in the prophetic phrasing, "The LORD made me understand by His hand upon me" in verse 19.[129] David serves in a similar yet more intensified role than that of Moses because the instructions are not for the movable, temporary tabernacle, but for the established temple that resides in Jerusalem.[130]

David's revelation progresses to Ezekiel's latter temple revelation in Ezekiel 40–48. In Ezekiel 40:1–2, the same phrase that was present in 1 Chronicles 28 is seen when Ezekiel recounts that in the twenty-fifth year of the exile, "the hand of the Lord was upon me... [and] in visions of God he brought me into the land of Israel and set me down on a very high mountain" (v. 2). God then tells Ezekiel to "describe the temple to the house of Israel...and let them measure the *plan* (43:10).[131] Ezekiel, in progressive fashion, describes another intensified typological event given that the temple that he sees is not the earthly tabernacle (Moses) or the earthly temple (David), but rather, the future-oriented eschatological temple. This progressive pattern begins with Moses in Exodus 25 and continues through the later prophet-priest servants, David and Ezekiel, and ultimately

---

127. While Jesus refers to himself as the temple, the author of Hebrews uses the tabernacle to further connote an eschatological orientation that points both forward and upward. The interchangeable nature of the tabernacle and temple is legitimate due to the fact that they both depict, in essence, the presence of God. Ramsey J. Michaels suggests that the reason for the usage of the tabernacle is to prevent readers from thinking that the comparison is that of a corrupt second temple with the true one ("Hebrews," in *1 Timothy, 2 Timothy, Titus, and Hebrews*, ed. Philip W. Comfort, CBC 17 [Carol Stream, IL: Tyndale House, 2009], 391–92). Instead, I suggest that the comparison is between a provisional one (i.e., earthly sanctuary) and a *better* one (heavenly sanctuary).

128. Martin J. Selman, *1 Chronicles: An Introduction and Commentary*, TOTC 10 (Downers Grove, IL: InterVarsity Press, 1994), 264. This is in contrast to passages where תַּבְנִית most likely means "form" or "likeness."

129. Ibid., 263.

130. John A. Thompson notes an additional intensification in that the temple is made of stone while the tabernacle was made of timber and skins (*1, 2 Chronicles*, NAC 9 [Nashville, TN: Broadman & Holman, 1994], 192).

131. The form here is not תַּבְנִית, but תָּכְנִית which can also be translated as *plan* or *measurement* (BDB, 1067; *NIDOTE* 4:292).

to Jesus Christ.[132] However, in the latter case, Jesus does not simply receive the revelation of God's heavenly tabernacle but *is himself* the revelation of God's presence. The mediatory function resides in Christ's offering of *himself,* a theme that the author of Hebrews will develop in 9:23–28.

5.2.2. Centering on the Heavenly Home

When the author of Hebrews activates Exodus 25:40 in 8:5, the believers heed back to the revelatory function of the tabernacle and are given the full revelation of God in Jesus Christ and with him, the very dwelling place of God. No longer is God's dwelling place concealed—limited only to a select few in the Old Testament and during the apocalyptic ascents.[133] God showcases his heavenly sanctuary but not simply for the believers to admire from afar. Rather, the tabernacle was ultimately revealed to showcase *their* heavenly home, where God dwells. The author showcases their future home where God no longer descends to dwell with them in the limited and temporary housing of the earthly tabernacle. Instead, it is they who ascend to dwell with him in a sanctuary made without hands (9:11). Like a bride who is given a preview of her future home, believers can find a new, expectant meaning in Jesus' promise to prepare a place for them (Jn 14:22).

The implications of knowing that an actual place exists for believers are highly motivating. The recipients of Hebrews are no strangers to a "great conflict of sufferings" (Heb. 10:32) including the seizure of their property (v. 34). This coupled with the exhortation to draw confidence in their possession of "the city of the living God, the heavenly Jerusalem" (12:22), reveals that they are in a state of liminality.[134] Liminality is a status of ambiguity, disorientation, and wandering in between places of stability. Those in liminality are often the marginalized in society which puts them in a place of danger (cf. Heb. 13:12–13). This status was shared amongst the Israelites in their wilderness wanderings, as well as the Christian community in Hebrews.

It is to this situation that the author of Hebrews presents believers with the actual existence of a spatial home in the heavenly tabernacle. This reorients their sense of place and belonging.[135] This sense of place is indispensable to their sense of identity. Anne Buttimer refers to this as "place identity," which comes from one's

---

132. One can continue tracing the trajectory through God's progressive revelation and include the author of Hebrews and John's later visions of the heavenly city in Revelation.

133. Apocalyptic literature, while varied in its message and themes, has a common feature in revelation that "unfolds directly the hidden things of God" (Rowland, *Open Heaven*, 14). Hebrews 8:5 (Exod. 25:40) intensifies the content of revelation in that not only do believers have access to the knowledge of these mysteries, but also have spatial access into the presence of God by way of Jesus' initial entry.

134. Asumang provides a helpful grid to interpret believers' situation under three phases of migration: separation, liminality, and entrance (*Unlocking Hebrews*, 47–51, 147–55).

135. See Isaacs, *Sacred Space*, 62.

need for spatial security such as that of the home.¹³⁶ As a result, people engage in "centering," a process where deeper meaning is assigned to whatever space people believe themselves to be occupy. It provides a base of reference from whence they can perform all their activity within their reach.¹³⁷ The heavenly descriptions of the tabernacle (8:1–5) and the cultic activity that takes place within (9:1–28) serve to assist them in this process.

Centering is possible for believers because there is an actual space prepared for them. The heavenly tabernacle becomes more than a metaphor or an abstraction because God has revealed its actual existence throughout redemptive history.¹³⁸ Furthermore, he has provided a way *into* it by believers' union with Christ. In fact, they occupy that space spiritually during the eschatological, already/not-yet age. Their obedience and perseverance in the face of liminality is maintained as they center their lives around Jesus, who is the anchor of the occupancy in the heavenly sanctuary (6:19).¹³⁹ Therefore, believers can maintain their sights and their centeredness when they look upward (and forward in consummation) to a far better country—one that exists in reality (Heb. 11:16).

In conclusion, the interpretative tradition of Exodus 25:40 in Hebrews 8:5 supports the notion of a standing, physical heavenly tabernacle (τὸν τύπον/תַּבְנִית), which God revealed to Moses on Mt. Sinai (Firstspace). In particular, the Jewish apocalyptic and intertestamental literature utilize spatial language for the participant's heavenly ascent and spatial descriptions for the heavenly structure itself. The Secondspace import is God's initiating revelatory act of showcasing the heavenly tabernacle as a dwelling for his people. This showcasing enables a centering of believers' identities and spatial standing with Christ in the heavenly sanctuary. In the next chapter, we focus on the activity and the details of Christ's high priestly ministry in that tabernacle space.

---

136. Anne Buttimer, "Home, Reach, and the Sense of Place," in *The Human Experience of Space and Place* (London; Croom Helm, 1980), 166–87; cf. Geoffrey R. Lilburne, *A Sense of Place: A Christian Theology of the Land* (Nashville, TN: Abingdon Press, 1989), 77.

137. As a result, certain spaces have different meanings to those living *within* that space compared to those outside. This base of reference is akin to how an athlete "visualizes" the field as they practice their motions or how a performer imagines himself to be in a well-accustomed place in order to enter a musical "groove."

138. To illustrate, a child may be told about all the details of a fairytale land, and while the story may successfully communicate all of that land's wonderful aspects, the story will enact a considerably greater response if that child is told that this fairytale land actually exists and that one day, he will live in it.

139. The kingdom of God follows Jesus' physical presence—both in his earthly ministry (cf. Schreiner, *Body of Jesus*, 24–27) and his heavenly ministry. Hence, Lilburne rightly suggests that we consider the base location of the kingdom to ultimately be tied to Christ where he dwells bodily in the heavens (*Sense of Place*, 101). While I agree with Lilburne, I suggest that the evidence of God's kingdom also becomes manifest in believers' priestly ethics on earth (Chapters 7–8).

Chapter 6

THE GREATER AND MORE PERFECT TENT: HEBREWS 9:1–14

So far, we have examined spatial Firstspace and Secondspace features that comprise Christ's journey beginning with his ascension in passing through the heavens (4:14) and extending to his arrival in the transcendent heavens that houses an already-existing tabernacle structure (8:5). Now, Christ takes the next step in his itinerary to secure believers' redemption, which consists of his actual entrance into the heavenly tabernacle to engage in heavenly, cultic activity. This section will examine 9:1–14, a passage that describes in more detail the activity of Christ's high priestly ministry with respect to believers' atonement. Observing these verses spatially, the physical features of heavenly tabernacle Firstspace are essential elements in arguing for the efficacy of Christ's redemptive activity. This becomes clearer when we see how verses 1–14 support the notion of Christ entering a physical heavenly tabernacle (Firstspace). This then allows the heavenly tabernacle's Secondspace features to come to the fore by recognizing the ritual correspondence between the levitical and heavenly cults. Acknowledging this correspondence enables believers to realize that they, too, have spiritually entered into the heavenly tabernacle through their Spirit-wrought union with Christ.

6.1. Firstspace: Entering Once and for All

In Hebrews, the author's intended meaning for σκηνή has been a topic of controversy, debate, and interest.[1] Because of the various possibilities, Lincoln Hurst writes, "The interpretation of 9:11 is so contentious that it would be hazardous to build any theory of the heavenly tent upon it."[2] Similar to how the heavenly

---

1. Cody, *Heavenly Sanctuary and Liturgy*, 156; Simon J. Kistemaker, *Exposition of the Epistle to the Hebrews*, NTC (Grand Rapids, MI: Baker Book House, 1984), 248; Schenck, *Cosmology and Eschatology*, 147, 155; Swetnam, "Greater and More Perfect Tent," 91.

2. Hurst, "Eschatology and 'Platonism,'" 51. Nevertheless, it is a crucial part of the author of Hebrews' overarching argument. Albert Vanhoye believes the central part of

tabernacle has been interpreted generally in Hebrews, there have mainly been two approaches to interpreting its meaning in verses 1–11:[3] (1) as a metaphor that symbolizes the heavenly cosmos, the incarnational/eucharistic/glorified body of Christ, the church,[4] or the events of Christ's ministry, death, and resurrection; (2) as an actual tent whether it be in blueprint form (e.g., a Platonic or idealized model) or a spatially realized, physical tent in substance.[5] How one understands σκηνῆς in 9:11 depends on how one understands the background and context of the passage. Either the true tent is reduced to merely a metaphor, or when the author of Hebrews says that Jesus entered a tent, he actually entered a sanctuary within the heavenly places.[6]

When examining the author's rhetorical strategy in 9:1–14 and especially verses 11–14, it becomes apparent that the author explicates Christ's high priestly ministry based on the notion that the tabernacle exists as a standing, physical structure. It is precisely this structure which Christ *enters* in accordance with high priestly cultic activity that takes place within its walls. To help us examine the author's argumentation, we begin with a translation of verses 1 and 11–14 which I will refer to in this section. We then examine key features of the passage that provide a Firstspace understanding of the heavenly tabernacle.

¹ Εἶχεν μὲν οὖν καὶ ἡ πρώτη δικαιώματα λατρείας τό τε ἅγιον κοσμικόν...
¹¹ Χριστὸς δὲ[7] παραγενόμενος ἀρχιερεὺς τῶν γενομένων[8] ἀγαθῶν διὰ τῆς μείζονος

Hebrews itself to be found in 9:1–14, which unsurprisingly draws attention to Christ himself (*Structure and Message of Hebrews*, 36).

3. For the presentation of the various views, see Kubo, "Hebrews 9:11-12," 97–104; Calaway, *The Sabbath and the Sanctuary*, 110–11; Roger L. Omanson, "A Superior Covenant: Hebrews 8:1-10:18," *RevExp* 82.3 (1985): 365–66.

4. This position taken by Brooke Foss Westcott will not be presented in detail due to the fact it can easily be dismissed (*The Epistle to the Hebrews: The Greek Text with Notes and Essays*, 3rd ed., CCGNT [London: Macmillan, 1903], 259). It is unlikely that Christ gains access to the presence of God *through* or *by means* of the church. It is, in fact, the other way around, where the church and its believers are granted access to God through Christ (cf. Hughes, *Hebrews*, 287).

5. See Hurst, "Eschatology and 'Platonism,'" 48.

6. Ibid., 49; Schenck, *Cosmology and Eschatology*, 159.

7. Due to the μὲν...δὲ construction of vv. 1–10 and 11–12, which will be further discussed later, it is best to translate δὲ as, "on the other hand" or "in contrast with all of this" (Paul Ellingworth and Eugene A. Nida, *A Handbook on the Letter to the Hebrews*, UBS Handbook Series [New York: United Bible Societies, 1983], 190).

8. Two options are presented: γενομένων or μελλόντων, both of them having textual support, which disallows an immediate and decisive preference for one (Rick Brannan and Israel Loken, *The Lexham Textual Notes on the Bible*, LBRS [Bellingham, WA: Lexham Press, 2014], Heb. 9:11; Roger L. Omanson and Bruce M. Metzger, *A Textual Guide to the Greek New Testament: An Adaptation of Bruce M. Metzger's Textual Commentary for*

καὶ τελειοτέρας σκηνῆς οὐ χειροποιήτου, τοῦτ' ἔστιν οὐ ταύτης τῆς κτίσεως, ¹² οὐδὲ δι' αἵματος τράγων καὶ μόσχων διὰ δὲ τοῦ ἰδίου αἵματος εἰσῆλθεν ἐφάπαξ εἰς τὰ ἅγια⁹ αἰωνίαν¹⁰ λύτρωσιν εὑράμενος.¹¹ ¹³ εἰ γὰρ τὸ αἷμα τράγων καὶ ταύρων¹² καὶ σποδὸς δαμάλεως ῥαντίζουσα τοὺς κεκοινωμένους ἁγιάζει πρὸς τὴν τῆς σαρκὸς καθαρότητα, ¹⁴ πόσῳ μᾶλλον¹³ τὸ αἷμα τοῦ Χριστοῦ, ὃς

the Needs of Translators [Stuttgart: Deutsche Bibelgesellschaft, 2006], 460). The variant chosen will impact the force of the participial verb and particularly its temporal reference. Either the good things (ἀγαθῶν) *have come* (γενομένων, ESV, HCSB, NIV, and the NRSV) or they are *to come* (μελλόντων, NASB, LEB, KJV). However, γενομένων, the more difficult reading, is favored due to the age and diversity of manuscript types (Kistemaker, *Hebrews*, 253; Lane, *Hebrews 9–13*, 229; Metzger, *Textual Commentary*, 598) and the likelihood that scribal editing took place due to the phrase, τῶν μελλόντων ἀγαθῶν, in 10:1 (Johnson, *Hebrews*, 234; Metzger, *Textual Commentary*, 598). The first option, from γίνομαι, appears as an active, middle, participle in the genitive only here in the entire book of Hebrews whereas μελλόντων is present in 10:1 and 11:20.

9. Substantival adjective.

10. Manuscript P adds the words των αγιων to form the phrase "Holy of Holies" (cf. Johnson, *Hebrews*, 234 n. i).

11. The aorist participle, εὑράμενος, can connote one of three kinds of temporal actions: antecedent, coincidental, or subsequent. Cf. Lane, *Hebrews 9–13*, 230, who takes the view of subsequent or coincident action, "thus obtaining eternal redemption." The first option is preferred since a coincidental understanding implies that the *act of entering* is what secures redemption, while the shedding of his own blood (διὰ δὲ τοῦ ἰδίου αἵματος) accomplishes it. The subsequent view implies that redemption occurs after his entrance, which confuses the order of his incarnation, crucifixion, and ascension into the heavenly places. Furthermore, 9:24 is one of two other instances (e.g., 6:20) where εἰσῆλθεν is in the aorist, indicative form, and here it denotes the idea of Christ who entered into heaven, *now* (νῦν) to appear in the presence of God. The closest appearance of redemption (ἀπολύτρωσις) in v. 15 also corresponds the effect of that redemption with the *death* of Christ (ὅπως θανάτου γενομένου εἰς ἀπολύτρωσιν), not his entrance into the heavenly sanctuary (cf. Peterson, *Hebrews and Perfection*, 137). Finally, 9:25 subsequently clarifies that Christ's self-sacrifice is not to be performed often (πολλάκις), which implies that redemption had been accomplished *before* his entrance, and that after entering, Jesus appears in the presence of God *for believers*. Thus, Christ's entering εἰς τὰ ἅγια does not mean he carries along any of the redemptive, propitiatory act of the cross, which was already accomplished.

12. "Goats and bulls" are in the plural because the author is referring to the cumulative number of bulls and goats that were sacrificed every year. In each instance there is one bull sacrificed for the high priest and one goat for the people (cf. Hughes, *Hebrews*, 355).

13. Dative of degree of difference (Kistemaker, *Hebrews*, 254).

διὰ πνεύματος αἰωνίου[14] ἑαυτὸν προσήνεγκεν ἄμωμον τῷ θεῷ, καθαριεῖ τὴν συνείδησιν ἡμῶν[15] ἀπὸ νεκρῶν ἔργων εἰς τὸ λατρεύειν θεῷ ζῶντι.

¹ Now even the first covenant had requirements of divine worship and the earthly sanctuary... ¹¹ But on the other hand, when Christ appeared as a high priest of the good things that have come, [entering] through the greater and more perfect tabernacle—not made with hands, which is not of this creation— ¹² he entered the holy place once for all, not through the blood of goats and calves, but through his own blood, having obtained eternal redemption. ¹³ For if the blood of goats and bulls and the sprinkling of the ashes of a heifer upon those who have been defiled sanctify for the purification of the flesh, ¹⁴ how much more will the blood of Christ, who through the eternal Spirit offered himself without blemish to God, cleanse our conscience from dead works to serve the living God?

6.1.1. Through the Tabernacle or By Means of the Tabernacle?

The author of Hebrews first describes the characteristics of the heavenly tent introduced in chapter 8 by calling it the *true* tabernacle (σκηνῆς τῆς ἀληθινῆς, v. 2). His next description appears in 9:11 calling it the greater and more perfect tabernacle (τῆς μείζονος καὶ τελειοτέρας σκηνῆς). Grammatically, how one understands the force of the preposition, διά, in verse 11 affects how one understands what is meant by this description. Διά can indicate a passage *through* (spatially), or a passage *by means of* (instrumentally).[16] The majority of those who take the latter,

---

14. Some copyists replace αἰωνίου with ἁγίου (a difference of only three letters) as the latter is a more commonly used reference to the Spirit. Thus, αἰωνίου is the more difficult reading since copyists would have no reason to change πνεύματος αγιου to πνεύματος αἰωνίου (Metzger, *A Textual Commentary*, 598–99; Omanson and Metzger, *A Textual Guide*, 460). However, αἰωνίου still refers to the Holy Spirit, whom the writer wishes to convey as conferring the eternal implications of Christ's sacrifice unto believers.

15. The external evidence of manuscripts is evenly balanced for ἡμῶν and ὑμῶν but the prior is preferred due to the hortatory tone of the letter (Lane, *Hebrews 9–13*, 230; Kistemaker, *Hebrews*, 254; Metzger, *A Textual Commentary*, 668; Omanson and Metzger, *A Textual Guide*, 461).

16. A third option, the "modal" view argued by Kenneth Schenck, is not considered because it is similar to the instrumental view in that σκηνῆς allegorically represents the corresponding age of salvation history; hence, "by a greater and more perfect way than the ἅγιον κοσμικόν" (*Cosmology and Eschatology*, 164). If there is an allusion in 9:11 to Hag. 2:9, "The latter glory of this house shall be greater than the former," then there is a similar reference to the "things that cannot be shaken" in Heb. 12:26–27 (G. K. Beale and Mitchell Kim, *God Dwells Among Us: Expanding Eden to the Ends of the Earth* [Downers Grove, IL: InterVarsity Press, 2014], 184). This then introduces the difficulty of reconciling Schenck's allegorical (metaphorical-only) interpretation of σκηνῆς, because how can a metaphor "not be shaken?"

instrumental view argue for the referent being Christ's body or the earthly events leading to his ascension.[17] This translation would be, "*by means* of the greater and more perfect tent." Scholars such as Hugh Montefiore and Brooke Westcott prefer the instrumental usage because of the two occurrences of διά followed by a genitive in verse 12 (δι' αἵματος and διὰ δὲ τοῦ ἰδίου αἵματος), both of which are clearly instrumental.[18] However, contextual proximity alone should not determine the force of a given preposition.[19] For example, in Hebrews 13:11, blood is brought in *by the high priest* (διὰ τοῦ ἀρχιερέως) and soon following in 13:12, Jesus sanctifies *through his own blood* (διὰ τοῦ ἰδίου αἵματος). The two instances of διά here, though close in succession, contextually call for different usages. Therefore, it is more important to consider how διά is being used in its *rhetorical* context.

The strongest argument against the notion that σκηνῆς refers to Christ's body is that the author immediately qualifies this tabernacle as not being made by hands and not of this creation (οὐ χειροποιήτου, τοῦτ' ἔστιν οὐ ταύτης τῆς κτίσεως).[20] This reasoning not only rules out Jesus' earthly body as being the σκηνῆς, but also the visible sky or the heavenly firmament, both of which are features of the tabernacle under the cosmological view. More often, the designation "not made with hands" is often used in contrast to that which is earthly.[21] Furthermore, it is not customary for the author of Hebrews to use such cryptic language when referring

---

17. Among those who take the instrumental view are John Calvin, *Commentary on the Epistle of Paul the Apostle to the Hebrews*, trans. John Owen (Bellingham, WA: Logos Bible Software, 2010), 202; Church, *Hebrews and the Temple*, 412; Cody, *Heavenly Sanctuary and Liturgy*, 161; Hugh Montefiore, *A Commentary on the Epistle to the Hebrews*, HNTC (New York: Harper & Row, 1964), 151–52; John Owen, *An Exposition of the Epistle to the Hebrews*, 24 vols., ed. W. H. Goold, Works of John Owen (Edinburgh: Johnstone & Hunter, 1854), 6:266–67; James Swetnam, "Hebrews 9:2 and the Uses of Consistency," CBQ 32.2 (1970): 214–15; Albert Vanhoye, *The Letter to the Hebrews: A New Commentary* (New York: Paulist Press, 2015), 144; and Westcott, *Hebrews*, 258. Other early church figures also took this view such as Chrysostom and Theodoret (Hughes, *Hebrews*, 284; Peterson, *Hebrews and Perfection*, 141).

18. Montefiore, *Hebrews*, 151–52; Westcott, *Hebrews*, 258; also Spicq, *L'Épître aux Hébreux*, 2:256; Swetnam, "Greater and More Perfect Tent," 99.

19. It is not unusual for the same preposition in the same context to take two different senses (Attridge, *Hebrews*, 245; also Laub, "Ein für allemal hineingegangen," 81, who takes the locative view).

20. Also Kistemaker, *Hebrews*, 249.

21. Cf. Mk 14:58; Acts 7:48; 17:24; Eph. 2:11. This does not necessarily mean that the tabernacle is *immaterial*, rather, that it is not made with *human* hands (*pace* Spicq who writes that the celestial temple, erected by God himself, "can only be immaterial") (Spicq, *L'Épître aux Hébreux*, 2:235): "Celui-ci, étant érigé par Dieu même, ne peut être qu'im5 matériel." Moses, the one who has seen God's original sanctuary, sings in Exod. 15:17: "The place, O LORD, which You have made for Your dwelling. The sanctuary, O Lord, which *Your hands have established*" (מִקְּדָשׁ אֲדֹנָי כּוֹנְנוּ יָדֶיךָ). Here we see that in contrast to an earthly sanctuary, there is a *heavenly* one that God created with *his* hands.

to Christ's body.²² His "characteristic term is σάρξ, 'flesh,' 'body' (2:14; 5:7; 10:20)."²³ More importantly, this interpretation attempts to understand σκηνῆς apart from the context of the author's argument, as we will examine later.

Albert Vanhoye argues that σκηνῆς indeed refers to Christ's body, but the body being referred to is not Christ's incarnational body but his glorified body. It is Christ in the "transformation of his humanity,"²⁴ marked by the article, τῆς. Hence, it is *the* greater tent, which is none other than the resurrected body of Christ who grants access to God.²⁵ For Vanhoye, this interpretation appreciates the passage's emphasis on the death and blood of Christ, which corresponds to his subsequent resurrection.²⁶ James Swetnam takes this idea further and identifies the referent as being Christ's *eucharistic* body.²⁷ Swetnam derives much of his support from biblical references outside of Hebrews such as when Jesus refers to his body as a temple (Mk 14:56; 15:29; Mt. 26:61; Jn 2:19).²⁸ Vanhoye also looks to the Gospels to import the notion that Christ himself is the "tent." However, we must account for the difference between Christ as *temple* in the Gospels and Christ as *tabernacle* in Hebrews.²⁹

It is better to first read our passage within the contextual argument of Hebrews before importing a theological concept from the Pauline or Synoptic traditions.³⁰ Behind his argument, Swetnam asserts a eucharistic foreshadowing that takes

---

22. Harold Attridge notes this kind of reading as an "allegorical" understanding of σκηνή as the body of Christ ("The Uses of Antithesis in Hebrews 8-10," *HTR* 79.1-3 [1986]: 6 n. 16).

23. Lane, *Hebrews 9-13*, 237.

24. Vanhoye, *Structure and Message of Hebrews*, 66. Although Vanhoye admits that the "letter of the text" (la lettre du texte) in v. 11 could be understood as a concrete structure in the heavens, he argues that the author of Hebrews conveys eschatological ideas using concrete terms but in diverse ways as metaphors: "Certes, il utilise plus d'une fois des termes concrets pour désigner les biens eschatologiques, mais la diversité même de ses expressions indique qu'il les entend comme des metaphors" ("Par la tente plus grande," 5).

25. Vanhoye, *Hebrews*, 143-44.

26. Ibid., 146.

27. Swetnam, "Greater and More Perfect Tent," 91-106.

28. Note that Jesus is referring to his body as a *temple* and not a *tabernacle*, which should lead us to think that the context of Jesus' statement is different than the one in our passage. Swetnam also cites Acts 17:24; 1 Cor. 15:47, and Phil. 3:21, all of which are outside of Hebrews (cf. ibid., 94).

29. Vanhoye does state at one point that compared to the temple (i.e., ναός), the tabernacle metaphor better fits the context of the Mosaic institution and is more easily applied to a human body (Vanhoye, "Par la tente," 25): "au lieu de ναός, l'auteur dit σκηνή, terme qui se rapporte plus directement à l'institution mosaïque et qui se prête plus facilement à une application métaphorique au corps de l'homme."

30. Within Hebrews, Christ is never referred to *as* the tabernacle; rather, he is identified as the λειτουργὸς of the heavenly tabernacle in 8:2 (Johnsson, "The Heavenly Sanctuary—Figurative or Real?," 48).

place even from the time of Moses.³¹ While he is correct to emphasize the role of blood in the New Covenant, he misses the sacrificial, atoning nature of Christ's blood that was *already* shed and offered self-sacrificially (v. 14). This is referring not to Christ's cultic institution of the Lord's Table or a sacerdotal notion of the Eucharist; but rather to his once-for-all atoning sacrificial death that took place on the cross and the subsequent implications in the heavenly places (vv. 12–13).

Aelred Cody, instead of identifying σκηνῆς as Christ's body, sees the word referring to the entire *humanity* of Christ used to accomplish the work of salvation.³² The tabernacle simply evokes the humanity of Christ as an instrument for salvation. The tabernacle, then, "is not exactly to be equated with the body of Christ or the humanity of Christ, but it is a figure primarily of the humanity of Christ as an instrument in the work of salvation (διά, instrumental) and secondarily of the entire span of Christ's saving passage through the earthly plane (διά, local) and onto heaven."³³ However, it is implausible to think that a substantive noun such as σκηνῆς would refer specifically to the incarnation, ministry, death, and resurrection of Jesus Christ. There is no example of this kind of usage in the New Testament. Only if the context referred to progressive events in Christ's humanity could one make such an inference; no such mentioning of this is found in Hebrews 9.

The instrumental usages of διά also becomes unlikely from a linguistic perspective. Lincoln Hurst rightly notes that the earthly tabernacle is a symbol (cf. 8:5, οἵτινες ὑποδείγματι καὶ σκιᾷ λατρεύουσιν τῶν ἐπουρανίων) for the heavenly tabernacle. If such is the case, how can the heavenly tabernacle in verse 11, then, be a symbol for *another* referent? We have a successive linkage of metaphors— what Hurst calls a "symbol of a symbol."³⁴ Against such complexity, a metaphor is most effective when there is a single referent, and for the author of Hebrews to have multiple layers of metaphorical referents would call into question the coherency and perspicuity of the passage.³⁵ The earthly tabernacle cannot be a symbol for the heavenly tabernacle, which is then a symbol for something else.

Finally, it must be noted that Christ's body or his humanity themselves, in their strictest definitions, are not what secures eternal redemption (αἰωνίαν λύτρωσιν εὑράμενος, v. 12). It is rather, the sacrificial act of self-offering done *in Christ's humanity* that secures it. While his sacrifice assumes Christ's incarnational body and humanity, the distinction must be upheld, given the context and contrast of

---

31. In his example, Exod. 24:8 is a foreshadowing of the eucharistic event by Moses with the Israelites (Swetnam, "Greater and More Perfect Tent," 98–100).

32. Cody, *Heavenly Sanctuary and Liturgy*, 163.

33. Ibid., 164–65.

34. Hurst, "Eschatology and 'Platonism,'" 49. This kind of metaphorical linkage is made "by using one metaphor (the tent for the body) as the basis for another metaphor (the body for church), with the consequence that the exegesis has a distinctly mystical quality" (Hughes, *Hebrews*, 286).

35. Eva Feder Kittay, *Metaphor: Its Cognitive Force and Linguistic Structure*, CLLP (New York: Clarendon Press, 1987), 40–95.

Christ's sacrifice over the Old Covenant sacrifices presented in verses 1–10, and given the main thrust of the author's argument in verse 12.

Moving on from the instrumental view, interpreting διά spatially with a locative genitive produces two interpretations: (1) a cosmic understanding of the visible heavens,[36] or (2) an actual, spatially realized heavenly tabernacle.[37] The first interpretation states that "the writer divided the heavenly world into two parts, corresponding to the two tents of the tabernacle. Christ passed through the heavenly regions (4:14)[38] on the way to the Holy of Holies (διεληλυθότα τοὺς οὐρανούς), which is the very presence of God (cf. 8:1; 9:24)."[39] However, this interpretation again disregards the fact that the tabernacle is not of this creation—meaning it is not of this world, which includes the visible entry-point of the heavens (Acts 1:11). The second, and preferred, interpretation[40] takes into consideration the language of space in its surrounding context, and thus understands it in a local sense, "through the compartment."[41]

Under this view, there is an actual tent, which is the outer part of a sanctuary in heaven (cf. 9:2–3).[42] In order for Jesus to get to the Holy of Holies, he must pass through a physical, spatially realized outer tabernacle.[43] This corresponds to

---

36. This may include a tripartite view of the heavens (cf. 2 Cor. 12:2). See earlier discussion on the author of Hebrews' implied cosmology in Section 4.1.2.

37. Hurst, "Eschatology and 'Platonism,'" 52; Jamieson, *Jesus' Death and Heavenly Offering*, 84; Moffitt, *Atonement and Resurrection*, 222 nn. 10–12, 225; Mackie, "Heavenly Sanctuary Mysticism," 178–79; Ribbens, *Levitical Sacrifice*, 114–15.

38. While I agree that Christ passes through the heavenly firmament as presented in 4:14 and discussed in Chapter 4 of this study, it would be odd for the author of Hebrews to now introduce σκηνῆς as the heavenly firmament without distinguishing it from τοὺς οὐρανούς used in 4:14.

39. Omanson, "A Superior Covenant," 366. For further discussion on this interpretation, see Attridge, *Hebrews*, 247; Cody, *Heavenly Sanctuary*, 148–50; Wilhelm Michaelis, "Σκηνή," *TNDT* 7:376–77; Kistemaker, *Hebrews*, 248.

40. Attridge, *Hebrews*, 246–47; Ellingworth and Nida, *Hebrews*, 191; Gäbel, *Kulttheologie*, 280; Lane, *Hebrews 9–13*, 237–38; also Schenck, *Cosmology and Eschatology*, 157. However, Schenck does not see the division of compartments in the heavenly sanctuary.

41. Lane, *Hebrews 9–13*, 229; Johnsson, *Defilement and Purgation*, 298–97; Peterson, *Hebrews and Perfection*, 141.

42. Against those who view the outer tent to be a metaphor for the entire created order (cf. Stegemann and Stegemann, "Cultic Language in Hebrews," 22). Kenneth Schenck sees the two tents serving as a "parable for the two ages of salvation history" (*Cosmology and Eschatology*, 132). This ultimately results in too sharp of a division between the Old and New Covenant epochs without recognizing the already/not-yet schema of eschatology. Thus, he believes that the outer tent is parabolically associated with the "fleshly" and the inner sanctum with the "realm of spirit" (ibid., 155, 180).

43. Peterson sees διὰ τῆς μείζονος καὶ τελειοτέρας σκηνῆς in v. 11 as the means and the εἰς τὰ ἅγια of v. 12 as the ends, which is a similar syntactical formulation of 9:2–7. Thus, the outer part of the tabernacle provides initial access into the second, Holiest of Holies, 9:7

"a realistic understanding of Exod. 25:40 and related texts, according to which a spatially conceived sanctuary consisting of two compartments existed in heaven and had provided the pattern for the desert sanctuary."[44] In sum, strong evidence for a localized view of διά into the heavenly tabernacle is seen in (1) the spatial imagery that is consistent with 4:14 and other spatially described verses (6:19–20; 9:24–25), (2) the qualification that it is not made with hands, and (3) the syntax that demands a distinction between the front and inner compartments.[45] Continuing our observation of the preceding context of our passage, we now examine verses 1–10, which further support the spatial or locale use of διά for a spatially realized outer tabernacle.

6.1.2. The Antithetical Schema of Hebrews 9:1–10 and 11–14

The cohesiveness of verses 11–14 is seen in the passage's construction as two long sentences in the Greek.[46] In 9:1, the presence of the particle μέν prepares the reader to expect a relative clause that follows—in our passage, an adversative,[47] which is introduced by the conjunction δέ in verse 11. Therefore, the author intentionally includes μέν for the effect of creating *anticipation* in response to the descriptions of the earthly sanctuary. The expectation of a comparison is thus established by the description of the earthly sanctuary and its rites in verses 1–10.[48] Steven Runge states that "the overly specific description of the sanctuary as 'earthly' creates the expectation of some other kind of sanctuary to follow, otherwise there would be no need for the distinction."[49] What is the content of this "overly specific description?" They are the descriptions of the spatial properties and ritual activities of the earthly and heavenly tabernacles. Therefore, verses 11–14 must be interpreted

---

(*Hebrews and Perfection*, 141). Although Peterson takes διά instrumentally, his interpretation is compatible with the local use (i.e., *by means* of a physical, outer tent). Rather than seeing two independent tents, they are best seen as two compartments separated by the δεύτερον καταπέτασμα (v. 3) (Otfried Hofius, "Das 'erste' und das 'zweite' Zelt: Ein Beitrag zur Auslegung von Hbr 9:1-10," *ZNW* 61.3-4 [1970]: 271–77). Hofius notes that πρώτη and δεύτερον are similarly used in Josephus to designate two compartments of the temple (ibid., 274–75; cf. Josephus, *War* 5:194–95).

44. Lane, *Hebrews 9–13*, 237–38.
45. Ibid., 238.
46. Cockerill, *Hebrews*, 387; Ellingworth and Nida, *Hebrews*, 189.
47. Steven E. Runge, *Discourse Grammar of the Greek New Testament: A Practical Introduction for Teaching and Exegesis*, LBRS (Peabody, MA: Hendrickson, 2010), 79.
48. Laub makes similar observations stating that in vv. 1–10, two things are of main importance for the author of Hebrews: the spatial arrangement (*räumliche Anordnung*) of the sanctuary tent along with its furnishings (vv. 1–5) and secondly, the act of atonement (*Suhnehandeln*) that takes place there on Yom Kippur (vv. 6–10) ("Ein für allemal hineingegangen," 69).
49. Runge, *Discourse Grammar*, 79.

against this backdrop.⁵⁰ While the content of verses 1–10 and 11–14 is enough to draw the contrast, the author makes the contrast more explicit with the inclusion of the μὲν...δέ construction.⁵¹

Before the author introduces the contrast in verse 11, verse 10 completes the description of the earthly sanctuary and its regulations by the phrase "until a time of reformation" (μέχρι καιροῦ διορθώσεως ἐπικείμενα), which signals the completion of the *protasis* of verses 1–10 before the *apodosis* of verses 11–14. Hence, in verse 11, the author begins to delineate what consisted in the coming of that reformation, which is marked by the coming of the high priest (παραγενόμενος ἀρχιερεύς). Following this, verses 11–14 continue the rhetorical strategy of comparison by drawing at least five points of contrast: "tent" (σκηνῆς), "blood" (αἷμα), "occurrence of the sacrifice" (ἐφάπαξ), "cleansing" (καθαρίζω), and "works of service" (νεκρῶν ἔργων/λατρεύειν θεῷ).⁵² Verses 11–14, then, must not be considered simply as a statement of fact, but as the *apodosis* of contrast to the entire sacrificial system performed in the earthly tabernacle, which was limited to regulations on the body (vv. 1–10).⁵³

---

50. Albert Vanhoye views the comparisons as being between institutions, while others see the comparison as one of persons (i.e., earthly priests versus the high priest). Ellingworth is right to say that the comparison of persons and institutions are not at odds with one another, and that the comparison should rather be seen as all-inclusive. He writes, "[T]here is a rigorous antithetical parallelism between vv. 1–10 and 11–14, namely between the old and new tabernacles; the old and new high priests; the blood of sacrifice under the two dispensations; the animal sacrifice and the self-offering of Christ; flesh and spirit; and the power of Christ's sacrifice to purify the conscience, something which the old sacrifices could not do" (Ellingworth, *Hebrews*, 445; cf. Vanhoye, *Hebrews*, 147–60).

51. Runge, *Discourse Grammar*, 79. Those who agree with this view include Attridge, "Uses of Antithesis in Hebrews 8–10," 6; Ellingworth, *Hebrews*, 445; Johnson, *Hebrews*, 235; Lane, *Hebrews 9–13*, 229. Lane sees the comparison beginning in 8:1–2, with the theme of Christ's entrance into the heavenly sanctuary (ibid., 202). While thematically this is true, we must not overlook the immediate grammatical construction. Ellingworth and Nida suggest the translation, "in contrast with all of this" or "on the other hand" for the adversative δέ (Ellingworth and Nida, *Hebrews*, 189). At the same time, the thematic overtones of 8:1–2 can very well be carried into ch. 9, which does not completely disqualify Lane's interpretation. Philip Church sees a contrast of vv. 11–12 with vv. 6–10 (*Hebrews and the Temple*, 417). This is due to noting the contrast between the former time of correction to the present time of eternal redemption, accentuated by the word *entering* (εἰσίασιν, v. 6) of the levitical priests with the once-for-all *entering* (εἰσῆλθεν, vv. 11–12) of the high priest.

52. Also noted by Ellingworth and Nida, *Hebrews*, 189.

53. This analysis aligns with Gäbel's argument that posits the importance, continuation, and utilization of cult theology in Hebrews. The absence of the Jerusalem Temple may lead some to conclude that the author of Hebrews was not at all interested in cult theology.

Linguistically, it is important to note that when two elements are contrasted, there must also be a level of commonality in order to draw the contrast. For example, the contrast between the levitical priest and the high priest shares the common category of being priests; however, they belong to entirely different priestly orders (levitical genealogy compared to an indestructible life like that of Melchizedek).[54] In a likewise manner, verses 11–14 can be subsumed under the same categories of description as verses 1–10, while, at the same time, they make antithetical distinctions *within* those categories.[55]

In addition to labeling these verses as antithetical statements (e.g., positive–negative [+/-]), they are also *a fortiori* arguments, whereby an initial *protasis* is stated and the later *apodosis* of the same category is presented in a way that is greater than the first.[56] What are the shared categories from verses 1–10 that we must maintain when reading verses 11–14? *They are the physical, spatial descriptions of the earthly tabernacle (vv. 1–5), the ritual acts of the levitical priests (vv. 6–7), and the effects that arise from the ritual acts that have taken place in the earthly tabernacle (vv. 8–10).*

Therefore, the author of Hebrews contends that Jesus' ministry is much more excellent (διαφορωτέρας) than the former ministry that took place on earth. As mentioned, for something to be "better," the author must establish two subjects within the same category first, and *then* discuss how the latter is better while operating under that same category. Without establishing a shared category, the latter does not become *better* but simply *different*. In the author's rhetorical strategy, he establishes shared categories between the Mosaic tabernacle with the heavenly tabernacle, and *then* argues how the latter is better. For example, the two tabernacles are entry points into the presence of God (shared category), but the heavenly one is better because God does not come down in his *shekinah* glory to believers; rather, *they* are brought into his direct presence through their

---

Contrary to this, the author of Hebrews does not disregard the earthly cult but rather draws attention to its deficiency to redirect the audience's attention to the "superiority" (*Überlegenheit*) and "permanent validity" (*bleibende Geltung*) of the cult event that takes place in the heavenly sanctuary (*Kulttheologie*, 471).

54. In the subordinate clauses of our passage, there is a "relative degree of continuity and discontinuity between the action of Christ and that of the Levitical high priest" (Lane, *Hebrews 9–13*, 236).

55. This is a feature also present in Leviticus. As Mayjee Philip writes, "The complexity of juxtaposing these antithetical concepts is what creates the world of Leviticus, where holiness is physically symbolized by the pure/clean, while the profane is represented by the impure/clean… In Leviticus, holiness is mirrored by the concepts of covenant (sacred space – tabernacle), sacrifice (sacred ritual, time), and priesthood (sacred personnel)" (*Leviticus in Hebrews*, 25).

56. A common feature found in Hebrews (e.g., 2:1–3; 3:3; 8:6 and 10:28–29) as noted by Ellingworth and Nida, *Hebrews*, 189.

union with the ascended Christ. As another example, the two tabernacles house the priestly activity for atonement (shared category), but the heavenly one is better because that activity is performed by the one greater than Melchizedek (5:6) and is administered with blood of more value than that of bulls and goats (9:12).[57]

The same rhetorical strategy is used regarding the nature of the two tabernacles. They are both material structures located in space (shared category), but what makes the heavenly one better is that it is made directly by God (ἣν ἔπηξεν ὁ κύριος, οὐκ ἄνθρωπος, 8:2b), has better sacrifices (κρείττοσιν θυσίαις, 9:23b), is more efficacious regarding the conscience (κατὰ συνείδησιν τελειῶσαι τὸν λατρεύοντα, 9:9b), and is itself the original pattern of the former (κατὰ τὸν τύπον, 8:5b). Altogether, these examples constitute what the author sums up in 9:11, that Christ, the greater and more perfect high priest, has come and entered into this greater and more perfect tabernacle (μείζονος καὶ τελειοτέρας σκηνῆς).

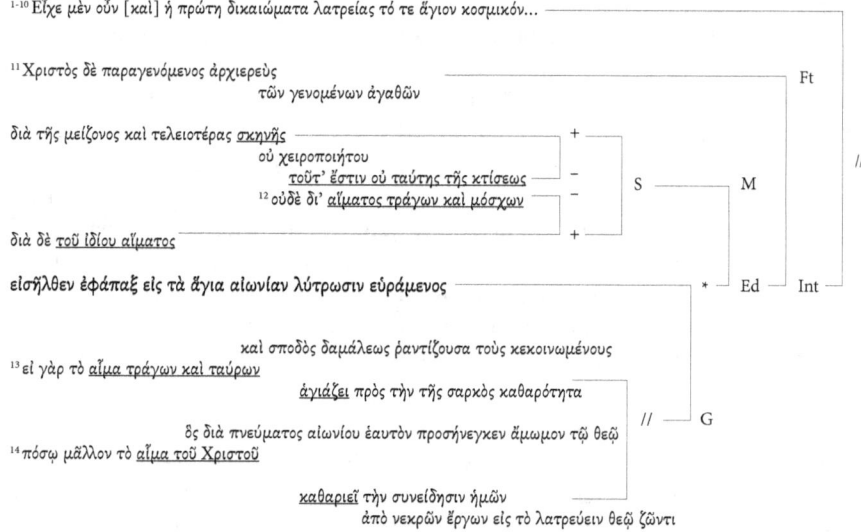

Figure 6.1. Rhetorical Analysis of Hebrews 9:11–14[58]

57. The author uses this rhetorical strategy for other topics throughout the epistle. For example, the content of God's revelation to the fathers and prophets is the same as that which we have received in these last days (shared category), but what we have now is *better* because that revelation is spoken to us by God's Son (Heb. 1:1–2).

58. Terms based on G. K. Beale, Daniel Brendsel, and William A. Ross, *Interpretive Lexicon of New Testament Greek: Analysis of Prepositions, Adverbs, Particles, Relative Pronouns, and Conjunctions* (Grand Rapids, MI: Zondervan, 2014). Note that bold and underlined words indicate the point of comparison in either the positive–negative (+/-) or *a fortiori* (//).

With this antithetical schema in view, the passage can be diagrammed according to a rhetorical analysis (see Figure 6.1). Verses 11–14, taken as a whole, make a contrasting assertion about the heavenly sanctuary against verses 1–10. The syntactical transition is introduced by verse 11a, which (not coincidentally) is introduced by the coming of Christ as high priest. His high priestly advent marks the division between the Old and New Covenants—a time of reformation from the old into the new.[59] That fact is then further interpreted by verses 11b–14. In its interpretation, the antithetical schema is continued by drawing a positive-negative comparison between (1) the greater and perfect tabernacle versus the tabernacle made with hands, and (2) the blood of bulls and goats versus the blood of the high priest. Having accomplished this, Jesus has entered (εἰσῆλθεν, vv. 12 and 24) into the Holy Place obtaining eternal redemption, which syntactically is prominent in this passage (marked by the bold typeface). This is the content of the main clause of the author's argument, further explained by giving the grounds for that clause in verses 13–14. Verses 13–14 similarly makes an *a fortiori* comparison regarding the blood sacrifice of earthly goats and bulls versus the sacrifice of Christ and their effects.

Considering the content of verses 1–10, we must not overlook the physical description of the earthly sanctuary, which also included the outer tabernacle (vv. 1–5). Σκηνή, in its proximate verses, is used to designate the outer tabernacle (9:2, 6, 8) and the inner tabernacle into the Holy of Holies (9:3). If verses 12–14 are a comparison to the sacrificial ritual presented in verses 6–10, it is also likely that the author makes similar comparisons between the physical, spatial descriptions between verses 1–5 and verse 11.[60] If the author simply wanted to communicate that the earthly tabernacle as a whole was insufficient, then one questions why he would have taken the effort to make such detailed descriptions of the outer and inner compartments (vv. 2–3); the lampstand, table, and

---

59. The contrasts in vv. 11–12 are between the "cultic spaces" and "mediums of approach" in the tabernacles from their corresponding epochs (Lane, *Hebrews 9–13*, 237).

60. For v. 6, this coheres with the understanding that priests served in the outer tent while the high priest entered the inner tent once a year. Similarly, Christ does not only enter the outer heavenly tabernacle, but the inner Ἅγια Ἁγίων as well. In v. 8, τῆς πρώτης σκηνῆς serves as a "double entendre" where the physical, outer tabernacle symbolically represents the earthly levitical order (Philip Church, "The Temple in the Apocalypse of Weeks and in Hebrews," *TynBul* 64.1 [2013]: 122). The author of Hebrews affirms this in v. 9: ἥτις παραβολὴ εἰς τὸν καιρὸν τὸν ἐνεστηκότα. This "double entendre" is another way of affirming reference to the tabernacles' temporal and spatial properties rather than having to choose only one (e.g., the divisions being only metaphors for periods of time). Koester makes similar observations stating that the terms "first" and "second" are useful because "they could be used both temporally and spatially" and the author masterfully utilizes both nuances for the sake of his argument (*Dwelling of God*, 158–59; cf. also Ellingworth, "Jesus and the Universe," 344).

sacred bread (v. 2); the golden altar of incense, the ark of the covenant, golden jar, Aaron's rod, and the tables of the covenant (v. 4); and the cherubim overshadowing the mercy seat (v. 5).[61] The specific references to these architectural descriptions similarly presented in Exodus 25–27 are too similar to ignore (see Table 6.1 where examples depicting these parallels are shown). The presence of these detailed descriptions within the antithetical schema then suggests that the author continues with physical and spatial categories as he begins his contrasting rhetoric in verse 11.[62]

Table 6.1 Architectural Descriptions of the Earthly and Heavenly Tabernacles

καὶ θήσεις τὴν τράπεζαν ἔξωθεν τοῦ καταπετάσματος καὶ τὴν λυχνίαν ἀπέναντι τῆς τραπέζης ἐπὶ μέρους τῆς σκηνῆς τὸ πρὸς νότον καὶ τὴν τράπεζαν θήσεις ἐπὶ μέρους τῆς σκηνῆς τὸ πρὸς βορρᾶν (Exod. 26:35 LXX).	σκηνὴ γὰρ κατεσκευάσθη ἡ πρώτη ἐν ᾗ ἥ τε λυχνία καὶ ἡ τράπεζα καὶ ἡ πρόθεσις τῶν ἄρτων,[63] ἥτις λέγεται Ἅγια[64] (Heb. 9:2)
καὶ γνωσθήσομαί σοι ἐκεῖθεν καὶ λαλήσω σοι ἄνωθεν τοῦ ἱλαστηρίου ἀνὰ μέσον τῶν δύο χερουβιμ τῶν ὄντων ἐπὶ τῆς κιβωτοῦ τοῦ μαρτυρίου καὶ κατὰ πάντα, ὅσα ἂν ἐντείλωμαί σοι πρὸς τοὺς υἱοὺς Ισραηλ (Exod. 25:22 LXX).	ὑπεράνω δὲ αὐτῆς Χερουβὶν δόξης κατασκιάζοντα τὸ ἱλαστήριον· περὶ ὧν οὐκ ἔστιν νῦν λέγειν κατὰ μέρος (Heb. 9:5)

61. The author explicitly states that he refrains from discussing the tabernacle's spatial features in more detail (v. 5), from which we can infer that there are additional characteristics he could have described. He does, however, refer back to the topic of tabernacle furnishings in verse 23.

62. "The descriptive terminology in v. 2 indicates the writer envisages the sanctuary in use: entering the tabernacle from the courtyard, the appointed priest enters first the Holy Place and then passes through the separating second curtain into the Most Holy Place" (Lane, *Hebrews*, 219; cf. D'Angelo, *Moses*, 226–27).

63. Codex Vaticanus and Sahidic manuscripts insert the phrase, "and the golden incense altar" (και το χρυσουν θυμιατηριον) most likely due to removing it from 9:4 and placing it here in 9:2. This stems from the traditional understanding that the golden altar was not in the Holy of Holies as stated in 9:4, but rather outside of it in the Holy Place (Philip W. Comfort, *New Testament Text and Translation Commentary: Commentary on the Variant Readings of the Ancient New Testament Manuscripts and How They Relate to the Major English Translations* [Carol Stream, IL: Tyndale House, 2008], 706).

64. Some manuscripts have τὰ ἅγια (B) or ἅγια ἁγίων ($\mathfrak{P}^{46}$, A, D*, vg[mss]) due to an attempt to clarify the anarthrous ἅγια as the Holy Place or the Holy of Holies, respectively. While the Holy of Holies is the more difficult reading with earlier witnesses, it conflicts with v. 3 where the author of Hebrews transitions to the activity in the Holy of Holies (Ἅγια Ἁγίων). The anarthrous Ἅγια may be acting similarly to the anarthrous σκηνή, which similarly denotes a specific (earthly) tabernacle in v. 2a (Ellingworth, *Hebrews*, 423).

A priestly act cannot be separated from the *place* where he performs those acts.[65] A priest's sacrificial offerings are made effectual, in part, by the very fact that he performs them within the confines of the tabernacle, and only afterwards, does he enter the Holy of Holies behind the second veil. The sacrificial system of the Old Testament is partly dependent upon the locative aspect of the earthly sanctuary.[66] Likewise, the heavenly high priest is, in part, tied to his location,[67] which is why the author emphasizes Christ's entry (εἰσῆλθεν, v. 24a).[68] He is the *heavenly* high priest because he has entered and has enacted the ritual service performed in the *heavenly* tabernacle.

This suggests the presence of an actual, spatially realized heavenly tabernacle with architectural arrangements corresponding to those of the earthly. On the other hand, if Christ's high priestly act does not take place in an actual location, then we have difficulty locating the actual, physical, glorified body of Christ. William Lane writes, "The superiority of Christ's cultic action derives from the uniqueness of the sanctuary that he entered and from the uniqueness of the sacrifice that he presented."[69] Therefore, σκηνῆς in verse 11 is a physical, spatially realized heavenly outer tabernacle, which is the greater and more perfect location where Christ enters for the cleansing of believers' consciences from dead works to serve the living God.

6.1.3. On the Character of the Transcendent Heavens

In our investigation, we have defined the heavenly tabernacle's Firstspace features as an actualized, physical structure that is localized in the transcendent heavens.[70] This naturally leads us to question the character of the transcendent heavens themselves. I do not define transcendent as *invisible*, but rather as something that surpasses our limited and normal experience. The contrast is not between transcendence and physicality but between transcendence and immanence/

---

65. "[O]ne could see the true tent in Hebrews as a basically *functional* entity. In other words, the sanctuary and the events within it are not to be separated" (Hurst, "Eschatology and 'Platonism,'" 63; emphasis original). I discuss this concept further in Chapter 8.

66. "In 9:24–25, the parallel with 9:7 becomes explicit: Just as the high priest entered the inner sanctum with blood, which he offered there, so Christ entered the heavenly inner sanctum in order to offer himself there" (Jamieson, *Jesus' Death and Heavenly Offering*, 51).

67. "Hebrews's consistent usage of the term to refer to a *place*; the author repeatedly draws a contrast between the *location* of two types of priestly service, between earthly and heavenly ministries (Heb. 8:5, 9:1–14)" (Keene, "Heaven Is a Tent," 18; emphases original).

68. Note the aorist indicative form to signify a completed action.

69. Lane, *Hebrews 9–13*, 237.

70. There may exist another realm that is distinct from the created earth and the heavenly firmament (Heb. 4:14) which houses the "architecture of the tabernacle." Furthermore, it is a place where "created things" may exist since God has prepared such a realm for his people (David A. deSilva, *Perseverance in Gratitude: A Socio-Rhetorical Commentary on the Epistle "to the Hebrews"* [Grand Rapids, MI: Eerdmans, 2000], 28–29).

attainability.⁷¹ Hence, I suggest using the terms *created/transcendent* rather than *visible/invisible* when distinguishing the two kinds of heavens.⁷² This implies that the transcendent heavens may or may not be invisible, and that a physical and transcendent heaven remains a possibility. While the idea of a physical and transcendent heaven may sound unfamiliar, the concept is not absurd. Jesus, in his glorified resurrection body, retains his physicality, as can be seen in the disciples' ability to visually recognize him and touch him (Jn 20:24–29). He is also able to physically eat a fish (Lk. 24:41–43). At the same time, Jesus is transcendent in his imperishable body (1 Cor. 15:42) and able to walk through closed doors (Jn 20:19).

This physical, glorified Jesus currently resides in the locale of the transcendent heavens. If such is the case, should we not be open to the idea of the physicality of his heavenly environment? If Christ is the *axis mundi* and central figure of the heavenly kingdom,⁷³ and furthermore, if the future consummation of that kingdom does not exclude a physical state, then we should not assume a non-physical intermediate.⁷⁴ Thomas Torrance writes, "As the Incarnation meant the entry of the Son into space and time without the loss of God's transcendence over space and time, so the Ascension meant the transcendence of the Son over space and time without the loss of His incarnation involvement in space and time."⁷⁵

Therefore, at the least, it can be asserted that a wholly other dimension may exist where physicality and transcendence are not mutually exclusive. At the same time, we should not take physicality to mean earthly since the language of that which resides in heaven is described as being greater and made without hands (Heb. 9:11). What may be the case could be outside of our comprehension while retaining characteristics of what we do understand about physicality. On the topic of the Trinity, C. S. Lewis writes a helpful analogy:

> A world of one dimension would be a straight line. In a two-dimensional world, you still get straight lines, but many lines make one figure. In a three-dimensional world, you still get figures but many figures make one solid

---

71. John M. Frame, *The Doctrine of God*, A Theology of Lordship (Phillipsburg, NJ: Presbyterian & Reformed, 2002), 107–14. "The heavenly sanctuary (ἐπουρανίων; 8:5) with heavenly things (τοῖς οὐρανοῖς; τὰ ἐπουράνια; 9:23) and spiritual beings (πνεύματα; 1:14) is not anti-material, but seems to have a kind of materiality that can be revealed and/or perceived by the senses)" (Ribbens, *Levitical Sacrifice*, 129 n. 211).

72. Contra Beale, *Temple and Church's Mission*, 36–37.

73. Jesus' body is the "*axis mundi* where heaven and earth collide" (Schreiner, *The Body of Jesus*, 134; emphasis original).

74. In Jewish apocalyptic literature such as 1 and 2 Enoch, the ontological distinctions between humans and heavenly spirits are maintained. In other words, the ontological distinction of the human body is not erased but rather transformed and glorified (Moffitt, *Atonement*, 179).

75. Thomas F. Torrance, *Space, Time, and Incarnation* (Edinburgh: T&T Clark, 1997), 31.

body. In other words, as you advance to more real and more complicated levels, you do not leave behind you the things you found on the simpler levels: you still have them, but combined in new ways—in ways you could not imagine if you knew only the simpler levels.[76]

Similarly, we may retain what we know about the physicality of the heavenly sanctuary while not claiming exhaustive knowledge of how it exists physically in the transcendent heavens. This understandably raises questions regarding the nature of the physicality of the transcendent heavens. Revelation 21:1–2 speaks of the holy city of Jerusalem coming down out of heaven but does not explain whether it is a preexisting physical structure that is the transcendent heaven itself or merely a part of it.[77] Furthermore, Hebrews' spatial focus is not on the characteristics of heaven itself but on the heavenly tabernacle. In Hebrews 1:11–12 (Ps. 102:26) and 12:27, there is reference to a discontinuity between the present world and the world to come, which suggests the possibility of "new time and space as something altogether different/de novo."[78] However, this does not refer to the *present,* transcendent heavens. Thus, while it is appropriate to argue for the physicality of the heavenly tabernacle, the question of the physicality of the transcendent heaven is an area for further research.

6.2. Secondspace: From the Cross to the Sanctuary

As we now consider Secondspace features, we turn to Christ's interaction with the heavenly tabernacle. The anchoring clause of verses 11–12 is marked by the aorist verb, εἰσῆλθεν. Grammatically, both preceding and following participles modify this verb, which is why some translations supply the phrase "he entered/went."[79] Rhetorically, Christ's high priestly appearance (v. 11a) and the positive/negative comparisons of verses 11b and 12a are the means through which he is able to enter into the holy place. In other words, both Christ's appearance and his functioning as high priest result in his entrance, which takes place with him having obtained eternal redemption (ἐφάπαξ εἰς τὰ ἅγια αἰωνίαν λύτρωσιν εὑράμενος). The high priest now has entered into the Holy of Holies. Although it does not explicitly

---

76. C. S. Lewis, *Mere Christianity* (1952; repr., New York: HarperOne, 2000), 161–62.

77. Some scholars assert that in Jewish thought, the heavenly Jerusalem always existed (Barrett, "Eschatology," 375). Gäbel, in his study of Exod. 15:17, comments that this verse emphasizes the pre-existing nature of God's heavenly dwelling place before the earthly temple (*Kulttheologie*, 31): "Sie betont den gegenüber dem irdischen Tempel präexistenten Charakter der himmlischen göttlichen Wohnstatt."

78. Moffitt, *Atonement*, 81 n. 83. Asserting the physicality of the tabernacle also attributes a temporality to it as well: "The temporal aspects of the heavenly sanctuary [i.e., Jesus' approach and entrance, liturgical activity] are demonstrated by the events, actions, and changes in the heavenly realm" (Ribbens, *Levitical Sacrifice*, 129 n. 211).

79. NASB, NLT, and NRSV.

say Ἅγια Ἁγίων as in verse 3,[80] the articular usage of τὰ ἅγια draws us back to this designation, especially given the distinction between the high priest's activity outside of the inner sanctuary and his entrance that follows. While τὰ ἅγια can have a general connotation, simply as "sanctuary," it is likely that "a more specific location within the Sanctuary is in view."[81]

Secondspace features become prominent in Hebrews 9:1–14 in light of Christ's physical entrance into the standing heavenly tabernacle. That is, Christ's entrance into the heavenly tabernacle accentuates the self-offering of his blood, which was secured in his death on the cross. This, in turn, purifies the tabernacle from the contamination of sin introduced by God's people, which in turn enables believers to spiritually enter into that tabernacle space now and to enter later physically in eschatological consummation.

The completion of Christ's heavenly itinerary is not primarily about his return to the heavenly throne (i.e., from heaven, to earth, back to heaven). The intent is ultimately to redeem God's people so that they, too, can dwell within God's midst.[82] Furthermore, this dwelling in God's midst is not a return to Old Testament instances of God coming down to earth to dwell with his people temporarily; rather, it is God's people going up to heaven to dwell with him eternally. The problem, however, lies in the contamination of the sanctuary introduced from the sins of the people (v. 23).[83] Entrance is barred until Christ performs and

---

80. In 9:2, the author designates the innermost sanctuary as such because he had already designated the tabernacle as the Holy Place. In v. 12, no such designation is necessary because the articular referent has already been established as the place that the high priest enters in as a result of his priestly activity which took place outside the Holy of Holies.

81. Keene, *Heaven Is a Tent*, 22, who admits that while the author is likely referring to the Holy of Holies or, at the very least, a separate compartment within the sanctuary, the generic translation, "the sanctuary," is still adequate; cf also. Richard M. Davidson, "Christ's Entry 'within the Veil' in Hebrews 6:19-20: The Old Testament Background," *AUSS* 39.2 (2001): 180–81; Schenck, *Cosmology and Eschatology*, 146–47. This is often argued because τὰ ἅγια in the LXX and other Greek literature of Judaism refers to the whole or general sanctuary. Peterson writes, "Although there appears to be an identification of τὰ ἅγια [in 9:12c] and τῆς σκηνῆς [τῆς] ἀληθινῆς in 8:2, it does violence to the syntax of 9:11f to suggest that the greater and more perfect tent and τὰ ἅγια are one and the same thing here" (*Hebrews and Perfection*, 141).

82. Eskola argues that Christ's exaltation is ultimately a cultic act because the place of his throne (cf. Ps. 110) is the mercy seat in the heavenly Holy of Holies. "Therefore it becomes a place for atonement in the manner of the original mercy seat in the Jerusalem Temple" (Eskola, *Messiah and the Throne*, 269).

83. There is debate around the meaning of v. 23 regarding the "cleansing of the heavenly things" (καθαρίζεσθαι...τὰ ἐπουράνια). For a survey of interpretive options and further discussion, see David MacLeod, "The Cleansing of the True Tabernacle," 152.605 (1995): 60–71; Gäbel, *Kulttheologie*, 569–87; William G. Johnsson, *Defilement and Purgation in the Book of Hebrews*, SJCL (Dallas, TX: Fontes Press, 2020). It is suggested that Nadab and

completes a once-for-all atonement on their behalf. Hence, one of the important features of Christ's entry is the cleansing and purification he brings to the Holy of Holies "just as the earthly priest cleansed the earthly tabernacle when he entered its inner sanctum."[84] Salvation in Hebrews is presented not only as received, but as a "distinctly *local* concept."[85]

Christ's spatial entrance then allows for the self-offering of his blood for the atonement for his people.[86] There has been recent scholarly discussion around the timing and location of the atonement, which was sparked by David Moffitt's revised doctoral dissertation, *Atonement and the Logic of Resurrection in the Epistle to the Hebrews* (2013).[87] In spite of Hebrews not having any explicit references to Christ's resurrection, Moffitt argues that the resurrection is crucial to the author of Hebrews' argument.[88] The presentation of Jesus' indestructible life in his "perfected, glorified humanity" is "the event that results in purification and opens the way for other human beings to enter fully into God's presence."[89] In

---

Abihu's offense consisted of their prohibited entrance or, specifically, the corpse pollution caused by their deaths (Morales, *Who Shall Ascend?*, 147 and 163). The need for cleansing is related to the contamination that sinners bring into the sanctuary (Jamieson, "Hebrews 9.23," 577). Hence, the author mentions how Moses sprinkled the blood on the book, all the people (v. 19), the tabernacle and all of its vessels (v. 21), which altogether entails "cult inauguration," that is, enacting by blood purification (ibid., 576–77).

84. Jamieson, "Hebrews 9.23," 578.

85. Laansma, "Cosmology of Hebrews," 131; emphasis original.

86. While the vertical movement of Christ's ascension can find parallels in the OT and intertestamental literature, Hebrews is unique in developing a spatial language that is horizontal and typological. Both spatial language is present in Hebrews (Ellingworth, "Jesus and Universe," 349).

87. Moffitt, *Atonement*. I list works engaging with Moffitt's work below although the "atonement question of Hebrews" has been debated ever since the Socinian controversy of 1578 (Ribbens, "Ascension and Atonement," 2 n. 3): George H. Guthrie, "Time and Atonement in Hebrews," in Laansma, Guthrie, and Westfall, eds, *So Great a Salvation*, 209–27; Jamieson, "When and Where Did Jesus Offer Himself?," 38–68; Kibbe, "Is It Finished?," 25–61; Nicholas J. Moore, "Sacrifice, Session and Intercession: The End of Christ's Offering in Hebrews," *JSNT* 42.4 (2020): 521–41 along with David Moffitt's response, "Jesus as Interceding High Priest and Sacrifice in Hebrews: A Response to Nicholas Moore," *JSNT* 42.4 (2020): 542–52; Jean-René Moret, "Le rôle du concept de purification dans l'Épître aux Hébreux: une réaction à quelques propositions de David M. Moffitt," *NTS* 62.2 (2016): 289–307; Westfall, "Space and Atonement," 228–48. Jamieson's taxonomy of scholarship on the timing and location of the atonement is also helpful (Jamieson, "When and Where Did Jesus Offer Himself?," 4–15). A bibliography of less recent works can be found in Ribbens' article, "Ascension and Atonement," 2 nn. 3, 5.

88. However, it is implied when speaking of Christ's ascension (cf. Heb. 1:3–5, 13; 2:9; 4:14) or as Spicq notes, "the eternal permanence of the perfect humanity" in Christ (Spicq, *L'Épître aux Hébreux*, 1:95): "la permanence éternelle de la parfaite humanité."

89. Moffitt, *Atonement*, 2.

other words, it is Christ's resurrection that qualifies him to be the heavenly high priest,[90] which in turn places the atonement, or at least its completion, not at the cross but in heaven.[91]

R. B. Jamieson adds a corrective to Moffitt's thesis by reinforcing the importance of Christ's death on the cross by arguing that what Jesus' death achieved is in fact what he gives to God in heaven. What Jesus offers God in heaven is the life he gave in death.[92] Therefore, it is Christ's blood that provides a "means of access to the Holy of Holies and material that is offered."[93] However, I contend that this does not mean that Christ's high priestly ministry is active only during his presence in the heavenlies.[94] To do so narrowly ties Christ's high priestly status and role to only when he performs his priestly activities in the heavenly tabernacle. Jesus' high priestly ministry cannot be reduced to either *only* the earthly act of

90. Ibid., 43.

91. I am not affirming the Socinian view, which denies any kind of efficacy for atonement in Christ's death and attributes such efficacy *only* to Christ's priesthood in heaven. The error here is not necessarily one concerning the importance of Christ's heavenly entry and ritual but is rather due to its "severing the death from the priesthood." As Geerhardus Vos aptly writes, "The principle to be strenuously maintained is that the priestly activity of Christ in heaven rests on the preceding sacrifice and therefore derives from the latter a strictly propitiatory character" ("The Priesthood of Christ in the Epistle to the Hebrews," in *Redemptive History and Biblical Interpretation: The Shorter Writings of Geerhardus Vos*, ed. Richard B. Gaffin Jr. [Phillipsburg, NJ: Presbyterian & Reformed, 2001], 154). Moffitt and especially Jamieson attempt to strengthen the connection between Christ's death and his ascension/heavenly entrance, which Ribbens refers to as the "sequential view." Ribbens argues that the sequential view should not be mistaken with the Socinian error of separating "Christ's death from the sacrifice offering and the sacrificial efficacies" (Ribbens, "Ascension and Atonement," 18).

92. Jamieson, *Jesus' Death and Heavenly Offering*, 14–20. Jamieson calls Christ's blood the "material content of his heavenly offering" which is a metonym for his death (ibid., 62–63, 128–33). Gäbel states similarly that Christ's self-sacrifice is the "Inhalt seines himmlischen Opfers" but also includes "Christi auf Erden gelebtes Leben sowie seine nicht-opferkultische Hingabe bis zum Tod" (*Kulttheologie*, 473). The inclusion of Christ's obedient life on earth is essential to the qualitative nature of Christ's self-sacrifice.

93. Ibid., 160. This notion, which Gäbel deems "extraordinary," has been present since his commentary on the cult theology of Hebrews: "Ganz außergewöhnlich ist schließlich die Deutung des Eintritts ins Allerheiligste mit Blut im Sinne einer Darbringung von opfermaterie in Hebr 9, 7" (*Kulttheologie*, 277).

94. The question on the timing of Christ's priesthood is a debated issue. While the author of Hebrews describes Christ's high priesthood having culminated in his entrance into the heavenly sanctuary, he also identifies Christ as such prior to his entrance. For example, Spicq notes places such as Heb. 6:20 where the aorist participle (ἀρχιερεὺς γενόμενος) "evokes the incarnation and the sacrifice of the cross," as part of his priestly activity (Spicq, *L'Épître aux Hébreux*, 2:165): "évoque l'incarnation et le sacrifice de la Croix".

sacrifice or *only* his heavenly self-offering.⁹⁵ Jean-René Moret, in his discussion on the meaning of blood and purification in Hebrews, argues against a simplistic view that equates blood to either death or life. Christ's blood indeed represents death; however, "death has value as it is the gift of life."⁹⁶ To put it another way, "the gift of life implies the death of its owner."⁹⁷

This ultimately sheds light on the tabernacle's Secondspace features by connecting Christ's heavenly entrance with the tabernacle's cultic activity. Hebrews 9:12 clarifies the meaning (*Bedeutung geklärt*) of eternal redemption by affirming that "because and by entering into the heavenly Most Holy; he did this by virtue of His own blood and with it."⁹⁸ Therefore, from the perspective of Hebrews, we cannot sever the content of Christ's offering (blood) from the cultic ritual of entering into the Most Holy Place and offering it for the redemption for his people.⁹⁹ This Secondspace spatial perspective is made possible only when we ground Christ's entrance and the securing of eternal redemption in tabernacle Firstspace.

Οὐδὲ δι' αἵματος τράγων καὶ μόσχων διὰ δὲ τοῦ ἰδίου αἵματος (v. 12) continues the negative/positive comparison that was introduced with the comparisons of the tabernacles (σκηνῆς) in verse 11. If we maintain that σκηνῆς is the outer tabernacle in the manner of Exodus 26:33, the transition to the topic of blood sacrifice is expected.¹⁰⁰ It is in the outer curtain where the levitical priests carried out their ministry, including the sacrificial offering of bulls and goats. The question then arises: What kind of comparison is the author of Hebrews making regarding the sacrificial offerings? He makes it explicit: the qualitative substance of the blood is completely different. It is *not* the blood of goats and calves but the high priest's own blood. The author is not making any distinction between the relative placement of where the sacrifice takes place. Both happen in the outer tabernacles, albeit one earthly and one heavenly. Therefore, Christ completes his self-sacrifice

---

95. In Heb. 5:5, Christ's identification and appointment as high priest begins with his "begottenness" (γεγέννηκά), and immediately after in v. 7, include the days of his flesh where he offered up "prayers and supplications" (δεήσεις τε καὶ ἱκετηρίας).

96. Moret, "Le rôle du concept de purification dans l'Épître aux Hébreux," 299: "La mort a une valeur en tant que don d'une vie."

97. Ibid.: "Le don de la vie implique la mort de son propriétaire." He also refers to Luke Timothy Johnson's statement: "The shedding or effusion of blood is ritual synecdoche for the offering of one's life" (Johnson, *Hebrews*, 237).

98. "Weil und indem er in das himmlische Allerheiligste eintrat; er tat das kraft seines eigenen Blutes und mit diesem" (Gäbel, *Kulttheologie*, 288).

99. "The consummation of God's saving purposes is depicted as entry into the holy of holies, the most sacred part of Israel's sanctuaries, where God was understood to be especially present" (Craig R. Koester, "God's Purposes and Christ's Saving Work According to Hebrews," in Mackie, ed., *The Letter to the Hebrews*, 445).

100. "Not only is there a correspondence between heaven and earth in terms of the cultic location (sanctuary), there is also correspondence between heaven and earth in terms of cultic activity" (Ribbens, *Levitical Sacrifice*, 130).

outside of the holy space spatially (i.e., on the cross), and *before* his entrance into the heavenly sanctuary temporally.[101] If the corresponding earth/heaven analogy is compromised, there is the danger of thinking that Christ's self-sacrifice was not complete prior to his entrance into the Holy of Holies and that his atoning work requires repetition or is not completed once for all. The genius of the author's argumentation is the utilization of the Yom Kippur framework to present a high priestly Christology and the theology of heavenly cult which surpasses that of the levitical order in efficacy. As Gäbel writes:

> Die kulttheologische Deuteung der Erhöhung Christi ist bestimmt durch die Jom Kippur-Typologie: Die Erhöhung Christi ist sein Eintritt ins himmlische Allerheiligste, seine hohpriesterliche Investitur und so auch die Darbringung seines Selbstopfers. Dieses bewirkt die Annullierung der Sünden. Deren Wirkung erstreckt sich auf alle Zeit von Grundlegung der Welt bis zur Parusie. So bleiben Gegenwart und Zukunft durch das zurückliegende Ereignis der Ehöhung Christi bestimmt. Auch das findet seinen Ausdruck im Rahmen der Jom Kippur-Typologie: Die Gegenwart entspricht der Zeit, während Derer der Hohepriester am Jom Kippur nach vollzogenem Sühnakt im Heiligtum Fürbitte hält; die Parusie wird dem Hervortreten des Hohenpriesters aus dem Heiligtum entrsprechen. Die Hohepriesterchristologie des Hebr erschließt durch die kulttheologische Deuteung der Erhöhung deren unüberbietbare soteriologische Bedeutsamkeit.[102]

The one corrective to Gäbel's statement is that soteriological significance does not begin with Christ's entrance into the Holy Place; rather, it begins with the altar of sacrifice. The altar that corresponds to Christ's entrance into the Holy of Holies is none other than the cross on earth, where Christ's self-sacrifice was finalized and culminated.[103]

---

101. Hughes notes that the analogy must be kept intact with the earthly ritual. The altar for the high priests took place *before* the entrance into the Holy of Holies (*Hebrews*, 337).

102. "The theological interpretation of the heavenly cult is determined by the Yom Kippur typology: Christ's exaltation consists of his entry into the heavenly Holy of Holies, his appointment as the heavenly High Priest, and thus, his self-sacrificial offering. This brings about the forgiveness of sins, which is applied from the foundation of the world until the Parousia. Therefore, both the present and the future are determined by the event of Christ's past exaltation. This also finds its expression within the framework of the Yom Kippur typology: The present corresponds to the time when the high priest interceded in the sanctuary on Yom Kippur after the completion of the act of atonement; the Parousia corresponds to the appearance of the high priest from the sanctuary. Through the theological interpretation of the heavenly cult, the matchless soteriological significance of the high priestly Christology of Hebrews is revealed" (Gäbel, *Kulttheologie*, 319).

103. The relation between an earthly and heavenly cultic activity is not a novel one. While heavenly temple liturgy is prevalent in Jewish writings, the sacrifice and offering of blood is new (Eskola, *Messiah and the Throne*, 251 and 266). However, T. Levi 3:5–6 makes

The question then arises, how can the actual event of Jesus' death on the cross correspond to the heavenly altar that exists in the outer tabernacle?[104] Here the distinction is not a merely a correspondence between the material (cross) and immaterial (outer tabernacle), since the argument presented thus far regards the heavenly tabernacle as both spatial and spiritual. Can the altar of the cross be spatially at two places at once—one on earth and one in the heavenly, outer tabernacle? While a metaphysical explanation lies within the realm of speculation, an understanding of the *referential* correspondence between the cross and the outer tabernacle is helpful. Geerhardus Vos writes, "This brings the act out of the sphere of abstractions into the realm of the concrete, and so the question is not, '*Where did Christ die?*,' but rather, '*Where was the sanctuary which was held in view in His*

---

mention of archangels making "propitiatory sacrifices to the Lord on behalf of all the sins of ignorance of the righteous ones" by presenting a "pleasing odor, a rational and bloodless oblation." There was, in the Old Covenant, legitimacy of the earthly, levitical cultic system precisely because it was modeled after the heavenly one. Hence, the rituals that were performed in the earthly tabernacle were efficacious based on the heavenly—namely, the proleptic priestly ministry of Christ (Ribbens, *Levitical Sacrifice*, 82–148). The cross then is the "antitypical altar" in the court of the heavenly sanctuary (Davidson, *Typology in Scripture*, 354 n. 1).

104. Kenneth Schenck believes the author of Hebrews uses metaphors to describe Christ's death and ascension by giving them a "new semantic pertinence by means of an impertinent attribution" (*Cosmology and Eschatology*, 92; cf. also Church, *Hebrews and Temple*, 435). Elsewhere, Schenck asserts that true atonement takes place in a heavenly, yet "abstract" space. Whatever literal referent there is to the heavenly tabernacle, it is heaven itself ("An Archaeology of Hebrews' Tabernacle Imagery", 239). However, this view is too simplistic and assumes a 'substitutionary view' of metaphors (i.e., a one-to-one correlation between metaphor and its referent). For more on the substitutionary view of metaphors, see Max Black, *Models and Metaphors: Studies in Language and Philosophy* (Ithaca, NY: Cornell University Press, 1981), 29–38 and "More About Metaphor," in *Metaphor and Thought*, ed. Andrew Ortony, 2nd ed. (New York: Cambridge University Press, 1993), 22.

In such cases, the metaphor is an alien (*allotrios*) use of a term that deviates from its original usage, which brings in the notion of the idea of substitution (cf. Aristotle's definition in *Poetics*, LCL 199 [Cambridge, MA: Harvard University Press, 1995], 21.105). "The metaphorical word takes the place of a non-metaphorical word that one could have used (on condition that it exists); so it is doubly alien, as a present but borrowed word and as substitute for an absent word" (Paul Ricœur, *The Rule of Metaphor: Multi-Disciplinary Studies of the Creation of Meaning in Language*, UTRS 37 [Toronto: University of Toronto Press, 1977], 18–19). However, the heavenly tabernacle is far from an alien usage; rather, the heavenly and earthly tabernacles are in close correspondence, as we have seen in Heb. 8:5. Given the author of Hebrews' extended comparison between the heavenly and levitical cults, and the detailed implications of Christ's heavenly sanctuary entrance, it is more appropriate to see them as analogical correspondents (cf. earlier Section 5.1.3). For further arguments, see Stegemann and Stegemann, "Cultic Language in Hebrews," 18–23.

death?"[105] This entails a ritual reference, which he deems as "ritual geography," to his death that places the *center* of his priesthood—hence, the sanctuary—in heaven. Vos draws these conclusions from Hebrews 8:4, where the author clearly writes that if Christ was on earth, he would not be a priest at all.[106] Vos concludes by stating, "The author in this verse by no means states or implies that Christ could not *act* as a priest on earth, but only that He could not really *be* a priest on earth."[107]

Therefore, in strict earthly geographical terms, the self-sacrifice of Christ took place on the altar of the cross. However, its ritual reference took place in the heavenly outer tabernacle where the ritual effects of that sacrifice went into effect. There is a corresponding analogy with the levitical priests and the Yom Kippur typology of the Old Testament.[108] The priestly act of the high priest took place locally in the Holy of Holies. Vos summarizes in the follow statement:

> This corresponds exactly with Christ's priestly act, which He performed outside the sanctuary, that is, outside of heaven, on Calvary. This one act does not lower the priesthood nor does it in any way imply that the true [geographical] location of that priesthood is the heavenly sanctuary. Again, as the Old Testament act was performed with reference to the Holy of Holies, so Christ's act on Calvary had its ideal reference to the sanctuary in heaven.[109]

---

105. Vos, *Teaching of Hebrews*, 113; emphasis original.

106. "For Hebrews, Jesus is really a high priest, who really offers a sacrifice, in a real sanctuary. The differences derive from the uniqueness of Christ's self-offering, not from metaphorical deployment of Levitical categories to describe the cross" (Jamieson, *Jesus' Death and Heavenly Offering*, 93).

107. Vos, *Teaching of Hebrews*, 113; emphases original.

108. "The Yom Kippur typology is consistently carried out. The description of the earthly event is, unlike the description found in Lev. 16, presented with its heavenly equivalent in view. The details need not be repeated. The emphasis is entirely on the entrance into the Holy of Holies, which Hebrews presents as an offering and thus, the completion of Christ's heavenly sacrifice" (Gäbel, *Kulttheologie*, 292): "Die Jom Kippur-Typologie ist konsistent durchgeführt. Schon die Schilderung des irdischen Geschehens ist, anders als die Schilderung in Lev. 16, auf dessen himmlische Entsprechung hin entworfen. Die Einzelheiten brauchen nicht wiederholt zu werden. Das Gewicht liegt ganz auf dem Eintritt ins Allerheiligste, den Hebr als Darbringung, damit als Vollzug des himmlischen opfers Christi, versteht."

When the levitical high priests entered into the inner sanctuary on Yom Kippur, on that day "the High Priest enters the 'other world,' into the very presence of God. He must therefore dress as befits the occasion" (Gordon J. Wenham, *The Book of Leviticus*, NICOT [Grand Rapids, MI: Eerdmans, 1979], 230).

109. Vos, *The Teaching to the Hebrews*, 113.

6.3. Summary

So far in Chapters 4–6, I set out to examine the Firstspace and Secondspace features of the heavenly tabernacle. First, I considered the historical, literary, and structural context of key passages where the heavenly tabernacle is mentioned. The audience of Hebrews was familiar with the Old Testament cultus and the levitical order. The author of Hebrews, likewise, was aware of this common milieu and utilized his audience's understanding of the earthly tabernacle to present Christ's high priestly ministry that takes place in a far greater and better tabernacle in the heavens.

As such, the earthly tabernacle was a visible and physical manifestation of inaccessibility. The Old Testament tabernacle presented two realities regarding believers' ability to dwell with God. In physical form, it communicated strongly the inability for sinful Israel to access God's presence. The compounding instructions and regulations for the levitical priesthood and the prohibition warnings to the rest of the Israelite community communicated this inaccessibility. Yet at the same time, the tabernacle served as the very means through which Israel could, in fact, commune with God. It was accessible—albeit in a limited sense—by God's initiating act of drawing near to his people. By virtue of the mediating sacrifice performed by the high priest, the Israelites—in shadowy and proleptic fashion—received atonement for their sins and their relationship with Yahweh was restored. The limitations of this access were both spatial and temporal. The inner courts were accessible only to appointed priests during dedicated times and seasons. Nevertheless, as Hebrews makes clear, this system was temporary and inadequate to maintain continual access to the heavenly throne.

Acknowledging this backdrop, the author of Hebrews then presents Christ as the one who provides access as the heavenly high priest according to the order of Melchizedek. In his resurrection and exaltation, Christ paves the way by crossing the chasm that is physically insurmountable to God's people (Heb. 4:14). In his heavenly ascent, Jesus passes through the created, heavenly firmament which itself served as the gateway to God's transcendent dwelling. That Jesus crossed the physical chasm of heaven (Firstspace) not only means that the path has been cleared, but the path has been cleared for his people (Secondspace). Hence the author of Hebrews can confidently exhort believers to draw near to God because Christ, the forerunner, has gone before them to provide direct and continual access with God. The heavenly ascent is made possible for believers.

Next, I investigated Hebrews 8:5 and its use of Exodus 25:40 to depict the archetypal pattern (τὸν τύπον/תַּבְנִית) for the earthly tabernacle. This pattern is none other than the actual heavenly tabernacle itself. This was concluded based on the numerous accounts in Jewish apocalyptic and other intertestamental literature of heavenly ascents and their encounters with a standing, physical tabernacle/temple in the transcendent heavens. I particularly noted the use of spatial language to describe both the journey itself and the tabernacle structure. Therefore, what God had shown Moses was not merely a metaphorical pattern or the *idea* of a typical structure; rather, it was an "analogue,"[110] where the heavenly structure was both the pattern and the source of the earthly structure (Firstspace). That God initiates this revelation of the heavenly tabernacle to his people by way of Moses' mediatory role means that such a place exists. Furthermore, such a place exists *for believers*, so that they may center their identities and their spatial standing with Christ in direct presence with the Lord (Secondspace).

Finally, I examined the relationship between the spatiality of the heavenly tabernacle with Christ's entrance into that space. Patrick Schreiner's comment on the spatial features of Jesus' body in the Gospel of Matthew rings true also for the Jesus' bodily entrance and presence in the heavenly tabernacle: "The Christian religion is not the religion of salvation *from* places, it is the religion of salvation *in* and *through* places."[111] Christ's entrance through the outer courts and into the Holy of Holies (Firstspace) signified the heavenly ritual of atonement in response to the contamination due to believers' sins (Secondspace). This was affirmed by the comparison which the author of Hebrews makes between the levitical ritual of atonement and the far greater, better atonement secured in a far greater tabernacle. The journey from the cross to the inner sanctuary completes Jesus' heavenly itinerary, which in turn enables believers to stand with him now spiritually and later physically in the eschatological consummation. Until that day, believers are encouraged to draw near and realize their spatial identity as priests living in the already/not-yet eschatological age. They are already present with Christ through their spiritual union with him (Chapter 7), and yet are exhorted to serve as priests through their ethical and communal living for the sake of those observing their lives (Chapter 8).

How do the preceding findings encourage us to understand the heavenly tabernacle? (1) First, reference to the heavenly tabernacle is a pedagogical device used by the author of Hebrews to communicate the qualitative difference between Christ's high priestly ministry and the levitical cult.[112] This pedagogy is based on a structure that actually exists both locally and materially in the transcendent heavens. (2) Second, the heavenly tabernacle is the final destination in Christ's itinerary, which originated with his incarnation (2:9) and continued in his heavenly ascent (4:14) and his traveling through the tabernacle outer courts to arrive at the Holy of Holies (9:11). Just as it is important to affirm the physicality and the locale of Christ's incarnation, ministry, and death, we must likewise affirm these features in his ascent and heavenly session. (3) Third, the heavenly tabernacle is not only the place where the redemptive act of Christ's death culminates and is secured for believers, but it is a place of *their* dwelling in the presence of God. This began with God's revelatory initiative in showing Moses and the people of God the *pattern* of his heavenly dwelling and culminates with that very space being made accessible to those who are united with Christ.

---

110. As discussed in Section 5.1.3.
111. Schreiner, *The Body of Jesus*, 88; emphases original.
112. See also Ribbens, *Levitical Sacrifice*, 139–40; She, *Use of Exodus in Hebrews*, 134.

If such is the case, the heavenly tabernacle is used to convey the eschatological situation of believers. It is a prime example of how they can live in the overlap of two ages—not only temporally, but positionally as well. Temporally speaking, until the consummation of the ages, believers presently live in an age when redemption is accomplished and secured. Yet, the vestiges of sin remain. Positionally, they are in two places at once. Spiritually, they reside with Christ and are seated with him in the heavenly places (Heb. 10:19–22; cf. Eph. 2:6), while they physically live out the implications of their newly obtained spiritual identity as cohabitors with Jesus. The heavenly tabernacle therefore conveys an eschatology that is both spatial and temporal. Furthermore, it serves as "the *ontological* ground to construct the temporal-heavenly and spatial-heavenly dimensions of *Auctor's* metanarrative."[113] The heavenly tabernacle is able to exhibit both the discontinuity and continuity of the Old and New Covenants. It operates on the assumptions of what the levitical order could and could not do. It then becomes the device through which believers can comprehend the magnitude of Christ's redemptive work in crossing the chasm between God and sinners and allowing them present and spatial access to God. This indicates that the "Heavenly Sanctuary must be viewed as a typical piece of NT inaugurated eschatology"[114] by signifying that what is future is now, and what is future is already present in heaven.[115]

Scholars have noted that these two eschatological dimensions (spatial and temporal) have been difficult to reconcile.[116] From the observations made thus far in these previous chapters, a way forward is possible when we begin to consider the sense in which we examine the tabernacle's spatial and temporal properties. A simplistic conflation of these two properties will create more difficulties. But when we see how the tabernacle's spatiality is both present and future and examine how it is so in each respect, we can begin to envision believers' relationship with the spatial tabernacle in the present and in the future.

---

113. She, *Use of Exodus in Hebrews*, 133–34; emphases original.

114. Mackie, *Eschatology and Exhortation*, 157.

115. Andrew T. Lincoln, "Sabbath, Rest, and Eschatology in the New Testament," in Mackie, ed., *The Letter to the Hebrews*, 177.

116. Koester, *Dwelling of God*, 153.

PART III
THIRDSPACE

Chapter 7

BELIEVERS' SPATIAL AWARENESS

We all occupy space; it is an unavoidable phenomenon that we participate in every moment of our lives. Oftentimes, we are unaware of how space affects us and, in turn, how we affect the space around us. Consider religious adherents who visit holy sites and the sense of awe they have as they approach such places. When they are spatially oriented toward a particular site, their behavior and attitude changes. The site becomes more than a standing structure occupying a piece of land. They perceive its historical and religious importance. They consider all the other followers who visited before them. They are being transformed and, if they allow it, they go on to transform the spaces around them in their journey home. This depends on how one perceives space.

The benefit of Edward Soja's spatial trialectics is the interpretive grid that allows us to examine an object's spatial features from different vantage points. A one-dimensional approach to a structure's spatial features accentuates some features, but it disregards others. In other words, a structure's physical or Cartesian properties cannot account for all the spatial features that make it unique. Such a view results in a simplistic approach to one's interaction with space.

For example, when someone physically enters a certain space, it can be said that they occupy that space. However, there is still the question of their engagement with that space. They may physically be in that location while their thoughts and emotions be "somewhere else." Spatial trialectics allows us to think of space in a much more nuanced manner that involves the physical, emotional, spiritual, and phenomenal implications of being in space. How does space impact all these areas in a person's life?

This spatial question allows us to look at Hebrews eschatology from different vantage points, including its vertical and horizontal dimensions[1] that involve spatial and temporal implications in believers' salvation. This chapter will examine the nature of believers' entrance into the heavenly tabernacle and how we can

---

1. Again, by vertical I mean the provisionally realized standing structure in the heavenly tabernacle. The horizontal dimension is concerned with how the tabernacle impacts believers now and in the future.

think about their occupancy in two places at once (heaven and earth). Then we will consider how believers themselves look toward two directions during their time on earth: (1) above to heavenly space, and (2) forward to its eschatological consummation. In sum, the interplay of their First-, Second-, and Thirdspace provides a heuristic for giving full consideration to both the vertical and horizontal dimensions of eschatology.

7.1. Complete Access and Full Entry

The extent of believers' entry and access into the heavenly tabernacle is debated among scholars.[2] Much of the discussion is centered around the terms, προσέρχομαι (to draw near) and εἰσέρχομαι (to enter).[3] A pivotal work that investigates these words' usage in the Old Testament (including the LXX) and Hebrews is John Scholer's *Proleptic Priests* (1991).[4] Scholer argues that εἰσέρχομαι in Hebrews "expresses the access available to believers, although it primarily describes an access afforded to those who have died and who now reside in the presence of God (e.g., 12.22–24)."[5] On the other hand προσέρχομαι "refers to a preliminary access into the holy of holies, into the direct presence of God through inner spiritual service such as worship and prayer, to be superseded by a still future and greater access."[6] Προσέρχομαι is reserved for living believers while εἰσέρχομαι speaks of Jesus and believers who have died.[7] If such is the case, living believers have obtained only preliminary or proleptic access (προσέρχομαι) in the present, while they look forward to full entry and access (εἰσέρχομαι) at either their deaths or Christ's second coming.

Scholer's sharp distinction of believers' access in this life with that in the life to come arises from his observation of the heavy parallels made with the ascent accounts in Jewish apocalyptic literature where heavenly access was prohibited or limited. For example, "bodiless and spiritual ascents stop short of entry into

---

2. Moore, "'In' or 'Near,'" 187. In addition to believers' spatial entrance in the heavenly tabernacle, scholars have wrestled with believers' perfection and the attainment of eschatological rest (cf. Peterson, *Hebrews and Perfection*, 1–20 for a historical survey).

3. Mackie, "Let Us Draw Near," 19. I will discuss all instances of these occurrences in Hebrews in Chapter 8.

4. John M. Scholer, *Proleptic Priests: Priesthood in the Epistle to the Hebrews*, JSOTSup 49 (Sheffield: JSOT Press, 1991).

5. Ibid., 11.

6. Ibid. Along with Scholer, others also argue that the author of Hebrews "maintains a careful and deliberate distinction between these terms" (Mackie, "Let Us Draw Near," 19). Cf. Isaacs, *Sacred Space*, 219; David A. deSilva, "Entering God's Rest: Eschatology and the Socio-Rhetorical Strategy of Hebrews," *TrinJ* 21.1 (2000): 28–29; *Perseverance in Gratitude*, 337; Moore, "'In' or 'Near,'" 187–90.

7. Such a view states that εἰσέρχομαι is used primarily for Jesus' entrance (6:20; 9:12, 24, 25) while believers' entry remains in the future (4:1, 3, 4, 9).

the highest heaven, most holy place, or throne room."[8] This limited access that was true for the levitical cult in the earthly tabernacle continued to be prominent concerning access into the heavenly cult in Second Temple and early Jewish traditions.[9] In response to Scholer, I agree that the apocalyptic genre lies in the backdrop of the audience's and the author's minds. However, Hebrews also presents Christ's high priestly ministry as inaugurating soteriological benefits that have never been available before. Hence, we must note the similarities *and* differences.[10] Scott Mackie's statement reflects such nuance: "The author's conception and construction of 'sacred space' has not only been shaped by the prevalent Jewish cult as well as regnal depictions of heaven (Isa. 6; 1 Kgs. 22:19), but it also seeks to transform those traditions christologically."[11]

While retaining this notion of prohibited access from Jewish apocalyptic literature, the author of Hebrews presents a high priestly Christology in Jesus' bodily resurrection. This resurrection entails "glorification or transformation," which allows full access for himself and for his people.[12] In fact, in Jewish apocalyptic ascents, there are accounts that suggest how such an entrance could be made possible. In both of their accounts, Moses and Enoch were wrapped in glory in their ascension. "Mortal human bodies do not belong in heaven. Thus, when Enoch's body goes up to heaven, something has to happen to it for him to be fit to remain in those realms."[13] Such instances suggest the concept of bodily transformation (glorification) in order to obtain access into God's innermost dwelling place (i.e., Jesus' resurrection and ascension).

In sum, Hebrews shares a symbolic world with Jewish apocalyptic; however, these symbols have been "adopted in the service of Christology."[14] It is this latter fact that elevates Hebrews above the ascent traditions of apocalyptic literature. Up through Hebrews 9, the author of Hebrews develops a rich Christology on various facets of Christ's character: (1) his divine superiority over the angels (1:4; 2:5–9), (2) his unique sonship to the Father (1:5–13; 5:5); (3) his eternal priesthood (5:6–10; 7:15–28; 8:1–6); and (4) the efficacy of his priestly sacrifice (9:11–14). What is new is the application (and culmination) of Jewish cultic soteriology in light of the resurrected Christ.

---

8. As observed by Nicholas Moore ("Heaven's Revolving Door," 203).
9. Moffitt, *Atonement*, 146.
10. Cf. Cockerill, *Hebrews*, 27–28.
11. Mackie, "Heavenly Sanctuary Mysticism," 82.
12. Moore, "Heaven's Revolving Door," 203; cf. Moffitt, *Atonement*, 163–81. Another distinct feature of Christ as the Messiah is that he ascends to the heavenly throne, a regnal characteristic that is not present in traditional messianology (Eskola, *Messiah and the Throne*, 90). Furthermore, the theme of resurrection is not a significant theme in Jewish mysticism and ascension stories (ibid., 155).
13. Moffitt, *Atonement*, 177. However, no ascension account applies deification or assumes such for its participants (Eskola, *Messiah and the Throne*, 155).
14. Ibid., 155, 159.

Against Scholer's notion of preliminary entrance of believers, Scott Mackie argues that such a separation between Christ's entrance and believers' entrance should not be made.[15] He argues that preliminary or proleptic access of believers does not hold the weight of the strong, hortatory language of passages such as Hebrews 4:14–16, 10:19–23, and 12:22–24.[16] "Thus, the thoroughgoing emphasis on a full and confident entry in 10:19–23, which is based on profound architectural, psychological, and mystical/experiential changes effected by Jesus' high priestly accomplishment, is severely attenuated by appeal to a dubious reading of one word, προσέρχομαι."[17]

Essentially, this debate is centered around the nature of the already/not-yet eschatology of believers in regards to their heavenly access. While Scholer maintains what Mackie calls a "restrictive architecture" of the heavenly sanctuary that reserves a "still future and greater" access, Mackie sees evidence of the "now" being emphasized in the author's exhortations.[18] Only if the emphasis is on the present will Hebrews' "entry exhortations begin to make sense" and commands such as "draw near" correspond to the actual experience of the author and the community.[19]

This is where a spatiotemporal eschatology of the heavenly sanctuary is helpful. Thinking in Soja's categories help nuance the question of the already/not-yet access of believers. It asks, "In what sense do believers have access and in what sense do they not?" To begin answering this question, we affirm that in their spirit, believers genuinely occupy the heavenly sanctuary along with Jesus. This is not referring to their entry in a strictly metaphorical or idealized sense. It is the physical, glorified, and resurrected Jesus who materially resides in the heavenly sanctuary. In turn, believers dwell with him spiritually in that actualized sanctuary.

One's view of spatiality will impact their reading of προσέρχομαι and εἰσέρχομαι. If spatiality is solely based on a positivist, locational understanding of place, then one must *either* choose that believers have entered in the holy place with Jesus or that believers are outside as they await full entrance in the eschatological future. Some opt for a middle ground and argue that though believers are not yet in the heavenly sanctuary with Jesus, they have nevertheless drawn near (προσέρχομαι) and are on the threshold of entering.[20] On the other hand, if we expand our notion

---

15. Mackie, "Let Us Draw Near," 19.

16. Ibid., 21–30; esp. 25. By highlighting the community's participation in the divine adoption ceremony that is inaugurated by Jesus' exaltation, it is essential to assume their joint presence with Christ himself (Mackie, "Heavenly Sanctuary Mysticism," 96).

17. Mackie, "Let Us Draw Near," 21.

18. This is an example that is subsumed under the larger debate between an over- and under-realized eschatology.

19. Ibid., 34.

20. For example, Moore diminishes the force of εἰς τὴν εἴσοδον by translating it as "with regard to an entrance that awaits" ("'In' or 'Near,'" 195). However, this stands at odds with the *present* confidence that believers have and the series of exhortations that

of spatiality as per Lefebvre and Soja, spatiality is more than a physical location (i.e., Firstspace). We can consider how believers have indeed entered the sanctuary *spiritually* through their identification with Jesus as their forerunner.

Jesus and the sanctuary are both physical. And yet, believers dwell spiritually with Jesus in this physical, heavenly realm. So in this sense, have they entered? I would agree with Mackie that the answer is a full-fledged "yes" in a Secondspace sense. This does not avoid the question of an actual, existential entrance into the heavenly tabernacle unless to "be somewhere" is solely based on a person's physical placement.[21] This does not mean that we ignore the tabernacle's physical existence in Firstspace. As Soja explains, "the knowledge of this material reality is comprehended essentially through thought" or Secondspace.[22]

If such is the case, the knowledge of believers' entrance into the heavenly tabernacle is comprehended through their spiritual entrance by way of their union with Christ.[23] Richard Gaffin argues that union with Christ is basically and primarily *existential* (i.e., experiential) in nature for the believer.[24] In includes the crucifixion, death, burial, resurrection, and if I may add, spiritual ascension and entrance into the heavenly sanctuary along with Christ (Eph. 2:6; Col. 2:12). Believers realize this through the transformation of their conscience from one of guilt to confidence. The manner in which they approach God and ethically live out their priestly duties confirms their spiritual entrance with Christ.[25]

Spiritual cohabitation with Christ is not the final state in which believers can experience all that is in the heavenly sanctuary. Physically, they have not entered and, therefore, they are still exhorted to draw near as they wait for the culmination

---

the author of Hebrews gives as a result of this reality. Note the present subjunctive verbs and corresponding participles in vv. 21–25: προσερχώμεθα, κατέχωμεν, κατανοῶμεν, μὴ ἐγκαταλείποντες, παρακαλοῦντες. The author does not refer to a future change of status when believers *will* have a sincere heart and a purified conscience; rather, they already possess it. Therefore, they have confidence to (presently) *enter* the holy place by the blood of Jesus.

21. Consider how one's mind and heart may be somewhere else other than the space his body occupies or the experiences of someone who engages in virtual reality. While that person may be physically in a chair, he is still experiencing the spaces of what his mind perceives virtually. Hence, there is more to space than physical occupancy.

22. Soja, *Thirdspace*, 79.

23. I discuss more on believers' union with Christ in the section entitled, "Partakers of Christ through the Spirit" found later in this chapter.

24. Richard B. Gaffin, *The Centrality of the Resurrection: A Study in Paul's Soteriology* (Grand Rapids, MI: Baker Academic, 1978), 46–52.

25. More on believers' conscience and confidence in Section 8.2 of this study. Access into the inner sanctuary is indicated by the Holy Spirit (Heb. 9:8). Hence, not only is believers' access made possible by the Spirit, but it is Trinitarian. It is the "blood of Christ" offered "through the eternal Spirit" and "without blemish to God," which then "purify our consciences from dead works to serve the living God" (Heb. 9:14). This purified conscience is necessary for the believers' priestly ethics.

of their entrance that consists of *both* physical and spiritual access. So while present believers do not "physically" occupy the inner parts of the heavenly sanctuary, by virtue of their union with the high priest, they are—in a sense—actually occupying the "architecture" of the holy place. Only in the future consummation will they physically occupy the holy space which they had access to all along spiritually. Only in such nuanced explanations can we maintain the tension and balance of an already/not-yet theology of access.[26] Only by recognizing what is true and not-yet true in nuanced spatial terms can we say "yes" and "no" with respect to believers' access. Therefore, in Soja's terms, believers can be said to be present in tabernacle space in relation to its Secondspace while they will occupy it physically in the future in relation to its Firstspace.[27]

A. The Spatial Basis for Hortatory Commands

This explains why, in the context of believers' conscience and sin, the author of Hebrews uses strong hortatory language to be confident and to draw near towards the throne of grace. This is an example of how the author interweaves his doctrinal expository material with complementary hortatory commands. For example, *because* Christ is greater than the angels and is God's unique Son, believers are

26. This reality can be explained using the terminology of "positional" or "existential" standings with Christ. A positional standing refers to the redemptive-historical manner in which believers are considered or declared to have progressed into the celestial Holy of Holies in Christ (Beale and Kim, *God Dwells Among Us*, 129–30, esp. 130 n. 43). An existential standing includes this but also much more, which is what I am trying to convey through Secondspace categories. In this way, the Holy Spirit bridges the link between believers and the celestial Holy of Holies so we can "see the Spirit as having brought the church into the initial phase of the end-time temple, where their physical existence in the world is the outer court and their spiritual existence is in the heavenly dimension of the Holy Place that invisibly extends to earth" (ibid.).

27. Related, there is much debate around the issue of whether believers have entered into their "rest" (3:7—4:13). My assertion that Christ has led believers into the heavenly sanctuary is not an attempt to provide conclusive evidence that they indeed have entered consummate rest. It is precisely this tension of a consummate rest that awaits yet is already obtained that characterizes Hebrews eschatology. One observation may be helpful when considering Soja's categories of space. Hebrews' language of movement and rest does not strictly mean that rest is solely a location to enter. In other words, to claim that believers have entered the *locale* of rest, at least spiritually speaking, does not mean they have obtained the *final state of rest*. This tension is precisely what produces the appropriate Thirdspace response of "striving" to enter definitive rest (4:11) while at the same time being exhorted and having confidence to do so. To illustrate this, one may physically be on vacation at a beach resort but still have uncompleted work that he did not finish. His mind in his current state is not one of rest although physically, he is in a place of rest. This does not mean that he cannot enjoy all that the beach resort offers. Yet, there is a qualitative difference in the state of rest he is in.

to pay close attention to what has been heard (2:1). Regarding Christ's high priestly ministry, complementary exhortations are spatial in character. The author affirms the believers' spatial standing with Christ in the heavenly sanctuary while exhorting them to draw near (4:16; 7:19, 25; 10:1, 22). "That the community's entry is always mimetically aligned with and empowered by Jesus' own pioneering entry into the heavens lends crucial coherence, clarity, and confidence to these entry exhortations."[28]

Evidence of this doctrinal and hortatory interweaving can be seen in the passages we observed detailing the heavenly tabernacle. The author's selection of artifacts used to describe the earthly tabernacle in 9:1–5 is carefully placed immediately before his argument for the superiority of Christ's priestly ministry in the heavenly tabernacle. The artifacts described are the lampstand, the bread of the Presence, the golden altar of incense,[29] and the ark of the covenant. There were certainly other artifacts present in the tabernacle (e.g., utensils, woven curtains, pillar furnishings). However, the author selectively mentions these, not randomly, but to highlight the communion that is established between God and his people. The ark is the "central point of contact between heaven and the tabernacle" and the "supreme post-Sinai symbol of the Presence of Yahweh."[30] Next, the bread of the Presence symbolizes the intimate communion of partaking of a meal with God. Finally, the continual burning of the lampstand symbolizes God's active and perpetual presence amongst his people.[31] The lampstand is modeled after the tree motif, where one is reminded of God's presence in the form of a fire being perpetually burned in the "unburning" bush (Exod. 3:2–3). Therefore, the increasing "intensity" of communion is portrayed by these artifacts.[32]

The foreshadowing of this communion in Heb. 9:1–5 and the greater efficacy of Christ's high priestly ministry in verses 6–10 prepare the appetite for Christ's climactic appearance and entrance into the heavenly tabernacle in verse 11.[33] As a result of his entrance into the Holy of Holies and the corresponding ritual atonement in those spaces, it is now possible for believers to commune with the living God in that sanctuary. Earlier I asserted the efficacy of Christ's atoning

---

28. Mackie, "Introduction to Part 2," *The Letter to the Hebrews: Critical Readings*, 142.

29. The altar and believers' participation in the priestly sacrifice will be discussed in detail in the next chapter.

30. Enns, *Exodus*, 511; cf. Durham, *Exodus*, 350.

31. Enns, *Exodus*, 511.

32. The outer courts contained the vessels (i.e., wash basin and the altar of burnt offering) required for the preparations one must take in order to draw successively closer to God.

33. "Heaven itself is the location where both regal and cultic conceptions of Christ are joined (cf. 8:1–2 and 10:12–13). It is "the spatial setting for the definitive sacrifice that inaugurated the new covenant and the new age and is where Christ reigns and lives to make salvific intercession" (Stewart, "Cosmology, Eschatology, and Soteriology," 550).

sacrifice through the "ritual geography" of the cross. The purpose of cleansing believers' sins is not only to make a change in their existential status; it also entails the cultic condition to stand in the presence of God. This is all made possible due to believers' union with Christ through Spirit-wrought faith. Mackie goes as far as saying that the "central purpose motivating Hebrews' elaborate priestly Christology, and its attendant heavenly locale, is found in the author's hortatory proclamation of the experiential, soteriological benefits of Jesus' sacrifice, which are primarily intended to facilitate access to God in the heavenly sanctuary."[34] This is especially marked in the author's concluding section on Christ's high priestly ministry regarding the implications and exhortations he gives to believers to enter the holy place by the blood of Jesus (10:19, ἔχοντες οὖν, ἀδελφοί). As Benjamin Ribbens states, "This transition demonstrates that the main point the author has been making relates to the heavenly sanctuary, as his main exhortatory conclusion is the ability of believers to enter God's presence, the heavenly sanctuary."[35]

The author of Hebrews makes such claims because he believes (1) Christ has entered into the innermost sanctuary (v. 12), and (2) believers are inseparably joined to Christ through the Spirit (v. 14).[36] Therefore, it is appropriate to say that where Christ goes, believers follow. Earlier I outlined the itinerary of Jesus' heavenly journey from his ascension into the spaces of the heavenly tabernacle (Chapter 4). This journey encompasses a "situation of solidarity" with his people, thus "bringing in his train a humanity liberated from sin and the power of death."[37] Hence, Jesus' words in his entrance are his declarations of

---

34. Mackie, "Heavenly Sanctuary Mysticism," 83–84. Hence, Jon Laansma states that in Hebrews, salvation is a distinctly local concept that is tied to the destination of the people of God—that is, the idea of sacred space ("Cosmology of Hebrews," 131).

35. Ribbens, *Levitical Sacrifice*, 83. This reading differs from Otto Glombitza's translation of entering the holy place to have access to the "goods" offered in salvation (*Heilsgütern*) ("Erwägungen zum kunstvollen Ansatz der Paraenese im Brief an die Hebräer 10:19-25," *NovT* 9.2 [1967]: 134, 138). However, this can be reconciled if we interpret the outcome of salvation as dwelling in the presence of God.

36. It is the same Holy Spirit that reveals the truth of "free and unimpeded access into God's presence (9:8)" (Martin Emmrich, "Pneuma in Hebrews: Prophet and Interpreter," in Mackie, ed., *The Letter to the Hebrews*, 84). The genius of Hebrews is in how it retains temple/tabernacle symbolism and its associated liturgical action, while at the same time elevates the "celestial order of salvation, an order in which men can have access to the presence of God, to union with God, through the action of Jesus Christ under the power of His eternal spirit" (Cody, *Heavenly Sanctuary and Liturgy*, 155).

37. Aitken, "Body of Jesus Outside the Eternal City," 201–202. While I agree with Aitken's proposal of believers' shared itinerary with Jesus, her understanding is similar to Mark George's social reading of the tabernacle—that is, the way to occupy true tabernacle space is through the reimagining of their occupied, monumental space of the city of Rome (ibid., 206–208).

"bringing many sons to glory," and "Behold, I and the children whom God has given me" (2:13).[38] Such declarations are appropriate because Jesus stands in the midst of the congregation, his brothers, and he sings praise (v. 12; cf. Ps. 22:22). This is hardly speaking of believers standing outside of where Jesus resides in a preliminary or proleptic sense. Rather, the solidarity between believers and Jesus is attested. "Rather than the high priest entering alone, the audience's itinerary is mapped onto Jesus's itinerary, so that the holy of holies becomes a highly populated space."[39]

B. The "Good Things" that Have Come

This coheres naturally with what the author writes in Hebrews 12:22–24. There he makes an inseparable connection between the believers' access to God and the perfection of their spirits. They *have* come (προσεληλύθατε)…to God along with the spirits of the righteous made perfect (Heb. 12:22; cf. 10:14).[40] This is not a novel concept in Hebrews. As mentioned earlier, this falls in line with God's intent ever since the construction of the tabernacle in Leviticus, which was to bring God's people into his presence.[41] To truncate that process and place believers outside of God's throne room threatens the efficacy of Christ's once-for-all atoning sacrifice. If the analogy between the heavenly and earthly cult is to be maintained, then we may say without reservation—speaking in the language of Secondspace—that believers share the same sanctuary space with Christ.

Therefore, the author can boldly claim that believers have come to the heavenly city (προσεληλύθατε). As a double-entendre, this is true both in the present and in the future when in a Firstspace, Secondspace, and Thirdspace sense, they have *fully* arrived. Christ's sacrifice that perfects and sanctifies believers (10:19–22) has "effectively removed the spatial barrier separating heaven and earth and the temporal barrier separating the old age and the new by enabling believers in the present to access both sacred space (heaven itself) and sacred time (the new age and the coming world)."[42] In using such language, the "good benefits" have already come in this age (9:11; 10:1).

---

38. In John's Gospel, Jesus tabernacled (ἐσκήνωσεν) among his people, and thus his incarnation became the "locus of God's word and glory among humankind" (Koester, *Dwelling of God*, 102). In Hebrews, the same concept of tabernacling glory is maintained, except now believers ascend with Christ to dwell with him in glory. Believers' participation in Christ's exaltation and entrance into God's presence can be seen in the shift from the second person to the third person "which depicts the Son conferring family membership on the community (2:12–13)" (Mackie, "Heavenly Sanctuary Mysticism," 96).

39. Aitken, "Body of Jesus Outside the Eternal City," 202.

40. This perfection is accomplished for believers living on earth since Hebrews emphah sizes the *spirits* of the righteous (Schenck, *Cosmology and Eschatology*, 136).

41. Morales, *Who Shall Ascend?*, 109–10.

42. Stewart, "Cosmology, Eschatology, and Soteriology," 556.

Because this is true in Secondspace categories,⁴³ believers' present cohabitation with Christ is why the author of Hebrews speaks of the good things that have already come. The author states this during his comparison of Christ's high priestly ministry in the greater tabernacle over the earthly one (Heb. 9:12). In the previous verse, 9:11, γενομένων is the preferred text-critical choice over μελλόντων.⁴⁴ In addition to the textual evidence, the former fits the author's eschatological schema to speak of the *good things* (ἀγαθῶν) that have already come with the inauguration of Christ's high priestly ministry.

Here, it is important to consider the vantage point from which one can read this phrase. From the viewpoint of those under the Old Covenant, they strictly look *forward* to the fulfillment of eschatological blessings. Whether they looked forward to an earthly, physical fulfillment or a better country, that is, a heavenly one, depended on the individual's faith (11:16). On the other hand, the author can speak from the vantage point of New Covenant believers who look at the present good things that have come in Christ (spiritual),⁴⁵ *and* forward to the *consummation* of those good things (a fullness that is both spiritual and physical).⁴⁶

Considering the context, the author draws a contrast between those under the New and Old Covenants. The point of difference between the two peoples is the fact that New Covenant believers can look presently to the spiritual blessings that were inaugurated by the death and resurrection of Jesus Christ. These good things (ἀγαθῶν) are further delineated in the subsequent verses of 10:1 and following. Ironically, 10:1 is the very verse that scribes considered to justify their redaction from γενομένων to μελλοντων. They failed to recognize that 10:1-4 describes the situation of those under the Old Covenant sacrificial system, whereas 9:11-14 describes those under the New Covenant, which is set against the Old Covenant sacrificial system presented in 9:1-10. The vantage points are different between 9:11-14 and 10:1.⁴⁷ Therefore, the external text-critical support along with the

---

43. In the next chapter I will present how believers' standing is closely related to their identity as priests and therefore is also true in a Thirdspace sense.

44. See my translation and textual criticism in Section 6.1.

45. The "good things" are further specified in later verses, specifically 9:24, where the author speaks of the spiritual reality of being in the presence of God by Christ's high priestly mediation. This refers to an experience as opposed to material things (Ellingworth and Nida, *Hebrews*, 191).

46. Thus, it is best to take παραγενόμενος as an inceptive, aorist tense. Since Christ appeared, the good things have begun and believers continue to enjoy them under his high priestly ministry (cf. Lane, *Hebrews 9-13*, 229). Philip Hughes partially agrees that this is from the vantage point of New Covenant believers; however, he prefers the translation, "to come," where believers look forward to the consummation of eschatological blessings, rather than the already-present inauguration of those blessings (Hughes, *Hebrews*, 326-27).

47. Such ambiguity between the selection of γενομένων or μελλοντων does not necessarily compromise the integrity of the author's main point. Both potentially fit into the eschatological already/not-yet schema and are equally true depending on the vantage point one wishes to take. They are the eschatological blessings that have come in the present or

contrasting elements against the Old Covenant sacrificial system suggest that γενομένων is the preferred reading. This includes and is not limited to the idea that believers have already received the "good thing" of access into presence with God in the heavenly tabernacle.[48]

C. Partakers of Christ through the Spirit

Naturally one may wonder: if the heavenly tabernacle is a materialized structure in the heavenlies, how can believers be certain of their occupancy in a space that is physically out of sight? It is possible only when believers understand their Secondspace positional standing due to their Spirit-wrought union with Christ, *who is there* in his physical body and spirit (Rom. 6:5–6; Col. 2:12; 1 Jn 4:13). This "mystical union" entails possessing both Christ and all his benefits.[49] One such benefit is believers' shared occupancy with Christ in the heavenly sanctuary. This is, at the least, partly what is meant by the author's notion that believers have become *partakers of Christ* (3:14). Following the structure of the epistle, this participatory language is introduced by way of Christ's incarnation when he became like his brothers yet without sin (2:9–17; 4:15). This language continues with Christ bringing believers with him along his heavenly itinerary (4:14). Finally, because believers are ingrafted into the body of Christ himself, they can confidently enter the holy place by the atonement secured through the blood of Jesus (10:19).[50]

---

definitely will have come in the future. While it is acceptable to say that the "good things" are *yet to come*, my point is that these exclusively future blessings are not what is referred to in v. 11.

48. This is why the author of Hebrews can state elsewhere that believers have come to Mt. Zion and to the city of the living God in the presence of angels and, most importantly, in the presence of God with righteous spirits made perfect (Heb. 12:22–23). It is appropriate to see the temple/sanctuary and the tabernacle as synonymous with Mt. Zion as the eschatological temple (Rev. 21:2–3; cf. Beale, *Temple and Church's Mission*, 302–303).

49. Following Benjamin J. Ribbens, "Partakers of Christ: Union with Christ in Hebrews," *Pro Ecclesia* 31.3 (2022): 284; cf. John Calvin, *Institutes of the Christian Religion*, ed. John T. McNeill, trans. Ford Lewis Battles (Louisville, KY: Westminster John Knox Press, 2011), 3.2.24 and 3.9.10. Ribbens argues that the participatory relationship with Christ is "consistent with how union with and participation in Christ is described elsewhere in the New Testament (particularly in Pauline literature)" ("Partakers of Christ," 284). These benefits include spiritual union with Christ, participation in the events of Christ's narrative, identification of believers in the realm of Christ's domain, and incorporation of membership into Christ's body (Constantine R. Campbell, *Paul and Union with Christ: An Exegetical and Theological Study* [Grand Rapids, MI: Zondervan, 2012], 406–20).

50. While the author of Hebrews does not utilize the "in Christ" language found in Paul, he does have a "thoroughgoing concept of access to the divine presence in the heavenly temple that is grounded in the ontology and history of the Incarnate Son, the heavenly High Priest" (Grant Macaskill, *Union with Christ in the New Testament* [Oxford: Oxford

This bond with Christ is made possible by the agency of the Holy Spirit. The Spirit becomes the means through which the blood of Christ becomes efficaciously applied to believers for all eternity. Hence, the author refers to the Spirit as being "eternal" (9:14) in order to "bring out the (extraordinary) eschatological significance" of the Spirit's role in Christ's high priestly action.[51] Furthermore, this bond is inseparable. During Christ's movement from the lower to the higher sphere, the "bond between the believers and Christ is so close" that in addition to the shared interest of soteriological benefit, a "severance of his *actual life* from the celestial Christ-centered sphere is unthinkable."[52]

As Martin Emmrich argues, the Spirit's prophetic exhortation to the community in utilizing Psalm 95 is an "eschatological event" speaking in the "last days."[53] In these last days, God speaks through the Son. Hence, it coheres well with the conclusions of our study that Christ, in his high priestly exaltation and occupancy in the heavenly sanctuary, continues to speak through the Spirit in an eschatological manner. It is a voice that continually assures believers of their standing with him in the presence of God. It is also a voice that continually urges them to be faithful to live out their calling as priests who worship both vertically through hymns and prayers and horizontally through communal ethics. It is that same Spirit who bears witness to God's univocal covenant promise in 10:15–18, which, without coincidence, leads to the result of believers confidently entering the holy places of God. They can do so only by the blood of Jesus because their evil consciences have now been sprinkled clean (10:19–22). Furthermore, their understanding and assurance of their vertical status in the heavenly sanctuary

---

University Press, 2013], 186). This is what I have been arguing regarding the relationship between believers' union with Christ and their shared entrance and occupancy with Christ in the heavenly tabernacle. While I have been utilizing the "union with Christ" theme to argue for believers' presence in the tabernacle, Macaskill argues in the opposite direction by arguing for believers' union with Christ by way of their occupancy in the heavenly tabernacle! Macaskill writes, "Access to the presence of God in the heavenly temple is the primary image of participation [in Christ] in Hebrews" (ibid., 179).

51. Martin Emmrich, "'Amtscharisma': Through the Eternal Spirit (Hebrews 9:14)," *BBR* 12.1 (2002): 32.; Albert Vanhoye, "Esprit éternel et feu du sacrifice en He 9:14," *Biblica* 64.2 [1983]: 274, who also includes a summary on the history of interpretation of διὰ πνεύματος αἰωνίου.

52. Vos, *Pauline Eschatology*, 37; emphasis original. It is the Holy Spirit that enables us to think of Christ being "historically absent and as actually present" (Thomas F. Torrance, *Space, Time and Resurrection*, Cornerstones [London: T&T Clark, 2019], 135). Furthermore, "[i]t is through the Spirit that things infinitely disconnected by the 'distance' of the ascension are nevertheless infinitely closely related. Through the Spirit Christ is nearer to us than we are to ourselves, and we who live and dwell on earth are yet made to sit with Christ 'in heavenly places,' partaking of the divine nature in him" (ibid.).

53. Emmrich, "Pneuma in Hebrews," 76–80.

with Christ in the presence of God necessarily result in their horizontal practice of "stirring up one another to love and good works" and "encouraging one another" as the day draws near (10:24).

Believers participate in more than a shared interest of salvation in Christ. It is participation in the actual life that he lives in the heavenly realms. As Geerhardus Vos writes, "As soon as the direction of the actual spiritual life-contact becomes involved, the horizontal movement of thought on the time-plane must give way immediately to a vertical projection of the eschatological interest into the supernal region."[54] Therefore, Christ's ascension inaugurates the vertical eschatology for believers. Their eschatological center moves to heaven because Christ resides there,[55] and therefore "heaven has a new status in the age structure simply because of Christ's presence there until the parousia."[56] It is the community's actual presence in the heavenly sanctuary that presents the climax of the author's comparisons between the earthly and heavenly cultus. It is an access that "qualitatively supersedes" that of the Jewish cultus which, at best, utilizes entry terminology purely in metaphorical (or proleptic) terms.[57] This ultimately grounds believers' sense of place, which then transforms their conscience from one of guilt to confidence and enables them to serve as living priests.

7.2. First-, Second-, and Thirdspace Interplay

7.2.1. The Grounding of Firstspace

Before considering the priestly implications that believers' heavenly occupancy has on their conscience and their ethics (Chapter 8), I now turn to how tabernacle First-, Second-, and Thirdspace interact with one another.[58] These three features are not separate categories for understanding space; rather, they altogether present a holistic view of the heavenly tabernacle's features. These features involve, influence, and impact believers as they understand their occupancy in that sacred space. Edward Soja goes so far to call them "three moments of the ontological trialectic" that subsume each other.[59] Furthermore, one of these should not have epistemological privilege over another. While this is true when considering the entirety of an object's spatial features, this cannot be true in one's investigation of space. Even when one engages space, they do not possess an ultimate view of all three in a comprehensive sense.

---

54. Vos, *Pauline Eschatology*, 37.
55. Lincoln, *Paradise Now and Not Yet*, 172.
56. Ibid.
57. Mackie, "Heavenly Sanctuary Mysticism," 84.
58. So far, we have considered only First- and Secondspace. By introducing Thirdspace, Soja ensures that a binary, reductionistic view of space is avoided (*Thirdspace*, 72).
59. Ibid.

Nevertheless, there must be a logical or existential priority in Firstspace—meaning that a sequential order must be established after considering the physical localization of the subject material.[60] To illustrate this, two people may refer to Secondspace and Thirdspace characteristics of an object. Even if they are in agreement concerning these characteristics, there is still no certainty that the two people are referring to the same thing. Or as another example, if one logically or existentially begins with Thirdspace, then Firstspace and Secondspace are contingent upon the "lived out" experiences of its participants' experience. This ultimately results in a myriad of Firstspace potentialities, since one person's subjective experiences are different from those of another. Space, then, becomes the creation of communities, which can only go as far as creating mental representations or commonly agreed upon understandings of such a space.[61] Such a logical priority of Thirdspace over First- and Secondspace cannot be utilized in Hebrews because it may dismiss the historical existence of Jesus' resurrected body along with the heavenly tabernacle space where he resides.[62] On the contrary, Firstspace features of the tabernacle's physicality and heavenly locale enable believers to have a sense of groundedness in their positional standing with God.[63]

Therefore, believers' sense of place is not anchored by merely holding onto the "certain and unchangeable Promise of God."[64] A promise, by definition (though it is guaranteed due to the character of God's faithfulness), is located in the future. I propose strengthening that future promise by acknowledging that a believer's sense of place is presently anchored by an actual, heavenly place. It is the difference between the "idea" of a home and an *actual* place that exists.[65] Therefore, the soteriological benefits that arise from Jesus' high priestly ministry include a sense of place that is grounded in believers' own spiritual standing in the throne room

---

60. Henri Lefebvre insists on an all-inclusive "theoretical unity" between the fields of the spatial triad. He terms this "logico-epistemological space" (*Production of Space*, 11–12). This logic flows from the physical localization of the subject into its Secondspace and Thirdspace features.

61. This is why Lefebvre saw an inevitable connection between space and a Marxist theory of power/social relations (ibid., 26).

62. This may precisely be why the author of Hebrews begins with expositional material that grounds the readers in the historicity and reality of Jesus' incarnation, ascension, and session (2:5–18). Only after establishing Firstspace and Secondspace realities does he shift to hortatory commands that are "lived out" in light of those realities (e.g., Heb. 3:1, 7–13).

63. The reality of Christ's ministry in the heavenly sanctuary is the ontological grounding of believers' proleptic priesthood on the earth (She, *Use of Exodus in Hebrews*, 137–38).

64. Asumang and Domeris, "Migrant Camp of the People of God," 24.

65. In his discussion on the Christian religion, Lefebvre asks, "What is an ideology without a space to which it refers, a space which it describes…?" (*Production of Space*, 44).

of God. This explains why "an emphasis on spatial orientation to either heaven or earth resides primarily in the expositional material,"[66] which focuses on Christ's high priestly ministry. As believers are united to Christ by faith in the Spirit, they tap into the eschatological hope that stems from tabernacle space.[67]

In Matthew Sleeman's work, *Geography and the Ascension Narrative in Acts* (2009), he argues that Jesus' heavenly presence anchors the narrative of the growth of the early church in the book of Acts.[68] Similarly, the earthly tabernacle grounded the Israelite community during their wilderness journey as they set up and established the tabernacle's centralized location. While their situation and surroundings were different throughout the Sinai Desert, their social and spiritual positioning around God's presence was to be a constant source of encouragement, hope, and perseverance. Similarly for New Covenant believers, the heavenly tabernacle serves as a far greater source of these benefits than the earthly tabernacle because of its nature, and because of believers' spiritual participation *within* the confines of the tabernacle by way of their union with Christ. Therefore, just as Jesus' ascension shapes believers' spatiality and "understanding of space both within and beyond the church"[69] in the book of Acts, the heavenly tabernacle shapes believers' understanding of their eschatological positioning and future hope in the Epistle to the Hebrews.[70] In other words, if Jesus' ascension functions as an ordering of space within Acts, the heavenly tabernacle functions as an eschatological ordering of believers' space in Hebrews.

7.2.2. Mutual Cooperation of Spatial Trialectics

As discussed in Section 1.2.4, there are two dangers in the interpretation of Hebrews eschatology: bifurcation and abstraction. Such dualistic oppositions of space and time have influenced our understanding of space.[71] For Hebrews, the

---

66. Guthrie, *Structure of Hebrews*, 121.

67. This eschatological hope is not limited to NT believers. Meredith Kline states that the peculiar forms of "intrusion" in the OT age are coherent and comprehensive. The divine administrations in the OT period "point to a reality that was (as an archetype in the heavens) and that is to come (in the Messianic age). They are antitype in relation to the reality that was. They are symbol in relation to the core of the present Old Testament Intrusion of that reality. And they are type in relation to that reality as it is to come" ("The Intrusion and the Decalogue," *WTJ* 16.1 [1953]: 4).

68. While Hebrews is a not strictly a narrative, scholars such as Kenneth Schenck have noted the narrative structure underlying Hebrews (cf. *Cosmology and Eschatology*, 10–23).

69. Sleeman, *Geography and Ascension*, 5.

70. Incidentally, this study's assertions fall in line with Sleeman's conclusion that the central location in Acts shifts from the earthly temple to the heavenlies.

71. Lefebvre attributes this to dualisms found in philosophy such as Descartes' *res cogitans* and *res extensa*, and the Ego and non-Ego of Kant (*Production of Space*, 39).

difficulty lies in the reconciliation of space and time in its eschatology. Giving consideration to the spatial characteristics of the heavenly tabernacle helps to remedy this problem.[72] Having done so, how do we view the relationship among the tabernacle's spatial features?

Lefebvre argues against seeing the spatial triad as an abstract model. Instead, he argues, the three "realms" should be interconnected so that the one perceiving space "may move from one to another without confusion."[73] Believers must be comfortable in understanding their spatial identity that encompasses both their heavenly earthly situations. By believing in a physical space occupied by a physical, resurrected Jesus (Firstspace), they see themselves occupying that space spiritually (Secondspace). In a reciprocal fashion, their spiritual identity and gaining of confidence further feeds into their belief of their co-occupancy with Christ. This mutual interaction between First and Secondspace becomes "concrete" in "spatial practice" (Thirdspace).[74] This does not require believers to be constantly conscious of their spatial presence in the heavenly tabernacle. The interconnections can also be "unconscious" and "give utterance" through their actions, words, and self-understanding.[75]

Thirdspace responses come as a result of one's occupancy and perceived understanding of Firstspace and Secondspace. The interplay can also be the case in the opposite direction. Jon Berquist states that Thirdspace can even resist and challenge Secondspace, which allows "engaging in the imaginative and active work of seeing and living differently."[76] If such is the case, Thirdspace practice that does not reflect God's commands can negatively impact one's view of Secondspace. Positively, faithful obedience in Thirdspace practice has the potential to affirm and strengthen believers' view of their Secondspace standing with Christ in the heavenly tabernacle.

If these kinds of mutual interactions amongst the spatial triad are ignored, an atomistic approach to heavenly tabernacle spatiality may result. For example, an overly Firstspace-heavy reading is similar to the Jewish apocalyptic belief that their eschatological hope resides in a nationalistic, future (horizontal-only),

---

72. The heavenly tabernacle is an example of the "vertical typology that pervades Hebrews" which allows us to see how the "earth/heaven axis intersects the horizontal time-continuum." Therefore, eschatology along with Hebrews' Christological-soteriological characteristics are "present in the vertical typology as in the horizontal perspective" (Davidson, "Typology in the Book of Hebrews," 135).

73. Lefebvre, *Production of Space*, 40. "Lefebvre opens the way to a *trialectics of spatiality*, always insisting that each mode of thinking about space, each 'field' of human spatiality—the physical, the mental, the social—be seen as simultaneously real and imagined, concrete and abstract, material and metaphorical" (Soja, *Thirdspace*, 64–65).

74. Lefebvre's terms; he also calls this practice a form of spatial production (*Production of Space*, 46).

75. Ibid.

76. Berquist, "Critical Spatiality and the Uses of Theory," 9.

physical temple.[77] An overly Secondspace-heavy reading of the heavenly tabernacle's symbolism and spiritual representations may neglect the physical, spatial descriptions of the tabernacle texts and reduce them to Platonic categories.[78] Finally, a Thirdspace-dominant reading results in a socially constructed understanding of the tabernacle (i.e., an anthropocentric view of space discussed in Section 2.2.1). It is only by considering all three features together that we are able to appropriate each of these characteristics.

Christ's high priestly access entry for believers allows us to see how spatial features mutually inform one another.[79] For example, the rhetorical power that arises from the metaphorical and symbolic significance of the heavenly tabernacle (Secondspace) is reinforced by the fact that there is an actualized, spatial temple. Believers' Firstspace reality gives ongoing assurance of Jesus' high priestly activity that is efficacious for their atonement, entry, and co-occupancy with him. As we will further see in the next chapter, this assurance is what enables believers to exemplify tabernacle Thirdspace in priestly participation in heaven and priestly living on earth. This interplay, along with believers' participation in this reality, is an integral feature of Hebrews eschatology.

Acknowledging this interplay affirms the two-dimensional nature of Hebrews eschatology, which consists of its vertical and horizontal planes or spatial and temporal elements.[80] G. K. Beale writes, "In the light of the spatial perspective, the end-time temple, for example, can be viewed both as a reality in present time that extends spatially from the heavenly dimension into the earthly and also as an invisible spatial dimension different from that of the material, earthly dimension (Heb. 9:1–10:26) because of the work of Christ."[81] His observation concerning the spatial and temporal planes of eschatology correlates well with Edward Soja's trialectics. Soja has argued for the overlap and even the subsumption of the spatial triad.[82] Reconciling Beale and Soja's contributions, the eschatological grid for Hebrews eschatology can be illustrated in Figure 7.1.

---

77. Similarly, Rabbinic literature looks forward to a restored Jerusalem under earthly conditions (Barrett, "Eschatology," 374).

78. This results from an overly literal one-to-one correlation between the earthly and heavenly without a forward-looking, typological view of Christ's activity. One example would be the Seventh-Day Adventist view of two phases of Christ's heavenly ministry being related to the two ministries of the earthly priests. For example, see Frank B. Holbrook, "Daniel and Revelation Committee Report," in Holbrook, ed., *Issues in the Book of Hebrews*, 11.

79. "Space is no longer thought of in an absolute or abstract way, but in a dialectic of the physical, the social, and even the imaginative" (Schreiner, "Space, Place, and Biblical Studies," 360).

80. Beale, *New Testament Biblical Theology*, 144, who calls this a striking feature of the eschatology in Hebrews (ibid., 143).

81. Ibid., 144.

82. Soja, *Thirdspace*, 72.

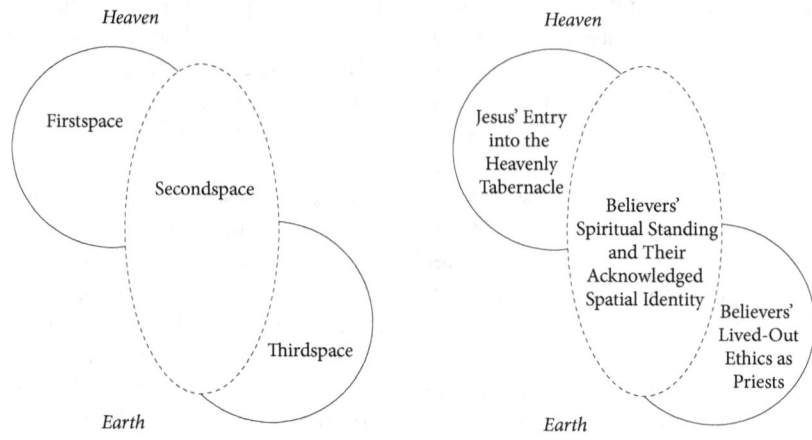

Figure 7.1. Spatial Overlap of the Heavenly Tabernacle

As mentioned earlier, Beale believes in a cosmological interpretation of the heavenly tabernacle, where the tabernacle's three dimensions represent the invisible Holy of Holies, the Holy Place ("the spiritual dimension that extends to earth"), and the outer court (the physical world).[83] While I agree there may be an analogical correlation between the heavenly tabernacle and the cosmos, I propose that the correlation is grounded in an actual original tabernacle that physically resides in heaven.[84] This coincides with what Beale considers to be important characteristics of each dimension: The Holy of Holies is the "center of gravity for God's presence," and the spiritual dimension extends to God's people who function as a "kingdom of priests," as "lampstands" shining God's revelation to the world; and the "outer court" is the setting for such obedient practice.[85] All this points to the fact that the three spatial dimensions do not simply exist alongside one another; rather, they contribute towards one another in a holistic sense for the believer.

---

83. Beale and Kim, *God Dwells Among Us*, 129.

84. As previously mentioned in Section 1.2.1, there are certainly cosmic implications. These "cosmic overtones should not be allowed to obliterate the redemptive framework of the sanctuary/temple and the typological relationship that obtains between the earthly sanctuary/temple and its heavenly counterpart" (de Sousa, "Heavenly Sanctuary/Temple Motif," 39). A structure in the heavens can both exist while also corresponding to various sections of the cosmos. See my discussion on analogical and paramorphic metaphors in Section 5.1.3.

85. Beale and Kim, *God Dwells Among Us*, 129.

7.3. Upward- and Forward-Looking

We shift our attention to the perspective of the audience of Hebrews. How do they perceive their place in the eschatological present and future, and between earth and heaven?[86] Chapters 4–6 argued that the original type of the earthly tabernacle is a standing structure in heaven. However, spiritual entrance into that tabernacle is not the culmination of God's redemptive promises. Furthermore, the salvific efficacy of Christ's high priestly ministry is not limited to a vertical-only dimension of the heavenly tabernacle.[87] There is also a forward-looking anticipation for the consummation of these benefits that will become the fullness of their entrance both spiritually and physically. The difficulty lies in reconciling these two dimensions without overly emphasizing one over the other. To have a vertical-only view removes Christ's atoning sacrifice and is in danger of having a Gnostic/Platonic position regarding salvation. To have a horizontal-only view results in a dispensational view of the re-creation of an earthly temple. In contrast, Hebrews eschatology presents the horizontal that is "inextricably tied to the vertical dimension in eschatology, Christology-soteriology, and ecclesiology. The vertical dimension provides an understanding of the link between heaven and earth in the unfolding of God's plan of salvation."[88]

Believers are in a unique position on earth where they can look in two directions—upward and forward. As Old Testament believers continually looked upward and forward in the shadowy types of the levitical cult, they "temporally related to the true ministry of Christ."[89] In other words, even their vertical, symbolic understanding of the levitical cult pointed forward to the accomplishment of Christ's earthly ministry. New Testament believers, too, concurrently look in two directions. However, their sight forward surpasses that of the Israelites under the Old Covenant; they look forward to the final culmination of salvation already received because Christ's death, resurrection and ascension have already occurred. Therefore, when they look upward, they do not simply see Christ as a "mediator standing between the real and phenomenal worlds" but as "an actor in the eschatological drama of redemption."[90]

Believers' participation in this eschatological drama is seen in the spatial and temporal realities portrayed by the heavenly tabernacle. There is no separate future eschatological tabernacle that is different in kind from the vertical, heavenly one that exists now—rather, only in degree. In these last days (1:1), believers see themselves in the overlap of two temporal ages. Similarly, they must see

---

86. Church, "Wilderness Tabernacle," 101. There is a lack of consensus regarding the relevance and the primacy of either Hebrews' spatial or temporal categories (Asumang and Domeris, "Ministering in the Tabernacle," 2–3; cf. Koester, *Hebrews*, 98).

87. To clarify, it is not the location itself that secures salvation; rather, it is the resurrected and exalted Christ who offers his blood in the heavenly sanctuary.

88. Davidson, "Typology in the Book of Hebrews," 149.

89. Barrett, "Eschatology," 385.

90. Ibid., 389.

themselves in the overlap of two spatial realities (heaven and earth). These dimensions "intermingle" as Geerhardus Vos writes:

> [H]eaven and earth more or less intermingle for the Christian. The Christian already anticipates his heavenly state here on earth. But if this is true of believers, as a merely redemptive acquisition, how much more must it be true of Christ, who is Himself directly a heavenly Person? The act, therefore, was performed in the milieu of heaven, since Christ Himself was a piece of heaven come down to earth.[91]

It is crucial to reconcile both spatial and temporal realities in Hebrews eschatology. In the bookends of Hebrews, there is a "dynamic relationship between the temporal and spatial elements of Hebrews's foundational story."[92] In Hebrews 2:5 the author references a world to come (τὴν οἰκουμένην τὴν μέλλουσαν) which "functions equally as spatial reference to the world (τὴν οἰκουμένην) that Christ was exalted to (1:6) and where he is presently reigning (1:13)."[93] In Hebrews 12:27, the present world will be shaken in order to prepare for the coming of that vertical abode. In other words, the present, heavenly abode of God will one day be the world that believers receive. By being present spiritually in heaven and physically on earth, believers know that "two spatial realities exist (heaven itself and the created universe) in correspondence with the existence and temporal overlap of two ages."[94] This already/not-yet schema is possible precisely because there is an actual heavenly tabernacle that serves as the locale for Christ's high priestly ministry for believers. "Hebrews has turned expressions that, in Platonic contexts, have primarily ontological meaning and spatial resonances into expressions with ontological, spatial, and temporal dimensions... The earthly tent, rites, and law correspond spatially and temporally to both heavenly and future realities."[95]

Where do the ontological, spatial, and temporal dimensions converge? It is precisely in the heavenly tabernacle. Temporally speaking, the outer section of the earthly tabernacle (9:8–9) is a symbol for the present time, where the heavenly tabernacle became accessible during a time of reformation, having an everlasting effect.[96] Ontologically, it will never pass away, for it is not made with hands or of

---

91. Vos, *The Teaching of Hebrews*, 114.
92. Stewart, "Cosmology, Eschatology, and Soteriology," 550.
93. Ibid.
94. Ibid. The future world is already in the process of being received by believers (12:28) while its full attainment lies in the future (13:14). In Rev. 21:2, the New Jerusalem comes down from heaven onto earth to be established forever.
95. Calaway, *Sabbath and Sanctuary*, 109. Calaway sees these characteristics as belonging to Jewish apocalyptic; however, they are also descriptions of Christian eschatology.
96. "The first tent is the current age, characterized by lack of access to the heavenly holy of holies, with only the mediation of the annual high priestly activities; the second tent is

earthly creation (v. 11). Spatially it is not found on this earth but in the heavenly places—the place where the ritual reference of Jesus' death resides. "The heavenly tabernacle, therefore, is eschatological for Hebrews in that it is the context for the new-covenant relationship established between God and his people via the sacrifice of Christ as our high priest."[97]

If such is the case, the question that Thomas Keene poses must be asked: "Why does the author of Hebrews, in contrast to every other NT author (including, perhaps, himself, Heb. 12:18-24), make Israel's tabernacle the backdrop for his discussion of the work of Jesus? To put it bluntly, would not the temple serve the author's purposes as well or better?"[98] Affirming his similarly arrived conclusion, it is precisely because the tabernacle was a portable structure that reflected the wilderness situation of the Israelites that it forced them to look forward to the establishment of God's permanent dwelling presence amongst the people.[99] In addition, through the tabernacle's levitical rites, the Israelites were urged to look upward to the spiritual realities that the ritual types signified. If the author of Hebrews had utilized the temple motif instead of the tabernacle, he would have undermined the exhortation to *continue* looking upward and forward for the fulfillment of the eschatological heavenly temple.

The tabernacle is used to further the argument of how the Old Covenant was only provisional and pointed forward to the need for a better covenant. However, we need not go as far as to say that the "relationship between the two sanctuaries is essentially a temporal one"[100] or that "Hebrews converts the vertical typology to the horizontal, eschatological schema by identifying the heavenly with the new age."[101] At the same time, we need not see the earthly tabernacle merely as a heavenly copy in a vertical dualism like that of Plato or assume that the author of Hebrews adapts "Platonic language to his own Jewish-Christian apocalyptic framework."[102]

---

the age to come (or that has come)... [and with Jesus' coming] there is a temporal ambiguity between the current age and the age to come, as both ages overlap in the audience's present" (ibid., 110).

97. Guthrie, "Hebrews," 970.

98. Keene, "Heaven Is a Tent," 46.

99. The earthly tabernacle is thoroughly vertical *and* horizontal, for by virtue of it being a copy (τύπος) of the heavenly one, it served as a "training device for orienting the Old Covenant people toward their New Covenant heavenly home" (Stuart, *Exodus*, 581).

100. Lane, *Hebrews 1–8*, cxxiii.

101. E. E. Ellis, "Quotations in the NT," *ISBE* 4:24. Scholars such as Horace Hummel have addressed how Hebrews scholarship tends to dismiss vertical typology as "an unassimilated remnant of paganism" and that biblical typology is often accepted as primarily horizontal. Allegory is primarily vertical and "history-escaping" while typology retains both vertical and horizontal elements ("The Old Testament Basis of Typological Interpretation," *BR* 9 [1964]: 39, esp. 39 n. 49).

102. deSilva, "Hebrews," 226.

Rather, from one point of view, the heavenly tabernacle is an "eternal archetype" that directs believers' attention upward to the locality of the already accomplished and ongoing ministry of the high priest. From another, it is an eschatological event where they look forward to the culmination of those events. This dual vantage point of the heavenly tabernacle supports the author's contention that, in Christ, believers have an already-established communion bond with God through his high priestly mediation.[103] At the same time, believers wait in expectancy for the fullness of that communion bond in its consummation as they strive to enter their Sabbath rest.

This is a crucial reminder for the recipients of Hebrews given their current situation living in the Roman Empire. Scholars have observed that the audience was in a state of disorientation and loss.[104] For example, James Thompson argues that the community had been deemed as outsiders to the Greco-Roman world around them. Hence, the author of Hebrews intends to replace their symbolic world by redirecting their attention to the "reality that is not of this creation (9:11; cf. 9:1), thus not perceptible to the senses (2:8c; 11:1; 12:18), in an attempt to rebuild their symbolic world."[105] In response, the author reasserts their "insider" status as a cultic community whose participation in the heavenly cultus gives them an alternative symbolic world and an identity that distinguishes them from the dominant culture.[106]

Because of the social challenges that his audience's occupied earthly spaces bring, the author points to the better space of the heavenly tabernacle. He does not point to the future as if a space does not yet exist; rather, he points upward as it currently exists and forward to its full consummation. In the present, the believers' access is affirmed. The paraenetic passages that warn the believers to continue to strive to enter eschatological rest had been established in earlier passages such as 3:12–4:16 and 6:1–20. While not straying from the sobering tone of his warnings, the author also points the readers *upwards* to the inauguration of eschatological promises that they already have received. Hence, the believers look not only forward to a *new creation* of the eschatological sanctuary by way of the temple, but they also look first *upward* to the already, spatially realized eschatological tabernacle as they wait for its consummation.[107]

---

103. The author's worldview includes "his perception of the temporal and spatial dimensions of the metanarrative undergirding reality and the unfolding of history" (Stewart, "Cosmology, Eschatology, and Soteriology," 546).

104. Thompson, "Insider Ethics," 211. Marie Isaacs writes that the author relocates the sacred territory that was once located geographically on earth to a beatific state in heaven. In other words, he is "re-locating the holy" (*Sacred Space*, 78–86).

105. Thompson, "Insider Ethics," 211.

106. Ibid., 212.

107. "Both types of thinking are ways of relating the transcendent to the earthly, and in a mature theological perspective it may be that both are necessary" (Hurst, "Eschatology and 'Platonism,'" 47) and for the horizontal, "the manifestation of such things is put off until the future" (ibid., 48).

Therefore, for New Testament believers, the potential error is not that they "look in hope to the building of another temple in Jerusalem composed of earthly 'bricks and mortar,'"[108] but that they look exclusively to the heavenly bricks and mortar in the consummated temple in the future eschaton. Thus, they were not wrong in *what* they were looking for but rather *where* they were looking for it.[109] It is in the vertical sense that Christ's inauguration into the heavenly holy place keeps open a way for believers so that the "right of access never grows obsolete."[110] This access must remain open in order for Jesus' disciples to faithfully order the space around them.[111] What is then physically out of sight is compensated by the Holy Spirit who communicates and extends the presence of Christ.[112]

While invisible to the eye, believers' certainty in the attainment of the heavenly sacred space is tied to Christ himself. Geoffrey Lilburne presents a theological praxis of Jesus' incarnation by presenting it as the locus for our notion of time and space.[113] If God entered into time and space through the incarnation, then our reality of time and space is reestablished in our connection to Christ. If such is the case, then there are implications for Jesus' resurrection as well. If our sense of place is tied to Christ's body, then our sense of place must be tied to where Christ's body is located—in the heavenly tabernacle.

---

108. Beale, "Eden, Temple, and Church's Mission," 20; *New Testament Biblical Theology*, 634.

109. Yet the line of sight will change from being towards the heavens to the earth when the New Jerusalem descends (Rev. 21:2). The affinity that the heavenly tabernacle has with its Jewish apocalyptic background lies in the temporal element that includes a progression of events (e.g., Jesus' entrance into the sanctuary [9:11], the ongoing cultic activity in the heavens [1:14], the coming of future judgment [10:30], and the continual participation of sacrifices [13:15–16]; cf. Ribbens, *Levitical Sacrifice*, 94). Mackie writes that while both spatial and temporal dimensions are present in Jewish apocalyptic, individual texts may emphasize one over the other. For example, 1 Enoch brings the spatial dimension to the fore while 4 Ezra and 2 Baruch bring out the temporal. However, "in almost all apocalyptic works both dimensions mutually cohere" (*Eschatology and Exhortation*, 32). The idea of future, end-time benefits residing as present realities in heaven is reflected in texts such as 4 Ezra 7:14, 26, 83; 8:52; 13:18; 2 Bar. 4:6; 21:12; 48:49; 51:8; 52:7; 1 En. 1:36; 42:8; 46:3 (Beale, *New Testament Biblical Theology*, 246 n. 43; Lincoln, *Paradise Now and Not Yet*, 43, 101, 149; Mackie, *Eschatology and Exhortation*, 6 n. 16).

110. David J. MacLeod, "The Present Work of Christ in Hebrews," *BSac* 148.590 (1991): 190.

111. Sleeman, *Geography and the Ascension Narrative*, 12. Sleeman refers to Jesus' place in heaven and the rich functionality of that notion shaping the earthly settings within Acts. As Gäbel aptly states, "Auch das gegenwärtige Leben der Adressaten soll, seiner Ausrichtung auf den Himmel unbeschadet, auf Erden gelebt warden" (*Kulttheologie*, 483).

112. Charles F. D. Moule, *The Origin of Christology* (1977; repr., Cambridge: Cambridge University Press, 1995), 104; cf. Sleeman, *Geography and the Ascension Narrative*, 13.

113. Lilburne, *Sense of Place*, 107–10.

In conclusion, the author urges the believers to see Christ (2:9; 12:2) and, through faith, have the assurance of things hoped for (11:1).[114] This is the same exhortation given to Moses who obeyed God by "seeing him who is unseen" (τὸν γὰρ ἀόρατον ὡς ὁρῶν ἐκαρτέρησεν, 12:27).[115] This is how the community perseveres and maintains their identity as priests on earth. The more they understand their heavenly standing with Christ, the more they can see him in what Mackie calls "mystical visuality."[116] This term befits the believers' sense of place within the heavenly tabernacle:

> From thinking of the eschatological state as future, the Christian mind is led to conceive of it as actually present but situated in a higher sphere. The horizontal, dramatic way of thinking gives place in part to a process of thought moving in a perpendicular direction and distinguishing not so much between before and after, but rather between higher and lower.[117]

This is crucial for the believer, as the question that existed for the Old Testament Israelites remained true for the recipients of Hebrews: the question of reconciliation between the transcendent God and man's earthly limitations. The heavenly tabernacle as a feature of Hebrews' vertical and horizontal eschatology addresses that gap. As Horace Hummel reflects, "What is at stake in the insistence on the integrality of the vertical dimension, I think, is that sense of the transcendent within the immanent, of eternity in time, that constitutes the biblical concept of 'Heilsgeschichte' and structures its eschatology."[118] Hebrews eschatology is both spatial and temporal and demands attention both vertically and horizontally. It is the bridge between what is transcendent and what is immanent for believers. Furthermore, these implications result in believers embracing their spatial identity as occupants of the heavenly sanctuary. As I will argue in the next chapter, this spatial identity is a priestly identity—one they will actualize in practice on earth (i.e., Thirdspace priestly activity).

---

114. Cf. Mackie, "Heavenly Sanctuary Mysticism," 79. The author of Hebrews warns his audience that a life that does not exhibit peace with others and holiness results in not being able to *see* the Lord (οὗ χωρὶς οὐδεὶς ὄψεται τὸν κύριον, 12:14).

115. Ibid.

116. Ibid.

117. Vos, *Redemptive History and Biblical Interpretation*, 198.

118. Hummel, "OT Basis," 39 n. 4.

Chapter 8

THIRDSPACE PRIESTLY ACTIVITY

One of the notable features of Hebrews is how the author interweaves doctrinal exposition with hortatory commands.[1] As a result, one might presume that the salvific benefits of Christ's high priestly ministry immediately result in believers' lived-out ethics. In spatial terms, this equates to assuming that believers' spatial grounding in the heavenly tabernacle directly leads to obeying the author's exhortations found especially starting from Hebrews 10:19. However, a crucial intermediary step must be acknowledged, that is, the believers' self-understanding of their identity as priests.

Prior to the climactic presentation of Christ's high priestly sacrifice and salvation conferred to believers, the author of Hebrews redefines the legitimacy of the priesthood in Hebrews 7:1–28.[2] This is the first in-depth explanation of the extension of the priesthood outside of the Levites. The author of Hebrews asserts Christ's priestly qualifications, which are based not on a legal requirement derived

---

1. In contrast with a more sequential presentation (i.e., indicative-imperative paradigm) as that of Paul's letters in Ephesians 1–3 and 4–6, and Romans 1–11 and 12–15. Michel also notes this "shift in emphasis" (Akzentverschiebung) but goes too far in stating that the theological thought in Hebrews reaches its culmination in its paraenesis (*Der Brief an die Hebräer*, 27).

2. It can be argued that the role of the priesthood existed in Adam even before the Levites existed. Michael Morales and G. K. Beale state that Adam's role within Eden (the garden-temple) was a priestly one. Hence, he was commanded to "worship and obey" (Gen. 2:15), which also describe the duties of the Levites pertaining to the tabernacle in Num. 3:7-8; 8:26; 18:5-6 (Beale, *New Testament Biblical Theology*, 620–21, 639; *Temple and the Church's Mission*, 66–82; Morales, *Who Shall Ascend?*, 53). Jason Hood writes, "The paradisical place of God's royal presence on earth in Eden and the temple mirrors God's heavenly paradise from which he reigns…" ("The Temple and the Thorn: 2 Corinthians 12 and Paul's Heavenly Ecclesiology," *BBR* 21.3 [2011]: 361). If we utilize this analogy, my proposal that the priesthood is tied to the sanctuary is strengthened. Adam's role as priest presumes his presence *within* Eden to guard and protect from outside evil, and to worship God while remaining in it. It is unsurprising that when Adam's role as priest is taken away,

from one's physical descent but based on the power of indestructible life (7:16).³ The reason for the inadequacy of the *former* priests is that they were prevented by death from continuing (v. 23).⁴ Therefore, Christ, the one who possesses this indestructible life who descends from Judah (v. 14), becomes the basis for the New Covenant priesthood. As a result, all those who share a spiritual genealogy with him are by association, priests.⁵ It is not coincidental that Psalm 110 lies in the background of Hebrews 7 where David foreshadows the messianic king who combines both kingly and priestly qualities. The lineage that is traced begins with "Melchizedek, followed by David, his descendants, and culminating in Christ" and they "represent and foreshadow the fulfillment of the promise made in Exodus 19:6, 'you shall be to me a kingdom of priests and a holy nation.'"⁶

The author's rhetorical intent is to argue for the everlasting efficacy of Christ's priesthood (vv. 23–26), which also detaches the priesthood from the levitical order and opens the possibility of the priesthood to others. Namely, those who are born again to an indestructible life are qualified to be priests. Redefining the qualifications for the priesthood is part of the author's larger rhetorical strategy. There is a change in the priesthood because of the necessary change in the law (7:12). Hence, the inauguration of a new cultus between God and mankind is based on the person of Christ who has "unmediated communion with God himself."⁷ Therefore, the "age-old covenantal traditions, symbols, paraeneses and promises are transformed into realities of the new age; it is also the day of the new priesthood of meeting 'face to face', a priesthood after the order of Melchizedek."⁸

he is also expelled from the tabernacle-garden sanctuary, which ultimately is exile from God's presence. His access to the garden goes hand-in-hand with his identity and role as the Edenic priest.

3. The term ἀκατάλυτος occurs only here in the NT and once in 4 Macc. 10:11: "But you, because of your impiety and bloodthirstiness, will endure unceasing (ἀκαταλύτους) tortures." Note the alpha privative of καταλύω, which connotes the idea of being endless and not able to be destroyed (Friedrich Büchsel and Otto Procksch, "ἀκατάλυτος," *TDNT* 4:338).

4. Num. 3:5–10; 18:1–7.

5. Christ is the true Son, and he calls New Covenant believers his "brethren" and "fellow sons brought into glory" (2:10–12).

6. Lacy K. Crocker, "A Holy Nation," *RTR* 72.3 (2013): 200. Based on this reading, Crocker suggests that any sacerdotal activities demonstrated by David reflect the priesthood of believers, which in turn are rooted in Christ.

7. Dunnill, *Covenant and Sacrifice in Hebrews*, 256.

8. Ibid., 257. For Second Temple understandings of Melchizedek, see Steeve Bélanger, "L'Épître aux Hébreux dans le contexte spéculatif sur la figure de Melchisédech durant la période du Second Temple de Jérusalem (IIᵉ siècle avant notre ère - Iᵉʳ siècle de notre ère)," *ASE* 33.1 (2016): 31–77. Bélanger concludes that the Melchizedek figure was well known in different Judean circles of the Second Temple period although the "speculation of a super-human figure" (*les spéculations sur une figure suprahumaine*) was limited to only certain Judean circles (ibid., 76).

A person's identity arises from the "indicative" of facts that is personally applicable to him. An awareness of this indicative brings about a transformation of his self-understanding, which results in his lived-out ethic (i.e., imperative). In other words, what Christ has done affects who believers are, and the fact of who believers are in turn impacts how they live. Spatially speaking, believers' positional standing in the heavenly tabernacle qualifies them as priests (i.e., where they are impacts how they live). This heavenly based identity is what qualifies, enables, and empowers believers to live out as priests on earth (i.e., to live out priestly Thirdspace).

This chapter will investigate the evidence that suggests the identification of believers as priests in Hebrews.[9] I will argue that the language applied to them is cultic language that has its roots in priestly language pertaining to the levitical order.[10] An important link is believers' entrance into the heavenly, holy sanctuary (προσέρχομαι/ἔρχομαί/εἴσοδος), which marks their classification as priests. As this identification is established, the commands for believers are priestly commands: λειτουργέω, λατρεύω, and διακονέω. Believers are able to embrace their identity and heed these exhortations due to their purified conscience and renewed confidence by holding fast and being grounded in Christ's spatial occupancy in the holy sanctuary. Having done so, they can proceed in obeying the priestly commands associated with spatial movement: to offer up (vertical

---

9. I acknowledge that the identification of believers as priests is not the sole or not even the primary application given to the audience of Hebrews. There are others, such as their identity as God's sons (Heb. 12:5–7). For example, Amy L. B. Peeler, *You Are My Son: The Family of God in the Epistle to the Hebrews*, LNTS 486 (New York: T&T Clark, 2015). But in such cases, these themes complement each other. For example, Franz Laub argues that Jesus' sonship, including his pre-existence, humiliation, and exaltation, is the foundation upon which the author of Hebrews lays his high priestly Christology. As such, they are all soteriologically relevant (*soteriologisch relevante*) ("Ein für allemal hineingegangen," 66). Similarly, Helmut Feld presents the entire Christology of Hebrews under three sections: the Son of God (*Der Sohn Gottes*), the earthly Jesus (*der irdische Jesus*), and the High Priest (*der Hohepriester*) (*Der Hebräerbrief*, ErFor 228 [Darmstadt: Wissenschaftliche Buchgesellschaft, 1985], 65–81). William Loader, in his revised dissertation, argues that the author of Hebrews utilized various traditions to present Jesus Christ as both son and high priest. At the same time, the author also acted as a "creative theologian" (*schöpferischer Theologe*) who was cognizant of the situational demands of his readers (*Sohn und Hoherpriester: Eine traditionsgeschichtliche Untersuchung zur Christologie des Hebrierbriefes*, WMANT 53 [Neukirchen-Vluyn: Neukirchener, 1981], 259).

10. I am not referring to Cesla Spicq's assertion that the recipients of the letters of Hebrews were converted Jewish or Essene priests stemming forth from Acts 6:7 and the warning to not return to Judaism (*L'Épître aux Hébreux*, 1:226–31, 1:238–42; cf. Ellingworth, *Hebrews*, 26–27). Spicq bases this speculation on the errant assumption that only priests have the intelligence and taste for a theology of the priesthood as presented in Hebrews: "Seuls des prêtres ont suffisamment l'intelligence et le goût de cette théologie du sacerdoce pour qu'on puisse leur écrire" (*L'Épître aux Hébreux*, 1:226).

priestly service), and to minister to one another (horizontal priestly service). This is the Thirdspace outcome of the existing physical Firstspace features of the heavenly tabernacle and the believers' Secondspace occupancy within it. In other words, the author of Hebrews utilizes powerful spatial language of the heavenly tabernacle to affirm believers' co-occupancy with the heavenly high priest. This "priestly union with Christ" in turn solidifies their identity as priests and impels them to live in priestly obedience.

8.1. Thirdspace Cultic Language

The general priesthood of believers[11] is explicitly found in both Old and New Testament passages: Exodus 19:5–6; Isaiah 61:6; 66:21;[12] 1 Peter 2:5; and Revelation 1:6; 5:10; 20:6.[13] While Hebrews is the only New Testament letter in which Christ is explicitly described as a priest, in a somewhat surprising fashion, the believers are not.[14] This has led scholars such as Marie Isaacs to claim that in Hebrews, nowhere "are [believers] designated 'priests,'" and "the notion of the priesthood of believers is never explicitly developed in Hebrews."[15] Such statements are countered in works such as John Scholer's *Proleptic Priests* (1991),[16]

---

11. I equate this term with βασίλειον ἱεράτευμα, which applies to the entire (Israelite or Christian) community as it "denotes priestly corporation" being distinguished by the spiritual sacrifices offered through the community (Gottlob Schrenk, "ἱεράτευμα," *TDNT* 3:250). I will further propose in Section 8.3 that, in Hebrews, this also includes reciprocal activity amongst believers. The term βασίλειον "means that it belongs to the King" (ibid.).

12. In Isa. 66:21, the Lord declares that even Gentiles will be priests of God.

13. Subsequent writings after the writing of Hebrews also show evidence of the concept of a general priesthood. For example, Philo opines that during the Passover festival the entire nation of Israel functions as priests because "there is nothing more beautiful than that the divine cult should be performed by all in harmony" (*Quaest. in Exod.* 1:10).

14. This is perhaps due to the author of Hebrews wanting to exclusively reserve the *high priestly* identification to Christ alone. Furthermore, believers are not called to be priests through any acts of their own but passively so based on Christ's active priestly mediation (cf. Enrique Nardoni, "Partakers in Christ (Hebrews 3.14)," *NTS*. 37.3 [1991]: 468).

15. Isaacs, "Hebrews 13:9–16 Revisited," 283. See also Attridge, *Hebrews*, 288; Moore, "Heaven's Revolving Door?," 187–207; "In or Near," 185–98; James Swetnam, Review of *Proleptic Priests: Priesthood in the Epistle to the Hebrews* by John Scholer," *CBQ* 54 (1992): 799–800.

16. Scholer, *Proleptic Priests*. Older and less comprehensive works that argue for the general priesthood of believers in Hebrews are Ernest Best, "Spiritual Sacrifice: General Priesthood in the New Testament," *Int* 14.3 (1960): 273–99; Nils Alstrup Dahl, "A New and Living Way: The Approach to God According to Hebrews 10:19-25," *Int* 5.4 (1951): 401–12; Lambertus Floor, "The General Priesthood of Believers in the Epistle to the Hebrews," *Neot* 5 (1971): 72–82; and Olaf Moe, "Der Gedanke des allgemeinen Priestertums im Hebräerbrief," *TZ* 3 (1949): 161–69.

which is the most comprehensive and recent work arguing for the general priesthood of believers in Hebrews. To do so, Scholer argues that the cultic language used in Hebrews is analogous to the LXX's presentation of the levitical cult.[17]

Based on the author of Hebrews' argumentation, at first glance, it may be tempting to dismiss the levitical order altogether. But we must recognize how the author skillfully utilizes the language and concepts of the levitical system to communicate New Covenant realities for the believer, which include believers' identity as priests. The author of Hebrews argues not against the concept of the priesthood at large, but rather, against the material offered, such as the blood of bulls (10:4).

A heavenly cult, a heavenly tabernacle, and a heavenly high priest continue to exist. In fact, these are the ultimate spiritual reality and basis (the archetype/antitype) upon which the Old Covenant order was modeled. Believers undergo the spiritual purification rites to obtain access to the sanctuary that are akin to the purification requirements for levitical priests.[18] That believers undergo such priestly rites implies both their access into the sanctuary and, along with it, their sacrifice (Christ's blood on their behalf) is effective before God.[19] Hence, their "cleansing of the flesh," effected by the blood of Christ and offered through the eternal Spirit (9:13–14), instates believers to serve as New Covenant priests with spiritual offerings that are acceptable due to their purified consciences.[20] When we look at the cultic language applied to believers, explicit priestly designations such as βασίλειον ἱεράτευμα (1 Pet. 2:9) are not necessary. Olaf Moe puts it well by drawing our attention to the cultic orientation of the addressed community in Hebrews:

> Wenn wir aber beobachten, daß die ganze Orientierung des Gedankenganges im Hebraerbrief eine kultische ist und als das Ziel des sacerdotium Christi das Nahen der Gemeinde zu Gott, der Gottesdienst des Gläubigen, die Darbringung ihrer Opfer bestimmt wird, dann ist es von vorherein wahrscheinlich, daß die Gemeinde eben als ein priesterliches Volk und die einzelnen Christen als Priester betrachtet warden.[21]

---

17. Hebrews uses cultic, priestly language to depict believers' status while also making clear that the expiatory act of sacrifice is reserved to Christ (Gerald O'Collins and Michael Keenan Jones, *Jesus Our Priest: A Christian Approach to the Priesthood of Christ* [Oxford: Oxford University Press, 2010], 56; cf. also Gäbel, *Kulttheologie*, 428; Scholer, *Proleptic Priests*, 205).

18. See Lev. 21:16–24.

19. Moret, "Le role," 302: "Le sanctuaire est le lieu de la présence de Dieu, la mise en place d'une classe sacerdotale accédant dans le sanctuaire permet d'affirmer ou de symboliser que le sacrifice a une efficacité devant Dieu."

20. Grässer, *An die Hebräer*, 1:258.

21. "But if we observe that the entire orientation of the train of thought in Hebrews is cultic and the goal of Christ's priesthood is drawing the congregation to God, the worship of believers, and their sacrifices, then it is probable that from the beginning the

8.1.1. προσέρχομαι and εἰσέρχομαι

Earlier I interacted with John Scholer's distinction between προσέρχομαι and εἰσέρχομαι with regard to the status of believers' entry into the heavenly tabernacle.[22] While I do not agree with his sharp distinction between a preliminary access of believers (προσέρχομαι) and Jesus' full entry (εἰσέρχομαι), his correlation of Hebrews' priestly language with the cultic language of the LXX is helpful.[23] He observes that every occurrence of προσέρχομαι in the LXX lies within the cultic context associated with access into God's presence through spiritual acts such as worship and prayer.[24] He concludes, "To 'draw near' is descriptive therefore of the ministering, sacrificing, and offering function of the priest.... We may conclude, therefore, that the cultic uses of *qareb* [קרב] and *niggaš* [נגש] in the LXX make reference to the priestly access to the sanctuary, altar and first tent, in order to minister for the people by making offerings."[25]

---

congregation was viewed to be a priestly one and individual Christians as priests" (Moe, "Der Gedanke des allgemeinen," 161).

22. Cf. Section 7.1. Following Scholer's work, there have been debates around his designation of προσέρχομαι and εἰσέρχομαι as distinct references to "approach" and "entrance" into the sanctuary (cf. Mackie, "Let Us Draw Near," 17–36; Moore, "Heaven's Revolving Door?," 187–207).

23. Although Scholer's work is the most comprehensive, he was not the first to propose cultic connotations of προσέρχομαι in Hebrews. For example, Moe notes that προσέρχομαι, which occurs six times (actual number of occurrences is seven), points to a "cultic direction" (*kultischer Richtung*) given places in the LXX such as Num. 18:4 and Jer. 7:16 ("Der Gedanke des allgemeinen Priestertums im Hebräerbrief," 162; also Kuss, *Der Brief an die Hebräer*, 155).

24. The two Hebrew words translated as προσέρχομαι are קרב and נגש, which refer to an approach towards the altar of burnt offerings (Scholer, *Proleptic Priests*, 91–93). Out of the eighty occurrences of προσέρχομαι, thirty-nine are translated from קרב and twenty from נגש. While Scholer's claim is true for most of the occurrences, there are incidences when the action is not attributed to the levitical priest. For example, "If the thief is not caught, then the owner of the house shall appear before God" (προσελεύσεται ὁ κύριος τῆς οἰκίας ἐνώπιον τοῦ θεοῦ, Exod. 22:7 LXX). Still other instances contain commands for the entire Israelite community to "not approach" certain unclean persons, although one may make the case that this is related to the notion of ritual purity as it pertains to priestly functions (e.g., Lev. 18:6, 19; 20:16). Nevertheless, the term is most frequently used to describe a priestly approach in the sacrifice cultus (Best, "Spiritual Sacrifice," 281).

25. Scholer, *Proleptic Priests*, 93–94. In his commentary on 4:16, Grässer doubts the priestly connotation for believers because "als term. techn. für das Nahen des Priesters zu Gott wird προσέρχομαι weder vom Alten (vgl. Ex 16,9; Lev. 9,5) noch vom Neuen Testament gebraucht" (*An die Hebräer*, 1:259). However, see Lev. 9:7–8 LXX: καὶ εἶπεν Μωυσῆς τῷ Ἀαρών Πρόσελθε (προσέρχομαι) πρὸς τὸ θυσιαστήριον...καὶ προσῆλθεν (προσέρχομαι) Ἀαρὼν πρὸς τὸ θυσιαστήριον; Deut. 5:27 LXX: πρόσελθε (προσέρχομαι) σὺ καὶ ἄκουσον ὅσα ἐὰν εἴπῃ κύριος ὁ θεὸς ἡμῶν; and esp. Deut. 21:5 LXX: καὶ προσελεύσονται (προσέρχομαι)

The command to enter is designated with εἰσέρχομαι, translated from בוא.²⁶ It is a particular usage of εἰσέρχομαι, used of the high priest during the Day of Atonement—namely for the purposes of bringing in blood as part of the sin-offering ritual.²⁷ Because such rituals took place in the inner tabernacle (past the second curtain), only the high priest performed this unique ritual.²⁸ Therefore, προσέρχομαι and εἰσέρχομαι have different and particular usages. The former refers to a preliminary access outside the inner sanctuary, and the latter refers to a full entry reserved for the high priest.

I intend to build upon Scholer's work and draw attention to the recipients of the entry commands in the Old Testament. The command to draw near is often given to Aaron, the high priest in relation to instructions regarding sacrificial offerings (Exod. 16:9; Lev. 9:7; 21:17–23; Num. 18:3–4, 22). The command is also given to Aaron's sons, the priests, for the purpose of priestly ministry: "Then the priests, the sons of Levi, shall come near (ינגשׁו/προσελεύσονται), for the LORD your God has chosen them to serve Him and to bless in the name of the LORD; and every dispute and every assault shall be settled by them" (Deut. 21:5). In other words, there is never an occasion when priests are exhorted to "draw near" *unless* there is a priestly function tied to it.²⁹ Furthermore, for all the occurrences of εἰσέρχομαι used in association with the tabernacle in the book of Leviticus, the recipient is Aaron (e.g., Lev. 16:3, 23). Therefore, I agree with Scholer that the commands to draw near and enter are part of the LXX cultic, priestly language.³⁰ I suggest, however, that these commands are especially given to designated priests (i.e., Aaron and his sons) in association with priestly service that takes place inside the tabernacle.

A. Προσέρχομαι *in Hebrews*

Out of the seven occurrences of προσέρχομαι in Hebrews, six of them explicitly have believers as the subject drawing near to the throne of grace (4:16),³¹ to God

---

οἱ ἱερεῖς οἱ Λευῖται—ὅτι αὐτοὺς ἐπέλεξεν κύριος ὁ θεός σου παρεστηκέναι αὐτῷ καὶ εὐλογεῖν ἐπὶ τῷ ὀνόματι αὐτοῦ.

26. Exod. 26:33; 28:29–30, 43; Lev. 4:5-7, 16-19; 6:23; 9:23; 10:18; 16:2–3, 12–28.

27. Scholer, *Proleptic Priests*, 150–52.

28. I am sympathetic to Scholer's desire to isolate the atonement ritual to Christ (the high priest); however, the ultimate purpose of entering the inner sanctuary is not to enact atonement but to be close with God (also Mackie, "Let Us Draw Near," 23). Hence, we can affirm believers' entrance into the innermost sanctuary though they themselves do not offer up blood but rely on Christ's mediatory self-sacrifice.

29. Exod. 19:22; 28:43; 30:20; Lev. 21:21–23.

30. Similarly in Hebrews, this cultic language is the "dominant motif that characterizes the exhortations of Hebrews" (Asumang, *Unlocking Hebrews*, 121).

31. Spicq, in his discussion on Heb. 4:16, notes here the "cultic nuance" (*la nuance cultuelle*) of προσέρχομαι (קרב) (*L'Épître aux Hébreux*, 2:94).

(7:25; 11:6), or to the eschatological mountain/city of the living God[32] (12:18, 22).[33] On the other hand, εἰσέρχομαι occurs seventeen times with five of these referring to Christ's entrance into the heavenly sanctuary.[34] Therefore, Scholer ultimately reserves entrance language (εἰσέρχομαι) for Christ, and looks elsewhere to connect the levitical priesthood to New Testament believers. He turns to explicit commands given to general priests in the Old Testament: to draw near (προσέρχομαι) to God in worship (Exod. 16:9; 24:2; Lev. 9:5; Num. 3:38; 4:19) and prayer (Jer. 7:16; Pss. 31:9 and 118:169; Zeph. 3:2 LXX), which are "sacerdotal circumstances."[35] He then applies these commands to New Testament believers to argue for their priestly identity.

Scholer's evidence for designating προσέρχομαι as a priestly command when spoken to levitical priests is convincing. However, one wonders if the same connection can be made for the entire Israelite community when they are given the same command. Drawing near to God, worship, and prayer are not, by themselves, priestly commands.[36] These are given to the Israelites as a general command that sets them apart as God's *chosen people* and not necessarily because

32. The temple was often understood as the architectural embodiment of the cosmic mountain, so similarly, the tabernacle represented the holy mountain of God (Morales, *Who Shall Ascend*, 52). Because of the perfect tense in the statement that believers "have come" (προσεληλύθατε), there is an "intimate connection and unity between the church in heaven and earth" (Ian C. Macleod, "Christ's High Priesthood and Christian Worship in Hebrews," *PRJ* 8.1 [2016]: 163).

Scholer believes that the city may be synonymous with the heavenly sanctuary elsewhere in Hebrews, but he does not specify where (*Proleptic Priests*, 141). I suggest this statement holds true, turning to Rev. 11:1-2, 19; 21:2-22, esp. v. 22. David Peterson believes an actual transfer takes place in believers' conversion and writes, "The relationship with God that believers may now enjoy, by virtue of Christ's finished work, involves as its implied end the transfer of believers to the heavenly city" (Peterson, *Perfection*, 166).

33. Hebrews 10:1 refers to the levitical priests who were not made perfect when they drew near, and 10:22 is directed to believers while the object is implicitly referred to as the space within the inner veil.

34. When believers are the subject, the object of their entrance is "rest" (3:11, 18-19; 4:1-11). Though these two verbs have varying objects of destination, what they share is the motif of the accessibility of God's presence in sacred space (Knut Backhaus, "How to Entertain Angels: Ethics in the Epistle to the Hebrews," in Gelardini, ed., *Hebrews*, 156).

35. Scholer, *Proleptic Priests*, 94.

36. Gareth Cockerill also suggests that the analogous relationship seems to be between New Testament believers and only the levitical priests based on Scholer's examples ("Review of Proleptic Priests: Priesthood in the Epistle to the Hebrews by John Scholer," *JBL* 112.1 [1993]: 172). Elsewhere Scholer defines the "unique and primary role of the priest" as his worship and sacrifice through which he serves as a mediator (*Proleptic Priests*, 19). Hence, I propose that generic worship and prayer are not what qualify one's priesthood, but rather, it is such cultic acts with the purpose of facilitating the relationship between God and others in the specified place of mediation (see Section 8.3.2).

they are official priests.³⁷ In the Old Testament, non-priests were allowed to perform priestly duties such as sacrifices at open-air altars (cf. Pss. 4:5; 50:13, 14, 23; 51:17; 141:2; Isa. 1:11-15; Hos. 6:6; Mic. 6:6-8).³⁸ The key difference lies in the location of such sacrifices; it was only the levitical priests who performed such sacrifices in the confines of the tabernacle and the temple. Altars for sacrifice and worship were not always attached to the tabernacle or temple. As Menahem Haran writes:

> Those who officiated in a temple, or at an altar adjoining a temple, were exclusive functionaries from priestly families, while at solitary altars, as we shall see later on, any Israelite could serve. The solitary altars were numerous and scattered throughout the country; there was probably no settlement without its altar, and altars could even be found outside cities, in the countryside.³⁹

This emphasizes the importance of one's location within the tabernacle structure to qualify both his acts and his identity as a priest. What gives προσέρχομαι its cultic and priestly connotations is that these acts are done in association with the spaces of the tabernacle/temple. It is when the high priest draws near to God by entering the Holy of Holies that these acts are marked as a sacerdotal function. It is when worship and prayer are offered up on behalf of the people at the altar. Hence, I suggest that Scholer's category of "sacerdotal circumstances" not be limited only to priestly acts but also be tied to their location—the tabernacle/temple structure. In other words, Scholer's argument holds true not based on the priestly functions *alone* between Old Testament and New Testament believers. Rather, it is reinforced when we draw connections between the levitical priests and New Testament believers by examining their priestly qualification *due to their entering sanctuary space*. Lambertus Floor's statement therefore better encapsulates the legitimacy of the general priesthood in Hebrews:

> In connection with the general priesthood of believers the Epistle to the Hebrews points out two things: (a) a sanctuary in which the priest of the new covenant is supposed to perform his duty; (b) a specific priestly service which has to be performed. If we are to formulate this in more homiletical terms, the Epistle to the Hebrews concerns the place and the pattern, the 'locus' and the 'modus' of the priesthood of believers.⁴⁰

---

37. Ernest Best writes, "Though priesthood is not mentioned in these contexts, and these spiritual sacrifices are at times set alongside the Temple sacrifices and not opposed to them, an opening is made for the existence of a general priesthood…" ("Spiritual Sacrifice," 276).
38. As noted by Best (ibid.).
39. Haran, *Temples and Temple-Service*, 16.
40. Floor, "General Priesthood," 73.

B. Εἰσέρχομαι in Hebrews

As mentioned previously, some hold to the position that believers are limited to preliminary access. If such is the case, the argument for the priesthood of believers is weakened. Sanctuary access and the identity of priests are inseparable.[41] The notion of believers' priesthood comes out of the identification and service of Old Testament priests in the tabernacle/temple.[42] Just as the tabernacle required specialized servants set aside for the task of priestly mediation, the presence of priests necessitated the place of such practices. The tabernacle was simultaneously the holy dwelling place for God and the place for holiness and priestly service. This leads to two observations regarding the use of priestly, cultic language for believers.

(1) First, if we observe the author of Hebrews' usage of προσέρχομαι for believers, the object of destination is never the first curtain or a general approach to the larger tabernacle structure.[43] Rather, the language already assumes their entrance. For example, in Hebrews 4:16, the author speaks to believers and exhorts them to draw near with confidence *to the throne of grace* (τῷ θρόνῳ τῆς χάριτος) to find mercy and grace.[44] This "throne of grace" is the same one located within the confines of God's innermost sanctuary as seen in passages such as Psalm 11:4: "The LORD is in his holy temple; the LORD's throne is in heaven" (cf. also Ps. 102:19; Isa. 6:1; 16:5; 66:1; Jer. 17:12; Ezek. 1:26; esp. 43:6–7; Dan. 7:9; Zech. 6:13). When we consider these references with the preceding and subsequent verses that distinguish Christ as the high priest (4:14 and 5:1), we can situate the locative setting of Christ and that of believers to be one and the same: the inner sanctuary of the heavenly tabernacle. It is precisely because Christ himself has passed through the heavens into the sanctuary

---

41. A sharp distinction between προσέρχομαι and εἰσέρχομαι overlooks how closely related προσέρχομαι is to εἰσέρχομαι. Both of them imply getting closer to God himself. Hence, the point is not simply to enter into the sanctuary but to enter in to meet God.

42. Beale and Kim, *God Dwells Among Us*, 113. Beale does not only have in mind the levitical priests but begins with Adam's work as a priest in the sanctuary of Eden and traces the priestly duty through to the call for God's people to be a nation of priests (Exod. 19:6).

43. Nicholas Moore argues for believers' preliminary entrance because, in the LXX, προσέρχομαι is used to describe the approach to the altar outside the sanctuary or the tabernacle in general and never into the Most Holy Place ("Heaven's Revolving Door," 198–99). However, it is unnecessary to force the full spectrum of meaning of προσέρχομαι in the LXX upon Hebrews. We must consider the contextual usage of προσέρχομαι in Hebrews itself.

44. Mackie notes similarly that in 10:19–23, the text provides "the most architectural detail of the entry exhortations" and "utilizes this wealth of architectural detail to convince the community of their ability to freely and confidently access God and his Son in the heavenly sanctuary" ("Let Us Draw Near," 27).

and believers' joint itinerary with him that they are able to draw near to God's throne.⁴⁵ This throne is located in the confines of a heavenly structure, that is, God's holy sanctuary.⁴⁶

Other locative designations are also used to connote the idea of heavenly destination (cf. 12:18–22). When a locative object is not explicit, believers are told to draw near to God (7:9, 25; 11:6)⁴⁷ or to draw near in a condition or manner described in cultic terminology such as "cleansing," "sprinkled," or "washed with pure water" (10:1, 22). These are all practices performed on the levitical priests for their consecration and ordination (cf. Lev. 8:6–13).⁴⁸ The levitical priests could only draw near by the blood of another. This priestly condition applies for believers who draw near by the blood of Christ.⁴⁹ As such, there is a contrast between those who draw near now (προσέρχομαι) and

---

45. Describing the throne as one of "grace" is unique in Hebrews, which the author utilizes to reinforce the idea that this approach is only made possible by the gracious, salvific benefits secured by Christ.

46. Moore does concede and state that the exhortation to approach this throne is the "closest Hebrews comes to suggesting that believers actually do enter the heavenly sanctuary" ("Heaven's Revolving Door," 203).

47. If προσέρχομαι is strictly tied to believers' preliminary entrance just outside the tabernacle gateway, then we would have to assume that is where God resides as well, since the author of Hebrews commands them to draw near to God.

48. The context is more specifically the Day of Atonement (Scholer, *Proleptic Priests*, 129; cf. Lev. 4:6, 17; 5:9; 16:14–15, 34). The priestly activities of ministering, sacrificing, and offering are not the end goal; they are the means through which the priest may stand in the presence of God. Through their mediatory role, the people of God are granted such access, as can be seen in their commands to "draw near to God" or, in the case when atonement has not been made, to *not* draw near to him (Exod. 3:5; 22:8; 24:2; Num. 16:5; Deut. 4:11; 5:27). Exodus 19:10–15 lies in the background of Heb. 12:18–22; the Israelites are commanded to approach the mountain but not go up on it or touch it. Before they approach, they must be consecrated by washing their garments and refraining from sexual activity. Interestingly, priestly consecration rites are applied to the entire Israelite congregation. Only after consecration takes place does God call the Israelites a kingdom of priests and a holy nation (Exod. 19:15–16). Dahl believes the background in Heb. 10:19–22 is the sprinkling of blood on the Israelites at Mt. Sinai prior to the inauguration of God's covenant, which later developed into the initiation of priests ("New and Living Way," 406, esp. n. 25). In Heb. 12:18–21, the same warning is present regarding the mountain. This time, however, the mountain that was untouchable is now accessible. In fact, believers have already come to the mountain (v. 22, ἀλλὰ προσεληλύθατε Σιὼν)!

49. In a similar manner to his contrasting the earthly and heavenly tabernacles, the author of Hebrews contrasts the former priests with believers; their respective "sprinklings" and "washings" differ.

the old priests—"a parallelism that in itself argues for a priestly designation."[50] Altogether, these practices comprise the sacerdotal activity performed at the altar which finds its culmination in the sacrificial rituals in the inner sanctuary.[51]

(2) The second observation is noting the differences in the entry of access between the Old Testament priests and New Testament believers. Because Scholer sees προσέρχομαι in the LXX reserved for levitical priests who stood outside the tabernacle entrance, and not referring to the high priest who enters, he attributes the same spatial status to New Testament believers with regards to the heavenly tabernacle. However, he overlooks a crucial fact which exponentially elevates the situation of New Testament believers. That is, while the Israelites and their priests were at best, given preliminary access at sundry times, New Testament believers are given full, continual access due to their union with Jesus Christ. Therefore, we need not apply the Old Testament situation to New Testament believers in a strict, one-to-one fashion.

This is precisely why the author of Hebrews utilizes the following logic: (1) First, Christ, as the high priest, has definitively entered the heavenly sanctuary (Heb. 4:10; 6:19–20; 9:12, 24). (2) Following, believers, by holding fast to Christ, have also entered that same sanctuary and therefore are able to draw near to God himself.[52] This may explain why the author of Hebrews reserves the usage of εἰσέρχομαι to Christ only, so the recipients of the letter are reminded that only Jesus has *actively* entered the inner sanctuary, while they have done so *passively* through their association with him.[53]

This also explains why the author of Hebrews affirms that Christ *has entered* into the inner sanctuary as a *forerunner* for believers (6:19) and later, that believers themselves have the confidence *to enter* the holy place by the blood of

---

50. Scholer, *Proleptic Priests*, 124.

51. There is also a connection to Christ's prayers at the culmination of his earthly priestly ministry before his death (ibid., 108).

52. Mackie argues that the background of Heb. 6:18–20 is the asylum granted to manslaughterers who take refuge in cities and seize the horns of the altar (Num. 35; cf. also 1 Kgs 1:50; 2:29) (Mackie, "Let Us Draw Near," 32). Moore contests this by locating the altar in 1 Kings as being outside the sanctuary proper ("Heaven's Revolving Door," 198). However, Mackie's argument is not based on identifying the object of κρατῆσαι as the altar of burnt offering in 1 Kings; rather, he is simply reinforcing the idea that "holding fast" necessitates an object (e.g., Jesus or the hope) for refuge. Thus, this passage, along with others, "forges a mimetic and linguistic link between the community and Jesus as their 'forerunner'" (Mackie, "Let Us Draw Near," 33).

53. Others have noted that εἰσέρχομαι is never used "directly" of the audience (Cockerill, "Review on Proleptic Priests," 172). As a result, Scholer attributes full entry only to deceased Christians who are consciously and spiritually in the heavens (*Proleptic Priests*, 11, 149). This creates a problem whereby there are two classes of Christians—those living on earth and those who have died. Furthermore, this view fails to acknowledge that what dead believers currently experience in heaven is qualitatively different from what believers should expect to experience in Christ's second advent (cf. Rom. 8:18–25).

Jesus (10:19).⁵⁴ If we maintain Scholer's preliminary threshold access against a full-fledged entry, then the usage of προσερχώμεθα in Hebrews 10:22's creates an interpretive problem: How can believers draw near to God if they are merely standing at the threshold of God's throne room as Scholer contends? Or, if God is the goal, how can the author boldly exhort believers to draw near to him if he locates them as being at the "outside?"⁵⁵ The context of verse 19 is filled with priestly language comprising of purification acts performed upon believers. Their hearts are *sprinkled clean* and their bodies are *washed with pure water*. This is the kind of consecration performed upon Aaron and his sons; therefore, in Hebrews 10:19–22, προσερχώμεθα carries "its full significance and refers to the approach of the priest to God."⁵⁶

In conclusion, Scholer's work is significant for its comprehensive study on the priestly commands of access for believers. By tracing their usages throughout the LXX and intertestamental literature, he argues for the general priesthood of believers. While I agree with his conclusions, there is further support to be made that goes beyond simply making connections of generic "priestly activities" such as worship, prayer, and approach to God. This is possible by localizing such activities specifically within the spaces of the tabernacle. Scholer at least recognizes the challenge of spatially orienting the believers when he writes that the perfect indicative usage of προσέρχομαι in Hebrews is a "problem," asking

---

54. That εἴσοδον is associated with entrance into God's realm is further supported in 1 Pet. 1:11, where the accusative preposition εἰς specifies the place of entrance: ἡ εἴσοδος εἰς τὴν αἰώνιον βασιλείαν. Scholer has difficulty explaining the application of such strong entrance language to believers in passages like Heb. 10:19–22 and suggests that the author uses entry verbs simply because of its "high-priestly context" (*Proleptic Priests*, 182). Grässer also notes how ἐγκαινίζω (10:20) has cultic overtones in the OT (cf. Num. 7:11 LXX; 1 Esd. 7:7 LXX; Dan. 3:2 LXX) (*An die Hebräer*, 3:14).

55. One could possibly argue that the exhortations are *presently* made in light of a *future* entrance. In response, (1) this would temporally separate the hortatory command from the doctrinal reality, which seems at odds with how the author of Hebrews interweaves the two throughout the epistle (cf. Section 7:1; MacLeod, "The Literary Structure of the Book of Hebrews," 185–97; Punt, "Hebrews, Thought-Patterns and Context: Aspects of the Background of Hebrews," 121; Stanley, "The Structure of Hebrews from Three Perspectives," 247–49). Instead, it is more accurate to make a distinction between what believers can currently do *spiritually* and will later do *physically*. (2) the salvific benefits that the author of Hebrews espouses are contingent on believers' union with Christ. Hence, to not assume believers' full entrance into the heavenly tabernacle potentially diminishes their "partaking of Christ" (Heb. 3:14).

56. Best, "Spiritual Sacrifice," 281. "The levitical priesthood passes into the priesthood of Christ, and through him into the priesthood of Christians, who are sprinkled with his blood and washed in baptism (10:22), and who are installed by his single offering (10:14); the members of the church are thus successors to the levitical priests" (ibid., 286).

how believers can be considered to have been "brought in" while they still reside on earth.[57] His solution is to attribute their access to their experiential spheres (i.e., priestly acts).[58] This, however, replicates the levitical system whereby their priestly access to God is granted by way of their own cultic activity. In other words, it dismisses the priestly work of Christ by which believers are granted priestly access. It is not by the way of believers' priestly activity that they are recognized as priests, but by a new and living way that Christ has inaugurated through his flesh (10:20). It is only *after* they have been granted priestly access that they can appropriate their priestly identity through their activity of priestly service.

8.1.2. λειτουργός and λατρεύω

The invitation for believers to enter the heavenly sanctuary is also an invitation to participate in the liturgical activity that takes place within. In describing the kinds of activity that the author attributes to believers there, he makes a "continual usage of sacrificial and cultic language" that implies succession from the levitical priesthood.[59] In Section 4.2, I discussed the co-sharing of space between Christ and the believers in Hebrews 2:10–12. There, both Christ and believers are identified as having one Father. Therefore, Christ is not ashamed to call them brothers and together, as one family of God, they sing praise *in the midst of the congregation* (ἐν μέσῳ ἐκκλησίας).

By itself, ἐκκλησίας refers to the larger community of Israelites, and any specification to a subgroup within them depends on the immediate context. In Hebrews 2:12, the quotation from Psalm 22 describes a votive feast, which follows the instructions given in Leviticus 7:16.[60] In light of God's answers to prayers, a vow is made, followed with a sacrifice, which is then followed by a feast. Throughout the procedure, the Levites participate in joint congregational praise, proclaiming what the Lord has done on their behalf. Hence, Psalm 22:25–26 is a congregational liturgy whereby the psalmist invites the congregation who is present with him to sing praises to God.[61] If such is the case, it is not surprising that the psalmist (or Jesus, in the context of Heb. 2:11–13) calls upon his fellow

---

57. Moore also notes that this dual portrayal could be at best confusing and at worst contradictory ("In or Near," 185).

58. Scholer, *Proleptic Priests*, 143–44, 181–82. Hence, believers are "proleptic" in that full priestly participation lies in the future (ibid., 145–46; cf. Johnsson, "Defilement and Purgation," 332–33).

59. Best, "Spiritual Sacrifice," 280.

60. Derek Kidner, *Psalms 1–72: An Introduction and Commentary*, TOTC 15 (Downers Grove, IL: InterVarsity Press, 1973), 126.

61. Peter C. Craigie, *Psalms 1–50*, 2nd ed., WBC 19 (Nashville, TN: Nelson, 2004), 200–201. Gäbel writes that the addressees see themselves as taking part in the "cult community" (*Kultgemeinde*) of the heavenly Jerusalem (*Kulttheologie*, 472).

brethren to join the heavenly liturgy in the presence of God.[62] This is likely the same setting in Hebrews 12:23, where believers are told that they have already come to Mt. Zion, where they join with a myriad of angels and the general assembly of the firstborn (ἐκκλησίᾳ πρωτοτόκων) in the presence of God.[63] Hence, Jesus' call for praise is an invocation to "induce the recipients to enter into and participate in the heavenly drama."[64]

This liturgical drama consists not only of praise, but of commands to serve and minister as priests.[65] As previously mentioned, Hebrews does not explicitly describe believers as priests; rather, they are described as priests *implicitly* through their spatial orientation/identity and by their priestly activity attributed to them. The focus in the following section will be on λειτουργός and λατρεύω, two words used to describe priestly activity in the sanctuary. In Sections 8.2-3, we will see what such priestly activity entails, to be categorized under believers' vertical offering of worship and/or their horizontal ethics towards others within the Christian community.

A. λειτουργός in Hebrews

The first instance of priestly service language appears in Hebrews 1:7, where God calls the angels "ministers, a flame of fire" (τοὺς λειτουργοὺς αὐτοῦ πυρὸς φλόγα), and in 1:14, where the author calls them "ministering spirits" (λειτουργικὰ πνεύματα). The context is the author's description of the activity of the heavenly angels on behalf of those who inherit salvation.[66] The cultic role of angels also

---

62. Mackie notes the reciprocal confession between the Son's confession of the Fatherhood of God, and the Son's conferral of family membership upon believers. This reinforcement of believers' identity as the Son's siblings is also an invitation for them to participate in the symbolic universe of liturgical invocations in the heavenly sanctuary ("Confession of the Son of God," 115).

63. Philip Church also notes the shared liturgical worship between humans and angels in 12:22-24 but suggests this is possible due to the heavenly temple "encompassing heaven and earth" ("Wilderness Tabernacle," 134). Hence, true worship is one and the same in both heaven and earth as the believers join in with the genuine *Engelgemeinschaft* (ibid., 117). See also Crispin H. T. Fletcher-Louis, *All the Glory of Adam: Liturgical Anthropology in the Dead Sea Scrolls*, STDJ 42 (Leiden: Brill, 2002), 307-9.

64. Mackie, "Confession of the Son of God," 122, who also suggests that entry commands such as προσέρχομαι and εἰς τὴν εἴσοδον are cultic invitations to participate in the aforementioned liturgical drama. Grässer interprets the approach to the throne of grace in Heb. 4:16 as an invitation to the heavenly festal assembly (*himmlischen Festversammlung*) (*An die Hebräer*, 1:258).

65. Spicq writes that the "life of a Christian is that of a priest, purified and consecrated to God" (*L'Épître aux Hébreux*, 2:259): "La vie du chrétien est celle d'un prêtre, purifié et consacré, uni à Dieu."

66. Jonathan Klawans writes that "where we find a belief of a temple in heaven, we will also find a developed angelology" (*Purity, Sacrifice, and the Temple: Symbolism and*

comes to the forefront in 12:22.⁶⁷ Taken together, the angels' service on behalf of believers in these verses is primarily mediatory, which has been the function of the priests in relation between God and his people. The angels are depicted as messengers who communicate the hand of God behind creation (cf. Ps. 104:4) and the unalterable word concerning salvation (Heb. 2:2–4).⁶⁸ Interestingly, prior to the angels' mention of priestly service, they are contrasted with Jesus, who is the unique Son of God. Though Jesus and the angels occupy the same heavenly space, they are ontologically different, which in turn makes Christ's priestly designation exponentially greater.

Another instance of λειτουργός occurs in Hebrews 8:2, where Christ himself is called the minister (λειτουργός) of the heavenly sanctuary. While the term can be used as a general term for service on behalf of a larger body of people,⁶⁹ it has a priestly connotation when the context calls for it.⁷⁰ Due to Jesus' identification as high priest in the previous verse (8:1) and the stated location of the ministry (the sanctuary and true tent), λειτουργός is certainly used in a priestly sense in 8:2. As Léopold Sabourin states, "Ces textes invitent à conclure que selon viii. 2 notre grand prêtre est appelé τῶν ἁγίων λειτουργός précisément parce qu'il est entré dans le sanctuaire."⁷¹ Seeing that its usage can be applied to *both* angels and Christ, that same priestly connotation can be shared outside of Jesus. It is not an

---

Supersessionism in the Study of Ancient Judaism [New York: Oxford University Press, 2006], 112). If such is the case, as David Moffitt points out, the depiction of angels ministering in heaven in Hebrews 1–2 "is significant" because this further suggests a concrete presence of a heavenly structure where God dwells (*Atonement*, 180).

67. Ellingworth, *Hebrews*, 133.

68. In the Testament of Levi, Levi ascends to the presence of the Most High and is told that he will be a priest who will tell forth God's mysteries to men (T. Levi 2.10). Furthermore, the angel confirms his said status by declaring that he will be [to God] a son to him, as minister and priest in his presence (T. Levi 4.2) who directly sees the holy sanctuary (T. Levi 5.1–2). Later, Levi is also adorned in priestly garments (T. Levi 9:3). This heavenly ascent is part of the commission God gives him to serve as a priest of the earthly temple (Mackie, "Heavenly Sanctuary Mysticism," 89–90).

69. Especially in non-biblical Greek (Hermann Strathmann, "λειτουργέω, λειτουργία, λειτουργός, λειτουργικός," *TDNT* 4:216, 219, 229–30). This sense appears once in the NT in Rom. 13:6.

70. See Exod. 37:19; Num. 7:5; 8:22; 16:9 and 18:4–6, described specifically as the "service of the tabernacle"; 1 Chron. 6:33; 9:13–28; 28:13; 2 Chron. 31:2–4; 35:16; and esp. Isa. 61:6; 2 Esd. 7:24; 20:39; Sir. 7:29–30; Ep. Ar. 95. See also Ellingworth, *Hebrews*, 132, who notes that this idea included ethical and spiritual service in rabbinic Judaism; cf. also Church, *Hebrews and the Temple*, 399. The term may at times also be used as a cultic title (Strathmann, "λειτουργέω, λειτουργία, λειτουργός, λειτουργικός," 4:230).

71. "These texts suggest the conclusion that according to 8:2, our high priest is called τῶν ἁγίων λειτουργός precisely because he entered the sanctuary" (Sabourin, "Liturge du sanctuaire," 89).

official title given only to the high priest, but rather describes the activity of those who reside in the heavenly sanctuary in its liturgical drama, with Christ being the prominent actor.

While believers are not explicitly referred to as λειτουργός in Hebrews, the term occurs in Romans 15:16: εἰς τὸ εἶναί με λειτουργὸν Χριστοῦ Ἰησοῦ εἰς τὰ ἔθνη... ἵνα γένηται ἡ προσφορὰ τῶν ἐθνῶν εὐπρόσδεκτος.[72] That Paul refers to himself as a "minister" of Christ performing the "priestly" service of God reveals that the term's usage does not refer merely to general service.[73] Here Paul considers his service to the Gentiles both a priestly service and an acceptable offering to the Lord. Furthermore, even Gentile believers are described as ministering to their Jewish-Christian benefactors in Romans 15:27.[74] In the LXX, λειτουργία is often used to describe priestly service,[75] especially at the place of the altar.[76] Therefore, an investigation of λειτουργός in Hebrews opens the door for the priestly term to be applied outside of Jesus—namely, to believers.

B. λατρεύω in Hebrews

The other instance of priestly service language is λατρεύω found in Hebrews 8:5; 9:9, 14; 10:2 and 13:10. Out of the six occurrences, half the times it is best understood as "worship," while the other half carry a more specific, priestly meaning of service. In 9:14, 10:2, and 13:10, the term is used to describe believers' actions.[77] Priestly service is the immediate response to the purification of their consciences, away from dead works, and in service to the living God (9:14). Furthermore, it is a service that exceeds the kind of priestly service that was performed by the levitical priests in the earthly tabernacle (13:10). In Hebrews 10:2, the participle

---

72. The phrase εἰς τὰ ἔθνη is omitted in Codex Vaticanus whereas its inclusion is "extremely well attested in the Greek textual tradition" (Richard N. Longenecker, *The Epistle to the Romans: A Commentary on the Greek Text*, ed. I. Howard Marshall and Donald A. Hagner, NIGTC [Grand Rapids, MI: Eerdmans, 2016], 1026).

73. Other Pauline usages support a priestly sense (e.g., 2 Cor. 9:12; Phil. 2:17).

74. David J. Downs, *The Offering of the Gentiles: Paul's Collection for Jerusalem in Its Chronological, Cultural, and Cultic Contexts*, WUNT 2/248 (Tübingen: Mohr Siebeck, 2008), 154–58, who also notes the strong, intentional usage of cultic language in the offering of the Gentiles in Rom. 15:14–32. See also Downs' article, "'The Offering of the Gentiles' in Romans 15.16," *JSNT* 29.2 (2006): 173–86. For that passage's OT background, see Danillo Santos' chapter entitled, "The Priesthood of Gospel Ministry: Isaiah 66.18 in Romans 15.16," wherein he argues for Isa. 66:18–24 as being a source for Paul's priestly metaphor, which categorizes Paul's and believers' offering up of their new-creation selves as priestly ministry ("Ministers of Christ Jesus: A Cognitive Account of Priestly Language in Paul" [PhD diss., Westminster Theological Seminary, 2021], 50–118).

75. Strathmann, "λειτουργέω, λειτουργία, λειτουργός, λειτουργικός," 4:215.

76. MacLeod, "Present Work of Christ in Hebrews," 187.

77. Hebrews 8:5 refers to the levitical priests' service in the tabernacle, but in such a way as to rhetorically compare their service with the greater priestly service of Christ.

τοὺς λατρεύοντας combines the meanings of worship and service, which suggests that the two concepts must not be strictly separated.[78] Outside of Hebrews, Revelation 7:15 describes the martyrs serving in the temple (λατρεύουσιν αὐτῷ ἡμέρας καὶ νυκτὸς ἐν τῷ ναῷ αὐτοῦ) with the great multitude from every nation and tribe.[79] Later, in Revelation 22:3, the martyrs are again described as recipients of everlasting life[80] who will serve the Lord while being in his direct presence. Both references describe believers worshiping and serving before God's throne. This again supports the notions that priestly service and worship are intrinsically linked and that such priestly service takes place in the presence of God within the tabernacle/temple sanctuary.[81]

While we observed the terms λειτουργός and λατρεύω separately, both are often used together or interchangeably to connote priestly service.[82] When considering these words and the spatial commands of access (προσέρχομαι/εἰσέρχομαι), we may conclude that the cultic language traditionally used for priests is applied to the believers in Hebrews. This includes the language for spatial commands of access (προσέρχομαι/εἰσέρχομαι) and for service (λειτουργός/λατρεύω). The giving of such priestly commands is enough to expect obedience on the believers' part; nevertheless, the author of Hebrews draws their attention to the confidence and boldness they now have as a result of their priestly identity. Their consciences are now purified, and they therefore should not be inhibited in living out as New Covenant priests.

8.2. Confidence, Boldness, and Conscience

Christ's high priestly ministry on behalf of his people does not pertain to access only. It also shapes the manner in which they approach God. The author utilizes the words, συνείδησις and παρρησία, which are used in the context of either movement towards God (4:16), the heavenly cult (9:9–14), or both (10:1–3,

---

78. In the LXX, it is used almost exclusively "to denote the service of the people in worship" (Best, "Spiritual Sacrifice," 282), which combines the two distinct usages found in Hebrews. Therefore, both elements may be in view.

79. Note also the reference to their purity exemplified by their pure, white robes, washed by the blood of the Lamb (Rev. 7:15). John writes that "For this reason" (διὰ τοῦτό), they are before the throne of God, and they serve (λατρεύουσιν) him in the temple. Therefore, the consecration rite of priests is performed upon the believers through the ceremonial washing of Christ's blood. There is also the language of consecration (ἐγκαινίζω) in Heb. 10:20, where Christ inaugurated the inner sanctuary through the veil. Again, this links the place of priestly practice with its access granted to believers.

80. This is similar to the inheritance of indestructible life that qualifies one to be priest (Heb. 7:16).

81. Other priestly references throughout Revelation are attributed to believers in 8:3–5 and 19:8.

82. Floor, "General Priesthood of Believers," 76, although he contends that at times, λειτουργεῖν is a specified usage for Jesus' priestly service.

19-22).⁸³ We observe from these passages that (1) movement towards God is prohibited by one's guilty conscience⁸⁴ and (2) the combination of that movement and the cleansing of conscience leads to priestly service (λατρεύω).⁸⁵ In this section, we will look at each occurrence of these words and further observe how Christ is the source of believers' purification.

A. Hebrews 4:16

In Hebrews 4:16, the conscience is associated with the believer's ability to draw near to God in the heavenly sanctuary. The image of God's throne uniquely appears in this passage. Interestingly, this description of God's throne is part of the exhortation given to believers to draw near. Earlier, I showed that προσέρχομαι is almost always used in a cultic (and therefore priestly) sense in Hebrews.⁸⁶ If such is the case, the three levels of limited access come into view (see Section 3.2): (1) Common Israelites are permitted outside, while (2) general priests are granted access to the outer altar. (3) Finally, only high priests are given access to the inner altar, which consisted of the mercy seat of the ark. Some have suggested that the ark is symbolic of God's throne.⁸⁷ Furthermore, the throne is often associated with God's judgment, and even more so when the preceding verses (vv. 3–7 and 12–13) are considered.⁸⁸ There, the word of God judges the thoughts and intentions of the heart. No creature is hidden from his sight (vv. 13–14). Notwithstanding, believers are encouraged to draw near as priests to that very throne,⁸⁹ and they are to do so with confidence.⁹⁰

---

83. Also Heb. 13:18, which shows the relationship between one's conscience and one's conduct. Prior to 13:18, συνείδησις occurs four times in the letter, with each instance functioning "prominently in one of the book's major expositions" and shows the term's importance in the author's presentation of Christ's high priestly ministry (Gary S. Selby, "The Meaning and Function of Syneidēsis in Hebrews 9 and 10," *ResQ* 28.3 [1985]: 146).

84. In direct contrast to external and ceremonial defilement, συνείδησις deals with man's internal faculty that prevents one's approach to God (ibid., 148).

85. In the Yom Kippur typology in Hebrews 9, two paths are presented: One is a negagtive strand that consists of one's inability to gain access to the heavenly Holy of Holies and the inability to purify the conscience. The opposite is the positive strand, in which one is granted access to the Holy of Holies and receives forgiveness (Gäbel, *Kulttheologie*, 282).

86. Also noted by Ellingworth, *Hebrews*, 269; Lane, *Hebrews 1–8*, 115.

87. Bruce, *Hebrews*, 116; *DBL*, 43 and 838.

88. In addition to the cultic nuance of these verses, Spicq is also open to a tribunal imagery whereby believers present themselves before God on the tribunal throne, which itself is a "l'emblème de l'autorité et de la dignité" (*L'Épître aux Hébreux*, 2:94). Hence, there need not be a strict separation between cultic and judgment imagery.

89. William Lane suggests that this very throne is also the place where mercy emanates as a result of the high priest's (i.e., Christ's) ministry of atonement on behalf of the people (cf. Lev. 16:2–34) (*Hebrews 1–8*, 115).

90. Spicq even uses the language of being united with God ("lui permet de s'unir à Dieu"), emphasizing the relational implications of believers' entry (*L'Épître aux Hébreux*, 2:231).

B. Hebrews 9:14

In Chapter 6 of this study, we examined the spatial language used to draw contrasts between the earthly and heavenly tabernacles in Hebrews 9:1-14. In these verses, the author also incorporates the problem of the conscience related to sanctuary access. On the basis of Christ's sacrifice, the cleansing of the conscience allows for unhindered access to God without the aid of the levitical priest.[91] This connection between conscience and entrance is supported in that the author of Hebrews addresses the believer as τὸν λατρεύοντα (v. 9), which can be translated as either "minister" or "worshipper" given the cultic language of the passage.[92] This suggests that the author has in view the believer's role in priestly service and worship, which was initially prevented due to his tainted conscience (cf. Num. 19:11-22).[93] The levitical order was only adequate for the purification of the flesh (v. 13), but Christ's blood cleanses their consciences. This is not a cleansing simply for restored fellowship with God,[94] but rather, is a cleansing that draws believers away from dead works and enables them to serve (τὸ λατρεύειν) the living God (v. 14). The author's train of thought becomes clear. The defiled conscience is what keeps a person from serving God, which is a "fundamental presupposition" behind the author's concern for the perfection of believers.[95]

C. Hebrews 10:19-22

After presenting the efficacy of Christ's high priestly ministry in the heavenly tabernacle (Heb. 8-9), the author of Hebrews makes clear the insufficiency of the levitical sacrifices (Heb. 10). The fundamental problem is that they cannot make perfect those who draw near (10:1-2).[96] Here the author associates the consciences of those serving or worshiping (τοὺς λατρεύοντας, v. 2)[97] with spatial movement

---

91. Selby, "Meaning and Function," 150.
92. Earlier I discussed that both senses, "minister" and "worship," may be in view for λατρεύω. Verse 14 also describes the action as worshipping/ministering (εἰς τὸ λατρεύειν). However, the context of sacrificing blood and the comparison against "dead works" suggest the specific act of "ministering" to be more prominent. Furthermore, the term's usage in 8:5, 10:2, 12:28, and 13:10 shows that the "language of service has cultic connotations" (Attridge, *Hebrews*, 252).
93. There is an allusion to the sprinkled ashes of the heifer involved in the cleansing of an Israelite defiled by contact with a corpse (Lane, *Hebrews 9-13*, 239).
94. The restoring of fellowship is for the purpose of participating in the worshipping community once again (Peterson, *Hebrews and Perfection*, 138).
95. Ibid., 139.
96. The problem of a tainted conscience was especially a problem for OT priests. As Peterson writes, "Clearly, the power of the defiled conscience to keep a person from serving God effectively is a fundamental presupposition of our writer's teaching on the perfecting of believers" (ibid.).
97. Note again the priestly service language, "λατρεύω," applied to believers.

(τοὺς προσερχομένους τελειῶσαι, v. 1). This clarifies the issue: it is not solely the fact that their consciences are not perfected due to the inadequacy of the blood of bulls and goats. The issue is that this inadequacy prohibits them from drawing near to God in the inner sanctuary. After acknowledging this problem (vv. 1–4), the author asserts the removal (ἀναιρέω) of the first order and the establishment of the second based upon the offering of Christ's body, which is sufficient to take away sins once for all (vv. 5–18).

After asserting the sufficiency and efficacy of Christ's sacrifice, the author addresses the problem of the conscience once again in verse 19, indicated by the use of "therefore" to begin the section.[98] In the previous verses, God's people could not draw near because the continual sacrifices could not make their consciences perfect. Starting in verse 19, the author presents the reversal of that pattern; believers have confidence, which in turn qualifies them to enter.[99] He utilizes spatial language in describing the benefits now available to believers: They have confidence now *to enter* (εἰς τὴν εἴσοδον) the holy place, which is inaugurated *through the veil* (διὰ τοῦ καταπετάσματος) of Christ's flesh.[100] Now that they have this great priest *over the house of God* (ἐπὶ τὸν οἶκον τοῦ θεοῦ), they are to *draw near* (προσερχώμεθα), having their hearts sprinkled clean from an evil conscience and their bodies washed with pure water (v. 22).[101]

In addition to the removal of an evil conscience, the sprinkling of the hearts hearkens back to the inauguration of the Mosaic covenant at Sinai (Exod. 19:10–14).[102] Furthermore, the author of Hebrews links this inauguration to the washing with pure water, which "closely parallels another Old Testament ceremony, the

---

98. Indicated by the οὖν conjunction immediately following ἔχοντες and preceding ἀδελφοί, παρρησίαν.

99. Rather than ascribing a subjective aspect to παρρησίαν, Ellingworth prefers "complete freedom" or "right to enter" to connote the privilege of access that has been granted to believers (*Hebrews*, 517). This is further supported by the object immediately following: εἰς τὴν εἴσοδον ἁγίων. The preposition εἰς is used in a similar spatial sense (referentially) in 6:10; 7:14; 9:9; 12:3 (Attridge, *Hebrews*, 284 n. 15).

100. I take διὰ in the instrumental sense to represent Christ's humanity and, along with it, his self-sacrifice on the cross. Gäbel sees connections to Heb. 2:15 and 5:7 and suggests that διὰ τοῦ καταπετάσματος refers to the "earthly mode of existence that Christ accepted and took upon himself in his incarnation" (*Kulttheologie*, 206). For a survey of interpretive options, see Ellingworth, *Hebrews*, 518–22; Otfried Hofius, *Der Vorhang vor dem Thron Gottes: eine exegetisch-religionsgeschichtliche Untersuchung zu Hebräer 6, 19. f. und 10,19f*, WUNT 14 (Tübingen: Mohr Siebeck, 1972); Mark A. Jennings, "The Veil and the High Priestly Robes of the Incarnation: Understanding the Context of Heb 10:20," *PRS* 37.1 (2010): 85–97; David M. Moffitt, "Unveiling Jesus' Flesh: A Fresh Assessment of the Relationship between the Veil and Jesus' Flesh in Hebrews 10:20," *PRS* 37.1 (2010): 71–84.

101. Note again, the cultic language used to describe the benefits applied to believers.

102. The inauguration of the New Covenant is referenced in the preceding passage, vv. 16–18, which quotes Jer. 31:33–34 MT (38:34 LXX).

initiation of the priests."[103] The unique combination of these two Old Testament events is understood as what Dahl calls a "sacerdotal initiation," where now a priestly community has been formed.[104] Now that believers' identities as priests are established and they no longer deal with the guilt that bars them sanctuary access, they have the confidence to embrace their priestly identity and serve accordingly.[105] It is not surprising that immediately afterwards, the author exhorts his audience with practical instruction on what such living looks like in verses 24–25.[106] They are to consider how to stimulate one another to love and good deeds, continue to assemble together, and encourage one another.[107]

In sum, the logic runs as follows: (1) The problem of the conscience always existed in the levitical system. (2) Christ removes the levitical order and establishes a new one inaugurated by his high priestly role within the inner sanctuary of the heavenly tabernacle. (3) Since believers have such a high priest to whom they are to hold fast, their consciences and bodies are cleansed and perfected. (4) As a result, believers can confidently draw near having been granted priestly access to now live and serve as priests on earth within the Christian community. Both Hebrews 9:1–14 and 10:1–25 link one's access to God with the acknowledgement of what Scott Mackie calls a "decisive cleansing in the innermost depths of their psyche."[108] This is possible only due to believers' solidarity with Christ the high priest who solves the dilemma of sin and prohibited access.

---

103. Dahl, "New and Living Way," 406; cf. Exod. 29:4, 20–21; Lev. 8:6, 23-30. Dahl also notes how priests washed themselves each time they entered the sanctuary (cf. Exod. 30:17–21; 40:30–31; Num. 5:17), which correlates with Christian baptism in the New Covenant.

104. Ibid., 406–407. This is further supported by the use of παρρησία, which has an "eschatological nuance," connoting a "new, objective reality obtained by the Christian community by the death of Christ" (Lane, *Hebrews 9–13*, 283).

Christian Eberhart traces the sacrificial metaphors in the OT that are utilized in Hebrews and suggests that the author appropriates the sacrificial tradition but "reframes the contents of sacrificial metaphors by referring them explicitly to the death of Jesus." This, in turn, "purifies human beings so that they may approach the heavenly sanctuary" ("Characteristics of Sacrificial Metaphors in Hebrews," in Gelardini, ed., *Hebrews*, 38).

105. Having a good conscience means that God no longer remembers the sins committed under the Old Covenant (Heb. 8:12; 10:17) and it can be said that those sins are perfectly removed with regard to one's awareness of them (Stegemann and Stegemann, "Cultic Language in Hebrews," 21).

106. The "objective content" of the promised hope is the assurance that the believers may "draw near to God in priestly service" (Lane, *Hebrews 1–8*, 154).

107. More discussion on the reciprocal acts of priestly service, in Section 8.3.

108. Mackie, "Heavenly Sanctuary Mysticism," 85.

D. Christ, the Source of Believers' Priestly Identity

In the aforementioned passages, as well as Hebrews 6:19, Christ is prominently portrayed as the active benefactor who endows such priestly privileges. In Hebrews 4:14–16, the author makes clear that because believers have a great high priest (ἔχοντες οὖν ἀρχιερέα μέγαν), they have confidence to draw near to the throne of grace. It is he who passed through the heavens. The author further exhorts his audience to hold fast to their confession[109] which allows them such sanctuary access.

In Hebrews 6:19, Christ is the one who enters within the veil, not only for himself, but as a forerunner on behalf of his people. This mediatory act is what signifies his being a high priest forever according to the order of Melchizedek (v. 20b). The author further presents Jesus in two images: First, Christ is metaphorically depicted as an anchor, which connotes the certainty of believers' eschatological hope in his person.[110] This is evident in the τε καὶ construction that binds ἄγκυραν and ἀσφαλῆ τε καί βεβαίαν as one and the same thought.[111] The second imagery is that of Christ entering into the sanctuary, past the veil. These two images are not in tension with one another since the author of Hebrews is not hesitant in using "la complexité et l'enchevêtrement des tableaux."[112] Moreover, when these two images are considered together, a unique exhortation is conveyed wherein believers' hope is secure in the person of Jesus. At the same time, Jesus enters within the veil, which consequentially brings others in with him (πρόδρομος ὑπὲρ ἡμῶν εἰσῆλθεν Ἰησοῦς, v. 20b).

In Hebrews 10:21, the audience is reminded that they have a great high priest over the house of God. This qualifies them to draw near with a sincere heart in full assurance of faith, having the purification and consecration rites required of and characteristic of heavenly priests. In the context of the Day of Atonement present in these passages,[113] "the two essential functions of the Priest (to have access to the Holy Place and to offer sacrifice) are thus fulfilled by the Christian priest—but only through Christ."[114] Jesus' atoning sacrifice undergirds and empowers this entire process. It has provided a cleansing from sin and the removal of anything—even a defiled conscience—that might hinder a relationship with God. Jesus "confers a state of holiness necessary for interaction with a holy God in the most holy place."[115]

---

109. This designation of calling Christ their confession (τῆς ὁμολογίας) occurs two other times in Heb. 3:1 and 10:23.

110. Spicq, *L'Épître aux Hébreux*, 2:165: "On doit identifier l'ancre au Sauveur lui-même."

111. Cockerill, *Hebrews*, 290 n. 21.

112. "the complexity and the entanglement of representations" (Samuel Bénétreau, "Le symbolisme dans l'Épître aux Hébreux. Images et métaphores," *ETR* 90.2 [2015]: 162).

113. The combination of the high priest's entrance through the means of blood, past the veil into the sanctuary points to the Day of Atonement, which is confirmed by the parallel nature of Heb. 6:19–20 and 10:19–21 (Young, "Where Jesus Has Gone," 172).

114. Best, "Spiritual Sacrifice," 286.

115. Mackie, "Heavenly Sanctuary Mysticism," 86.

With these passages in view, Christ is the source of believers' priestly calling. Apart from him, such a priestly identity would not be possible, since the two problems remain of their tainted consciences and their barred entry from God's presence. Scholer writes:

> In fact, it would not be incorrect to affirm that all other cultic references and allusions in Heb. are ancillary to the high priestly category. Were Jesus Christ not high priest, there would be no reason for any further consideration of things cultic, much less any purpose in depicting the recipients of the Epistles as priests.[116]

Nevertheless, believers are not explicitly referred to as priests. Rather, they are implicitly so through the cultic benefits and their spatial designations with regards to the heavenly sanctuary. John Dunnill suggests that this is due to the precariousness of their position. The author does not want to suggest that they enjoy any kind of sacerdotal privilege apart from Christ. "All mediation is now exercised by Jesus Christ, through whom alone they draw near."[117] Olaf Moe makes a further observation that Christ is not called ἱερεύς μέγας, but ἀρχιερεύς because "er ist nicht der einzige Priester des Neuen Bundes; er ist nur im Vergleich mit den andern der große."[118]

The value of Christ's priesthood to believers is of the highest degree. Nevertheless, believers share a priesthood with him *in kind* precisely because their priesthood originates in Christ.[119] They share an identity with him as fellow brothers within the family of God, as well as being joint worshippers and ministers in the heavenly sanctuary. Such is heavenly sanctuary Secondspace. In turn, their acts and services are in essence the same as Christ's; they are to mediate God's presence to those around them. Such are the lived-out spaces of heavenly sanctuary Thirdspace.

8.3. Thirdspace Movement

Thirdspace is the lived-out practices of Firstspace and Secondspace. The ordering in which one views these three spatial properties of the heavenly tabernacle is important. First, the materialized presence of tabernacle Firstspace must be established so actual space is being discussed. This protects us from an idealized, Platonic concept of the heavenly cult. The physical manifestation of the tabernacle is supported by the resurrected and physical Jesus standing in its Holy of Holies,

---

116. Scholer, *Proleptic Priests*, 9.
117. Dunnill, *Covenant and Sacrifice*, 259.
118. "He is not the only priest of the New Covenant; he is the greater priest compared to the others" (Moe, "Der Gedanke des allgemeinen," 163).
119. Similarly, in the OT, the difference between priest and high priest was different not categorically, but only in degree (Scholer, *Proleptic Priests*, 34).

ministering on behalf of believers. Secondspace imports the salvific benefits from Christ's high priestly ministry conferred unto believers and spiritually places them with Christ in the sanctuary. This in turn qualifies them to be and to live as priests, which consequently affects the earthly world they live in.[120] This ordering is what is unique in Hebrews' presentation of the heavenly tabernacle and the general priesthood of believers.

The concept of a general priesthood has existed throughout the Old Testament, as well as intertestamental and rabbinic literature.[121] More recently with respect to the writing of Hebrews, the community at Qumran viewed themselves as genuine priests in response to the defiled state of the Jerusalem temple.[122] As a result, they attempted to artificially create tabernacle/temple space through their ethic and community practices—hence, reversing the order mentioned above. By the time of Qumran, while "a division existed between priestly and lay elements at Qumran, there was also the belief that the entire community was priestly. This is implied in particular texts by the atonement effected by the community, by the strict concern for community purity, and by a terminology that is perceptively sacerdotal."[123] There is one interesting example in 4QShirShabb where the reciter speaks as though praising while residing in the heavenly sanctuary. He calls upon the people: "Praise with the holy ones the foundations of the holy of holies the supporting columns of the highest vault, and all the corners of the building…. and its beams and its walls, all its structure, the work of its construction" (4Q405 f6:2–5).[124]

The community at Qumran believed they were without a temple—or at least, in their view, a pure temple.[125] On one hand, they looked forward to the establishment of the legitimate temple. On the other hand, they began to relocate

---

120. This is different from Gäbel's sequence of conditions required for sanctuary access. While he rightly notes the relation between Christ's earthly obedience with the exhortation to live obediently for believers, he states that this obedient living on earth grants them "access to the heavenly sanctuary and its cult, the path to heavenly glory" (*Kulttheologie*, 473: "Zugang zum himmlischen Heiligtum und Kult, der Weg zu himmlischer Herrlichkeit"; cf. also 478).

121. Scholer, *Proleptic Priests*, 13–63.

122. This "levitical or priestly ideology" (*idéologie lévitique ou sacerdotale*) finds its basis in Exod. 19:6 and accounted for the practices of ritual purity examined in places such as communal meals found in the Essenes and the Pharisees (Simon Claude Mimouni, "Le 'grand prêtre' Jésus 'à la manière de Melchisédech' dans l'Épître aux Hébreux," *ASE* 33.1 [2016]: 99).

123. Scholer, *Proleptic Priests*, 49–50.

124. Martínez and Tigchelaar, *Dead Sea Scrolls*, 2:829.

125. A constant question for the community was whether priests could function without a sanctuary (Alison Schofield, "Re-Placing Priestly Space: The Wilderness as Heterotopia in the Dead Sea Scrolls," in Mason et al., eds., *A Teacher for All Generations*, 1:473).

their cultic practices to the sanctuary that remains undefiled—the heavenly one.[126] Recitations such as those found in the Shabbath Shirot reflect their attempts to legitimize their priestly activity by tying their presence within the confines of the heavenly tabernacle/temple. Instead of performing sacrificial services like those which previously took place in the Jerusalem temple, they replaced them with "a general *'abôdāh* (service)," which allowed them to see themselves as operating in the cultic realm.[127] By establishing such practices, they saw themselves as being "absorbed into the ontology of the heavenly cult,"[128] and as a "priesthood serving simultaneously in the Judean desert and in the heavenly sanctuary."[129] Nevertheless, their attempts fall short compared to what New Covenant believers possess in terms of heavenly sanctuary access and activity.[130]

The association with the heavenly cult is also present for New Covenant believers; yet, their acts become "true sacrality [that] is transferred to heaven" and directly "participate in the heavenly cult."[131] What makes Hebrews different from Qumran is the approach given to believers for obtaining atonement and privileged access. Qumran saw their way of life as their means to atone for the sin that accumulated in the Jerusalem temple, while New Testament believers obtain their atonement through the high priestly work of Jesus.

New Covenant believers are not socially reconstructing a substitute priestly space following the rejection of the Jerusalem Temple; rather, they are reappropriating the priestly space that once existed in the earthly sanctuary when they are repositioned to spiritually occupy the archetypal priestly space made accessible by Christ's entrance (6:20). This has implications for how we understand cultic references, such as the altar spoken of in 13:10: ἔχομεν θυσιαστήριον ἐξ οὗ φαγεῖν οὐκ ἔχουσιν ἐξουσίαν οἱ τῇ σκηνῇ λατρεύοντες, which refers to an altar that resides in heaven.[132] The crux of the issue lies in Schofield's description of Qumran's priestly

---

126. Schofield writes that the Yahan (Qumran) community "re-inscribed the desert as a new priestly space, both conceptually and, for some, literally" (ibid., 470). Interestingly, Schofield applies spatial theory on the Yahad community to argue that they sought to create a new social heterotopia through *practice*, which she calls "regimentation of space." Hence, the desert became a counter-site, a place of otherness (Thirdspace) over against the dominance of the Jerusalem temple (ibid., 474–75).

127. Scholer, *Proleptic Priests*, 57.

128. Fletcher-Louis, *All the Glory of Adam*, 309.

129. Church, "Wilderness Tabernacle," 118.

130. At best, their worship takes place concurrently (*doppelte Korrespondenz*)—one in heaven and one on earth via their respective temples (Gäbel, *Kulttheologie*, 68).

131. Ibid., 474: "Auch für die Adressaten gilt, dass der wahre Kult, die wahre Sakralität in den Himmel verlegt sind…die Adressaten im himmlischen Allerheiligsten verankert und zum himmlischen Jerusalem hinzugetreten sind und so am himmlischen Kult teilnehmen."

132. Marie Isaacs identifies three groups of traditional interpretations of this verse: (1) an altar that resides in the heavenly sanctuary, (2) the eucharistic table as the locus of Christian worship, and (3) a reference to Christ's sacrificial death such as Golgotha

attempts: "Actions *define* a space," which in turn allowed the Yahad community to cement "their new priestly hierarchy through praxis."[133] For the Christian community, believers need not be concerned with creating a holy space; rather, they inherit it by virtue of Christ's finished work which comes as a result of their faith.[134] Furthermore, their priestly role is not an attempt to create any heavenly reality or transport them to one; rather, it is the natural outcome of their re-established identity as heavenly priests.[135]

8.3.1. Vertical or Horizontal Priestly Service

In this section, I will show that the outflow of priestly service is oriented in two directions: vertically and horizontally. Vertically, priestly service consists of unhindered worship, praise, and prayer to God that is motivated by thanksgiving (Heb. 2:12 [Ps. 22:22]). Horizontally, priestly service proceeds outward, toward the Christian community in reciprocal fashion (Heb. 10:23–25; 12:14–15). Furthermore, in a similar way as we see how the eschatology of the heavenly tabernacle is both vertical (spatial) and horizontal (temporal), we see cases where both vertical and horizontal, priestly service are one and the same (Heb. 12:28–29; 13:1–10, 13–18).[136] In other words, the reciprocal acts of service on behalf of others become an upward-oriented, priestly service to God.

A. Vertical Priestly Service (Hebrews 2:12)

In Hebrews 2:12, Jesus refers to believers as his fellow brothers and sings praise along with them in their midst. In the previous section, I argued that this

---

("Hebrews 13:9–16 Revisited," 273). Isaacs argues, however, that this altar of sacrifice/burnt offerings never existed within the tabernacle/temple, but outside of it. Therefore, "sacrifice is principally the means by which one enters sacred territory, not what goes on there once entry is attained" (ibid., 275). However, she does not see believers as having entered the sanctuary but instead, standing imminently close to it, which goes against what I have argued in the preceding sections.

133. Schofield, "Re-Placing Priestly Space," 487; emphasis original.

134. Elsewhere the author of Hebrews cites Cain and Abel to clarify that sacrificial offerings which are acceptable are those offered up in faith (11:4).

135. Best suggests that the general priesthood of believers does not consist in the *act* of priesthood but rather in a corporate *status* of belonging to the priesthood ("Spiritual Sacrifice," 279). I propose that the two are inseparable.

136. The heavenly tabernacle is spatially eschatological in that it physically resides above in the transcendent heavens, which will be consummated in experience temporally in the future. Nevertheless, the results and benefits with regards to believers' spiritual occupancy in the heavenly tabernacle are experienced and received in the present. Similarly, believers' priestly acts are oriented both to God who resides in the heavenly tabernacle (vertical) and to others on earth (horizontal). This also takes place in the present.

references the heavenly, liturgical drama of worship in which Christ, angels, and believers participate. This joint congregational worship is possible due to what the author writes in the preceding verses: Christ is the one who brings his people into glory and sanctifies them (vv. 10–11). When considering the psalm in the background for these verses, Christ's salvific benefits which are conferred to believers are in view. In Psalm 22:16–18 (21:17–19 LXX), David makes a messianic prophecy concerning Jesus' suffering on the cross (cf. Jn 19:24). In the foretelling of the Messiah's sufferings (Ps. 22:22, 25), David responds in praise that comes forth out of the *great congregation* (ἐκκλησίᾳ μεγάλῃ/ בְּקָהָל רָב). Therefore, congregational praise comes as a result of the sufferings inflicted upon the Messiah, *because* it provides salvific benefits upon believers.[137] One such benefit is that Christ's people are now able to join in congregational praise within the context of the heavenly liturgy. Not only that, but the one who sanctifies and the ones who are sanctified come from the same Father, indicating solidarity between them (v. 11).[138] This intrinsically ties a believer's familial identity with Christ and reserves them a spot within the congregation in liturgical worship, where they lift up such praises as priests.

Believers' prayers are not directed toward an empty space. Jesus continues to serve as the heavenly high priest—not for the sake of atonement, since his sacrifice requires no repetition, but as an intercessor of the prayers and petitions that are lifted up.[139] The altar in reference to where believers offer up sacrifices is not the one outside of the Most Holy Place (cf. Exod. 30:6). Rather, Hebrews explicitly refers to the altar as being in the Most Holy Place, the golden altar of incense (Heb. 9:3). This intentional change in Hebrews is due to the "sacral, ritualistic,

---

137. "It is appropriate to an experience of vindication and exaltation after suffering and affliction" (Lane, *Hebrews 1–8*, 59).

138. The designation of ἐξ ἑνός, which can be either masculine or neuter in gender, has been a debated issue since patristic times and continues to be debated (Ellingworth, *Hebrews*, 164–65, who provides a summary of positions). I agree with William Lane (*Hebrews 1–8*, 58), who notes the contextual references to God in v. 10. Furthermore, God is the referent in both vv. 12 and 13. For the position arguing for Abraham as the referent, see James Swetnam, "Ἐξ Ἑνός in Hebrews 2,11," *Biblica* 88.4 (2007): 517–25. The reference to God also coheres with Erich Grässer's notion that ἁγιάζων and ἁγιαζόμενοι have the "same origin and goal" (*Ursprung und das gleiche Ziel*) in an eschatological sense ("Mose und Jesus: Zur Auslegung von Hebr 3:1-6," *ZNW* 75.1–2 [1984]: 5). Hence, the identification of believers as ἀδελφοὺς is in regards to their "eschatological existence" (*eschatologische Existenz*) (ibid., 7).

139. Scholer, *Proleptic Priests*, 85; cf. also MacLeod, "Present Work of Christ in Hebrews," 198–99, who states that one major activity of Christ is the mediation of praise and thanksgiving. This activity is reciprocal because the power of God works *through* (διὰ Ἰησοῦ Χριστοῦ, genitive of personal means) the person of Jesus Christ (cf. Heb. 6:20; 7:25; 9:24; 2:18; 4:14 and esp. 12:24).

and intercessory significance of incense ascending directly into the presence of Yahweh upon his mercy seat."[140]

Hebrews is not the only place where the concept of believers offering sacrifices is present.[141] The notion of offering sacrifices need not always reference Christ's propitiatory death on the cross. In Ephesians 5:2, Jesus' sacrifice is described not only in terms of his death, but in reference to his entire life (περιπατεῖτε ἐν ἀγάπῃ, καθὼς καὶ ὁ Χριστὸς ἠγάπησεν ἡμᾶς).[142] This supports the notion that believers' priestly living does not mimic Jesus' sacrificial death but embodies a life of service (Rom. 12:1).

Furthermore, Gary Anderson suggests that in both Scripture and in Qumran, prayer and sacrifice are coordinated activities (cf. Ps. 141:2).[143] Unlike the modern tendency to view prayer as spontaneous and an "effervescent outpouring of one's feeling toward God," prayer was more often a "carefully prescribed cultic act."[144] Related, praise is not simply an attitude but also falls within the cultic rubric.[145] Praise and prayer are not isolated, but are often presented in conjunction with one's sacrifice. Interestingly, there is also a transformation from mourning to praise that correlates with one's spatial transition from Sheol to God's temple (Ps. 30).[146] Namely, praise results from being transferred to the confines of God's temple from a place of death. The same concept exists in Hebrews, crucially presenting Christ as the agent of this spatial move.

B. Horizontal Priestly Service (Hebrews 3:13 and 10:23-25)

In Hebrews scholarship, the priestly activity of the believers has mainly been viewed as acts of prayer, praise, and thanksgiving, which John Scholer constitutes as the entirety of believers' priesthood.[147] Because he wishes to emphasize believers' physical presence on earth, the "drawing near" of believers consists only in vertical acts of spiritual worship.[148] It does not consist of any mutual service

---

140. Harold S. Camacho, "The Altar of Incense in Hebrews 9:3-4," *AUSS* 24.1 (1986): 12; cf. Rev. 8:3-4. Similarly, Laub comments that it is unlikely that the author of Hebrews made a mistake in relocating the altar in the Holy of Holies. Rather, the author does so for his theological purposes ("Ein für allemal hineingegangen," 69).

141. See also Rom. 12:1; 15:16; 2 Cor. 2:14–17; Eph. 5:2; Phil. 2:17; 4:18.

142. Eberhart, "Characteristics of Sacrificial Metaphors in Hebrews," 55, 63.

143. Gary A. Anderson, "The Praise of God as a Cultic Event," in *Priesthood and Cult in Ancient Israel*, ed. Gary A. Anderson and Saul M. Olyan, JSOTSup 125 (Sheffield: JSOT Press, 1991), 15.

144. Ibid.

145. Even in the Psalter (cf. Pss. 27:6; 54:6, 8; 141:2), joyful praise was a veritable ritual commanded by circumstances (ibid., 17).

146. Ibid., 30.

147. Scholer, *Proleptic Priests*, 108; also Dahl, "A New and Living Way," 408.

148. In addition to Scholer, David deSilva believes "drawing near" specifically means, "prayer" (*Perseverance in Gratitude*, 329).

amongst the Christian community.¹⁴⁹ Similarly, Ernest Best writes that the "essential task of this priesthood is to offer worship; the main activity of the redeemed is the praise and adoration of God and the Lamb."¹⁵⁰ However, others have suggested that an interplay exists between heaven and earth so that believers participate in this interaction.¹⁵¹ For example, Lambertus Floor views the heavenly tabernacle as spanning both heaven and earth. By this he means that the church of Christ on earth is in "direct connection to heaven," while earth is the "place where the believers have to perform service as priests of a new covenant."¹⁵²

I suggest that believers' priestly activity comprises more than vertical movements of worship, praise, and prayer. The horizontal ethical instructions can also be classified as the believers' priestly service. Gerald O'Collins and Michael Keenan Jones hint at the horizontal implications of the general priesthood when they state that believers are "called to a priestly existence that involves ongoing sacrifice not only through their prayers of praise and confession of faith believers but also through 'doing good' and generously sharing with others."¹⁵³ After all, a priesthood by definition "implies a community on behalf of which the priesthood offers sacrifice."¹⁵⁴ Furthermore, the cultic order of instructions in Leviticus deals

---

149. Scholer acknowledges the command for believers to "meet together," but goes on to suggest that the gathering is ultimately for the purposes of worship (*Proleptic Priests*, 128).

150. Best, "Spiritual Sacrifice," 280.

151. When we think about space, it is never a blank canvas but is "inherently caught up in social relations" (Schreiner, *Body of Jesus*, 45). Therefore, to think of heavenly tabernacle space is also to think about the relationships amongst those who occupy it (i.e., the Christian community).

152. Floor, "General Priesthood," 76.

153. O'Collins and Jones, *Jesus Our Priest*, 56. However, they interpret Heb. 13:10–12 as referring to the Eucharist, which seems to be an overly literal interpretation of the altar. At the same time, we need not view the altar as pertaining strictly and only to the place of sacrifice. Søren Ruager notes places in the OT (i.e., Exod. 24:4–11) where the events of the sprinkling of blood and table fellowship (i.e., sharing a communal meal) both took place at the altar. He writes: "In ähnlicher Weise geht es auch im Neuen Bund nicht nur um die Auffindung eines Opfers und die Ausgießung von Blut und die Besprengung des Bundesvolkes damit...sondern es wird auch vorausgesetzt, daß das ganze Volk Gottes, und nicht bloß die Ältesten Israels, zum HERRN hinaufsteigen und daß sie in seiner Gegenwart essen und trinken." [In a similar way, the New Covenant is not just about obtaining a sacrifice and pouring out its blood and sprinkling it on the people of the covenant...but it also assumes that the entire people of God, and not just the elders of Israel, will ascend to the LORD, that they may eat and drink in his presence] ("'Wir haben einen Altar' (Hebr 13, 10): Einige Überlegungen zum Thema: Gottesdienst/Abendmahl im Hebräerbrief," *KD* 36.1 [1990]: 75).

154. Edward Gordon Selwyn, *The First Epistle of St. Peter: The Greek Text with Introduction, Notes and Essays* (Grand Rapids, MI: Baker Book House, 1981), 296. Richard Davidson argues that an ecclesiological structure is basic to the cultic argument prior in

also with ethical and communal matters. Michael Morales notes the transition from Leviticus 1–16 to 17–27, which includes such matters as the prospect of life in the land. He writes:

> While the cultic context never fades from view, it is the case that the second half of Leviticus addresses a wider angle of social and moral issues, from sexual immorality and idolatry, to murder, incest and, more positively, what it means to love one's neighbour. The laws describe a life that fits with YHWH's holy nature and that may be defined adequately as one of justice and love.[155]

The common denominator between the vertical and horizontal implications of the cultic order is that the "context and the purpose of these laws have YHWH as their focus."[156] The potential problem of equating the commands to "draw near" with vertical acts of prayer and worship is that, in essence, that would be an attempt to attain heaven from earth. This dismisses Hebrews' entire presentation that addresses how Christ bridged that gap by bringing his people into heaven's sanctuary. As Gäbel writes:

> Die Adressaten leben in der Welt als Fremde, bestimmt durch ihre Zugehörigkeit zum himmel. Sie sollen ausziehen aus der irdischen Stadt, fort von ihrem sakralen Zentrum, denn sie sind kultisch hinzugetreten zum himmlischen heiligtum und Kult… Die Kultheologie des Hebr zielt auf den himmlischen Kultvollzug der Kultgemeinde des neuen Bundes, deren Hoherpriester im Himmel ist.[157]

The priestly exhortations for believers assume an already-attained arrival within the heavenly sanctuary. It is from this "sacred center" (*sakralen Zentrum*) that believers are called to move out and implement the "cult community of the New Covenant," as representatives of the high priest in heaven. Therefore, the direction is not simply to aim upward to draw near to God; but having already attained access, they draw near to God horizontally in heavenly sacred space. As they do,

---

7:1–10:18. To be purified in one's conscience is to be united into an eschatological community so that both individual and corporate dimensions emerge out of Heb. 8:5 and 9:24 (*Typology in Scripture*, 351).

155. Morales, *Who Shall Ascend?*, 207.

156. Ibid. Morales further suggests that it is an anachronism to assume that ancient Israel had a sharp distinction between cultic and ethical requirements (ibid., 213).

157. "Those addressed live in the world as strangers though they belong to heaven. They are to move away from the earthly city—away from its sacred center, because they belong to the heavenly sanctuary and its cult… The cult theology of Hebrews aims at the heavenly cult consisting of the cultic community of the New Covenant, whose High Priest resides in heaven" (Gäbel, *Kulttheologie*, 466).

they go out horizontally to the spaces of the secular world to implement the holiness of their cult community of the New Covenant.[158]

Hebrews 3:13 and 10:23-25 are two passages where such horizontal, priestly acts of service are present. In Hebrews 3:13, the main command is to comfort (παρακαλεῖτε) one another daily so that none among them would be hardened by the deceitfulness of sin.[159] Hebrews 10:23-25 is similar in that the author encourages believers to stimulate one another to love and good deeds. This includes continual assembling so that they may comfort (παρακαλοῦντες) one another.[160] In both passages, the author is concerned with the danger of sin. Psalm 95 lies in the background of Hebrews 3:13, which the author quotes: "Today, if you hear his voice, do not harden your hearts as in the rebellion" (Ps. 95:7-11). He then explains the present danger for the community: an unbelieving heart will cause them to fall away from the living God.[161] The author then responds to this danger by immediately writing, "But [ἀλλὰ], encourage one another...*so that* [ἵνα] they would not be hardened by the deceitfulness of sin" (v. 13). In other words, the author makes known (1) the danger of sin that comes from an unbelieving heart, (2) the counter-response to that danger in the form of mutual encouragement, (3) and the result/purpose/outcome of their reciprocal, priestly service.

Similarly in 10:26, he begins with a γάρ clause, which explains the result of *not* stirring up one another to good works. The good works (καλῶν ἔργων) mentioned here recapitulates the works (ἔργου) which the author already described as "having ministered and ministering to the saints" (διακονήσαντες τοῖς ἁγίοις καὶ

---

158. Similarly in the OT, Israel enters a covenant relationship with God at Sinai, which brings a "new social organization manifested in space with reference to the tabernacle." As a result, this new "socio-spatial organization emanates outward, from the presence of the deity into the rest of the world" (Mark K. George, "Social-Spatial Logic and the Structure of the Book of Numbers," in George, ed., *Constructions of Space IV*, 24-25).

159. In Ps. 23:4, the Lord's comforting actions (נחמ/παρεκάλεσαν) may also be connected to a priestly designation in the "house of the Lord" and the "anointing of one's head" (vv. 5-6).

160. Both ἑαυτούς and ἀλλήλους are reciprocal ("one another") and not reflexive ("yourselves") (Ellingworth, *Hebrews*, 223; Lane, *Hebrews 1-8*, 87).

161. Priests were given the task of oracular instruction (i.e., guidance), beginning with Moses' consultation of oracles (Scholer, *Proleptic Priests*, 17). Scholer also references Num. 27:21 and Deut. 33:3, which shows that this task extended to priests such as Eleazar and Levi who sought God's guidance on behalf of the people (ibid., 28). Moe argues that apart from sacrifice, teaching was a main function of the Levitical priests by pointing to the following passages: Deut. 17:9-13; 33:10; Mal. 2:6-7 ("Der Gedanke des allgemeinen," 164). In Heb. 5:2, Christ "deals gently" (μετριοπαθεῖν) with the ignorant and misguided in his role as high priest (5:1). All this may be subsumed under the category of mediation, which certainly may include instruction and guidance (cf. also the proclamation of God's excellencies as part of the task of the general priesthood in 1 Pet. 2:9).

διακονοῦντες) in 6:10.[162] This is in contrast to the dead works mentioned earlier in 6:1 and 9:14.[163] In the context of these two verses, explicit cultic language describes the futility of dead works served out of a tainted conscience. With such dead works, they are not able to serve (λατρεύειν) the living God.[164] Instead, they can counter this by participating in mutual fellowship. Hence, the encouragement to continue meeting one another (10:25) is intentional, as it is reflective of the heavenly liturgy that they participate in with Christ (3:14). As William Lane writes, "The neglect of worship and fellowship was symptomatic of a catastrophic failure to appreciate the significance of Christ's priestly ministry and the access to God it provided."[165] The command to mutual responsibility—to urge and exhort one another—is not an isolated command. It first derives from Christ's priestly service on believers' behalf.

The definition of a priest, in part, is one who stands before others and mediates their approach to God. Furthermore, it is a role that involves "nature" and "experience"[166]—meaning, the priest must first have experienced that which is expected of his people. Therefore, a horizontal dimension of priestly service is evident in both Christ and, in turn, the believers. They are able to serve in such a way as beneficiaries of Christ's priestly service on their behalf.

8.3.2. Vertical and Horizontal Priestly Service

As discussed in the previous section, the author of Hebrews gives discrete exhortations that pertain to either vertical or horizontal acts of priestly service. Furthermore, these actions are performed by believers in light of Christ's priestly ministry towards them. Christ is both the source and model for their priesthood. In addition to the passages mentioned (Heb. 2:12; 3:13; and 10:23-25), there are instances where vertical and horizontal acts of priestly service converge. In other words, there is no separation between what is directed vertically towards God or what is directed horizontally toward others. They are often one and the same—meaning, their priestly acts and ethical living for the good of fellow believers serve as a vertical act of worship to God. Such is the practice presented in the following passages: 12:28-29 and 13:15-16.

---

162. "They are works of goodness beneficial and pleasing to those who receive them and appropriate and acceptable in the eyes of God" (Cockerill, *Hebrews*, 479).

163. Ellingworth, *Hebrews*, 527. The διὰ τοῦτο in 9:15 logically connects the sacrificial, priestly mediation of Christ in 9:11-14 to an explanation of how Christ is the διαθήκης καινῆς μεσίτης (see Gabriella Berényi, "La portée διὰ τοῦτο en He 9,15," *Biblica* 69.1 [1988]: 110-12). The author of Hebrews further explains that the sacrifices of the New Covenant are not offered according to the law (10:8) but as sacrifices of "good works" introduced in 10:14.

164. Note again the priestly term, λατρεύειν.

165. Lane, *Hebrews 9-13*, 290.

166. Vos, "Priesthood of Christ," 5-6.

A. Bidirectional Priestly Service (Hebrews 12:28-29 and 13:15-16)

Leading up to 12:28, the preceding verses beginning in verse 14 utilize purity language in the context of the cultic presentation in Hebrews.[167] The concern is the maintaining of their status of holiness which Christ has conferred unto believers. By utilizing the example of Esau, the author warns them against the defilement that comes from bitterness and strife. He then reminds them of the eschatological mountain to which they have arrived (προσέρχομαι), and of the heavenly liturgy which they take part in with the myriad of angels. Finally, the cultic metaphor of sprinkling with Jesus' blood qualifies their place amongst the heavenly, general assembly (cf. 9:19-21). Priestly language continues in verses 28-29 ("therefore," διό) in connection with the preceding cultic context. This time, the author makes it explicit that believers are to offer to God an acceptable service (λατρεύωμεν εὐαρέστως τῷ θεῷ) with reverence and awe. This is motivated by the gratitude that they have in light of Christ's mediatory work on their behalf. Hence, the author makes an intentional connection between gratitude and priestly offering.

G. K. Beale makes a similar connection: "In response to their inclusion in God's unshakeable kingdom and temple, Christians are to 'show gratitude' by performing the priestly duty of 'offering to God an acceptable service with reverence and awe' (12:28)."[168] It is their inclusion in the heavenly sanctuary that produces gratitude and secures their priestly identity. Interestingly, a couple of verses later, the author immediately expounds what such acceptable service entails. Without any formal introduction, the author begins a chain of imperatives in chapter 13: μενέτω, ἐπιλανθάνεσθε, μιμνήσκεσθε, μνημονεύετε, μιμεῖσθε, and μὴ παραφέρεσθε. These are not comprehensive commands entailing the whole of priestly ministry but representative acts that describe the entire domain of one's life.[169] After giving these commands, the author returns to using explicitly

---

167. Lane, *Hebrews 9–13*, 450–51.

168. Beale suggests an allusion to Hag. 2:6-7, which references the "house of glory," indicating a heavenly temple. What believers currently possess is not of this world and so the heavenly temple serves as the basis on which they can serve as priests (*Temple and the Church's Mission*, 306). In his study of μετάθεσις in the context of Heb. 12:1-29, Stefan Schapdick argues for an emphasis on the present state of affairs for the recipients of the letter rather than an eschatological future that is outstanding. Rather than looking to the future, "salvation is located beyond this world, in the eternal, unshakable world of God" ("Die Metathesis der erschütterbaren Dinge, 'damit Das Unerschütterbare bleibe' (Hebr 12,27), Verwandlung–Vernichtung–Wandelbarkeit? Zum Verständnis des Begriffs Μετάθεσις im Kontext von Hebr 12,1-29 (Teil II)," *BZ* 57.1 [2013]: 46–59): "Das Heil ist jenseits dieser Welt situiert, in der ewig-unerschütterbaren Welt Gottes."

169. Floor, "General Priesthood of Believers," 78–79. Note that the ethical imperatives (vv. 1–6) are presented in between the priestly, sacrificial language of 12:28–29 and 13:10–16. This is one example of how the concept of priesthood enables us to see how the hortatory and doctrinal concepts are presented in tandem. This is, however, not to say that the priestly concept is the sole or principal interpretive key in reconciling the hortatory

cultic language to remind his audience of their spatial positioning. He reminds them that they have an altar in their midst that is unlike the earthly one (v. 10).[170] Christ has secured such priestly privileges through his suffering outside the gate.[171] Furthermore, they have a heavenly eternal city already in their possession.[172] This in turn encourages the offering up (vertically) of a sacrifice of praise to God (13:15–16). Verses 15 and 16 especially capture the "great drama between heaven and earth" with regard to the everyday life of the Christian community under the pressures of the dominant culture.[173]

The sacrifice of praise mentioned here takes the phrase θῦσον τῷ θεῷ θυσίαν αἰνέσεως from Psalm 49:14 LXX,[174] which is presented in stark contrast to the flesh of bulls and blood of goats in the prior verse. Hence, the cultic imagery of sacrifice is reappropriated to discuss ethical concerns within the community. In doing so, the author oscillates between describing vertical and horizontal acts of priestly service. Furthermore, horizontal acts of service within the community *become* the offering of praise to God. These are the sacrifices that please the Lord (v. 16). They are the actions that manifest "mutual support in the midst of an unsupportive society" and gratitude in response to Christ's high priestly ministry. This new priestly status is manifested in that such acts "maintain their forward momentum on their momentous journey into the Heavenly Holy of Holies."[175]

The convergence of vertical and horizontal priestly service is supported by other passages in the New Testament. In Romans 12:1, the entire body is described as a living and holy sacrifice, which consists of the whole of man in both his inner and outer being. Such living *is* their spiritual service of worship (v. 1).[176] In Philippians 4:17–20, the horizontal act of generosity is captured in Epaphroditus' gift, which Paul equates to a fragrant aroma, an acceptable sacrifice, well-pleasing to

---

and doctrinal messages of the entirety of Hebrews (e.g., "The Spatial Basis for Hortatory Commands" in Section 7.1 of this study for another example).

170. I interpret τῇ σκηνῇ in v. 10 as the heavenly tabernacle. However, there have been other interpretations of the altar (e.g., eucharistic table or a metonym for Golgotha) (Isaacs, "Hebrews 13:9–16 Revisited," 273–77).

171. The ethical instructions cohere with the call to go outside the camp and bear Christ's shame in communal solidarity. These two aspects must be seen together as one experiences persecution from the outside world (Thompson, "Insider Ethics," 219).

172. Especially in the face of opposition, a sense of shared space is very closely related to a sense of shared identity. When believers see themselves as occupying the same tabernacle space, they are better able to heed the instruction for brotherly love (13:1), as noted by J. Cornelius de Vos, "Hebrews 3:7–4:11 and the Function of Mental Time-Space Landscapes," in *Constructions of Space III: Biblical Spatiality and the Sacred*, ed. Jorunn Økland, J. Cornelis de Vos, and Karen J. Wenell, LHBOTS 540 (New York: T&T Clark, 2016), 179.

173. Backhaus, "How to Entertain Angels," 168.

174. David A. deSilva, "The Invention and Argumentative Function of Priestly Discourse in the Epistle to the Hebrews," *BBR* 16.2 (2006): 316; cf. also Lev. 7:12 LXX.

175. Ibid., 317.

176. Best, "Spiritual Sacrifice," 287.

God. Not only is the gift itself an upward-facing act of worship, Paul responds to the Philippians' act of charity by himself praising God in verse 20. In Ephesians 5:2, the particular act of walking in love is again an offering and a sacrifice to God as a fragrant aroma. In 2 Corinthians 2:14–17 and Romans 15:16, Paul sees his ministry (λειτουργὸν Χριστοῦ Ἰησοῦ)[177] as a priestly service of the gospel that spreads the fragrance of Christ.[178]

Similarly to the passages oriented toward either vertical or horizontal priestly service, these converging acts of service are rooted in how Christ exemplified priestly service toward believers. Christ is the one who first suffered for his people by tasting death on their behalf (2:9). Even leading up to his death, he had been tempted in every respect that they are, yet without sin (4:15). As a result, he is able to help those who are tempted. Lastly, the gifts and sacrifices Christ offers up to God are presented in response to the sins committed by the ignorant and misguided (5:1–3). Furthermore, he deals gently with them as he himself is beset with weakness (v. 2). Therefore, the priestly commands to comfort, encourage, and suffer are not isolated commands but are presented in light of Christ's initial priestly service on their behalf.[179]

B. Priests to the Pagan World

Although the preceding passages focused on the reciprocal priestly behavior within the Christian community, such actions also impact the pagan world around them. This is part of the "symbolic counter-world that may direct and strengthen the cognitive self-affirmation of Christians [namely, their identity as priests] confronted with the claims of pagan society."[180] An important aspect of Thirdspace is its capacity to challenge the dominant space through resistance or presenting a "counterspace."[181] With the dominant space of the Roman Empire established, the Christian community serves as a mediatory priesthood—not only for themselves, but also to those watching from the outside.

For example, when faced with social pressure to conform to pagan society, the author of Hebrews rightfully warns his readers against returning back to their former idolatrous practices. Strategically, by "[e]ffectively elevating the believers

---

177. The same usage is found in Hebrews describing the priestly service of Jesus, the angels, and believers (cf. Section 8.1.2).

178. Best makes similar statements in these passages, which "imply the doctrine of a general priesthood" ("Spiritual Sacrifice," 287). In 2 Cor. 6:17–18, believers are referred to as God's living temple and following, to go out from the midst of the secular world and maintain their holiness (Isa. 52:11; Ezek. 11:17; cf. Beale and Kim, *God Dwells Among Us*, 114).

179. Priestly consecration is not "restricted in sense to the sphere of 'worship', but includes the life of faith, hope and love, as the proper response to God's grace" (Peterson, *Hebrews and Perfection*, 151).

180. Backhaus, "How to Entertain Angels," 160.

181. Soja, *Thirdspace*, 68.

to the status of priests who will themselves enter the heavenly Holy of Holies, the author can harness the power of purity codes and pollution taboos at this point to advance the responses to their situation that he favors."[182]

This is consistent with the author's command to go outside of the camp, which was known to be a marginal space "where the unclean lived and flagrant sinners were executed (Lev. 13:45–46; Num. 5:2–4; 12:14–15; 31:19–20)."[183] The bidirectional movements of "entering" the Holy of Holies and "going outside" the camp do not conflict with one another. Rather, as mentioned earlier, they are complementary.[184] Hence, following Jesus outside the camp is a command to actively live out as priests within an unclean and defiled pagan society, not to flee from it by retreating into their obtained holy spaces. This is considered their priestly witness. The priestly sacrifices and acts are pleasing sacrifices to God and simultaneously, "the expression of priestly witness."[185]

Heterotopia, or otherworldly living, can take varied forms, although two main forms can be identified.[186] The first is the heterotopia of crisis, in which individuals live in a stage of personal crisis with respect to their immediate society and environment. The other is the heterotopia of deviation, in which one's behavior is "deviant" from the social norms that are in place. Both forms of heterotopia are true of the audience addressed in Hebrews. As individuals, they are in a stage of personal crisis as their identity, values, and purposes stand in contrast to those of the Roman Empire. They realize that they have been tasked with the priestly duties of benevolence and priestly abstention from impure and sinful practices. All the while, there will be opposition and even consequences for their behavior from the dominant culture. This altogether is their heterotopia of deviation, since they are called not to conform to the world but to suffer outside of the camp (13:13). As "lived space," it can be filled with "meaning, emotion, and struggle."[187] Those most in tune with Thirdspace are those who think differently and, at times, challenge the conventional view of the space that surrounds them. This was certainly true for the audience of Hebrews living in the midst of persecution and suffering (10:32–34).

Thirdspace priestly living is similar to Jesus' "world-building activity" through which he performed his deeds and words during his earthly ministry.[188] Because space is not only absolute, but is also relational, there is a necessary interaction that takes place among the participants of that space. Jesus himself challenged the rulers of different spaces he encountered throughout his ministry. He did

---

182. deSilva, "The Function of Priestly Discourse," 313. See his discussion on the purity commands concerning matters such as cultic foods and marital purity in Hebrews 13 (ibid., 314).
183. Ibid., 315.
184. Cf. Gäbel, *Kulttheologie*, 466.
185. Beale and Kim, *God Dwells Among Us*, 121–22.
186. Soja, *Thirdspace*, 159–60.
187. Sleeman, *Geography and the Ascension Narrative*, 45; Soja, *Thirdspace*, 40 n. 18.
188. Schreiner, *Body of Jesus*, 120; cf. esp. "World-Building with Words," 93–136.

so by becoming the *axis mundi* of the eschatological kingdom, where in a sense, he brought heaven down.[189] In affirming believers' solidarity with Christ, then they too are to become the connective between heaven and earth.[190] This is only possible if the believers can truly call heaven their home—a place they know and occupy.[191] The result is the transformation of the earthly spaces around them. Geoffrey Lilburne describes this phenomenon as the "christification of holy space." Such acts "[indicate] both the substitution of the holiness of the person for the holiness of a place and, by extension, the process whereby new places became holy by virtue of their association with Christ."[192]

In conclusion, Thirdspace priestly living describes the christification of the spaces within and outside the Christian community. The author of Hebrews exhorts his audience to do so on the basis of their heavenly tabernacle standing with the resurrected Jesus. He is himself, "un prêtre qui s'adresse à des prêtres."[193] And to affirm their priestly identity, the author utilizes cultic language to assure them of their purified consciences, by which they can boldly draw near and serve the living God. He then explicates what that means through both vertical and horizontal acts of priestly activity. This is the word of exhortation which the author of Hebrews shares (13:22), in order that his recipients might live faithfully until they participate in the full consummation of tabernacle space, both spiritually and physically, at Christ's return.

189. Ibid., 134.
190. Schreiner makes similar suggestions for the disciples who were with Jesus during his earthy ministry in "world-building" Thirdspace living (ibid., 124).
191. If Jesus orients and redefines the space that is around him (Matthew Sleeman, "Mark, the Temple and Space: A Geographer's Response," *BibInt* 15.3 [2007]: 343; Schreiner, *Body of Jesus*, 14) then it may be that he continues to influence and guide believers who occupy the heavenly sanctuary so that they continue to live as obedient priests.
192. Lilburne, *Sense of Place*, 68. Thirdspace is a strategic location from which to encompass, understand, and potentially transform all spaces (Soja, *Thirdspace*, 68).
193. "a priest addressing to the priests" (Mimouni, "Le grand prêtre Jésus," 102).

Chapter 9

CONCLUSION

This study has sought to bring attention to the spatial aspects of Hebrews eschatology by particular focus on the heavenly tabernacle. This endeavor came as a result of the scarcity of material that positively discusses the provisionally realized final state in the heavens. This in no way diminishes the importance and value of the temporal aspects of eschatology (i.e., the already/not-yet overlap of the two ages).[1] Rather, I hoped to present a more holistic understanding of eschatology in Hebrews. To do so, I have argued the following thesis: the author of Hebrews presents the heavenly tabernacle along with all its high priestly activity, to eschatologically situate, orient, and ground believers both spatially and temporally. This eschatological orientation, and particularly the spatial features of the heavenly tabernacle, enables believers to actualize in practice their heavenly, priestly identity by serving as priests on earth.

9.1. Part 1: The Heavenly Tabernacle

In Chapter 1, I argued that spatial language is a prominent feature in the eschatology of Hebrews that is often perceived as being antithetical to its corresponding temporal features. This is seen in biblical scholars who overly assert a Platonic or Philonic influence upon the author of Hebrews, which in turn has caused many to neglect Hebrews' spatial features altogether. In response to this commonly assumed bifurcation, I presented the heavenly tabernacle as an interpretive key to help resolve this tension. The rest of the chapter consisted of a survey of scholarship on the heavenly tabernacle in five different categories. While each view makes helpful contributions to heavenly tabernacle scholarship, I proposed that the tabernacle is best understood as a spatially realized (i.e., localized and materialized) structure existing in the transcendent heavens.

---

1. As Geerhardus Vos writes, "It has sometimes been asserted that this deflection from the straight prospective line of vision to the upward bent towards the heavenly world represents a toning down of the eschatological interest. Nothing could be farther from the truth" (*Pauline Eschatology*, 39).

Chapter 2 presented Critical Spatial Theory as espoused by Henri Lefebvre and Edward Soja. In particular, I featured Soja's Thirdspace as a helpful interpretive tool to assess the heavenly tabernacle's spatial features. In doing so, I challenged the traditional view of space that has its roots in a static, Cartesian approach to geography. By studying the heavenly tabernacle's Firstspace, Secondspace, and Thirdspace, all of its spatial, symbolic, and social features can be appreciated. Therefore, in Lefebvre's terms, space is perceived, conceived, and lived (*l'espace perçu, l'espace conçu,* and *l'espace vécu*).

I then summarized significant biblical studies that have utilized Critical Spatiality and how we might use Soja's methodology without adopting an anthropocentric view of space. As it applies to the heavenly tabernacle, Firstspace is the physical, material place, that I argue exists as a standing structure in the heavens. Secondspace is the heavenly tabernacle's symbolic features, which consist in the implications of Christ's high priestly ministry on behalf of believers. This ultimately reinforces believers' spiritual standing with Jesus in the innermost sanctuary of the heavenly tabernacle. Finally, Thirdspace is the "lived-out" practice that results from a Firstspace and Secondspace grounding.

Chapter 3 examined the heavenly tabernacle in the context of Hebrews. Three features were considered: (1) its historical context, (2) literary context, (3) and the structure of the author's overall argument. Afterwards, I identified two important aspects of the tabernacle from the Old Testament that lay in the background of the author of Hebrews and his recipients. First, the tabernacle was a space of temporal and spatial limitations. These limitations consisted in the architectural divisions that prevented free access as well as the delineation of the appointed times when the otherwise inaccessible inner sanctuary was made accessible (i.e., the Day of Atonement). The second aspect is related to the first: that very tabernacle was, at the same time, the space and place where God descended to dwell with his people. Establishing these two notions allows us to appreciate the rhetorical force of the author's presentation of heavenly tabernacle eschatology.

9.2. Part 2: Firstspace and Secondspace

In Chapters 4–6, I examined specific passages pertaining to spatial features of the heavenly tabernacle. Each chapter was divided in two parts: Firstspace and Secondspace. In Chapter 4, I examined Jesus' heavenly ascent in Hebrews 4:14 and 6:19–20. There I argued that οὐρανός in 4:14 is best understood as the physical firmament that is the created heavens. Jesus, then, passes through the created heavens (διέρχομαι) to arrive at his final destination, the heavenly tabernacle. By presenting Jesus' heavenly itinerary, the author of Hebrews is then able to explicate Jesus' high priestly ministry that takes place in the heavenly sanctuary. The Secondspace features that arise from these passages is the astounding possibility that God's people can now traverse the same heavenly itinerary with Jesus as their forerunner. The insurmountable chasm that separated man from God has now been crossed and made traversable for believers.

In Chapter 5, special attention was given to Hebrews 8:5 along with the Old Testament background passage it references, Exodus 25:40. There I discussed the importance of the Old Testament and intertestamental literature to enlighten our understanding of Hebrews' intertextuality. I then traced the interpretive tradition of Exodus 25:40 through the Old Testament, Jewish apocalyptic literature, Qumran, and rabbinic sources. As a result, I concluded that a physical, standing structure (Firstspace) has been a well-accepted tradition by the time of the writing of Hebrews. As such is the case, the author of Hebrews showcases the heavenly tabernacle by centering the believers' spatial orientation (i.e., locating them) within its walls (Secondspace). Knowing that an actual place exists becomes a motivating factor in believers' understanding of their solidarity with Christ.

The last passage examined was Hebrews 9:11–14 in Chapter 6. These verses are part of the author's larger argument that shows why and how Christ's priestly ministry is far greater and better than the levitical order. To support his argument, the author of Hebrews presents Jesus as performing his ministry in the innermost Holy of Holies. This is in stark contrast to the earthly tabernacle, which was insufficient to house the once-for-all sacrifice that has eternal efficacy. The Secondspace import is the idea that Jesus entered the Holy of Holies by virtue of his death on the cross, which correlates to entrance into the heavenly tabernacle by way of ritual geography.

9.3. Part 3: Thirdspace

Chapters 7 and 8 discussed the implications of the heavenly tabernacle's Firstspace and Secondspace. First, in Chapter 7, I discussed believers' spatial awareness of their having entered the very place Christ occupies. A full understanding of this spiritual benefit contributes to the interplay of believers' Firstspace, Secondspace, and Thirdspace. This spatial triad is what enables believers to look upward and forward as they live out their heavenly identity. Furthermore, this spatial orientation is a key feature that enables believers to see themselves as heavenly priests and as a result to serve as such while living on earth.

Chapter 8 discussed what Thirdspace priestly activity entails. First, I argued that the cultic language utilized in Hebrews is intentional. It serves to describe the priestly identity and activity of believers. Both προσέρχομαι and εἰσέρχομαι are specialized terms to describe the priests privileged entrance into the inner sanctuary to minister on behalf of the people. These terms are applied to New Covenant believers as a result of Christ's atoning sacrifice which purifies and cleanses their conscience. Only after being consecrated in such priestly fashion are they now able to serve (λειτουργός, λατρεύω) as priests on earth. Such priestly acts consist of both vertical service (prayer, worship, and thanksgiving) and horizontal service (mutual service amongst the Christian community). Furthermore, the example of such priestly acts by believers serves as a witness to the unbelieving world around them (for the original audience, the Roman Empire).

9.4. Contributions, Implications, and New Avenues of Research

By bringing spatial features of the heavenly tabernacle to the forefront, I have sought to present a holistic presentation of Hebrews eschatology that is both vertical and horizontal. This has resulted in two primary contributions to Hebrews scholarship: (1) The first was the methodological application of Edward Soja's Tripartite Critical Spatial Theory to passages that discuss the heavenly tabernacle in Hebrews. While Critical Spatiality has been a helpful interpretive tool in biblical studies, it had never been applied to the heavenly tabernacle in a comprehensive manner. (2) The second contribution was theological. By arguing for the tabernacle's physical existence in the heavens, I showed that the provisional eschatological realities are indeed real. Furthermore, these benefits are made available to believers by the high priestly ministry of Christ. This includes believers' shared occupancy with Christ in the innermost sanctuary of the heavenly tabernacle. This then enables and empowers recipient believers to live out their priestly identity on earth.

The following implications arise from this study: First, the heavenly tabernacle is a fitting example of how eschatology is to be perceived in both spatial and temporal terms. Instead of overemphasizing one dimension over the other, we can begin to understand concepts such as the already (provisionally in heaven) and not-yet (on earth). This may be a reason why the tabernacle motif was utilized rather than the temple.[2] Furthermore, the tabernacle motif resonates with the audience's wilderness-like situation as displaced Christians throughout the Roman Empire living in a state of liminality. Second, we can better appreciate the impact of Christ's high priestly ministry. In addition to the atonement of sins which is conferred upon believers, Christ's high priestly ministry includes the invitation for believers to enter into the very presence of God. It provides a richer understanding of promises such as Jesus' preparation of a heavenly place for his disciples (Jn 14:2). Having attained this heavenly access, believers may now have a transformed self-understanding—not as sinners with guilty consciences, but as purified and consecrated priests who serve the living God. Third, while there may be different proposals as to how to structure the doctrinal and hortatory features of the letter, the spatiotemporal eschatological tabernacle allows us to see how doctrine naturally flows into the ethical commands for priestly living. For instance, the reality of believers' shared occupancy with Christ by way of his high priestly ministry is precisely what motivates them to live according to their identity. Believers are able to "live out" what they have become in Christ: heavenly priests.

Various areas of potential research arise from this study. The author of Hebrews intentionally uses the tabernacle motif to convey the richness of Christ's high priestly ministry. The question then arises: "Are there spatial aspects of the tabernacle that communicate certain ideas better than the temple would?"

---

2. This draws our focus on the author's rhetorical strategy rather than speculating on the existence or destruction of the Jerusalem Temple by the time of the writing of Hebrews.

Answering such questions may provide further explanation for the various wilderness themes present in the epistle. Additionally, the scope of this study was limited to the Epistle to the Hebrews. Another potentially fruitful study lies in spatial study of the temple in Revelation. How does the heavenly tabernacle in Hebrews deepen our understanding of the heavenly temple and heavenly Jerusalem in Revelation? How do the worship and offering depicted in Revelation inform our understanding of priestly service? How important is the concept of the general priesthood in Revelation, especially considering that the people of God are the eschatological temple?[3] Finally, it may be interesting to see how the heavenly tabernacle theme coincides with other themes found in Hebrews (e.g., familial language for believers, perseverance and perfection, warning passages).

With regard to broader scholarship of the New Testament, this study offers an example of how Critical Spatiality can be utilized to deepen our understanding of Scripture's spatial language. It invites us to consider the dynamic features of space that existed amongst the early Christian community. It also challenges us to think differently about space. Rather than being merely a locative setting to "house" doctrinal concepts, space becomes an active participant in the larger story of redemption. It also becomes an important feature in the lives of Christians today. Our view of heaven is not a far-off, distant place where spiritual ideas exist. It is a real place that houses a real God: Jesus, the resurrected high priest who intercedes for his people. Heaven does not become a cosmical heaven but a "thoroughly redemptive heaven, a heaven become what it is through the progressive upbuilding and enrichment pertaining to the age-long work of God in the sphere of redemption."[4]

---

3. The resurrection body of Jesus is the new temple and will reach its climax when humanity becomes God's dwelling place as the eschatological temple (Beale, *The Temple and the Church's Mission*, 388–93; Morales, *Who Shall Ascend?*, 304).

4. Vos, *Pauline Eschatology*, 40.

BIBLIOGRAPHY

Abegg Jr., Martin G. *Qumran Sectarian Manuscripts*. Bellingham, WA: Logos Bible Software, 2003.
Aitken, Ellen. "The Body of Jesus Outside the Eternal City: Mapping Ritual Space in the Epistle to the Hebrews." Pages 194–209 in *Hebrews in Contexts*. Edited by Gabriella Gelardini and Harold W. Attridge. AGJU 91. Leiden: Brill, 2016.
Aitken, Ellen. "Reading Hebrews in Flavian Rome." *USQR* 59.3–4 (2005): 82–85.
Aitken, J. K., ed. *T&T Clark Companion to the Septuagint*. New York: T&T Clark, 2015.
Algra, Keimpe. *Concepts of Space in Greek Thought*. Philosophia Antiqua 65. Leiden: Brill, 1995.
Allen, David L. *Hebrews*. NAC 35. Nashville, TN: Broadman & Holman, 2010.
Anderson, Gary A. "The Praise of God as a Cultic Event." Pages 15–33 in *Priesthood and Cult in Ancient Israel*. Edited by Gary A. Anderson and Saul M. Olyan. JSOTSup 125. Sheffield: JSOT Press, 1991.
Anderson, Gary A., and Saul M. Olyan, eds. *Priesthood and Cult in Ancient Israel*. JSOT 125. Sheffield: JSOT Press, 1991.
Aptowitzer, Victor. "The Celestial Temple as Viewed in the Aggadah." *Studies in Jewish Thought*. Edited by Joseph Dan. Binah 2. New York: Praeger, 1989.
Aristotle. *Physics, Volume I: Books 1–4*. Translated by P. H. Wicksteed and F. M. Cornford. LCL 228. Cambridge, MA: Harvard University Press, 1957.
Aristotle. *Poetics*. Translated by Stephen Halliwell. LCL 199. Cambridge, MA: Harvard University Press, 1995.
Asumang, Annang. "The Tabernacle as a Heuristic Device in the Interpretation of the Christology of the Epistle to the Hebrews." ThM diss. The South African Theological Seminary, 2005.
Asumang, Annang. *Unlocking the Book of Hebrews: A Spatial Analysis of the Epistle to the Hebrews*. Eugene, OR: Wipf & Stock, 2008.
Asumang, Annang, and Bill Domeris. "Ministering in the Tabernacle: Spaciality and the Christology of Hebrews." *Conspectus* 1 (2006): 1–25.
Asumang, Annang, and Bill Domeris. "The Migrant Camp of the People of God: A Uniting Theme for the Epistle to the Hebrews." *Conspectus* 3 (2007): 1–33.
Attridge, Harold W. *The Epistle to the Hebrews: A Commentary on the Epistle to the Hebrews*. Hermeneia. Philadelphia, PA: Fortress Press, 1989.
Attridge, Harold W. *Essays on John and Hebrews*. WUNT 264. Tübingen: Mohr Siebeck, 2010.
Attridge, Harold W. "The Uses of Antithesis in Hebrews 8–10." *HTR* 79.1–3 (1986): 1–9.
Bachmann, Michael. "Hohepriesterliches Leiden: Beobachtungen zu Heb 5:1-10." *ZNW* 78.3–4 (1987): 244–66.
Backhaus, Knut. *Der sprechende Gott: gesammelte Studien zum Hebräerbrief*. WUNT 240. Tübingen: Mohr Siebeck, 2009.

Backhaus, Knut. "How to Entertain Angels: Ethics in the Epistle to the Hebrews." Pages 149–76 in *Hebrews: Contemporary Methods, New Insights*. Edited by Gabriella Gelardini. BIS 75. Leiden: Brill, 2005.

Balz, Horst Robert, and Gerhard Schneider, eds. *Exegetical Dictionary of the New Testament*. 3 vols. Grand Rapids, MI: Eerdmans, 1990–93.

Barr, James. *The Semantics of Biblical Language*. Oxford: Oxford University Press, 1961.

Barrera, Julio C. Trebolle. *The Jewish Bible and the Christian Bible: An Introduction to the History of the Bible*. Grand Rapids, MI: Eerdmans, 1998.

Barrett, C. K. "The Eschatology of the Epistle to the Hebrews." Pages 363–93 in *The Background of the New Testament and Its Eschatology: Essays in Honour of C. H. Dodd*. Edited by W. D. Davies and D. Daube. Cambridge: Cambridge University Press, 1956.

Barth, Markus. "The Old Testament in Hebrews." Pages 53–78 in *Current Issues in New Testament Interpretation*. Edited by William Klassen and Graydon F. Snyder. London: SCM Press, 2013.

Beale, G. K. "The Descent of the Eschatological Temple in the Form of the Spirit at Pentecost: Part 1 The Clearest Evidence." *TynBul* 56.1 (2005): 73–102.

Beale, G. K. "Eden, the Temple, and the Church's Mission in the New Creation." *JETS* 48.1 (2005): 5–31.

Beale, G. K. *Handbook on the New Testament Use of the Old Testament: Exegesis and Interpretation*. Grand Rapids, MI: Baker Academic, 2012.

Beale, G. K. *John's Use of the Old Testament in Revelation*. JSNTSup 166. Sheffield: Sheffield Academic Press, 1998.

Beale, G. K. *A New Testament Biblical Theology: The Unfolding of the Old Testament in the New*. Grand Rapids, MI: Baker Academic, 2011.

Beale, G. K. *The Temple and the Church's Mission: A Biblical Theology of the Dwelling Place of God*. NSBT 17. Downers Grove, IL: InterVarsity Press, 2004.

Beale, G. K., and D. A. Carson, eds. *Commentary on the New Testament Use of the Old Testament*. Grand Rapids, MI: Baker Academic, 2007.

Beale, G. K., and Mitchell Kim. *God Dwells among Us: Expanding Eden to the Ends of the Earth*. Downers Grove, IL: InterVarsity Press, 2014.

Beale, G. K., William A. Ross, and Daniel J. Brendsel. *An Interpretive Lexicon of New Testament Greek: Analysis of Prepositions, Adverbs, Particles, Relative Pronouns, and Conjunctions*. Grand Rapids, MI: Zondervan, 2014.

Bélanger, Steeve. "L'Épître aux Hébreux dans le contexte spéculatif sur la figure de Melchisédech durant la période du Second Temple de Jérusalem (IIe siècle avant notre ère - Ier siècle de notre ère)." *ASE* 33.1 (2016): 31–77.

Bénétreau, Samuel. "Le symbolisme dans l'Épître aux Hébreux. Images et métaphores." *ETR* 90.2 (2015): 145–63.

Berényi, Gabriella. "La portée διὰ τοῦτο en He 9,15." *Biblica* 69.1 (1988): 108–12.

Berger, Peter L., and Thomas Luckmann. *The Social Construction of Reality: A Treatise in the Sociology of Knowledge*. New York: Anchor Books, 1990.

Bergh, Ronald H. van der. "A Textual Comparison of Hebrews 10:5b-7 and LXX Psalm 39:7-9." *Neot* 42.2 (2008): 353–82.

Berquist, Jon L. "Critical Spatiality and the Book of Hebrews." Pages 181–93 in *Hebrews in Contexts*. Edited by Gabriella Gelardini and Harold W. Attridge. AGJU 91. Leiden: Brill, 2016.

Berquist, Jon L. "Critical Spatiality and the Construction of the Ancient World." Pages 14–29 in *Imagining Biblical Worlds: Studies in Spatial, Social, and Historical Constructs in Honor of James W. Flanagan*. Edited by David M. Gunn and Paula M. McNutt. JSOTSup 359. New York: Sheffield Academic Press, 2002.

Berquist, Jon L. "Introduction: Critical Spatiality and the Uses of Theory." Pages 1–14 in *Constructions of Space I: Theory, Geography, and Narrative*. Edited by Jon L. Berquist and Claudia V. Camp. LHBOTS 481. New York: T&T Clark, 2007.

Berquist, Jon L., and Claudia V. Camp, eds. *Constructions of Space I: Theory, Geography, and Narrative*. LHBOTS 481. New York: T&T Clark, 2007.

Berquist, Jon L., and Claudia V. Camp, eds. *Constructions of Space II: The Biblical City and Other Imagined Spaces*. LHBOTS 490. New York: T&T Clark, 2008.

Best, Ernest. "Spiritual Sacrifice: General Priesthood in the New Testament." *Int* 14.3 (1960): 273–99.

Black, C. Clifton. "The Rhetorical Form of the Hellenistic Jewish and Early Christian Sermon: A Response to Lawrence Wills." *HTR* 81.1 (1988): 1–18.

Black, Max. *Metaphor and Thought*. Edited by Andrew Ortony. 2nd ed. New York: Cambridge University Press, 1993.

Black, Max. *Models and Metaphors: Studies in Language and Philosophy*. Ithaca, NY: Cornell University Press, 1981.

Bauer, W., F. W. Danker, W. F. Arndt, and F. W. Gingrich. *Greek-English Lexicon of the New Testament and Other Early Christian Literature*. 3rd ed. Chicago, IL: University of Chicago Press, 2000.

Bleek, Friedrich. *Der Brief an die Hebräer: erläutert durch Einleitung Uebersetzung und forlaufenden Commentar*. 2 vols. Berlin: Ferdinand Dümmler, 1828.

Block, Daniel. *The Book of Ezekiel, Chapters 25–48*. NICOT. Grand Rapid, MI: Eerdmans, 1997.

Borgen, Peder, Kåre Fuglseth, and Roald Skarsten, eds. *The Works of Philo: Greek Text with Morphology*. Bellingham, WA: Logos Bible Software, 2005.

Botterweck, G. Johannes, Helmer Ringgren, and Heinz-Josef Barry., eds. *Theological Dictionary of the Old Testament*. Translated by J. T. Willis, D. E. Green, and D. W. Scott. 15 vols. Grand Rapids, MI: Eerdmans, 1977–2012.

Brannan, Rick, and Israel Loken. *The Lexham Textual Notes on the Bible*. LBRS. Bellingham, WA: Lexham Press, 2014.

Brinkman, Johan Marie. *The Perception of Space in the Old Testament: An Exploration of the Methodological Problems of Its Investigation, Exemplified by a Study of Exodus 25 to 31*. Kampen: Kok Pharos, 1992.

Bromiley, Geoffrey W., et al., eds. *International Standard Bible Encyclopedia*. Revised edition. 4 vols. Grand Rapids, MI: Eerdmans, 1979–88.

Brown, Francis, Samuel Rolles Driver, and Charles Augustus Briggs. *Enhanced Brown-Driver-Briggs Hebrew and English Lexicon*. Oxford: Clarendon Press, 1977.

Bruce, F. F. *The Epistle to the Hebrews*. NICNT. Grand Rapids, MI: Eerdmans, 1990.

Büchsel, Friedrich, and Otto Procksch. "ἀκατάλυτος." *TDNT* 4:328–35.

Burnet, Régis. "La finale de l'épître aux Hébreux: une addition alexandrine de la fin du II siècle?" *RB* 120.3 (2013): 423–40.

Buttimer, Anne. "Home, Reach, and the Sense of Place." Pages 166–87 in *The Human Experience of Space and Place*. London: Croom Helm, 1980.

Calaway, Jared. *The Sabbath and the Sanctuary: Access to God in the Letter to the Hebrews and Its Priestly Context*. WUNT 2/349. Tübingen: Mohr Siebeck, 2013.

Calvin, John. *Commentary on the Epistle of Paul the Apostle to the Hebrews.* Translated by John Owen. Bellingham, WA: Logos Bible Software.
Calvin, John. *Institutes of the Christian Religion.* Edited by John T. McNeill. Translated by Ford Lewis Battles. Louisville, KY: Westminster John Knox Press, 2011.
Camacho, Harold S. "The Altar of Incense in Hebrews 9:3-4." *AUSS* 24.1 (1986): 5-12.
Campbell, Constantine R. *Paul and Union with Christ: An Exegetical and Theological Study.* Grand Rapids, MI: Zondervan, 2012.
Carson, D. A. *The Gospel According to John,* PNTC. Grand Rapids, MI: Eerdmans, 1991.
Casey, Edward S. *Getting Back into Place: Toward a Renewed Understanding of the Place-World.* 2nd ed. Studies in Continental Thought. Bloomington, IN: Indiana University Press, 2009.
Cashdan, Eli. *The Babylonian Talmud: Tractate Menaḥot.* Edited by Isidore Epstein. London: Soncino Press, 1948.
Charlesworth, J. H. *The Old Testament Pseudepigrapha.* 2 vols. New York: Yale University Press, 1983, 1985.
Childs, Brevard S. *The Book of Exodus: A Critical Theological Commentary.* OTL. Philadelphia, PA: Westminster Press, 1974.
Church, Philip Arthur Frederick. *Hebrews and the Temple: Attitudes to the Temple in Second Temple Judaism and in Hebrews.* NovTSup 171. Leiden: Brill, 2017.
Church, Philip Arthur Frederick. "The Temple in the Apocalypse of Weeks and in Hebrews." *TynBul* 64.1 (2013): 109-28.
Church, Philip Arthur Frederick. "Wilderness Tabernacle and Eschatological Temple: A Study in Temple Symbolism in Hebrews in the Light of Attitudes to the Temple in the Literature of Middle Judaism." PhD diss., University of Otago, 2012.
Clarke, Katherine. *Between Geography and History: Hellenistic Constructions of the Roman World.* Oxford: Clarendon Press, 1999.
Cockerill, Gareth Lee. *The Epistle to the Hebrews.* NICNT. Grand Rapids, MI: Eerdmans, 2012.
Cockerill, Gareth Lee. "Review of Proleptic Priests: Priesthood in the Epistle to the Hebrews by John Scholer." *JBL* 112.1 (1993): 171-73.
Cody, Aelred. *Heavenly Sanctuary and Liturgy in the Epistle to the Hebrews: The Achievement of Salvation in the Epistle's Perspectives.* St. Meinrad, IN: Grail, 1960.
Collins, John J. *The Apocalyptic Imagination: An Introduction to Jewish Apocalyptic Literature.* 2nd ed. Grand Rapids, MI: Eerdmans, 1998.
Collins, John J. "Towards the Morphology of a Genre: Introduction." *Semeia* 14 (1979): 1-20.
Combrink, H. J. B. "Some Thoughts on the Old Testament Citations in the Epistle to the Hebrews." *Neot* 5 (1971): 22-36.
Comfort, Philip W. *New Testament Text and Translation Commentary: Commentary on the Variant Readings of the Ancient New Testament Manuscripts and How They Relate to the Major English Translations.* Carol Stream, IL: Tyndale House, 2008.
Craigie, Peter C. *Psalms 1-60.* 2nd ed. WBC 19. Nashville, TN: Nelson, 2004.
Crocker, Lacy K. "A Holy Nation." *RTR* 72.3 (2013): 185-201.
Dahl, Nils Alstrup. "A New and Living Way: The Approach to God According to Hebrews 10:19-25." *Int* 5.4 (1951): 401-12.
Dan, Joseph, ed. *Studies in Jewish Thought.* Binah 2. New York: Praeger, 1989.
D'Angelo, Mary Rose. *Moses in the Letter to the Hebrews.* SBLDS 42. Missoula, MT: Scholars Press, 1979.

Davidson, Richard M. "Christ's Entry 'within the Veil' in Hebrews 6:19-20: The Old Testament Background." *AUSS* 39.2 (2001): 175–90.

Davidson, Richard M. "Typology in the Book of Hebrews." Pages 121–186 in *Issues in the Book of Hebrews*. Edited by Frank B. Holbrook. DARCOM 4. Silver Spring, MD: BRI, 1989.

Davidson, Richard M. *Typology in Scripture: A Study of Hermeneutical ΤΥΠΟΣ Structures*. AUSDDS 2. Berrien Springs, MI: Andrews University Press, 1981.

deSilva, David A. "Entering God's Rest: Eschatology and the Socio-Rhetorical Strategy of Hebrews." *TrinJ* 21.1 (2000): 25–43.

deSilva, David A. "Hebrews." Pages 199–257 in *The Bible Knowledge Background Commentary: John's Gospel, Hebrews-Revelation*. Edited by Craig A. Evans and Craig A. Bubeck. Colorado Springs, CO: Victor, 2005.

deSilva, David A. "How Greek Was the Author of 'Hebrews'? A Study of the Author's Location in Regard to Greek Παιδεία." Pages 629–50 in *Christian Origins and Greco-Roman Culture: Social and Literary Contexts for the New Testament*. Edited by Stanley E. Porter and Andrew W. Pitts. TENT 9. Leiden: Brill, 2013.

deSilva, David A. "The Invention and Argumentative Function of Priestly Discourse in the Epistle to the Hebrews." *BBR* 16.2 (2006): 295–323.

deSilva, David A. *Perseverance in Gratitude: A Socio-Rhetorical Commentary on the Epistle "to the Hebrews."* Grand Rapids, MI: Eerdmans, 2000.

Docherty, Susan E. *The Use of the Old Testament in Hebrews: A Case Study in Early Jewish Bible Interpretation*. WUNT 2/260. Tübingen: Mohr Siebeck, 2009.

Dodd, C. H. *According to the Scriptures: The Sub-Structure of New Testament Theology*. London: Fontana Books, 1965.

Downs, David J. *The Offering of the Gentiles: Paul's Collection for Jerusalem in Its Chronological, Cultural, and Cultic Contexts*. WUNT 2/248. Tübingen: Mohr Siebeck, 2008.

Downs, David J. "'The Offering of the Gentiles' in Romans 15.16." *JSNT* 29.2 (2006): 173–86.

Dozeman, Thomas B. "Biblical Geography and Critical Spatial Studies." Pages 87–108 in *Constructions of Space I: Theory, Geography, and Narrative*. Edited by Jon L. Berquist and Claudia V. Camp. LHBOTS 481. New York: T&T Clark, 2007.

Dunnill, John. *Covenant and Sacrifice in the Letter to the Hebrews*. SNTSMS 75. New York: Cambridge University Press, 1992.

Durham, John I. *Exodus*. WBC 3. Dallas, TX: Word, 1987.

Durkheim, Emile. *The Elementary Forms of Religious Life*. Translated by Karen E. Fields. New York: Free Press, 1995.

Eberhart, Christian. "Characteristics of Sacrificial Metaphors in Hebrews." Pages 37–64 in *Hebrews: Contemporary Methods, New Insights*. Edited by Gabriella Gelardini. BIS 75. Leiden: Brill, 2005.

Eisele, Wilfried. *Ein unerschütterliches Reich: Die mittelplatonische Umformung des Parusiegedankens im Hebräerbrief*. BZNW 116. Berlin: de Gruyter, 2003.

Ellingworth, Paul. *The Epistle to the Hebrews: A Commentary on the Greek Text*. NIGTC. Grand Rapids, MI: Eerdmans, 1993.

Ellingworth, Paul. "Jesus and the Universe in Hebrews." *EvQ* 58.4 (1986): 337–50.

Ellingworth, Paul, and Eugene A. Nida. *A Translator's Handbook on the Letter to the Hebrews*. UBS Handbook Series. New York: United Bible Societies, 1983.

Ellis, E. E. "The Old Testament Canon in the Early Church." Pages 653–90 in *Mikra: Text, Translation, Reading, and Interpretation of the Hebrew Bible in Ancient Judaism and Early Christianity*. Edited by M. J. Mulder and Harry Sysling. CRINT 1. Minneapolis, MN: Fortress Press, 1990.

Ellis, E. E. "Quotations in the NT." *ISBE* 4:18–26.

Emery, Gilles, and Matthew Levering, eds. *The Oxford Handbook of the Trinity*. New York: Oxford University Press, 2011.

Emmrich, Martin. "'Amtscharisma': Through the Eternal Spirit (Hebrews 9:14)." *BBR* 12.1 (2002): 17–32.

Emmrich, Martin. "Pneuma in Hebrews: Prophet and Interpreter." Pages 75–92 in *The Letter to the Hebrews: Critical Readings*. Edited by Scott D. Mackie. T&T Clark Critical Readings in Biblical Studies. London: T&T Clark, 2018.

Enns, Peter. *Exodus*. NIVAC. Grand Rapids, MI: Zondervan, 2014.

Epstein, Isidore, trans. *The Babylonian Talmud*. 35 vols. London: Soncino Press, 1935.

Eskola, Timo. *Messiah and the Throne: Jewish Merkabah Mysticism and Early Christian Exaltation Discourse*. WUNT 142/2. Tübingen: Mohr Siebeck, 2001.

Evans, Craig A., and Craig A. Bubeck, eds. *The Bible Knowledge Background Commentary: John's Gospel, Hebrews-Revelation*. Colorado Springs, CO: Victor, 2005.

Fairhurst, Alan Marshall. "Hellenistic Influence in the Epistle to the Hebrews." *TynBul* 7 (1961): 17–27.

Feld, Helmut. *Der Hebräerbrief*. ErFor 228. Darmstadt: Wissenschaftliche Buchgesellschaft, 1985.

Fish, Stanley E. *Is There a Text in This Class? The Authority of Interpretive Communities*. Cambridge, MA: Harvard University Press, 1980.

Flanagan, James W. "Ancient Perceptions of Space/Perceptions of Ancient Space." *Semeia* 87 (1999): 15–43.

Flanagan, James W. "Space." Pages 239–44 in *Handbook of Postmodern Biblical Interpretation*. Edited by A. K. M. Adam. St. Louis, MO: Chalice Press, 2000.

Fletcher-Louis, Crispin H. T. *All the Glory of Adam: Liturgical Anthropology in the Dead Sea Scrolls*. STDJ 42. Leiden: Brill, 2002.

Floor, Lambertus. "The General Priesthood of Believers in the Epistle to the Hebrews." *Neot* 5 (1971): 72–82.

Foucault, Michel. "Questions on Geography." Pages 63–77 in *Power/Knowledge: Selected Interviews and Other Writings*. Translated by Colin Gordon. New York: Pantheon Books, 1980.

Foucault, Michel, and Jay Miskowiec. "Of Other Spaces." *Diacritics* 16.1 (1986): 22–27.

Frame, John M. *The Doctrine of God*. A Theology of Lordship. Phillipsburg, N.J: Presbyterian & Reformed, 2002.

France, R. T. "The Writer of Hebrews as a Biblical Expositor." *TynBul* 47.2 (1996): 245–76.

Freedman, Harry, and Maurice Simon, eds. *Midrash Rabbah Exodus*. Translated by S. M. Lehrman. Vol. 3. London: Soncino Press, 1939.

Freedman, Harry, and Maurice Simon, eds. *Midrash Rabbah Numbers II*. Translated by Judah J. Slotki. Vol. 6. London: Soncino Press, 1939.

Friedeman, Caleb T., ed. *Listen, Understand, Obey: Essays on Hebrews in Honor of Gareth Lee Cockerill*. Eugene, OR: Pickwick Publications, 2017.

Gäbel, Georg. *Die Kulttheologie des Hebräerbriefes: Eine exegetisch-religionsgeschichtliche Studie*. WUNT 2/212. Tübingen: Mohr Siebeck, 2006.

Gaffin, Richard B. *The Centrality of the Resurrection: A Study in Paul's Soteriology.* Grand Rapids, MI: Baker Academic, 1978.
Gammie, John G. "Spatial and Ethical Dualism in Jewish Wisdom and Apocalyptic Literature." *JBL* 93.3 (1974): 356–85.
Gane, Roy E. "Re-Opening Katapetasma ('Veil') in Hebrews 6:19." *AUSS* 38.1 (2000): 5–8.
Garland, David E. *2 Corinthians.* NAC 29. Nashville, TN: Broadman & Holman, 1999.
Gelardini, Gabriella. "Charting 'Outside the Camp' with Edward W. Soja: Critical Spatiality and Hebrews 13." Pages 210–37 in *Hebrews in Contexts.* Edited by Gabriella Gelardini and Harold W. Attridge. AGJU 91. Leiden: Brill, 2016.
Gelardini, Gabriella, ed. *Hebrews: Contemporary Methods, New Insights.* BIS 75. Leiden: Brill, 2005.
Gelardini, Gabriella, and Harold W. Attridge, eds. *Hebrews in Contexts.* AGJU 91. Leiden: Brill, 2016.
Genette, Gérard. *Palimpsests: Literature in the Second Degree.* Translated by Channa Newman and Claude Doubinsky. Stages 8. Lincoln, NE: University of Nebraska Press, 1997.
Gentry, Peter J. "The Septuagint and the Text of the Old Testament." *BBR* 16.2 (2006): 193–218.
George, Mark K., ed. *Constructions of Space IV: Further Developments in Examining Ancient Israel's Social Space.* LHBOTS 569. New York: T&T Clark, 2013.
George, Mark K. *Israel's Tabernacle as Social Space.* SBLAIL 2. Leiden: Brill, 2009.
George, Mark K. "Introduction." Pages xi–xvi in *Constructions of Space IV: Further Developments in Examining Ancient Israel's Social Space.* Edited by Mark K. George. LHBOTS 569. New York: T&T Clark, 2013.
George, Mark K. "Social-Spatial Logic and the Structure of the Book of Numbers." Pages 23–43 in *Constructions of Space IV: Further Developments in Examining Ancient Israel's Social Space.* Edited by Mark K. George. LHBOTS 569. New York: T&T Clark, 2013.
George, Mark K. "Space and History: Siting Critical Space for Biblical Studies." Pages 15–31 in *Constructions of Space I: Theory, Geography, and Narrative.* Edited by Jon L. Berquist and Claudia V. Camp. LHBOTS 481. New York: T&T Clark, 2007.
Gheorghita, Radu. *The Role of the Septuagint in Hebrews: An Investigation of Its Influence with Special Consideration to the Use of Hab 2:3-4 in Heb 10:37-38.* WUNT 2/160. Tübingen: Mohr Siebeck, 2003.
Glombitza, Otto. "Erwägungen zum kunstvollen Ansatz der Paraenese im Brief an die Hebräer 10:19-25." *NovT* 9.2 (1967): 132–50.
Goppelt, Leonhard. *Theology of the New Testament.* 2 vols. Grand Rapids, MI: Eerdmans, 1982.
Goppelt, Leonhard. "Τύπος, Ἀντίτυπος, Τυπικός, Ὑποτύπωσις." *TDNT* 8:246–59.
Grässer, Erich. *An Die Hebräer.* 3 vols. EKKNT 1–3/17. Zürich: Benziger, 1990–97.
Grässer, Erich. "Mose und Jesus: Zur Auslegung von Hebr 3:1-6." *ZNW* 75.1–2 (1984): 2–23.
Gray, Patrick. "Hebrews Among Greeks and Romans." Pages 13–30 in *Reading the Epistle to the Hebrews: A Resource for Students.* Edited by Eric F. Mason and Kevin B. McCruden. RBS 66. Atlanta, GA: SBL, 2011.
Greenlee, J. Harold, and David Alan Black, eds. *Scribes and Scripture: New Testament Essays in Honor of J. Harold Greenlee.* Winona Lake, IN: Eisenbrauns, 1992.
Greenspoon, Leonard J. "The Use and Abuse of the Term 'LXX' and Related Terminology in Recent Scholarship." *BIOSCS* 20 (1987): 21–29.

Gunn, David M., and Paula M. McNutt, eds. *Imagining Biblical Worlds: Studies in Spatial, Social, and Historical Constructs in Honor of James W. Flanagan*. JSOTSup 359. New York: Sheffield Academic Press, 2002.

Guthrie, Donald. *The Letter to the Hebrews: An Introduction and Commentary*. TNTC 15. Downers Grove, IL: InterVarsity Press, 1983.

Guthrie, George H. *2 Corinthians*. BECNT. Grand Rapids, MI: Baker Academic, 2015.

Guthrie, George H. "Hebrews." Pages 919–97 in *Commentary on the New Testament Use of the Old Testament*. Edited by G. K. Beale and D. A. Carson. Grand Rapids, MI: Baker Academic, 2007.

Guthrie, George H. "Hebrews' Use of the Old Testament: Recent Trends in Research." *CurBR* 1.2 (2003): 271–94.

Guthrie, George H. "Old Testament in Hebrews." *DLNT* 841–50.

Guthrie, George H. *The Structure of Hebrews: A Text-Linguistic Analysis*. NovTSup 73. Leiden: Brill, 1994.

Guthrie, George H. "Time and Atonement in Hebrews." Pages 209–27 in *So Great a Salvation: A Dialogue on the Atonement in Hebrews*. Edited by Jon C. Laansma, George H. Guthrie, and Cynthia Long Westfall. New York: T&T Clark, 2019.

Hanson, R. P. C. *Allegory and Event: A Study of the Sources and Significance of Origen's Interpretation of Scripture*. London: SCM Press, 1959.

Haran, Menahem. *Temples and Temple-Service in Ancient Israel: An Inquiry into Biblical Cult Phenomena and the Historical Setting of the Priestly School*. Winona Lake, IN: Eisenbrauns, 1985.

Hare, D. R. A. "The Lives of the Prophets: A New Translation and Introduction." In *OTP* 2:379–400.

Harvey, David. *The Condition of Postmodernity: An Enquiry into the Origins of Cultural Change*. Cambridge, MA: Blackwell, 1989.

Harvey, David. *Justice, Nature, and the Geography of Difference*. Cambridge, MA: Blackwell, 1996.

Himmelfarb, Martha. *Ascent to Heaven in Jewish and Christian Apocalypses*. New York: Oxford University Press, 1993.

Hockey, Katherine M., Madison N. Pierce, and Francis Watson, eds. *Muted Voices of the New Testament: Readings in the Catholic Epistles and Hebrews*. LNTS 565. New York: T&T Clark, 2017.

Holbrook, Frank B. "Daniel and Revelation Committee Report." Pages 1–12 in *Issues in the Book of Hebrews*. Edited by Frank. B. Holbrook. DARCOM 4. Silver Spring, MD: BRI, 1989.

Holbrook, Frank B., ed. *Issues in the Book of Hebrews*. DARCOM 4. Silver Spring, MD: BRI, 1989.

Hood, Jason B. "The Temple and the Thorn: 2 Corinthians 12 and Paul's Heavenly Ecclesiology." *BBR* 21.3 (2011): 357–70.

Hofius, Otfried. "Das 'erste' und das 'zweite' Zelt: Ein Beitrag zur Auslegung von Hbr 9:1–10." *ZNW* 61.3–4 (1970): 271–77.

Hofius, Otfried. *Der Vorhang vor dem Thron Gottes: eine exegetisch-religionsgeschichtliche Untersuchung zu Hebräer 6, 19. f. und 10,19f*. WUNT 14. Tübingen: Mohr Siebeck, 1972.

Howard, George E. "Hebrews and the Old Testament Quotations." *NovT* 10.2–3 (1968): 208–16.

Hubbard, Phil, and Rob Kitchin, eds. *Key Thinkers on Space and Place*. 2nd ed. Los Angeles, CA: Sage, 2011.

Hübner, Hans. "The OT Quotations in the New Testament." *ABD* 4:1096–1105.

Hughes, Philip E. *A Commentary on the Epistle to the Hebrews*. Grand Rapids; MI: Eerdmans, 1977.
Hughes, Philip E. "Review of Philo and the Epistle to the Hebrews by Ronald Williamson." *WTJ* 35.3 (1973): 349–51.
Hummel, Horace D. "The Old Testament Basis of Typological Interpretation." *BR* 9 (1964): 38–50.
Hurst, Lincoln D. *The Epistle to the Hebrews: Its Background of Thought*. SNTSMS 65. New York: Cambridge University Press, 1990.
Hurst, Lincoln D. "Eschatology and 'Platonism' in the Epistle to the Hebrews." *SBLSP* 23 (1984): 41–74.
Hurst, Lincoln D. "How 'Platonic' Are Heb. VIII.5 and IX. 23f.?" *JTS* 34.1 (1983): 156–68.
Isaac, Ephraim. "1 (Ethiopic Apocalypse of) Enoch: A New Translation and Introduction." In *OTP* 1:5–89.
Isaacs, Marie E. "Hebrews 13:9–16 Revisited." *NTS* 43.2 (1997): 268–84.
Isaacs, Marie E. *Sacred Space: An Approach to the Theology of the Epistle to the Hebrews*. JSNTSup 73. Sheffield: Sheffield Academic Press, 1992.
Jamieson, R. B. "Hebrews 9.23: Cult Inauguration, Yom Kippur and the Cleansing of the Heavenly Tabernacle." *NTS* 62.4 (2016): 569–87.
Jamieson, R. B. *Jesus' Death and Heavenly Offering in Hebrews*. SNTSMS 172. New York: Cambridge University Press, 2019.
Jamieson, R. B. "When and Where Did Jesus Offer Himself? A Taxonomy of Recent Scholarship on Hebrews." *CurBR* 15.3 (2017): 338–68.
Jennings, Mark A. "The Veil and the High Priestly Robes of the Incarnation: Understanding the Context of Heb 10:20." *PRS* 37.1 (2010): 85–97.
Jenson, Philip P. *Graded Holiness: A Key to the Priestly Conception of the World*. JSOTSup 106. Sheffield: JSOT Press, 1992.
Jobes, Karen H. "Rhetorical Achievement in the Hebrews 10 'Misquote' of Psalm 40." *Biblica* 72.3 (1991): 387–96.
Jobes, Karen H., and Moisés Silva. *Invitation to the Septuagint*. Grand Rapids, MI: Baker Academics, 2000.
Johnson, Luke Timothy. *Hebrews: A Commentary*. NTL. Louisville, KY: Westminster John Knox Press, 2006.
Johnsson, William G. *Defilement and Purgation in the Book of Hebrews*. SJCL. Dallas: Fontes Press, 2020.
Johnsson, William G. "The Heavenly Sanctuary—Figurative or Real?" Pages 35–52 in *Issues in the Book of Hebrews*. Edited by Frank B. Holbrook. DARCOM 4. Silver Spring, MD: BRI, 1989.
Josephus, Flavius. *The Works of Josephus: Complete and Unabridged*. Translated by William Whiston. Peabody, MA: Hendrickson, 1987.
Joslin, Barry Clyde. "Can Hebrews Be Structured? An Assessment of Eight Approaches." *CurBr* 6.1 (2007): 99–129.
Karrer, Martin. "The Epistle to the Hebrews and the Septuagint." Pages 335–53 in *Septuagint Research: Issues and Challenges in the Study of the Greek Jewish Scriptures*. Edited by Wolfgang Kraus and R. Glenn Wooden. SBLSCS 53. Atlanta, GA: SBL, 2006.
Karrer, Martin, and Wolfgang Kraus, eds. *Die Septuaginta: Texte, Kontexte, Lebenswelten*. WUNT 219. Tübingen: Mohr Siebeck, 2008.
Käsemann, Ernst. *The Wandering People of God: An Investigation of the Letter to the Hebrews*. Translated by R. A. Harrisville and I. L. Sundberg. Minneapolis, MN: Augsburg, 1984.

Kaufman, Stephen A., ed. *Targum Onqelos to the Pentateuch.* Cincinnati, OH: Hebrew Union College, 2005. Logos Bible Software.

Kaufman, Stephen A., ed. *Targum Pseudo-Jonathan to the Pentateuch.* Cincinnati, OH: Hebrew Union College, 2005. Logos Bible Software.

Kee, H. C. "Testaments of the Twelve Patriarchs: A New Translation and Introduction." In *OTP* 1:775–828.

Keene, Thomas. "Heaven Is a Tent: The Tabernacle as an Eschatological Metaphor in the Epistle to the Hebrews." PhD diss., Westminster Theological Seminary, 2010.

Kibbe, Michael. "Is It Finished? When Did It Start? Hebrews, Priesthood, and Atonement in Biblical, Systematic, and Historical Perspective." *JTS* 65.1 (2014): 25–61.

Kidner, Derek. *Psalms 1–72: An Introduction and Commentary.* TOTC 15. Downers Grove, IL: InterVarsity Press, 1973.

Kistemaker, Simon J. *Exposition of the Epistle to the Hebrews.* NTC. Grand Rapids, MI: Baker Book House, 1984.

Kistemaker, Simon J. *Psalm Citations in the Epistle to the Hebrews.* 1961. Reprint, Eugene, OR: Wipf & Stock, 2010.

Kittay, Eva Feder. *Metaphor: Its Cognitive Force and Linguistic Structure.* CLLP. New York: Clarendon Press, 1987.

Kittel, Gerhard, and Gerhard Friedrich, eds. *Theological Dictionary of the New Testament.* Translated by Geoffrey W. Bromiley. 10 vols. Grand Rapids, MI: Eerdmans, 1964–1976.

Klassen, William, and Graydon F. Snyder, eds. *Current Issues in New Testament Interpretation.* London: SCM Press, 2013.

Klawans, Jonathan. *Purity, Sacrifice, and the Temple: Symbolism and Supersessionism in the Study of Ancient Judaism.* New York: Oxford University Press, 2006.

Klijn, A. F. J. "2 (Syriac Apocalypse of) Baruch: A New Translation and Introduction." In *OTP* 1:615–52.

Kline, Meredith G. "The Intrusion and the Decalogue." *WTJ* 16.1 (1953): 1–22.

Koch, Klaus. "אֹהֶל." *TDOT* 1:129.

Koester, Craig R. *The Dwelling of God: The Tabernacle in the Old Testament, Intertestamental Jewish Literature, and the New Testament.* CBQMS 22. Washington, DC: Catholic Biblical Association of America, 1989.

Koester, Craig R. "God's Purposes and Christ's Saving Work According to Hebrews." Pages 438–59 in *The Letter to the Hebrews: Critical Readings.* Edited by Scott D. Mackie. T&T Clark Critical Readings in Biblical Studies. London: T&T Clark, 2018.

Koester, Craig R. *Hebrews: A New Translation with Introduction and Commentary.* AYBC 36. New Haven, CT: Yale University Press, 2008.

Kraus, Wolfgang, and R. Glenn Wooden, eds. *Septuagint Research: Issues and Challenges in the Study of the Greek Jewish Scriptures.* SBLSCS 53. Atlanta, GA: SBL, 2006.

Kubo, Sakae. "Hebrews 9:11-12: Christ's Body, Heavenly Region, Or…?" Pages 97–109 in *Scribes and Scripture: New Testament Essays in Honor of J. Harold Greenlee.* Edited by David Alan Black. Winona Lake, IN: Eisenbrauns, 1992.

Kuss, Otto. *Der Brief an Die Hebräer.* 2nd ed. RNT 8. Regensburg: Friedrich Pustet, 1966.

Laansma, Jon C. "The Cosmology of Hebrews." Pages 125–43 in *Cosmology and New Testament Theology.* Edited by Jonathan T. Pennington and Sean M. McDonough. LNTS 355. London: T&T Clark, 2008.

Laansma, Jon C. "Hidden Stories in Hebrews: Cosmology and Theology." Pages 9–18 in *So Great a Salvation: A Dialogue on the Atonement in Hebrews.* Edited by Jon C. Laansma, George H. Guthrie, and Cynthia Long Westfall. LNTS 516. New York: T&T Clark, 2019.

Laansma, Jon C., George H. Guthrie, and Cynthia Long Westfall, eds. *So Great a Salvation: A Dialogue on the Atonement in Hebrews.* LNTS 516. New York: T&T Clark, 2019.

Lane, William L. *Hebrews 1–8.* WBC 47A. Dallas, TX: Word, 1991.

Lane, William L. *Hebrews 9–13.* WBC 47B. Dallas, TX: Word, 1991.

Lane, William L. "Hebrews: A Sermon in Search of a Setting." *SWJT* 28.1 (1985): 13–18.

Laub, Franz. "'Ein für allemal hineingegangen in das Allerheiligste' [Hebr 9:12]: Zum Verständnis des Kreuzestodes im Hebräerbrief." *BZ* 35.1 (1991): 65–85.

Lefebvre, Henri. *La production de l'espace.* 2nd ed. 1974. Reprint, Paris: Éditions Anthropos, 1981.

Lefebvre, Henri. *The Production of Space.* Translated by Donald Nicholson-Smith. Cambridge, MA: Basil Blackwell, 1991.

Lefebvre, Henri. *The Survival of Capitalism: Reproduction of the Relations of Production.* Translated by Frank Bryan. New York: St. Martin's Press, 1976.

Levenson, Jon D. *Creation and the Persistence of Evil: The Jewish Drama of Divine Omnipotence.* Princeton: Princeton University Press, 1994.

Lewis, C. S. *Mere Christianity.* 1952. Reprint, New York: HarperOne, 2000.

Lilburne, Geoffrey R. *A Sense of Place: A Christian Theology of the Land.* Nashville, TN: Abingdon Press, 1989.

Lincoln, Andrew T. *Paradise Now and Not Yet: Studies in the Role of the Heavenly Dimension in Paul's Thought with Special Reference to His Eschatology.* SNTSMS 43. New York: Cambridge University Press, 1981.

Lincoln, Andrew T. "Sabbath, Rest, and Eschatology in the New Testament." Pages 171–83 in *The Letter to the Hebrews: Critical Readings.* Edited by Scott D. Mackie. T&T Clark Critical Readings in Biblical Studies. London: T&T Clark, 2018.

Loader, William. *Sohn und Hoherpriester: Eine traditionsgeschichtliche Untersuchung zur Christologie des Hebrierbriefes.* WMANT 53. Neukirchen-Vluyn: Neukirchener, 1981.

Löhr, Hermut. "'Umriss' Und 'Schatten': Bemerkungen Zur Zitierung von Ex 25,40 in Hebr 8." *ZNW* 84.3-4 (1993): 218–32.

Long, Philip J. "Holy of Holies." *The Lexham Bible Dictionary.* Bellingham, WA: Lexham Press, 2016. Logos Bible Software.

Longenecker, Richard N. *Biblical Exegesis in the Apostolic Period.* 2nd ed. Grand Rapids, MI: Eerdmans, 1999.

Longenecker, Richard N. *The Epistle to the Romans: A Commentary on the Greek Text.* Edited by I. Howard Marshall and Donald A. Hagner. NIGTC. Grand Rapids, MI: Eerdmans, 2016.

Lopez, Kathryn. "Standing Before the Throne of God: Critical Spatiality in Apocalyptic Scenes of Judgment." Pages 139–55 in *Constructions of Space II: The Biblical City and Other Imagined Spaces.* Edited by Jon L. Berquist and Claudia V. Camp. LHBOTS 490. New York: T&T Clark, 2008.

Macaskill, Grant. *Union with Christ in the New Testament.* Oxford: Oxford University Press, 2013.

Mackie, Scott D. *Eschatology and Exhortation in the Epistle to the Hebrews.* WUNT 2/223. Tübingen: Mohr Siebeck, 2007.

Mackie, Scott D. "Heavenly Sanctuary Mysticism in the Epistle to the Hebrews." *JTS* 62.1 (2011): 77–117.

Mackie, Scott D. "Introduction to Part 1." Pages 7–13 in *The Letter to the Hebrews: Critical Readings.* Edited by Scott D. Mackie. T&T Clark Critical Readings in Biblical Studies. London: T&T Clark, 2018.

Mackie, Scott D. "Introduction to Part 2." Pages 141–45 in *The Letter to the Hebrews: Critical Readings*. Edited by Scott D. Mackie. T&T Clark Critical Readings in Biblical Studies. London: T&T Clark, 2018.

Mackie, Scott D. "'Let Us Draw Near…but Not Too Near' A Critique of the Attempted Distinction between 'Drawing Near' and 'Entering' in Hebrews' Entry Exhortations." Pages 17–36 in *Listen, Understand, Obey: Essays on Hebrews in Honor of Gareth Lee Cockerill*. Edited by Caleb T. Friedeman. Eugene, OR: Pickwick Publications, 2017.

Mackie, Scott D., ed. *The Letter to the Hebrews: Critical Readings*. T&T Clark Critical Readings in Biblical Studies. London: T&T Clark, 2018.

MacLeod, David J. "The Cleansing of the True Tabernacle." *BSac* 152.605 (1995): 60–71.

MacLeod, David J. "The Literary Structure of the Book of Hebrews." *BSac* 146.582 (1989): 185–97.

MacLeod, David J. "The Present Work of Christ in Hebrews." *BSac* 148.590 (1991): 184–200.

Macleod, Ian C. "Christ's High Priesthood and Christian Worship in Hebrews." *PRJ* 8.1 (2016): 147–64.

MacRae, George W. "Heavenly Temple and Eschatology in the Letter to the Hebrews." *Semeia* 12 (1978): 179–99.

Martin, Ralph P., and Peter H. Davids, eds. *Dictionary of the Later New Testament and Its Developments*. Downers Grove, IL: InterVarsity Press, 1997.

Martínez, Florentino García, and Eibert J. C. Tigchelaar, eds. *The Dead Sea Scrolls Study Edition*. 2 vols. Leiden: Brill, 1997–98.

Mason, Eric F. "'Sit at My Right Hand': Enthronement and the Heavenly Sanctuary in Hebrews." Pages 901–16 in *A Teacher for All Generations: Essays in Honor of James C. VanderKam*. Edited by Eric F. Mason et al. 2 vols. JSJSup 153. Leiden: Brill, 2012.

Mason, Eric F. *"You Are a Priest Forever": Second Temple Jewish Messianism and the Priestly Christology of the Epistle to the Hebrews*. STDJ 74. Leiden: Brill, 2008.

Mason, Eric F., et al., eds. *A Teacher for All Generations: Essays in Honor of James C. VanderKam*. 2 vols. JSJSup 153. Leiden: Brill, 2012.

Mason, Eric F., and Kevin B. McCruden, eds. *Reading the Epistle to the Hebrews: A Resource for Students*. RBS 66. Atlanta, GA: SBL, 2011.

Massey, Doreen B. *For Space*. Thousand Oaks, CA: Sage, 2005.

Massey, Doreen B. *Space, Place, and Gender*. Minneapolis, MN: University of Minnesota Press, 1994.

Matthews, Victor H. "Physical Space, Imagined Space, and 'Lived Space' in Ancient Israel." *BTB* 33.1 (2003): 12–20.

McCaffrey, James. *The House with Many Rooms: The Temple Theme of Jn. 14, 2-3*. AnBib 114. Rome: Editrice Pontificio Istituto Biblico, 1988.

McCullough, J. C. "The Old Testament Quotations in Hebrews." *NTS* 26.3 (1980): 363–79.

McLay, R. Timothy. *The Use of the Septuagint in New Testament Research*. Grand Rapids, MI: Eerdmans, 2003.

McNamara, Martin, ed. *The Targum Onqelos to Exodus: Translated, with Apparatus and Notes*. Translated by Bernard Grossfeld. Vol. 7. Collegeville, MN: Liturgical Press, 1990.

Metzger, Bruce M. *A Textual Commentary on the Greek New Testament*. 2nd ed. Stuttgart: Deutsche Bibelgesellschaft, 1994.

Michaelis, Wilhelm. "Σκηνή." *TDNT* 7:376–77.

Michaels, Ramsey J. "Hebrews." Pages in 303–476 in *1 Timothy, 2 Timothy, Titus, and Hebrews*. CBC 17. Edited by Philip W. Comfort. Carol Stream, IL: Tyndale House, 2009.

Michel, Otto. *Der Brief an die Hebräer*. 12th ed. KEK 13. Göttingen: Vandenhoeck & Ruprecht, 1966.
Milik, J. T., and Matthew Black. *The Books of Enoch: Aramaic Fragments of Qumrân Cave 4*. Oxford: Clarendon Press, 1976.
Mimouni, Simon Claude. "Le 'grand prêtre' Jésus 'à la manière de Melchisédech' dans l'Épître aux Hébreux." *ASE* 33.1 (2016): 79–105.
Moe, Olaf. "Der Gedanke des allgemeinen Priestertums im Hebräerbrief." *TZ* 3 (1949): 161–69.
Moffatt, James. *A Critical and Exegetical Commentary on the Epistle to the Hebrews*. ICC. Edinburgh: T&T Clark, 1924.
Moffitt, David M. *Atonement and the Logic of Resurrection in the Epistle to the Hebrews*. NovTSup 141. Leiden: Brill, 2013.
Moffitt, David M. "The Interpretation of Scripture in the Epistle to the Hebrews." Pages 77–97 in *Reading the Epistle to the Hebrews: A Resource for Students*. Edited by Eric F. Mason and Kevin B. McCruden. RBS 66. Atlanta, GA: SBL, 2011.
Moffitt, David M. "Jesus as Interceding High Priest and Sacrifice in Hebrews: A Response to Nicholas Moore." *JSNT* 42.4 (2020): 542–52.
Moffitt, David M. "Serving in the Tabernacle in Heaven: Sacred Space, Jesus's High-Priestly Sacrifice, and Hebrews' Analogical Theology." Pages 259–82 in *Hebrews in Contexts*. Edited by Gabriella Gelardini and Harold W. Attridge. AGJU 91. Leiden: Brill, 2016.
Moffitt, David M. "Unveiling Jesus' Flesh: A Fresh Assessment of the Relationship between the Veil and Jesus' Flesh in Hebrews 10:20." *PRS* 37.1 (2010): 71–84.
Montefiore, Hugh. *A Commentary on the Epistle to the Hebrews*. HNTC. New York: Harper & Row, 1964.
Moore, Nicholas J. "Heaven's Revolving Door? Cosmology, Entrance, and Approach in Hebrews." *BBR* 29.2 (2019): 187–207.
Moore, Nicholas J. "'In' or 'Near' Heavenly Access and Christian Identity in Hebrews." Pages 185–98 in *Muted Voices of the New Testament: Readings in the Catholic Epistles and Hebrews*. Edited by Katherine M. Hockey, Madison N. Pierce, and Francis Watson. LNTS 565. New York: T&T Clark, 2017.
Moore, Nicholas J. "Sacrifice, Session and Intercession: The End of Christ's Offering in Hebrews." *JSNT* 42.4 (2020): 521–41.
Morales, L. Michael. *Who Shall Ascend the Mountain of the Lord? A Biblical Theology of the Book of Leviticus*. NSBT 37. Downers Grove, IL: InterVarsity Press, 2015.
Moret, Jean-René. "Le rôle du concept de purification dans l'Épître aux Hébreux: une réaction à quelques propositions de David M. Moffitt." *NTS* 62.2 (2016): 289–307.
Moule, Charles F. D. *The Origin of Christology*. 1977. Reprint, Cambridge: Cambridge University Press, 1995.
Moxnes, Halvor. "Landscape and Spatiality: Placing Jesus." Pages 90–106 in *Understanding the Social World of the New Testament*. Edited by Dietmar Neufeld and Richard E. DeMaris. New York: Routledge, 2010.
Moxnes, Halvor. *Putting Jesus in His Place: A Radical Vision of Household and Kingdom*. Louisville, KY: Westminster John Knox Press, 2003.
Mulder, M. J., and Harry Sysling, eds. *Mikra: Text, Translation, Reading, and Interpretation of the Hebrew Bible in Ancient Judaism and Early Christianity*. CRINT 1. Minneapolis, MN: Fortress Press, 1990.
Nardoni, Enrique. "Partakers in Christ (Hebrews 3.14)." *NTS* 37.3 (1991): 456–72.

Nauck, Wolfgang. "Zum Aufbau des Hebräerbriefes." Pages 199–206 in *Judentum, Urchristentum, Kirche; Festschrift Für Joachim Jeremias*. Edited by Walter Eltester. BZNW 26. Berlin: Töpelmann, 1960.

Neufeld, Dietmar, and Richard E. DeMaris, eds. *Understanding the Social World of the New Testament*. New York: Routledge, 2010.

Neusner, Jacob. *The Babylonian Talmud: A Translation and Commentary*. Peabody, MA: Hendrickson, 2011.

Nierengarten, Paul A. "Temple Scroll." *The Lexham Bible Dictionary*. Bellingham, WA: Lexham Press, 2016. Logos Bible Software.

Nomoto, Shinya. "Herkunft und Struktur der Hohenpriestervorstellung im Hebräerbrief." *NovT* 10.1 (1968): 10–25.

O'Collins, Gerald, and Michael Keenan Jones. *Jesus Our Priest: A Christian Approach to the Priesthood of Christ*. Oxford: Oxford University Press, 2010.

Økland, Jorunn, J. Cornelis de Vos, and Karen J. Wenell, eds. *Constructions of Space III: Biblical Spatiality and the Sacred*. LHBOTS 540. New York: T&T Clark, 2013.

Omanson, Roger L. "A Superior Covenant: Hebrews 8:1-10:18." *RevExp* 82.3 (1985): 361–73.

Omanson, Roger L., and Bruce M. Metzger. *A Textual Guide to the Greek New Testament: An Adaptation of Bruce M. Metzger's Textual Commentary for the Needs of Translators*. Stuttgart: Deutsche Bibelgesellschaft, 2007.

Owen, John. *An Exposition of the Epistle to the Hebrews*. Edited by W. H. Goold. 24 vols. Works of John Owen. Edinburgh: Johnstone & Hunter, 1854.

Peeler, Amy L. B. *You Are My Son: The Family of God in the Epistle to the Hebrews*. LNTS 486. New York: T&T Clark, 2015.

Penner, Ken M. *The Lexham Dead Sea Scrolls Hebrews-English Interlinear Bible*. Bellingham, WA: Lexham Press, 2016.

Penner, Ken M., and Michael S. Heiser. *Old Testament Greek Pseudepigrapha with Morphology*. Bellingham, WA: Lexham Press, 2008.

Pennington, Jonathan T. *Heaven and Earth in the Gospel of Matthew*. NovTSup 126. Leiden: Brill, 2007.

Pennington, Jonathan T., and Sean M. McDonough. "Conclusion." Pages 189–92 in *Cosmology and New Testament Theology*. Edited by Jonathan T. Pennington and Sean M. McDonough. LNTS 355. London: T&T Clark, 2008.

Pennington, Jonathan T., and Sean M. McDonough, eds. *Cosmology and New Testament Theology*. LNTS 355. London: T&T Clark, 2008.

Perkins, Larry J. "Exodus." Pages 43–51 in *A New English Translation of the Septuagint*. Edited by Albert Pietersma and Benjamin G. Wright. Oxford: Oxford University Press, 2007.

Perriman, Andrew C. "Review of Sacred Space: An Approach to the Theology of the Epistle to the Hebrews by Marie Isaacs." *Themelios* 20.1 (1994): 29–30.

Peterson, David. *Hebrews and Perfection: An Examination of the Concept of Perfection in the "Epistle to the Hebrews."* SNTSMS 47. New York: Cambridge University Press, 2005.

Pietersma, Albert, and Benjamin G. Wright, eds. *A New English Translation of the Septuagint*. Oxford: Oxford University Press, 2007.

Philip, Mayjee. *Leviticus in Hebrews: A Transtextual Analysis of the Tabernacle Theme in the Letter to the Hebrews*. Oxford: Peter Lang, 2011.

Philo of Alexandria. *Philo*. Translated by F. H. Colson, G. H. Whitaker, and J. W. Earp. 10 vols. LCL. Cambridge, MA: Harvard University Press, 1929.

Philo of Alexandria. *On Abraham. On Joseph. On Moses.* Translated by F. H. Colson. LCL 289. Cambridge, MA: Harvard University Press, 1935.

Philo of Alexandria. *On the Creation. Allegorical Interpretation of Genesis 2 and 3.* Translated by F. H. Colson and G. H. Whitaker. LCL 226. Cambridge, MA: Harvard University Press, 1929.

Philo of Alexandria. *On Flight and Finding. On the Change of Names. On Dreams.* Translated by F. H. Colson and G. H. Whitaker. LCL 275. Cambridge, MA: Harvard University Press, 1934.

Philo of Alexandria. *On the Special Laws, Book 4. On the Virtues. On Rewards and Punishments.* Translated by F. H. Colson. LCL 341. Cambridge, MA: Harvard University Press, 1939.

Philo of Alexandria. *Questions and Answers on Exodus.* Translated by Ralph Marcus. LCL 401. Cambridge, MA: Harvard University Press, 1953.

Porter, Stanley E., and Andrew W. Pitts, eds. *Christian Origins and Greco-Roman Culture: Social and Literary Contexts for the New Testament.* TENT 9. Leiden: Brill, 2013.

Poythress, Vern S. *The Shadow of Christ in the Law of Moses.* Phillipsburg, NJ: Presbyterian & Reformed, 1995.

Prinsloo, Gert T. M., and Cristl M. Maier, eds. *Constructions of Space V: Place, Space and Identity in the Ancient Mediterranean World.* LHBOTS 576. New York: T&T Clark, 2013.

Punt, Jeremy. "Hebrews, Thought-Patterns and Context: Aspects of the Background of Hebrews." *Neot* 31.1 (1997): 119–58.

Rahlfs, Alfred, ed. *Psalmi cum Odis.* Septuaginta: Vetus Testamentum Graecum. Auctoritate Academiae Scientiarum Gottingensis Editum 10. Göttingen: Vandenhoeck & Ruprecht, 1979.

Rascher, Angela. *Schriftauslegung und Christologie im Hebräerbrief.* BZNW 153. Berlin: de Gruyter, 2007.

Ribbens, Benjamin J. "Ascension and Atonement: The Significance of Post-Reformation, Reformed Responses to Socinians for Contemporary Atonement Debates in Hebrews." *WTJ* 80.1 (2018): 1–23.

Ribbens, Benjamin J. *Levitical Sacrifice and Heavenly Cult in Hebrews.* BZNW 222. Berlin: de Gruyter, 2016.

Ribbens, Benjamin J. "Partakers of Christ: Union with Christ in Hebrews." *Pro Ecclesia* 31.3 (2022): 282–301.

Ricœur, Paul. *The Rule of Metaphor: Multi-Disciplinary Studies of the Creation of Meaning in Language.* UTRS 37. Buffalo: University of Toronto Press, 1977.

Rowe, Kavin. "The Trinity in the Letters of St. Paul and Hebrews." Pages 41–54 in *The Oxford Handbook of the Trinity.* Edited by Gilles Emery and Matthew Levering. New York: Oxford University Press, 2011.

Rowland, Christopher. *The Open Heaven: A Study of Apocalyptic in Judaism and Early Christianity.* London: SPCK, 1982.

Ruager, Søren. "'Wir haben einen Altar' (Hebr 13, 10): Einige Überlegungen zum Thema: Gottesdienst/Abendmahl im Hebräerbrief." *KD* 36.1 (1990): 72–77.

Runge, Steven E. *Discourse Grammar of the Greek New Testament: A Practical Introduction for Teaching and Exegesis.* LBRS. Peabody, MA: Hendrickson, 2010.

Ryken, Leland, James C. Wilhoit, and Tremper Longman III, eds. *Dictionary of Biblical Imagery.* Downers Grove, IL: InterVarsity Press, 2000.

Sabourin, Léopold. "Liturgie du sanctuaire et de la tente véritable." *NTS* 18.1 (1971): 87–90.

Sack, Robert David. *Conceptions of Space in Social Thought: A Geographic Perspective*. Critical Human Geography. London: Macmillan, 1980.
Salevao, Iutisone. *Legitimation in the Letter to the Hebrews: The Construction and Maintenance of a Symbolic Universe*. JSNTSup 219. New York: Sheffield Academic Press, 2002.
Salvesen, Alison. "Exodus." *T&T Clark Companion to the Septuagint*. Edited by J. K. Aitken. New York: T&T Clark, 2015.
Sandmel, Samuel. "Parallelomania." *JBL* 81.1 (1962): 1–13.
Santos, Danillo Auguso. "Ministers of Christ Jesus: A Cognitive Account of Priestly Language in Paul." PhD diss., Westminster Theological Seminary, 2021.
Schapdick, Stefan. "Die Metathesis der erschütterbaren Dinge, 'damit Das Unerschütterbare bleibe' [Hebr 12,27], Verwandlung–Vernichtung–Wandelbarkeit? Zum Verständnis des Begriffs Μετάθεσις im Kontext von Hebr 12,1-29 [Teil II]." *BZ* 57.1 (2013): 46–59.
Schenck, Kenneth. "An Archaeology of Hebrews' Tabernacle Imagery." Pages 238–58 in *Hebrews in Contexts*. Edited by Gabriella Gelardini and Harold W. Attridge. AGJU 91. Leiden: Brill, 2016.
Schenck, Kenneth. *Cosmology and Eschatology in Hebrews: The Settings of the Sacrifice*. SNTSMS 143. New York: Cambridge University Press, 2007.
Schenck, Kenneth. "Philo and the Epistle to the Hebrews: Ronald Williamson's Study After Thirty Years." *SPhiloA: Studies in Hellenistic Judaism*. BJS 14. Providence, RI: Brown University Press, 2002.
Schofield, Alison. "Re-Placing Priestly Space: The Wilderness as Heterotopia in the Dead Sea Scrolls." Pages 469–90 in *A Teacher for All Generations: Essays in Honor of James C. VanderKam*. Edited by Eric F. Mason et al. 2 vols. JSJSup 153. Leiden: Brill, 2012.
Scholer, John M. *Proleptic Priests: Priesthood in the Epistle to the Hebrews*. JSOTSup 49. Sheffield: JSOT Press, 1991.
Schreiner, Patrick. *The Body of Jesus: A Spatial Analysis of the Kingdom in Matthew*. LNTS 555. New York: T&T Clark, 2016.
Schreiner, Patrick. "Space, Place and Biblical Studies: A Survey of Recent Research in Light of Developing Trends." *CurBR* 14.3 (2016): 340–71.
Schrenk, Gottlob. "ἱεράτευμα." *TDNT* 3:246–52.
Segal, Alan F. "Heavenly Ascent in Hellenistic Judaism, Early Christianity and their Environment." *ANRW* 23.2: 1333–94. Part 2, *Principat*, 23.2. Edited by Hildegard Temporini and Wolfgang Haase. Berlin: de Gruyter, 1980.
Selby, Gary S. "The Meaning and Function of Syneidēsis in Hebrews 9 and 10." *ResQ* 28.3 (1985): 145–54.
Selman, Martin J. *1 Chronicles: An Introduction and Commentary*. TOTC 10. Downers Grove, IL: InterVarsity Press, 1994.
Selwyn, Edward Gordon. *The First Epistle of St. Peter: The Greek Text with Introduction, Notes and Essays*. Grand Rapids, MI: Baker Book House, 1981.
She, King L. *The Use of Exodus in Hebrews*. StBibLit 142. New York: Peter Lang, 2011.
Silva, Moisés. *Biblical Words and Their Meaning: An Introduction to Lexical Semantics*. 2nd ed. Grand Rapids, MI: Zondervan, 1994.
Sleeman, Matthew. "Critical Spatial Theory 2.0." Pages 49–66 in *Constructions of Space V: Place, Space and Identity in the Ancient Mediterranean World*. Edited by Gert T. M. Prinsloo and Christl M. Maier. LHBOTS 576. New York: T&T Clark, 2013.
Sleeman, Matthew. *Geography and the Ascension Narrative in Acts*. SNTSMS 146. New York: Cambridge University Press, 2009.
Sleeman, Matthew. "Mark, the Temple and Space: A Geographer's Response." *BibInt* 15.3 (2007): 338–49.

Soja, Edward W. *Postmodern Geographies: The Reassertion of Space in Critical Social Theory*. New York: Verso, 1989.
Soja, Edward W. "Taking Space Personally." *The Spatial Turn: Interdisciplinary Perspectives*. Edited by Barney Warf and Santa Arias. Routledge Studies in Human Geography 26. New York: Routledge, 2009.
Soja, Edward W. *Thirdspace: Journeys to Los Angeles and Other Real-and-Imagined Places*. Cambridge, MA: Blackwell, 1996.
Soskice, Janet Martin. *Metaphor and Religious Language*. Oxford: Oxford University Press, 1985.
Sousa, Elías Brasil de. "The Heavenly Sanctuary/Temple Motif in the Hebrew Bible: Function and Relationship to the Earthly Counterparts." PhD diss., Andrews University, 2005.
Sousa, Elías Brasil de. "Sanctuary: Cosmos, Covenant, and Creation." *JATS* 24.1 (2013): 25–41.
Sowers, Sidney G. *The Hermeneutics of Philo and Hebrews: A Comparison of the Interpretation of the Old Testament in Philo Judaeus and the Epistle to the Hebrews*. BST 1. Richmond, VA: John Knox Press, 1965.
Spicq, Ceslas. "Ἄγκυραν et Πρόδρομος dans Hébr VI. 19–20." *ST* 3 (1951): 185–87.
Spicq, Ceslas. *L'Épitre aux Hébreux*. 2 vols. Paris: Gabalda, 1952.
Spicq, Ceslas. "New Testament Space/Spatiality." *BTB* 42.3 (2012): 139–50.
Stanley, Steve. "The Structure of Hebrews from Three Perspectives." *TynBul* 45.2 (1994): 245–71.
Stegemann, Ekkehard W., and Wolfgang Stegemann. "Does the Cultic Language in Hebrews Represent Sacrificial Metaphors? Reflections on Some Basic Problems." Pages 13–23 in *Hebrews: Contemporary Methods, New Insights*. Edited by Gabriella Gelardini. BIS 75. Leiden: Brill, 2005.
Stewart, Alexander. "Cosmology, Eschatology, and Soteriology in Hebrews: A Synthetic Analysis." *BBR* 20.4 (2010): 545–60.
Stewart, Eric Clark. *Gathered Around Jesus: An Alternative Spatial Practice in the Gospel of Mark*. Eugene, OR: Cascade, 2009.
Steyn, Gert J. "'On Earth as It Is in Heaven...' The Heavenly Sanctuary Motif in Hebrews 8:5 and Its Textual Connection with the 'Shadowy Copy' of LXX Exodus 25:40." *HTS Teologiese Studies/Theological Studies* 67.1 (2011): 1–6.
Steyn, Gert J. "An Overview of the Extent and Diversity of Methods Utilised by the Author of Hebrews When Using the Old Testament." *Neot* 32.2 (2008): 327–52.
Steyn, Gert J. *A Quest for the Assumed LXX Vorlage of the Explicit Quotations in Hebrews*. FRLANT 235. Göttingen: Vandenhoeck & Ruprecht, 2011.
Steyn, Gert J. "Which 'LXX' are We Talking about in NT Scholarship?" Pages 697–707 in *Die Septuaginta: Texte, Kontexte, Lebenswelten*. Edited by Martin Karrer and Wolfgang Kraus. WUNT 219. Tübingen: Mohr Siebeck, 2008.
Strathmann, Hermann. "λειτουργέω, λειτουργία, λειτουργός, λειτουργικός." *TDNT* 4:215–222, 226–31.
Stuart, Douglas. *Exodus*. NAC 2. Nashville, TN: Broadman & Holman, 2006.
Suh, Myung Soo. *The Tabernacle in the Narrative History of Israel from the Exodus to the Conquest*. StBibLit 50. New York: Peter Lang, 2003.
Swetnam, James. "Ἐξ Ἑνός in Hebrews 2,11." *Biblica* 88.4 (2007): 517–25.
Swetnam, James. "Greater and More Perfect Tent: A Contribution to the Discussion of Hebrews 9:11." *Biblica* 47.1 (1966): 91–106.

Swetnam, James. "Hebrews 9:2 and the Uses of Consistency." *CBQ* 32.2 (1970): 205–21.
Swetnam, James. "On the Literary Genre of the 'Epistle' to the Hebrews." *NovT* 11.4 (1969): 261–69.
Swetnam, James. "Review of Proleptic Priests: Priesthood in the Epistle to the Hebrews by John Scholer." *CBQ* 54 (1992): 799–800.
Tabor, James D. *Things Unutterable: Paul's Ascent to Paradise in Its Greco-Roman, Judaic, and Early Christian Contexts.* Studies in Judaism. Lanham, MD: University Press of America, 1986.
Talbot, Eduard Stuart. "Tabernacle (Jewish)." Page 1584 in *The Oxford Dictionary of the Christian Church.* Edited by F. L. Cross and Elizabeth A. Livingstone. New York: Oxford University Press, 2005.
Theissen, Gerd. *Untersuchungen zum Hebräerbrief.* SNT 2. Gütersloh: Gerd Mohn, 1969.
Thomas, Kenneth J. "Old Testament Citations in Hebrews." *NTS* 11.4 (1965): 303–25.
Thompson, John A. *1, 2 Chronicles.* NAC 9. Nashville, TN: Broadman & Holman, 1994.
Thompson, James W. "Insider Ethics for Outsiders: Ethics for Aliens in Hebrews." *ResQ* 53.4 (2011): 207–19.
Thurston, Robert W. "Philo and the Epistle to the Hebrews." *EvQ* 58.2 (1986): 133–43.
Torrance, Thomas F. *Space, Time, and Incarnation.* Edinburgh: T&T Clark, 1997.
Torrance, Thomas F. *Space, Time and Resurrection.* Cornerstones. London: T&T Clark, 2019.
Torrey, Charles Cutler. "The Authorship and Character of the So-Called 'Epistle to the Hebrews.'" *JBL* 30.2 (1911): 137–56.
Tov, Emmanuel. *The Parallel Aligned Hebrew-Aramaic and Greek Texts of Jewish Scripture - Alexandrinus and Theodotion Variants.* Bellingham, WA: Lexham Press, 2003.
Tov, Emmanuel. "The Septuagint." Pages 161–88 in *Mikra: Text, Translation, Reading, and Interpretation of the Hebrew Bible in Ancient Judaism and Early Christianity.* Edited by M. J. Mulder and Harry Sysling. CRINT 1. Minneapolis, MN: Fortress Press, 1990.
Tuan, Yi-Fu. *Space and Place: The Perspective of Experience.* 7th ed. Minneapolis, MN: University of Minnesota Press, 2011.
VanGemeren, Willem, ed. *New International Dictionary of Old Testament Theology & Exegesis.* 5 vols. Grand Rapids, MI: Zondervan, 1997.
Vanhoye, Albert. "Discussions sur la Structure de l'Épître aux Hébreux." *Biblica* 55.3 (1974): 349–80.
Vanhoye, Albert. "Esprit éternel et feu du sacrifice en He 9:14." *Biblica* 64.2 (1983): 263–74.
Vanhoye, Albert. *The Letter to the Hebrews: A New Commentary.* New York: Paulist Press, 2015.
Vanhoye, Albert. "L'οἰκουμένη dans l'Épître aux Hébreux." *Biblica* 45 (1964): 248–53.
Vanhoye, Albert. "Par la tente plus grande et plus parfaite (He 9,11)." *Biblica* 46.1 (1965): 1–28.
Vanhoye, Albert. *Structure and Message of the Epistle to the Hebrews.* SubBib 12. Rome: Editrice Pontificio Istituto Biblico, 1989.
Vos, Geerhardus. *The Pauline Eschatology.* Princeton, NJ: Princeton University Press, 1930.
Vos, Geerhardus. *Redemptive History and Biblical Interpretation: The Shorter Writings of Geerhardus Vos.* Edited by Richard B. Gaffin Jr. Phillipsburg, NJ: Presbyterian & Reformed, 2001.
Vos, Geerhardus. *The Teaching of the Epistle to the Hebrews.* Edited by Johannes G. Vos. Philipsburg, NJ: Presbyterian & Reformed, 1956.

Vos, J. Cornelius de. "Hebrews 3:7–4:11 and the Function of Mental Time-Space Landscapes." Pages 169–81 in *Constructions of Space III: Biblical Spatiality and the Sacred*. Edited by Jorunn Økland, J. Cornelis de Vos, and Karen J. Wenell. LHBOTS 540. New York: T&T Clark, 2016.

Wallace, Daniel B. *Greek Grammar Beyond the Basics: An Exegetical Syntax of the New Testament with Scripture, Subject, and Greek Word Indexes*. Grand Rapids, MI: Zondervan, 1996.

Wallace, James Buchanan. *Snatched into Paradise (2 Cor 12:1-10): Paul's Heavenly Journey in the Context of Early Christian Experience*. BZNW 179. New York: de Gruyter, 2011.

Walser, Georg. *Old Testament Quotations in Hebrews: Studies in Their Textual and Contextual Background*. WUNT 2/356. Tübingen: Mohr Siebeck, 2013.

Walton, John H. *Ancient Near Eastern Thought and the Old Testament: Introducing the Conceptual World of the Hebrew Bible*. Grand Rapid, MI: Baker Academic, 2006.

Warf, Barney, and Santa Arias, eds. *The Spatial Turn: Interdisciplinary Perspectives*. Routledge Studies in Human Geography 26. New York: Routledge, 2009.

Wenell, Karen J. *Jesus and Land: Sacred and Social Space in Second Temple Judaism*. LNTS 334. New York: T&T Clark, 2007.

Wenham, Gordon J. *The Book of Leviticus*. NICOT. Grand Rapids, MI: Eerdmans, 1979.

Westcott, Brooke Foss. *The Epistle to the Hebrews: The Greek Text with Notes and Essays*. 3rd ed. CCGNT. London: Macmillan, 1903.

Westerholm, Stephen. "Tabernacle." *ISBE* 4:698–706.

Westerholm, Stephen. "Temple." *ISBE* 4:759–76.

Westfall, Cynthia Long. *A Discourse Analysis of the Letter to the Hebrews: The Relationship Between Form and Meaning*. LNTS 297. New York: T&T Clark, 2005.

Westfall, Cynthia Long. "Space and Atonement." Pages 228–48 in *So Great a Salvation: A Dialogue on the Atonement in Hebrews*. Edited by Jon C. Laansma, George H. Guthrie, and Cynthia Long Westfall. LNTS 516. New York: T&T Clark, 2019.

Wevers, John William, ed. *Exodus*. Septuaginta: Vetus Testamentum Graecum. Auctoritate Academiae Scientiarum Gottingensis Editum II.1. Göttingen: Vandenhoeck & Ruprecht, 1991.

Wevers, John William. *Text History of the Greek Exodus*. MSU 21. Göttingen: Vandenhoek & Ruprecht, 1992.

Wilcox, Max. "'According to the Pattern (Tbnyt)...': Exodus 25:40 in the New Testament and Early Jewish Thought." *RevQ* 13.1–4 (1988): 647–56.

Williamson, Ronald. "Background of the Epistle to the Hebrews." *ExpTim* 87.8 (1976): 232–37.

Williamson, Ronald. *Philo and the Epistle to the Hebrews*. ALGHJ 4. Leiden: Brill, 1970.

Williamson, Ronald. "Philo and New Testament Christology." Pages 439–45 in *Studia Biblica 1978 III: Papers on Paul and Other New Testament Authors. Sixth International Congress on Biblical Studies, Oxford 3–7 April 1978*. Edited by E. A. Livingstone. JSNTSup 3. Sheffield: JSOT Press, 1980.

Williamson, Ronald. "Platonism and Hebrews." *SJT* 16.4 (1963): 415–24.

Wills, Lawrence M. "The Form of the Sermon in Hellenistic Judaism and Early Christianity." *HTR* 77.3–4 (1984): 277–99.

Winston, David. *The Wisdom of Solomon: A New Translation with Introduction and Commentary*. AB 43. Garden City, NY: Doubleday, 1979.

Wise, Michael Owen, Martin G. Abegg, and Edward M. Cook. *The Dead Sea Scrolls: A New Translation*. New York: HarperCollins, 2005.

Young, Norman H. "'Where Jesus Has Gone as a Forerunner on Our Behalf' (Hebrews 6:20)." *AUSS* 39.2 (2001): 165–73.

INDEX OF REFERENCES

Hebrew Bible/
Old Testament
Genesis
1–3	101
1:26	115
2:15	173
5:24	83, 98
11:4	87
47:31	56

Exodus
1–18	96
3:2–3	155
15:17	123, 135
16:9	178–80
19–24	96
19	66
19:5–6	176
19:6	174, 182, 197
19:10–15	183
19:10–14	193
19:10–11	65
19:12–16	65
19:12	65
19:15–16	183
19:17	65
19:18	66
19:20	65, 66
19:21	65
19:22	179
19:24	65
19:25	66
22:7	178
24	97
24:1–2	65
24:2	180
24:4–11	202
24:8	125
24:9–15	65
24:12	65
24:16–18	65
24:18	97
25–40	96, 114
25–31	67, 96, 97, 114
25–27	132
25	65, 97, 104, 105, 107, 108, 114, 116
25:1	97
25:2	97
25:8	95, 115
25:9	28, 56, 95–99, 102–10, 114
25:10–39	97, 98
25:10–22	97
25:22	114, 132
25:23–30	97
25:31–40	102
25:31–39	97
25:40	17, 31, 53, 54, 56, 90, 93–100, 102–104, 106–108, 110, 111, 113–15, 117, 118, 127, 143, 213
26:1	66
26:30	98
26:31–35	66, 86
26:33	17, 86, 139, 179
26:35	132
27:8	98
28:29–30	179
28:43	68, 179
29:4	194
29:14	68
29:20–21	194
29:45–46	66
30:6	200
30:17–21	194
30:20	179
33:7–11	21
33:18	68
35–40	67, 97
36:7	67
36:8	66
36:35	66
37:19	188
38:16–18	67
38:19–20	67
38:23	67
39:2–8	67
40:1–33	86
40:30–31	194
40:34	87
40:35	66

Leviticus
1–16	203
3:5	183
4:5–7	179
4:6	183
4:12	68
4:14	143
4:16–19	179
4:17	183

Index of References

Leviticus (cont.)		5:1	68	7:12	66
5:9	183	5:2–4	209	8:27	100
6:23	179	5:17	194	22:19	151
7:12	207	7:5	188		
7:16	186	7:11	185	2 Kings	
8:6–13	183	8:22	188	16:10	115, 116
8:6	194	8:26	173	16:19	116
8:17	68	9:15–23	87		
8:23–30	194	12:7	56	1 Chronicles	
9:5	178, 180	12:14–15	209	6:33	188
9:7–8	178	13:2	89	9:13–28	188
9:7	179	13:20	88	28	116
9:11	68	14:4	89	28:11–19	116
9:23	179	16:5	183	28:11–18	115
10:1–2	68	16:9	188	28:11	99, 116
10:18	179	18:1–7	174	28:12	116
13:45–46	209	18:3–4	179	28:13	188
13:46	68	18:3	68	28:19	116
16	142	18:4–6	188		
16:2–34	191	18:4	178	2 Chronicles	
16:2–12	86	18:5–6	173	31:2–4	188
16:2–3	179	18:7	86	35:16	188
16:2	86	18:22	179		
16:3	179	19:11–22	192	Psalms	
16:11–17	18	24:6	112	4:5	181
16:12–28	179	27:21	204	8:3–5	81
16:12	86	31:19–20	209	8:5–7	56
16:14–15	183	35	184	11:4	182
16:15	86			21:17–19 LXX	200
16:23	179	Deuteronomy		21:23	56
16:27	68	4:11	183	22	186
16:34	68, 183	5:27	178, 183	22:16–18	200
17–27	203	17:9–13	204	22:22	157, 199, 200
18:6	178	21:5	178, 179	22:25–26	186
18:19	178	23:10	68	22:25	200
20:16	178	26:15	98	23:4	204
21:16–24	177	32:35	56	23:5–6	204
21:17–23	179	32:36	56	27:6	201
21:21–23	179	32:43	56	30	201
22:8	183	33:3	204	31:9	180
24:2	183	33:10	204	39:7–9	56, 57
24:14	68			40:7–9	57
		Joshua		44:7	81
Numbers		18:1	112	49:14	207
3:5–10	174			50:13	181
3:7–8	173	1 Kings		50:14	181
3:38	180	1:50	184	50:23	181
4:19	180	2:29	184		

51:17	181	11:17	208	*Mark*	
54:6	201	40–48	116	1:9–11	84
54:8	201	40:1–2	116	1:10	78
94:7–11	56, 58	40:2	116	14:56	124
95	60, 160	41:1–3	86	14:58	123
95:7–11	204	41:3	86	15:29	124
101:26–28	56	43:6–7	182	15:38	82
102:19	182	43:10	116		
102:25–27	77			*Luke*	
102:26	135	*Daniel*		2:13	84
103:4	56	3:2	185	2:15	84
104:4	188	6:23	58	3:21–23	84
109:1	10	7	93	9:28–36	88
110	136, 174	7:9	182	9:33	88
110:1	113			23:43	101
118:169	180	*Hosea*		23:45	82
141:2	181, 201	6:6	181	24:41–43	134
144:12	98				
		Amos		*John*	
Proverbs		4:10	115	1:9	112
12:5	56			1:14	112
		Micah		1:32–34	84
Isaiah		6:6–8	181	2:19	124
1:11–15	181			6:32	112
6	151	*Habakkuk*		8:23	11
6:1	182	2:3–7	56	13:16	87
10:24	115			14:2	23, 214
10:26	115	*Zephaniah*		14:22	117
16:5	182	3:2	180	15:1	112
52:11	208			20:24–29	134
61:6	176, 188	*Haggai*			
66:1–2	100, 109	2:6–7	206	*Acts*	
66:1	82, 182	2:6	77	1:1–2	88
66:18–24	189	2:9	122	1:2	88
66:21	176			1:9–11	84, 88
		Zechariah		1:11	84, 126
Jeremiah		6:13	182	2:34	78
7:16	178, 180			6:7	175
17:12	182	*Malachi*		7:43	109
31:33–34	193	2:6–7	204	7:44	108, 109
38:31–34	57, 62			7:48	123
38:34 LXX	193	New Testament		7:56	78, 84
		Matthew		13	55
Ezekiel		3:13–17	84	13:6	80
1:22	99	3:16	78	13:13–41	55
1:26	182	26:61	124	13:14–41	55
8:3	102	27:51	82	13:15	54
10:8	115			14:24	80

Acts (cont.)		2:6	11, 145,	1:10	77
15:3	80		153	1:11–12	135
15:41	80	2:11	123	1:13	8, 10, 137,
16:6	80	4–6	173		168
17:24	123, 124	4:8–10	85	1:14	134, 171,
18:23	80	4:9–10	81		187
19:1	80	4:10	77	2:1–4	77
19:21	80	5:2	201, 208	2:1–3	60, 129
20:2	80			2:1	61, 155
20:25	80	*Philippians*		2:2–4	188
		1:24–26	11	2:3	60, 61
Romans		2:17	201	2:4	12
1–11	173	3:20–21	5	2:5–18	162
5:12	80	3:21	124	2:5–9	80, 81, 151
6:5–6	159	4:17–20	207	2:5	32, 168
8:18–25	184	4:18	201	2:6–9	85
8:19–25	5	4:20	208	2:6–8	56, 81
9–11	60			2:8	170
10:6–7	81	*Colossians*		2:9–17	159
12–15	173	2:12	153, 159	2:9	8, 31, 81,
12:1	201, 207	3:1–4	5		137, 144,
13:6	188				172, 208
13:11–14	5	*1 Thessalonians*		2:10–12	174, 186
15:16	189, 201,	4:13–18	5	2:10–11	200
	208	4:16–17	89	2:10	89, 90, 200
15:27	189			2:11–13	186
		2 Thessalonians		2:11	200
1 Corinthians		2:4–8	5	2:12–13	157
2:6–7	5			2:12	56, 157,
3:12–15	5	*1 Timothy*			186, 199,
7:29–31	5	6:17–19	5		200, 205
15:20–28	5			2:13	31, 157,
15:20	89	*Hebrews*			200
15:42	134	1–2	188	2:14	124
15:47	124	1:1–14	80	2:15	193
16:5	80	1:1–13	61	2:17–3:1	63
		1:1–2	113, 130	2:18	200
2 Corinthians		1:1	115, 167	3–4	13
2:14–17	201, 208	1:2	61, 115	3:1–4:13	61
4:16–18	5	1:3–7	60	3:1–6	89, 112
6:17–18	208	1:3–5	137	3:1	31, 162,
12:2–4	78, 85	1:3–4	61		195
12:2	79, 126	1:3	8	3:2–5	56
12:3	101	1:4	81, 151	3:3	129
12:4	102	1:5–7:28	63	3:5	115
		1:5–13	151	3:6	116
Ephesians		1:6	56, 168	3:7–4:13	154
1–3	173	1:7	56, 187	3:7–4:11	77
1:3	12	1:8	81	3:7–13	162
1:14	12	1:10–12	56, 77, 85	3:7–11	56, 58

3:7	8	6:1–20	170	8:1	62, 76, 80, 81, 94, 95, 111, 126, 188
3:11	8, 180	6:1	205		
3:12–4:16	170	6:4	12		
3:13	201, 204, 205	6:5	32		
		6:10	193, 205	8:2	95, 99, 111, 122, 124, 130, 136, 188
3:14	159, 185, 205	6:18–20	184		
		6:19–20	28, 32, 50, 54, 75, 82, 86, 89, 90, 127, 184, 195, 212		
3:18–19	180			8:3–10:18	113
4	9			8:3–4	112
4:1–11	75, 180			8:3	10
4:1–8	89			8:4	142
4:1–6	75	6:19	88, 118, 195	8:5	15, 20, 22, 31, 53, 54, 56, 93–95, 99, 108, 111–14, 117–19, 125, 130, 133, 134, 141, 189, 192, 203, 213
4:1	9, 10, 150				
4:3–7	191	6:20	9, 63, 76, 82, 86, 88, 121, 138, 150, 195, 198, 200		
4:3	9, 10, 150				
4:4	76, 150				
4:5	9				
4:9	150				
4:10–11	9	7–10	53		
4:10	184	7	174		
4:11	15, 154	7:1–10:18	203		
4:12–13	191	7:1–28	173		
4:13–14	191	7:9	183		
4:14–16	63, 88, 152, 195	7:11–28	94	8:6–13	61
		7:12	174	8:6	95, 111, 129
4:14	50, 54, 63, 70, 75–77, 80–86, 88, 90, 119, 126, 127, 133, 137, 144, 159, 182, 212	7:14	174, 193		
		7:15–28	151	8:7–13	95
		7:16	174, 190	8:8–12	57, 62
		7:19	155	8:12	194
		7:22	61	9	125, 128, 151, 191
		7:23–26	174		
		7:23	174	9:1–10:26	165
		7:25	61, 155, 180, 183, 200	9:1–28	103, 118
4:15	159, 208			9:1–14	22, 50, 63, 71, 82, 83, 111, 119, 120, 133, 136, 192, 194
4:16	50, 63, 76, 86, 89, 155, 178, 179, 182, 187, 190, 191	7:26–28	94		
		7:26	9, 77, 80–82		
		7:27	9, 30		
5–10	13	8–9	192	9:1–11	120
5:1–10:18	63	8	122	9:1–10	95, 120, 126–29, 131, 158
5:1–3	208	8:1–10:39	63		
5:1	182, 204	8:1–10:18	51, 113		
5:2	204, 208	8:1–6	94, 95, 151	9:1–5	18, 96, 111, 127, 129, 131, 155
5:5	139, 151	8:1–5	28, 33, 50, 63, 70, 83, 90, 111, 118		
5:6–10	151				
5:6	130			9:1	120, 127, 170
5:7	124, 193				
5:9	61	8:1–2	20, 95, 128, 155	9:2–7	126
5:11–6:12	77			9:2–3	126, 131

Hebrews (cont.)			150, 156,	10:15–18	160
9:2	99, 131,		158, 184	10:16–18	193
	132, 136	9:13–14	131, 177	10:17	194
9:3	82, 127,	9:13	192	10:18	62, 63, 95
	132, 136,	9:14	12, 50, 125,	10:19–13:25	51, 62
	200		153, 156,	10:19–39	77
9:4	132		160, 189,	10:19–31	63
9:5	132		192, 205	10:19–25	50, 63
9:6–10	12, 20, 127,	9:15	121, 205	10:19–23	152, 182
	128, 131,	9:19–21	206	10:19–22	50, 145,
	155	9:19	137		157, 160,
9:6–7	113, 129	9:21	137		183, 185,
9:6	9, 128, 131	9:23–28	117		191, 192
9:7–11	10	9:23–24	77	10:19–21	195
9:7	9, 126, 133,	9:23	28, 108,	10:19–20	28, 89
	138		111, 130,	10:19	63, 156,
9:8–10	129		132, 134,		159, 173,
9:8–9	168		136		185, 193
9:8	9, 71, 99,	9:24–28	31	10:20	82, 124,
	131, 153	9:24–25	127, 133		185, 186,
9:9–14	190	9:24	28, 32, 33,		190
9:9	9, 130, 131,		70, 85, 111,	10:21–25	153
	189, 192,		121, 126,	10:21	63, 195
	193		131, 133,	10:22	10, 50, 63,
9:10–12	85		150, 158,		155, 180,
9:10	128		184, 200,		183, 185,
9:11–14	26, 120,		203		193
	127–31,	9:25	9, 10, 121,	10:23–25	199, 201,
	151, 158,		150		204, 205
	205, 213	9:26	30	10:23	195
9:11–12	14, 28, 32,	9:28	33	10:24–25	31, 194
	85, 95, 120,	10	192	10:24	161
	128, 131,	10:1–25	194	10:25	10, 50, 205
	135	10:1–4	158, 193	10:26	204
9:11	20, 25, 33,	10:1–3	50, 190	10:28–29	129
	70, 85, 95,	10:1–2	192	10:30	56, 171
	113, 117,	10:1	10, 15, 121,	10:32–34	50, 209
	119, 120,		155, 157,	10:32	117
	122, 124–		158, 180,	10:34	22, 117
	28, 130–36,		183, 193	10:37–38	56
	139, 144,	10:2	189, 192	11:1–13:19	63
	155, 157–	10:4	177	11:1	170, 172
	59, 169–71	10:5–18	193	11:4	199
9:12–13	125	10:5–7	56, 57	11:6	10, 180,
9:12	18, 111,	10:8	205		183
	123, 125,	10:11	10	11:12	77
	126, 130,	10:12–13	155	11:16	118, 158
	131, 135,	10:12	10, 70	11:20	121
	136, 139,	10:14	157, 185,	11:21	56
			205	11:33	58

Index of References 241

12:1–29	206	13:22	28, 52, 55,	*2 Esdras*	
12:2	31, 76, 89,		76, 210	7:24	188
	90, 172	13:24	60	20:39	188
12:3	193	25–31	22		
12:5–7	175			*Wisdom of Solomon*	
12:5	56	*1 Peter*		4:10–11	79
12:14–15	199	1:11	185	9:8	99
12:14	50, 172,	1:17	11	9:10	100
	206	2:5	176	9:12	100
12:18–24	169	2:9	177, 204	9:15–17	99, 100
12:18–22	183	3:22	85		
12:18–21	183			*Ecclesiasticus*	
12:18	170, 180	*2 Peter*		7:29–30	188
12:22–24	150, 152,	3:5	78		
	157, 187	3:7	78	PSEUDEPIGRAPHA	
12:22–23	159	3:10	78	*1 Enoch*	
12:22	117, 157,	3:13	78	1:2–4	98
	180, 183,			1:36	171
	188	*1 John*		2:1–3	83
12:23	187	2:8	112	2:1	98
12:26–27	122	4:13	159	2:2	98
12:26	77, 85			14–19	78
12:27	135, 168,	*Revelation*		14:8–20	98
	172	1:6	176	14:8–9	83
12:28–29	199, 205,	2:7	101	14:8	79
	206	3:21	76	14:10	79, 99
12:28	168, 192,	5:10	176	14:16	99
	206	7:15	190	14:19–20	99
13	13, 51, 206	8:3–5	190	17	83
13:1–10	199	8:3–4	201	25:3	79
13:1–6	206	11:1–2	180	33–36	83
13:1	207	11:19	180	39–41	99
13:7–19	21	13:6	13	39:3–4	79
13:10–16	206	15:5	13	39:4	99
13:10–12	202	19:8	190	41:1–2	99
13:10–11	21	20:6	176	42:8	171
13:10	189, 192,	21:1–2	135	46:3	171
	198, 207	21:2–22	180	50	99
13:11	123	21:2–3	159	52:1	79
13:12–13	117	21:2	168, 171	71:1–9	99
13:12	123	21:3	13	71:6	99
13:13–18	199	21:22	180	72–82	83
13:13	50, 53, 68,	22:3	190	72:1–37	83
	209			77:1–9	79
13:14	13, 88, 168	APOCRYPHA/DEUTERO-		90	93
13:15–16	171, 205–	CANONICAL BOOKS			
	207	*1 Esdras*		*2 Baruch*	
13:15	207	7:7	185	4:1–7	101, 107
13:16	207			4:5–6	101
13:18	191			4:6	171

2 Baruch (cont.)

21:12	171
48:49	171
51:8	171
52:7	171
59:1–12	101, 107
59:3–4	101
59:3	101

2 Enoch

1–23	78
7:1	78
8:1	78, 85

3 Baruch

11:1	78

3 Enoch

1–2	78
17:1–3	78

4 Enoch

20	78

4 Ezra

7:14	171
7:26	171
7:83	171
8:52	171
13:18	171

4 Maccabees

10:11	174

Apocalypse of Moses

37:3	79

Aristeas the Exegete

95	188

Lives of the Prophets

3:14–19	102
3:15	102

Martyrdom and Ascension of Isaiah

7:1–37	78

Testament of Abraham

A 10	78

Testament of Levi

2–5	78
2:10	188
3:1–10	100
3:1	100
3:3–5	101
3:4	100
3:5–6	140
4:2	188
5:1–2	188
5:1	87
9:3	188

DEAD SEA SCROLLS

4Q301

f2b.5	103

4Q403

Frag. 1 i.41	103
f1 ii.10–16	85

4Q404

f5.8	103
f6.5	103

4Q405

f6.2–5	197

4Q417

Frag. 1 i	102
Frag. 1 i.16–17	102

4Q418

f43–45i.13	102

PHILO

De congressu eruditionis gratia

116	19

De gigantibus

52	18

Legum allegoriae

3:102–104	106
3:102	96, 106, 108, 112

De migratione Abrahami

104	18

De opificio mundi

82	17

Quaestiones et solutiones in Exodum

1:10	176
2:52	106, 107, 112
2:75–78	19
2:82	106
2:94	17

Quis rerum divinarum heres sit

197	19
2:221–25	19
2:226	19

De somniis

1:206	106, 108
2:231–233	18
2:232	18

De specialibus legibus

1:66	19
1:75–77	19

De vita Mosis

2:74–76	17, 106, 108
2:77	19
2:88	19
2:101–102	19
2:135	17
2:141	108
2:141	106

JOSEPHUS

Jewish Antiquities

3:123–50	19
3:179–87	19

Index of References

Jewish War
5:219	83
5:5:5	19

BABYLONIAN TALMUD
Hagigah
12b	78, 79

Menahot
29A	104

Shebu'oth
14b–15	107
14b–15a	105
14b	105

Sanhedrin
16b	105, 107

MIDRASHIM
Midrash Song of Songs
3:2	105

Midrash Exodus
25:3–6	105
35:3–6	105
35:6	105

Midrash Numbers
15:10	105

APOSTOLIC FATHERS
1 Clement
36:1–5	60

CLASSICAL AND ANCIENT CHRISTIAN LITERATURE
Aristotle
Physics
4:5:212a32–212b3	36

Calvin
Institutes
3.2.24	159
3.9.10	159

INDEX OF AUTHORS

Abegg, M. G., Jr. 103
Aitken, E. 21, 88, 156, 157
Aitken, J. K. 56, 57
Algra, K. 45
Allen, D. L. 88
Anderson, G. A. 201
Aptowitzer, V. 105
Arias, S. 38
Asumang, A. 4, 6–8, 18, 23–25, 27, 40, 77, 94, 107, 117, 162, 167, 179
Attridge, H. W. 57, 63, 87, 90, 123, 124, 126, 128, 176, 192, 193

Bachmann, M. 63
Backhaus, K. 28, 180, 207, 208
Balz, H. R. 999
Barr, J. 93
Barrera, J. C. T. 57, 60
Barrett, C. K. 3, 11, 28, 92, 135, 165, 167
Barth, M. 58
Beale, G. K. 4, 5, 10, 19, 65, 66, 82, 83, 95, 104, 122, 130, 131, 134, 154, 159, 165, 166, 171, 173, 182, 206, 208, 209, 215
Bélanger, S. 174
Bénétreau, S. 195
Berényi, G. 205
Berger, P. L. 999
Bergh, R. H. van der 57
Berquist, J. L. 21, 35, 37, 38, 40–42, 46, 47, 49, 50, 53, 164
Best, E. 176, 178, 181, 185, 186, 190, 195, 199, 202, 207, 208
Black, C. C. 55
Black, M. 79, 141
Bleek, F. 58
Block, D. 114
Borgen, P. 106, 110
Brannan, R. 120

Brendsel, D. 130, 131
Brinkman, J. M. 7, 36, 40
Bruce, F. F. 55, 60, 61, 94, 115, 191
Burnet, R. 60
Büschel, F. 174
Buttimer, A. 118

Calaway, J. 93, 99, 120, 168, 169
Camacho, H. S. 201
Campbell, C. R. 159
Carson, D. A. 23
Casey, E. 35, 37
Cashdan, E. 104, 105
Childs, B. S. 97
Church, P. A. F. 23, 61, 63, 64, 77, 80, 94, 99, 100, 103, 123, 128, 131, 141, 167, 187, 188, 198
Clarke, K. 45
Cockerill, G. L. 15, 55, 61, 63, 64, 77, 89, 127, 180, 184, 195, 205
Cody, A. 23, 68, 84, 87, 94, 119, 123, 125, 126, 156
Collins, J. J. 32, 91
Combrink, H. J. B. 58
Comfort, P. W. 132
Cook, E. M. 103
Craigie, P. C. 186
Crocker, L. K. 174

D'Angelo, M. R. 96, 132
Dahl, N. A. 176, 183, 194, 201
Dan, J. 999
Davidson, R. M. 5, 6, 94, 98, 108, 136, 141, 164, 167, 203
deSilva, D. A. 92, 101, 104, 133, 150, 169, 201, 207, 209
Docherty, S. E. 56, 57, 60
Dodd, C. H. 108

Index of Authors

Domeris, B. 24, 25, 27, 162, 167
Downs, D. J. 189
Dozeman, T. B. 43
Dunnill, J. 60, 61, 174, 196
Durham, J. I. 67, 97, 155
Durkheim, E. 38

Eberhart, C. 194, 201
Eisele, W. 15
Ellingworth, P. 10, 15, 16, 19, 55, 57, 60, 61, 63, 80, 81, 88, 92, 94, 96, 111, 120, 126–29, 131, 132, 137, 158, 175, 188, 191, 193, 200, 204, 205
Ellis, E. E. 56, 169
Emmrich, M. 156, 160
Enns, P. 97, 155
Eskola, T. 68, 78, 83, 94, 99, 136, 140, 151

Fairhurst, A. M. 17, 18
Feld, H. 175
Fish, S. E. 46
Flanagan, J. W. 37, 38, 42–44
Fletcher-Louis, C. H. T. 187, 198
Floor, L. 176, 181, 190, 202, 206
Foucault, M. 37, 40
Frame, J. M. 134
France, R. T. 64
Freedman, H. 105, 106
Fuglseth, K. 106, 110

Gäbel, G. 4, 16, 31, 65, 92, 113, 126, 129, 135, 136, 138–40, 142, 171, 177, 186, 191, 193, 197, 198, 203, 209
Gaffin, R. B. 153
Gammie, J. G. 83
Gane, R. E. 86
Garland, D. E. 79
Gelardini, G. 21
Genette, G. 24
Gentry, P. J. 56
George, M. K. 21, 22, 35, 36, 38, 39, 43, 45, 46, 204
Gheorgita, R. 55–57, 59, 60, 112
Glombitza, O. 156
Goppelt, L. 6, 94, 108
Grässer, E. 63, 177, 178, 185, 187, 200
Gray, P. 60
Greenlee, J. H. 999
Greenspoon, L. J. 57

Gunn, D. M. 44, 45
Guthrie, D. 61–64, 75, 79, 95, 96, 105, 137, 163, 169

Hanson, R. P. C. 16
Haran, M. 66–68, 181
Hare, D. R. A. 102
Harvey, D. 37, 38
Heiser, M. S. 102
Himmelfarb, M. 78, 99
Hofius, O. 127, 193
Holbrook, F. B. 165
Hood, J. B. 173
Howard, G. E. 56
Hubbard, P. 38
Hübner, H. 58, 112
Hughes, P. E. 16, 77, 78, 94, 120, 121, 123, 125, 140, 158
Hummel, H. D. 169, 172
Hurst, L. D. 16, 55, 91, 92, 119, 120, 125, 126, 133, 170

Isaac, E. 98
Isaacs, M. E. 5, 17, 18, 27–30, 78, 117, 150, 170, 176, 199, 207

Jamieson, R. B. 32, 33, 94, 95, 111, 113, 126, 133, 137, 138, 142
Jennings, M. A. 193
Jenson, P. P. 67
Jobes, K. H. 57, 59
Johnson, L. T. 80, 121, 128, 139
Johnsson, W. G. 30, 91, 113, 124, 126, 136, 186
Jones, M. K. 177, 202
Joslin, B. C. 62

Karrer, M. 58
Käsemann, E. 15
Kaufman, S. A. 109
Kee, H. C. 100
Keene, T. 12, 14, 17, 19, 20, 23, 26, 94, 133, 136, 169
Kibbe, M. 19
Kidner, D. 186
Kim, M. 122, 154, 166, 182, 208, 209
Kistemaker, S. J. 96, 119, 121–23, 126
Kitchin, R. 38
Kittay, E. F. 125

Klawans, J. 187, 188
Klijn, A. F. J. 101
Kline, M. G. 163
Koch, K. 67
Koester, C. R. 14, 19, 64, 66, 77, 82, 85, 88, 93, 94, 99, 108, 111, 114, 131, 139, 145, 157, 167
Kubo, S. 93, 120
Kuss, O. 81, 178

Laansma, J. C. 63, 84, 85, 91, 137, 156
Lane, W. L. 16, 55, 61, 62, 75, 80, 92, 95, 121, 122, 124, 126-29, 131-33, 158, 169, 191, 192, 194, 200, 204-206
Laub, F. 95, 123, 127, 175
Lefebvre, H. 37, 39-41, 162-64
Levenson, J. D. 20
Lewis, C. S. 135
Lilburne, G. R. 118, 171, 210
Lincoln, A. T. 3, 5, 78, 145, 161, 171
Loader, W. 175
Löhr, H. 94-96, 112
Loken, I. 120
Long, P. J. 66
Longenecker, R. N. 58, 95, 189
Lopez, K. 93
Luckmann, T. 46

Macaskill, G. 159, 160
MacLeod, D. J. 55, 62, 136, 171, 185, 189, 200
MacLeod, I. C. 180
MacRae, G. W. 27, 28, 92
Mackie, S. D. 8, 30, 31, 54, 60, 86, 88, 92, 94, 126, 145, 150, 151, 155-57, 161, 171, 172, 178, 179, 182, 184, 187, 188, 194, 195
Martínez, F. C. 102, 103, 197
Mason, E. F. 13
Massey, D. B. 38
Matthews, V. H. 45
McCaffrey, J. 87
McCullough, J. C. 57, 60
McDonough, S. M. 84
McLay, R. T. 56, 59, 60
McNamara, M. 109
McNutt, P. M. 44, 45
Metzger, B. M. 9, 120-22
Michaelis, W. 126

Michaels, R. J. 116
Michel, O. 12, 18, 55, 57, 85, 173
Milik, J. T. 79
Mimouni, S. C. 197, 210
Miskowiec, J. 37
Moe, O. 176, 178, 196, 204
Moffatt, J. 15, 17, 18, 57, 58, 94
Moffitt, D. M. 6, 13, 28-30, 32, 50, 56-59, 70, 94, 107, 113, 126, 134, 135, 137, 138, 151, 188, 193
Montefiore, H. 123
Moore, N. J. 13, 86, 93, 137, 150-52, 176, 178, 182-84, 186
Morales, L. M. 65, 66, 68-70, 83, 88, 90, 114, 137, 157, 173, 180, 203, 215
Moret, J.-R. 137, 139, 177
Moule, C. F. D. 171
Moxnes, H. 38, 44
Myung, S. S. 64

Nardoni, E. 176
Nauck, W. 62, 63
Neusner, J. 79, 104, 105
Nida, E. A. 120, 126-29, 158
Nierengarten, P. A. 66
Nomoto, S. 111

O'Collins, G. 177, 202
Omanson, R. L. 120, 122, 126
Owen, J. 123

Peeler, A. L. B. 175
Penner, K. M. 102, 109
Pennington, J. T. 77, 78, 84
Perkins, L. J. 95
Perriman, A. C. 29
Peterson, D. 11, 85, 121, 123, 126, 127, 136, 150, 180, 192, 208
Philip, M. 23-25, 129
Poythress, V. S. 68, 83
Procksch, O. 174
Punt, J. 55, 185

Rascher, A. 56
Ribbens, B. J. 14, 19, 33, 91-94, 126, 134, 135, 137-39, 141, 144, 156, 159, 171
Ricœur, P. 141
Ross, W. A. 130, 131
Rowe, K. 81

Rowland, C. 4, 78, 79, 91, 108, 117
Ruager, S. 202
Runge, S. E. 127, 128

Sabourin, L. 95, 188
Sack, R. D. 38
Salevao, I. 55
Salvesen, A. 56, 59
Sandmel, S. 16
Santos, D. A. 189
Schapdick, S. 206
Schenck, K. 11, 18–20, 23, 24, 92, 94, 113, 119, 120, 122, 126, 136, 141, 157, 163, 176
Schofield, A. 197–99
Scholer, J. M. 150, 176–80, 183–86, 196–98, 200–202, 204
Schreiner, P. 4, 35–39, 42, 44, 46, 47, 49, 118, 134, 144, 165, 202, 209, 210
Segal, A. F. 78, 83
Selby, G. S. 191, 192
Selman, M. J. 116
Selwyn, E. G. 202
She, K. L. 94, 113, 144, 145, 162
Silva, M. 16, 57, 59
Simon, M. 105, 106
Skarsten, R. 106, 110
Sleeman, M. 24, 37, 38, 44–46, 163, 171, 209, 210
Soja, E. W. 35, 37, 38, 40–45, 48, 50, 153, 161, 164, 165, 208–10
Soskice, J. M. 113
Sousa, E. B. de 20, 65, 166
Sowers, S. G. 17–19
Spicq, C. 5, 15–17, 55, 57, 58, 63, 64, 87, 112, 123, 137, 138, 175, 179, 187, 191, 195
Stanley, S. 55, 62, 63, 185
Stegemann, E. W. 89, 126, 141, 194
Stegemann, W. 89, 126, 141, 194
Stewart, A. 91, 155, 157, 168, 170
Stewart, E. C. 4, 46
Steyn, G. J. 59, 96, 100, 102

Strathmann, H. 188
Stuart, D. 98, 115, 169
Swetnam, J. 23, 55, 119, 123–25, 176, 200

Tabor, J. D. 78, 79
Talbot, E. S. 67
Theissen, G. 15
Thomas, K. J. 58, 59
Thompson, J. A. 116, 170, 207
Thompson, J. W. 51
Thurston, R. W. 15, 16
Tigchelaar, E. J. C. 102, 103, 197
Torrance, T. F. 134, 160
Torrey, C. C. 55
Tov, E. 56, 58
Tuan, Y.-F. 38

Vanhoye, A. 6, 20, 23, 27, 62, 120, 123, 124, 128, 160
Vos, G. 3, 5, 11, 60, 138, 142, 160, 161, 168, 172, 205, 211, 215
Vos, J. C. de 207

Wallace, D. B. 76
Wallace, J. B. 78
Walser, G. 57
Walton, J. H. 20
Warf, B. 38
Wenell, K. J. 44
Wenham, G. J. 142
Westcott, B. F. 120, 123
Westerholm, S. 66, 67, 98
Westfall, C. L. 6, 24, 27, 30, 31, 37, 52, 53, 62, 137
Whiston, W. 83
Wilcox, M. 94, 95, 102, 104, 108
Williamson, R. 15–18, 92
Wills, L. M. 55
Winston, D. 99
Wise, M. O. 103

Young, N. H. 86, 195

www.ingramcontent.com/pod-product-compliance
Lightning Source LLC
Chambersburg PA
CBHW071819300426
44116CB00009B/1367